3C2 — 3rd ed

W9-CNN-440

THE THEORY OF
INTERNATIONAL VALUES

THE
THEORY OF
INTERNATIONAL
VALUES

By Frank D. Graham

GREENWOOD PRESS, PUBLISHERS
NEW YORK

PREFACE

THE ensuing treatise has, as the farmer said of his pig-trough, mostly been made out of my own head. Such slight adumbration of its central ideas as I have found in the work of others has been an *ex-post* rather than an *ex-ante* discovery. The book is a straight exercise in what I conceive to be untutored logic. This is the principal reason for the relatively few references to earlier writers (except for purposes of refutation). I have, of course, long been reasonably well acquainted with the orthodox literature on international trade and values, and the corpus of classical doctrines is the certain source of the (heretical) tenets here developed. That corpus commands respect, but no reverence. The leading classical and neo-classical writers were, or are, learned, able, and ingenious men. They have, nevertheless, been caught in one of those mental fixations that so often, in the history of economic as of other theory, have led to the survival of ideas which, even on the supposition that their birth was not unfortunate, should long since have been interred. For the most part the ideas were abortive from the beginning but by skillful, if self-deceptive, resuscitating measures they were brought to apparent health.

Just as the untoward influence of Ricardo in diverting attention from the evils of recurrent deficiency of effective demand was a potent factor in economic thought, until the late Lord Keynes pointed out that Ricardo's victory over Malthus had been a purely rhetorical triumph, so also Ricardo can be charged with setting on the wrong path his followers in the field of international value theory though this doubtful honor should, perhaps, rather go to John Stuart Mill who, at any rate, kept them there. Once on the wrong path it is extraordinarily difficult for those who think the right turning has been made to recognize the error of their way. They push ahead, they know that they are making progress *somewhere*, they develop a vested interest in defense of their choice of route, and they exercise the most impressive ingenuity in explaining away the evidence, however manifest, that they are on the wrong road. No more convincing proof of these tendencies could perhaps be found than in the processes of my own thought. I am, I think, a natural skeptic and began very early to doubt the validity of the accepted doctrines on international values. But the subtle argumentation with which they were supported was so plausible, intriguing, and impressive, that it was only after many years, when I had painfully retraced my steps to the fork at which Ricardo and Mill stood (and took what I conceive to be the wrong turning), that the *nature* of the elaborated fallacies of the orthodox position became to me starkly clear.

By far the best statement of the classical position, modified to take account of practically every even partly cogent comment, is that of my colleague, Professor Jacob Viner, in his *Studies in the Theory of International Trade*.[1] This is a model of scholarship—acute, erudite, judicious, and careful—which scrupulously renders, and fairly criticizes, all of the opinions of others with which it deals and, at the same time, develops new doctrine of great interest and importance. When I differ with Viner, as will occur, the difference, in nearly every case, is in the marrow, and, provided only that we were at one on fundamentals, I should seldom disagree with him. I cannot say as much of Marshall, to whom, as the neo-classicist of greatest renown, I shall frequently refer, since Marshall is, in my opinion, not only awkward in his premises but frequently illogical in his reasoning from them.

The present book deals all but exclusively with matters not on the boundary of exploration in the field of the theory of international values but with those at its heart. The requisite task is to get the fundamentals straight. In going back to such fundamentals, and beginning anew at the beginning, the book is elementary and rough-hewn. It contains no geometry, algebra, or higher mathematics. It is, nevertheless, meant for advanced students of international trade, rather than the wholly uninitiated, and assumes on the part of the reader a certain familiarity with long-accepted doctrines. It is primarily concerned with "static" theory, and equilibrium conditions, which must be rightly conceived before it is possible to deal intelligently with kinetic, and pathological, phenomena. It therefore leaves untouched much that appears in orthodox texts on international trade where static and kinetic are freely mixed (to give nothing but confusion) and pathology is treated without a sound notion of what health would be. Tainted as is the theory of such texts it may have *some* value for analysis that attempts to lay a base for *ad hoc* therapy under kinetic general conditions. But it

[1] Harper, New York, 1937.

is worthless in explanation of norms and *it should never be forgotten that, whereas normal values are a potent and persistent factor in the market, market values have only a remote and intermediate influence, if any, on the norms to which they are steadily attracted.* The general pattern of international trade is established by the norms. The market deviations from these norms are analogous to the deviations of any drawn line from the ideal of straightness. But we must have that ideal, or norm, before we càn make any attempt to deal significantly with the facts. A new kinetic analysis will, I trust, evolve out of the principles here laid down.

As a more comprehensive, though less intensive, precursor of Viner's *Studies,* Professor James W. Angell's *The Theory of International Prices,*[2] ably surveys the broad literature with which it deals and has been very useful to me. Like Viner, Angell is frequently much more than just in comment on some of my writings. I should like here gratefully to acknowledge my debt to both of these books and to their authors. Two other books in the field are of outstanding importance and have been of great help. These are Gottfried Haberler's *Theory of International Trade*[3] and Bertil Ohlin's *Interregional and International Trade.*[4]

Professor F. W. Taussig is responsible for my early interest in the theory of international trade. I am recognizant to him not only on this account but also for his supreme virtues as a teacher and for his encouragement (though not necessarily acceptance!) of ideas which often traversed his own preconceptions.

To my graduate students over many years I am beholden for eager attention, informed inquiry, rational skepticism, and, not infrequently, fertile contributions on the treated topics. My only regret is that most of these students have been excessively deferential.

The administrators of the University Research Fund of Princeton University contributed to the expenses of preparation of the manuscript and for this I would now express my thanks. I wish also to acknowledge my debt to the authors and publishers of books, from which citations have been made, for their gracious permission to insert the quotations.

F. D. G.

214 The Western Way
  Princeton, N.J.

[2] Harvard University Press, Cambridge, Mass., 1926.   [3] Hodge, London, 1936.
[4] Harvard University Press, Cambridge, Mass., 1933.

CONTENTS

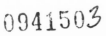

THE THEORY OF
INTERNATIONAL VALUES

CHAPTER I

THE theory of international values here presented is, in form, an elaboration but, in fact, a complete refutation of classical doctrines. Classical theory still commands the loyalty of *cognoscenti* despite the fact, of which they must be presumed to be unaware, that it imposes upon its adherents an acceptance of the thesis that changes in the relative values of internationally traded commodities will have no necessary, or even probable, effects upon their relative supply. This thesis, which violates all logic and experience, suggests that the classical doctrines *must* be wrong, and the present treatment is an essay at presenting a theory which does not require any such heroic contravention of patent truth.

The classical theory inferentially denies that relative supply will be affected by shifts in price relationships because, regardless of such shifts, it is so shaped as to *fix*, both absolutely and relatively, the supply of the traded goods. The general theory of values recognizes that, *for non-reproducible goods*, price, whether market or normal (if such there could be), is solely a function of the desires of competent buyers and sellers since it is obvious that nothing can have any influence in stimulating, or retarding, new supplies of the goods in question. For such goods (original) cost is irrelevant and for them there are, in consequence, no true norms. But this has always been held to be a special case of value and there is no reason to suppose that internationally traded goods, in general, fall within this category. For reproducible international, as for most domestic, goods, (marginal) desires, and values, are conditioned by supply and supply is conditioned by cost.

International values, nevertheless, have long been treated like the values of "old masters." This came about not by deliberate intention but as a result of the method of exposition of Ricardo, and of John Stuart Mill, who gave the cast to almost all of the succeeding discussion. Ricardo and Mill dealt all but exclusively with the trade between two countries only, in but two commodities, each of which was presumed to be solely produced in but one of the national trading entities, and *must* be so produced if international values were in fact fashioned according to the "principles" by them set forth.[1] Both writers assumed that each country would, at all times, produce as much of its specialty as it could and, with each country exclusively engaged in a single commodity, this means that, for any given status of population and the industrial arts, the evolving supply of each of the traded goods will remain substantially constant regardless of fluctuations in the ratio of exchange between them. In his inadequate treatment of complex trade, Mill asserted (wrongly) that such trade would proceed along the lines that he had (wrongly) alleged would apply to the simple case to which he had devoted his chief attention. Mill, however, left an edifice of theory which has been admired, rather than skeptically scrutinized, for more than a century.[2] The work, in this branch of theory, of later writers such as Marshall, Edgeworth, Bastable, Taussig, Viner, Haberler (to a lesser extent), and many others, though subtle, is essentially a process of elaboration, refinement, defense, and rehabilitation of the simple and shaky classical structure that Mill bequeathed to them. Persistent heretical attacks on this structure, including those of the mathematical school led by Cournot,[3] they

[1] It is true that Mill considered the possibility of production of both of the commodities in one of the countries but only to reject it as a special, and more or less irrelevant, case. His whole theory proceeds on the assumption that, for practical purposes, this case can be ignored. He also gave casual attention to more complex trade but thought that the (dubious or frankly erroneous) "principles" that he laid down for the trade between two countries, in but two commodities, were adequate to cover any conceivable degree of complexity.

[2] "Mill's exposition of the general theory . . . in his stupendous chapter on 'International Values' . . . is still unsurpassed." (F. Y. Edgeworth, *Papers Relating to Political Economy*, Macmillan and Co., Limited, London, 1925, Vol. II, p. 20.)

[3] The mathematical economists, *on the whole*, have not substantially departed from the orthodox position. This is, of course, not true of Cournot, but Cournot's work is not, though it well might have been, the better on that account. The best mathematical treatments of the topic known to me are those of Theodore O. Yntema, *A Mathematical Reformulation of the General Theory of International Trade* (University of Chicago Press, Chicago, 1931), which the author expressly declares to be "merely a mathematical exposition and development of the classical theory" (p. 103), and Jacob L. Mosak, *General-Equilibrium Theory in International Trade* (Principia Press, Bloomington, Ind., 1944), which seeks (appropriately) to integrate the theory of international trade with the general body of economic thought. Mosak's book is closely reasoned and clears up a number of disputed points but it does not depart as widely from classical theory as its author seems to suppose, nor as widely as it should. Its essential defect (which it shares with the classical school) lies in the inadmissible assumption that the potentiality of output of any given good, or group of goods, is the *property* of a given (national) group of producers. The output of any good may in fact be transferred from one to an entirely different (opportunity cost) environment, that is, from one to another, very differently situated, group of producers and exchangers. In complex trade this will have kaleidoscopic effects on the whole international trading position. These effects can, perhaps, not be handled with existing mathematical techniques. The algebraic method, moreover, presents *functions* and

steadily (and successfully) parried. The fencing was skillful and it is a matter of regret that it was not devoted to a better cause since the fencers' triumphs are attributable not to the virtues of the theory that was being defended but to the even greater vices of those by which it was recurrently challenged. Although the classical theory was highly vulnerable, it was, for the most part, attacked where it was strongest. The result is that an essentially spurious gospel is still orthodox, accredited, and prevalent.

One may perhaps be allowed to say that, for a century, we have done nothing but tread the same old Mill. Marshall, for instance, whose treatment of the subject is, "in the main an exposition and elaboration . . . of Mill's analysis,"[4] speaks of E's (England's or Ex's), and G's (Germany's or Generalia's), goods as mutually exclusive categories of commodities conceptually gathered into "representative bales" and, as such, traded the one against the other.[5] This implies that, though the proportions of the several goods in either E's or G's bale might, from time to time, be altered, the total evolving supply of the unique *set* of goods, produced either in E or in G, must remain unchanged in any given state of population and the industrial arts. Since, in Marshall's conception, these sets of goods are exchanged as units, each against the other, he is committed quite as fully as Ricardo and Mill to the assumption of fixed supplies of nationally segregated categories of internationally traded commodities.[6]

---

these not infrequently obscure, rather than reveal, facts which come to light in a presentation in definite, or absolute, terms. While, therefore, algebraic formulations of the theory have much to their credit they are better fitted to the elucidation of refinements than to the exposition of basic doctrines. Mathematics, moreover, is form rather than substance.

[4] Jacob Viner, *Studies in the Theory of International Trade*, Harper, New York, 1937, p. 541.

[5] A substitute for Marshall's "representative bale" is suggested by Edgeworth (*op. cit.*, Vol. II, p. 58). This is an "ideal article typical of the total volume of trade," but it would seem to have no conceptual, or any other, advantage over Marshall's composite.

[6] Since he was dealing with *sets* of goods Marshall is not necessarily precluded from positing changes in the relative supplies of the various commodities *within* any given set (representative bale) in response to price changes between the sets. But the envisaged price changes, *between* the sets, would tend equally to affect all commodities within any set (and, therefore, within any one nation) because the (normal) prices of the commodities within any set are bound together by (assumedly unchanging) cost relationships within each of the nations. There is, in the neo-classical as well as in the classical analysis therefore, no reason to suppose any change in the relative supply of the representative bales, or in the price relationships between the indi-

As a consequence of this doctrine, the classical and neo-classical theory is compelled not only to ignore, or to deny, any effects on relative supply of shifts in the ratio of exchange between internationally traded goods but neo-classical theory also perpetuates the ancient error of supposing that given goods "belong," more or less inevitably, to one country, and others to another. This has led to wholly fallacious doctrines not alone on international values but on reciprocal national demands, transfer problems, elasticities of "national demands," and disequilibrium in the international accounts. It will later appear that necessary adjustments in international trade are typically effected not, as the classicists contend, through a shift in the price relationships between the original exports and imports of any given country but rather through an alteration in the relative volume and in the composition of the country's exports and imports (with or without price changes that will, if present, run not at all along the lines alleged in the classical analysis).[7]

The *effect* of the classical concepts is to define international trade as trade between quasi-monopolistic national commercial entities whereas the classicists actually construed international trade not at all in this way but as competitive trade between private individuals across national boundaries over which productive resources do not freely move. The classical treatment is invalid for either conception of international trade though it is somewhat more applicable to that with which it did not affect to deal than to that for which it was specifically designed.

Because, in the classical conception, the supply of "E's goods," "G's goods," and also "A's goods," "B's goods," "C's goods," etc., is fixed, the only thing that could then affect the ratio of exchange between them would be a shift in "demand." Since this "demand," however, is conceived not in terms of the relative desires, and purchasing powers, of buyers, wherever located, for each of the various goods but in terms of the desire of each "country" for the goods of the other, the ratio at which internationally traded goods exchange,

---

vidual commodities of which each is composed, in response to an alteration in the exchange ratio between the bales (the price of one bale in terms of another).

[7] Where temporary price changes are necessary (usually the result of pathological monetary conditions) they will tend to occur not in the ratio between the export and import prices of any given country but in that between internationally traded goods as a whole and those which are purely domestic commodities.

on a presumed shift in these *national* demands, is necessarily alleged
to alter *en bloc*, with all of the goods exported by one country showing a substantially equal change in value in terms of all of the
goods exported by another (i.e. the *im*ports of the first country).
The exchange relationships between goods do not, in fact, alter in
this manner, and such a concept is wholly alien to the type of trade
which the classical economists were attempting to expound since
it is clear that in competitive trade between individuals, some of
which, in the case of each commodity, happens to pass over national
boundaries, there is no such thing as a segregatable *national* demand, and that, even if there were, it would be an irrelevance.
Practically all internationally traded goods are consumed in all of
the countries concerned; the significant demand for any good is
total demand; and it is of no consequence whatever for total demand
whether any given demander is of one nationality rather than
another. With the possible exception of complementary products,
moreover, no shift in the demand for, or the price of, any good
would ever be attended by a precisely similar shift in the demand
for, or the price of, any other commodity.

Not only is the form in which demand is assumed to come to
market expression erroneously developed in the classical theory but
the concept itself is superficially, even naïvely, treated. Demand is,
to a great extent, confused with desire. But demand involves not
merely desire but also the offer of a *quid pro quo*, and this implies
supply. The real question is what determines *supply*, and to this
the classicists gave anything but adequate, or acute, attention. Demand, supply, and value (price), in any actual exchange transaction, are identical things.[8] The identity is reached through what
Adam Smith described as the higgling of the market. In the theory
of domestic values Smith was not content to let the matter rest with
this but, in a search for natural, normal, equilibrium, or "long-run,"
values, looked behind the actual phenomena of momentary supply
to normal supply and the causes thereof. The determinants he
professed to find were in relative labor costs. The whole theory of
domestic values which Smith and his followers built up was a theory
not of market values but of natural, normal, equilibrium, or "long-
run" values (based on labor cost) on which higgling would be more

[8] See Appendix A. It is impossible to express demand, supply, or price, except in a
context which includes all three. They are a trinitarian entity.

or less precisely focused and around which market values would more or less closely cluster. Normal values express as identities not only demand, supply, and prices but also the costs that would prevail, in equilibrium, as the mode, or central tendency, of market phenomena.

For very good reasons, no doubt, Smith said nothing about international, as contrasted with domestic, values, and we may perhaps assume that he felt that for international values he could offer no explanation other than higgling.[9] The later classical, and the neo-classical, writers affected to offer a more satisfying exegesis but, with the possible exception of the assertion that the higgling would ordinarily take place somewhere within a wide zone or "circle"[10] the *limits* of which would be set by comparative costs of production of the traded commodities in the one country and the other, they made no real advance on Smith.

Smith had implied, in connection with domestic values, that, under conditions of constant labor-cost, the amount and the character of demand for the several commodities is irrelevant to normal value since, whatever the demand, the relative supplies of the various commodities would always be increased or diminished, in appropriate correspondence with any shift in demand schedules, to maintain identity of relative values with constant relative costs. The sequel will show that, under a valid concept of costs, this will hold true of international as well as of domestic values. The later classical and the neo-classical writers assert on the contrary that, regardless of relative costs, international values will alter with every shift in (international) "demand," and that, in the absence of a further shift in this demand, the alterations would be definitive inasmuch as, on their analysis, no compensatory tendency on the side of supply will ever come into operation.[11] This, if true, would imply either

[9] Since it was obvious that British exports did not tend to exchange against British imports on the basis of their respective labor costs, Smith was at a loss for an explanation of natural, or normal, values in the international field.

[10] "In . . . international trade, the correct figure by which to describe [the] action [of comparative costs] would be, not a point about which values move, but a circle within which they move." (J. E. Cairnes, *Some Leading Principles of Political Economy Newly Expounded*, Harper, New York, p. 353.)

[11] "In all such cases [of disturbance of equilibrium] a *definitive* change in the relative price levels [of the countries concerned] takes place . . . a new equilibrium is established, with . . . prices lower once for all in [the one] country, and higher once for all in the . . . [other] country." F. W. Taussig, "A Rejoinder" (to Jacob H. Hollander), *The Quarterly Journal of Economics*, Vol. xxxii, pp. 693-694.

that, with the notorious volatility of demand, there are *no* normal international values (and normal values are what these writers were professedly treating) or that, if there are, they are not established on any of the principles that have ever been alleged to be determinative of them. If the classical theory of international values is what it purports to be—a theory of normal values in competition[12]—it is then, at best, no more than embryonic inasmuch as it never gets beyond market values to a discussion of the (perhaps, in this case, peculiar) forces that determine norms, those fundamental value ratios from which market values temporarily deviate but to which they always tend to return.

So far as *market values at any given moment* are concerned, it is more or less legitimate to assume that supply is, for that moment, fixed. Cost is, then, more or less irrelevant, and relative marginal utilities will follow current relative marginal desires. But *normal* marginal desires and utilities are exclusively conditioned by actual or prospective variations in supply and (with or without any change in desire schedules) marginal desires, marginal utilities, and market values will always approach the norm set by cost as the supply of the goods in question is increased or diminished in response to prior deviations of market values from that norm. At the point of equilibrium, that is to say when no one has any incentive to shift from the supply of one thing to the supply of another, the relative marginal utilities of the several goods will be identical with their relative costs and with the ratios at which the goods will then exchange each against the others. It is *then* a matter of indifference whether we speak of reciprocal demand or of reciprocal supply as synonymous with, or of ophelimities or costs as determinative of, the relative values of the goods. The classical theory of international values, however, never gets close to any such equilibrium concept but, in contenting itself with the assumption of fixed supplies regardless of price relationships, flounders in the ephemeralities of market values

---

12 A limited competition, of course, since factors of production are assumed to be immobile as between countries.

"It may be well . . . to remind the reader that the subject of our . . . inquiry is normal, not market, values—the proportions in which nations exchange their products as a rule, or when trade is in a state of equilibrium, not those in which the exchange may take place on a particular occasion, or under the influence of exceptional conditions. [Normal value] has . . . been aptly represented by Adam Smith as a central point about which market values move, and toward which they gravitate" (J. E. Cairnes, *op. cit.*, pp. 343, 353). cf. Appendix A.

and can never consider the aberrations of market values as deviations from a norm which it is precluded from establishing through the faults in its analytical technique.

Normal cost ratios appear only when there are producers on the margin of indifference as between the output of one commodity and another.[13] The classicists failed to pursue their inquiries to the point of discovery of any such margin. Their failure is in part, though not fundamentally, attributable to the use of a labor-cost theory of value. When this defective theory is supplanted by an opportunity-cost explanation, the principle of substitution at the margin (which is essential to the notion of normal values) readily comes into its own in the international as in the domestic field.[14] An equilibrium based on identical opportunity costs of any two commodities in two or more countries is, in any given constellation of those costs, highly stable even in the face of great shifts in demand. The classical and neo-classical discussion of ready alteration in the (normal) terms of trade, through spontaneous or induced shifts in "national demands," is therefore unrealistic to the point of fantasy. It may, in fact, be flatly said that under the cost conditions assumed by the classicists, and in sharp contradiction of their doctrines, normal international values in a complex trading world would stand fast against all alterations in demand except such as are quite beyond the range of ordinary expectation.

The more complex the trade the more steady, on the whole, will the terms on which it is conducted tend to be. The difference between simple and complex trade is here, in fact, a difference in kind. Simple trade is markedly subject to vagaries in the respective bargaining powers of the parties concerned as well as to collusive action between any two or more of them. The matter has recently been

[13] The presence of producers on the margin of indifference will lead to a shift of output from the relatively depreciating to the relatively appreciating commodity whenever market values deviate from the relative costs of such producers. This shift in relative supply will bring market values into line with the norms.

[14] A labor-cost theory of value, however defective, would not *preclude* the establishment of cost-based norms in international values since there is no necessity for comparing actual labor-costs in one country with those in another but merely for comparing the *ratios* between the costs, in various countries, of the output of various commodities some of which are, or may be, produced in more than one of them. The relevant comparison, however, is automatically made when we think in terms of opportunity cost, and of equilibrium as established through the production of the various goods at equal opportunity cost as measured in some commodity put out in common by any two, or more, countries.

explored by Professors von Neumann and Morgenstern in a brilliant development of the theory of games and its application to the "game" of production and exchange.[15] A three-person game, they note, differs *fundamentally* from a two-person game, a four-person game from a three-person game, and so forth. Mill was wholly unjustified in asserting the contrary. Whenever the number of "players," or of participants in a social economy, increases, "the complexity of the economic system normally increases both in the number of commodities and services exchanged and in the processes of production employed." But, "when the number of participants becomes really great, some hope emerges that the influence of every particular participant will become negligible. . . ."[16]

The results of a so-called "simple," i.e. a two-person, game are indeterminate solely because such a game puts a premium on bluff, or bargaining, with more or less widely varying consequences.[17] A somewhat more complex game may *increase* the scope of strategy inasmuch as it permits of coalitions of some of the players against the others. But when a "game" approaches the highly complex state of free competition (as the economist understands the term) the possibility of employing strategy becomes negligible. There are too many players, on both sides of the market, to leave room for bargaining. No one, under perfectly free competition, can get anything by bluff. He can exert no influence over his competitors or customers, and his influence on the market is infinitesimal. In this situation, it is possible to lay down laws of the market and to reach determinate results. Just as in many branches of the physical sciences very great numbers of units permit the development of an exact theory (through the application of the law of statistical probabilities) so, in economics, a degree of determinateness may be attained in highly complex trade which is quite impossible in its simple "counterpart." In the ideal case of free competition "all solutions would be sharply and uniquely determined."[18] The "zones of indeterminateness (of ratios of exchange)—which undoubtedly exist when the number of

---

[15] John von Neumann and Oskar Morgenstern, *Theory of Games and Economic Behavior*, Princeton University Press, Princeton, 1944, *passim*.

[16] Von Neumann and Morgenstern, *op. cit.*, p. 13.

[17] cf. Alfred Marshall, *Principles of Economics*, 6th edn., Macmillan, London, 1910, Appendix F, pp. 791-793. Marshall (wrongly) attributes indeterminacy to the lack of the use of money in the exchanges he is considering.

[18] Von Neumann and Morgenstern, *op. cit.*, p. 14. It should be said that von Neumann and Morgenstern are not willing to concede that this is more than a possibility.

participants is small—narrow and disappear as the number increases."[19]

The theory of international values deals with a case of somewhat inhibited rather than perfectly free competition (some, or all, of the factors of production are assumed to be immobile as between nations). It therefore presents a problem which must be formulated, solved, and understood for small, but increasing, numbers of participants in an approach to a complex competition which, if still imperfect, goes far to abolish the possibilities of "strategy." This is the method employed in the present book. It yields results very different from those posited by the classical writers on international values; the inferences from it do not at all conform with those that have become traditional.

The two-country two-commodity model of international trade was not well developed by the classicists but, even if it had been, the ratio of exchange of products would not always have escaped indeterminateness since such trade, on occasion, offers a prime opportunity for setting the terms of trade at any one of many points within a presumptively wide zone. This zone, however, is narrowed almost to extinction as the number of countries, and the variety of commodities, increases, and, with its progressive disappearance, the determinateness of the ratio of exchange becomes practically absolute. The classicists and neo-classicists have persistently striven for such determinateness but, with their faulty instruments, it has always eluded them.

The present writer, in two exploratory articles in *The Quarterly Journal of Economics* in 1923 and 1932,[20] ventured to express skepticism of the classical doctrines, and Professor Bertil Ohlin, in his able and comprehensive *Interregional and International Trade*,[21] published in 1933, brought to the subject a training which all but inevitably resulted in a structure very different from that which had been built in the classical tradition. Ohlin does not fail to pay attention to costs. Yet it was from the method of the classical school that Ricardo's doctrines acquired that "simplicity and sharpness of outline, from which . . . [they] derived some of their seductive

---

[19] *loc. cit.* Here again, von Neumann and Morgenstern present this as an opinion (of others) which they would accept only with reservations, as unproved.

[20] "The Theory of International Values Re-examined," Vol. xxxviii, pp. 54-86; and "The Theory of International Values," Vol. xlvi, pp. 581-616.

[21] Harvard University Press, Cambridge (Mass.), 1933, *passim.*

charm" as well as "most of whatever tendency they may have [had] to lead to false practical conclusions."[22] Though Ohlin's aversion to this latter tendency is worthy of all commendation he has, in avoiding this Charybdis, fallen upon a Scylla of equivocacy which it was the chief object (by no means realized) of the classical economists to avoid. Determinate results are even less characteristic of Ohlin than of the classicists. The classicists were wrong; Ohlin avoids their errors only at the cost of precision.

Much of the recent writing on the theory of international trade, following that on economic theory in general, has been directed to economic pathology.[23] It has not, therefore, sought to reconsider the classical doctrines of normality or attempted a synthesis of the partially valid approaches both of the classicists and of Ohlin. On the contrary it has largely abandoned general theory for the discussion of special cases within, or outside, any such general scheme as can alone provide an organon for the phenomena of international trade in general. In the provision of such a scheme we need, first of all, the definiteness more or less characteristic of classical doctrine rather than the indeterminacy of Ohlin and, always holding fast to a definiteness purged of error, to graft upon it Ohlin's realism, without his vagueness, as circumstances may permit.

The Method of Attack

The task of laying a sound analytical foundation for so complex a structure as that of international trade is made arduous by the very processes of our thought. When we are confronted with an economic reality of a complexity so great that it cannot be compre-

---

[22] Alfred Marshall, *Principles of Economics, op. cit.,* p. 379n.

[23] The pathology is that of disequilibrium, frustrated adjustments, chronic instability, and cumulatively morbid conditions. Most of this is associated with disturbed international monetary relationships. It is worthy of note that the classical theory of *adjustment* in international trade, and of restoration of equilibrium after a disturbance arising from the advent of improvements, or a deterioration, in production, loans, indemnities, subsidies, export or import duties, bounties, and the like, runs in monetary terms. In the theory of the *establishment* of equilibrium, however, the classicists, for very good reasons, shunned a pecuniarily expressed exposition. It is quite as feasible to deal in non-pecuniary terms with the restoration as with the initial establishment of equilibrium. But to the classicists, whose view was obscured by clouds of their own making, this was so far from being obvious that a recourse to a monetary explanation, however much they recoiled from it, seemed unavoidable. The result is that the basic theory and that of the mechanism of adjustment to disturbance are stated in respectively incongruous terms.

hended immediately, accurately, and as a whole, there are several ways of grappling with it none of which is wholly adequate.

We may, first, segregate any given aspect of the matter and try to understand it *in vacuo*. The objection to this method (a method which has of late been rather fashionable) is that no aspect of any problem can be at all fully understood apart from its interconnections with essential phases of the problem which are, consciously or unconsciously, ignored. This is peculiarly true of economic, and specifically of value, problems where mutual interdependence is the keynote. The *ad hoc* investigator, in fact, brings to the attack on his problem a background of general ideas which he may or may not fully apprehend but which are inevitably arbitrary, probably erroneous, and either superficial or tendentious. The result can, at best, give but very limited satisfaction.

Another way of dealing with the problem is to assess as well as may be, and at a stroke, *all* of the facts and forces in the situation. The upshot of this method, if the probing goes at all below the surface, is an inability to draw any conclusion except that it is all very complex. This is more or less the method, and the outcome, of Ohlin. That values (including the whole complex of pecuniary relationships) are mutually interdependent there is no gainsaying. Values are therefore integrable into a system, and any value, or value norm, can be finally explained only by taking into account the *whole* of the commercial world. This, indeed, constitutes the importance of international trade theory in the development of any systematic treatment of values or prices.[24] But to integrate values into a system we

[24] The concept of the world integration of prices received only lip-service from the classicists, and its corollary, the shift in the composition of industry in the several national units as price relationships change, was completely ignored. The classicists separated, much too sharply, domestic from international trade as well as the theories appropriate to each. We should have but one basic theory of trade and values, applicable to the whole of the trading world, and theories of domestic trade and values, in the several component national units, are properly subordinate parts of this general theory. The classical economists assumed that competition was freer (the factors of production more mobile) in domestic than in international trade and, since they were building their systems on the assumption of competition, they began, naturally enough, with the system which was not only closer to them but, as they saw it, more in accord with their fundamental assumptions. They then went on to an independent consideration of international values and never succeeded in synthesizing the two categories of value. The mutual interdependence of values was faintly, if at all, reflected in the discrete theories which they built up, respectively, for domestic and for international trade. The theory of international values is not only a constituent member of a more general theory but is, in turn, affected by the whole of which it is a part. "The classical theory of international trade has

must concentrate on essentials and omit consideration of a variety of possible aberrations.

The third method of attack on a complex situation—the common method of science—is to confine our attention originally to what are observed, or at least conceived, to be basic and comprehensive facts and forces, to ignore the others until we can feel a measure of certitude about our inferences from those we have selected as basic, and then to deal, in each case severally, with the factors that are peculiar to that case. This—the method of abstraction of extraneous forces—is indispensable to any rational interpretation of phenomena and is indeed present, in some degree, even in the methods previously described. The three methods, in fact, differ rather in emphasis than in kind, the first attempting simplification by an undue limitation of the scope of the investigation, the second, in reaction, increasing the scope of the investigation at the expense of definiteness of

---

suffered from the basic defect of not being integrated into the general body of economic thought. Traditionally, one approach has been employed in the theory of a closed economy, and another in the theory of international trade. The reason for this difference has been well analyzed by Viner in his *Studies in the Theory of International Trade*. The classical theory of international trade was developed with a view to solving macrocosmic problems; the effects of trade between two countries, the effects of unilateral payments, the effects of tariffs, bounties, *etc.* For such problems the partial-equilibrium approach developed by the classical writers for dealing with a domestic economy was totally inadequate. Such an approach is satisfactory only if all other determining conditions do in fact remain substantially equal when there is a change in any one of them. By *assumption*, however, the problems in the field of international trade were such that all other determining conditions did not remain equal. Resort was therefore had to a form of general-equilibrium analysis in this field. . . . This form, however, differed markedly from the general-equilibrium analysis of a closed economy which was developed by the Lausanne [mathematical] school. It was, on the one hand, far less general than the Lausanne theory, but on the other, considerably more fruitful. The Lausanne theory was sufficiently general in that it could include any number of individuals, firms, and commodities. But the system which it developed was so complex that, on the whole, *the Lausanne theory satisfied itself with a demonstration of the possibility of equilibrium without analyzing the laws of its working. The classical theory of international trade, however, was basically concerned with the laws of change of the international equilibrium system.* It therefore resorted to extreme oversimplification. Most of its analysis was developed in terms of two representative individuals within two countries trading in two representative commodities. That such an analytical system is insufficient to lay bare the complexities of an economic system in which there are millions of different individuals, firms, products, and factors in hundreds of countries requires no emphasis. The classical theory simply assumed this whole problem away. This is clearly shown by . . . quotation from Edgeworth . . . 'A movement along a supply-and-demand curve of international trade should be considered as attended with rearrangements of internal trade; as the movement of the hand of a clock corresponds to considerable unseen movements of the machinery.' " (Jacob L. Mosak, *op. cit.*, pp. 179-180.) Italics mine.

outline, and the third, in compromise, seeking the fullest feasible attainment of both scope and clarity.

It is, in the present writer's judgment, not so much that the classical theories are simple, and unrealistically sharp in outline, but that they are in *essence* erroneous that has led to the false practical conclusions drawn from them. The postulates, and basic method, of the classicists are, for the most part, unobjectionable.[25] The argument in this book is therefore cast in the classical form in the conviction that the classicists did not fail because they were too rigorous in their abstractions but because they were not sufficiently rigorous in the reasoning based upon them.

The Results

The sequel will demonstrate:

1. that the (normal) values of internationally traded commodities are not determined by "reciprocal national demands";

2. that the very concept of "reciprocal national demands" is irrelevant to the type of trade which the classicists affected to treat;

3. that changes in the demand for internationally traded commodities, or for the current exports and imports of any given country, may have no effect on the terms on which they are exchanged;

4. that such changes in demand as affect the ratio of exchange of internationally traded commodities will not necessarily improve, but may worsen, the general "terms of trade" for many countries for whose current exports demand has increased relative to the demand for their current imports;

5. that the shifts in the national "terms of trade" posited by the classical economists are impossible, in the premises, whenever any two of the countries concerned have a common export;

6. that the export of products in common, by one or more countries, is, the classical presumption to the contrary notwithstanding, not only probable but necessary to the attainment of equilibrium and to the establishment of normal values;

7. that shifts in the ratio of exchange of international commodities will seldom, if ever, break along national lines but will

---

25 "It is obvious that without the use of special hypotheses, it would be impossible to work out any theory on so intricate a subject [as international trade]." (C. F. Bastable, *The Theory of International Trade*, Macmillan, London, 1903, p. 42.)

follow a course which, from the classical point of view, would appear to be random or chaotic;

8. that opportunity cost, rather than demand, is the significant factor in the determination of (normal) international values and that these values precisely correspond with such costs;

9. that international and domestic (normal) values are correlated on a cost basis and that the (normal) values of internationally exchanged commodities are proportional to real costs expressed in terms of opportunity;

10. that commodities might not only be exported from a country which had no comparative advantage in their output but that such export would be necessary to the attainment of equilibrium;

11. that a country may import certain commodities in which it has a comparative advantage in production;

12. that a variety of exports is evidence of an unfavorable ratio of exchange for the country concerned rather than a cause of a favorable ratio;

13. that small, or poor, countries tend to have a favorable ratio of exchange *solely* because they can concentrate on a few exports without "overloading" the market;

14. that comparative advantage and "the terms of trade" are interdependent, and, particularly, that comparative advantages are likely to shift with every shift in the terms;

15. that adjustments to disturbances of equilibrium are to a greater extent attained by shifts in the *number* of exports, relative to imports, than by alteration in the ratio of exchange;

16. that ratios of exchange of international commodities tend to be highly stable;

17. that the mechanism of restoration of equilibrium, after a disturbance, is not a shift in the ratio of exchange of the current exports to the current imports of any country but a shift in the ratio of domestic prices to those of international goods taken as a whole;

18. that the whole price-specie-flow analysis of classical theory is not only erroneous but inconsistent with the classical doctrine of the determination of values by reciprocal national demand;

19. that classical notions on the distribution of productive powers within a nation are circular and abortive;

20. that classical theory, while more applicable to market values

than to the normal values to which it was addressed, is unsatisfactory even in explication of market phenomena.

Theory and "Facts"

The question might be raised, on practical grounds, as to whether it is worth while to reformulate the classical theory of international values no matter how defective the earlier formulation may have been. The theory deals with conditions which have been subjected to so much invasion as, it is often alleged, to be no longer of any but antiquarian interest. Private and national monopolies or oligopolies, exerting indeterminate power, are now such highly familiar phenomena as to seem an integral part of the economic scene, and theories of (reasonably) free competition are therefore thought to be anachronistic. That this is not so may perhaps be clear when we reflect, for example, that *The Wealth of Nations* became a landmark in economic thought because it was the first successful attempt to deal with economic data in a systematic manner, with the use of abstractions, in an abstract regime of competition. In writing the book, Adam Smith was obviously not trying to explain existing phenomena. Far from being a description or explanation of things as they are, or were, *The Wealth of Nations* is a polemic against the then current economic institutions and an outline of an alternative, and, in Smith's view, better, economy. The theory of international trade that Smith presents is a (not very good) theory of the operation of what he conceived to be an ideal system and not, in any sense, a theory of prevailing, or even anticipated, practice.[26] It is clear that any "science" of human behavior "*must* describe *ideal* and not actual behaviour, if it is addressed to free human beings expected to change their own behaviour . . . as a result of the knowledge imparted."[27] The practical significance, if any, of such a science lies in the positing of norms, criteria, standards, or referents, for the determination of conduct. Description is well enough in its place, but description will never supply standards. A theory may, it is true, be employed as a basis of *explanation* of what is, or what will be, but, in dealing with human phenomena, such a theory should be sought in the realm

[26] "To expect, indeed, that the freedom of trade should ever be entirely restored in Great Britain is as absurd as to expect that an Oceana or Utopia should ever be established in it." (*Wealth of Nations*, Book IV, Chap. 2)

[27] Frank Hyneman Knight, *The Ethics of Competition and Other Essays*, Harper, New York, 1935, p. 278.

of individual or social psychology, biology, or some such kindred science. The description of how men act or the explanation of why they act as they do, in what we are pleased to call the economic phase of their lives, is not economics. On the contrary, how men act in "economic" affairs, and why they act as they do, is often *contrasted* with "truly" economic action. We then say that certain of their actions or motives are uneconomic even though they are concerned with what is generally conceded to be the subject-matter of economics. We could, however, not make this assertion without some independent criterion of the economic. This criterion it is one of the functions of economic theory to supply.

Any theory of ideal relationships will become realistic in the degree that actual conditions move toward the posited ideal. Popular acceptance of the classical theory of international trade, as an explanation of the facts, therefore waxed in the century following the appearance of *The Wealth of Nations* when facts and institutions were, on the whole, moving toward the postulates of the theory, but its popular repute has been waning since the trend toward correspondence with the postulates of the theory, and with the truly economic, was sharply reversed in the latter part of the nineteenth century.

The departure of the actual from postulated conditions does not, of course, make the theory any less valid for the situation with which it purports to deal. If the trend of facts is regarded as foreordained, or otherwise unalterable, the center of interest is, of course, bound to shift from a theory that has little relevance to reality to a theory which can more readily be applied to the existing or prospective situation. A fatalistic view of events, however, makes all attempts at amelioration vain. If things will be as they will be, regardless of human aspiration and striving, we are wasting time in seeking more economic means of accomplishing our ends. We could not then, indeed, have *any* ends, in the sense of choice between alternatives. Unless free will can play some role in human affairs all aspiration is fruitless. Theory would then be confined to an explanation and prediction of the course of events, while interest in events could spring from idle curiosity and idle curiosity alone.[28] There would, in such a world, be no place for economics, as a superior method of realization

---

[28] Even a passive adaptation to events would, except in foreordained fashion, be impossible in a completely foreordained world.

of chosen ends, since both the ends and the process of their realization would be prescribed. If, then, the classical theory postulates ideal conditions from which we have been retreating, we are logically bound, in spurning fatalism as fatal to economics as to any other striving, to condemn not the theory but the retreat from the conditions it postulates. Whatever the defects of classical theory, there is, therefore, no more reason to castigate it because, after a period of appropinquation, the facts have again departed from its suppositions than because its suppositions were as alien to the facts when it was first propounded as they have again become. There is equally little reason to deplore any lack of "realism" in a new effort along classical lines. If all the world should become less honest than of yore the theory that honesty is the best policy, however unheeded, might well, as a social precept, seem more valid than ever before. The fact that prevailing practice repudiated the theory would not, of itself, make the theory bad.

The ideal set forth in any social theory should, nevertheless, be not so remote from potential realization or approximation as to render the theory devoid of appeal as a criterion of practical action. A theory which is to be useful for positive, rather than merely adaptive, human action must, therefore, indicate not the probable response to a given situation but the response, appropriate to the most effective realization of given ends, which men might someday be expected to learn.

International Trade and National Business "Enterprise"

The classical economists did not very specifically define the ends to which their theory was germane but, whether under the influence of the doctrine of natural rights or, later, of the Utilitarian philosophy, their social goal was the rather vague "greatest good to the greatest number." This made it cosmopolitan. The pursuit of happiness was conceived to be a universal motivating force of human action and, since no one could be the judge of another's happiness, it was presumed that the greatest good to the greatest number would be attained where everyone was free to follow his own devices. It was obvious, however, that it would be impossible for everyone to follow his own devices if private individuals, or private groups, were permitted to coerce their fellows, or if governments should coerce any of their subjects to any end but the *equal* expansion of the liberties and opportunities of all. It is not too much, therefore, to say that the socio-economic method of attaining ends is essentially non-coercive and that any process involving coercion not equally imposed on all is *ipso facto* non-economic in the social sense of the word. In international affairs the coercion of one nation by another, however mild or indirect, is the counterpart of discriminating coercion of individuals within the nation.

When we say that the economic way of pursuing one's ends is to seek to realize them by work, trade, thrift, or some such non-coercive action, we are obviously using the word "economic" in a social, or cosmopolitan, sense, since from the point of view of the individual, or nation, it might be much more effective for the realization of the given ends to resort to privilege, robbery, conquest, chicane, or other such "political" methods. The transfer of goods from one individual to another may take place on terms running from unblushing robbery or privilege to what the common law designated as "bargaining at arms' length." The latter, in which neither force, fear, fraud, favor, nor loyalty may exert any influence, and contract is free, is the prerequisite to *trade*, in contradistinction to some form of robbery, status, or charity.

The exchange between a slave and his master is akin to straight robbery. So far as the master is single-minded in the pursuit of what he conceives to be his advantage he will take from the slave all that he can get and will give him in exchange only so much as will keep the slave submissive and his productivity at the point which will show the maximum spread between what he produces and what he is suffered to consume. The terms of exchange, the conditions of employment, what the slave produces and what he consumes, will be decided by the master solely in his own interest. This we should hardly call trade nor should we say that it is "economic," even if it resulted in a greater output of *material* commodities than could be attained in any other way. Exploitation may shade away from this extreme to varied, widely current, and *relatively* innocuous forms of status, private or national monopoly, or other restriction, but, whenever either of the parties to an exchange is subject to the power of the other, whether it is exerted directly or impersonally in the market, positively or negatively, the conditions of true trade, and of the economic, are absent. If, therefore, we seek a theory of trade, rather than a theory of exploitation, we must deal with free and competitive trade between individuals none of whom, whether by crude or subtle means in sole or collective action, is able to compel or cajole any of the others or in any way to rig the market. So far as we depart from these conditions we inject into the analysis an element of power of men over men which transforms the exchange of goods into a more or less thoroughgoing form of exploitation.

There is no doubt that the use of power by any strategically placed state may often, at the expense of other nations, improve the material returns of the state in a position effectively to employ it. From a *nationalistic* point of view, therefore, and on material considerations only, the case for restraints on trade is sometimes formidable. Just as the monopolist in domestic trade can frequently batten on the impotence of his fellows, so also the nation that can exert some form of monopoly power in international commerce may be able to extract a larger return from the rest of the world than it could obtain under a regime of free trade.

The classical advocacy of free trade, as a certain method of increasing, or maximizing, the *national* economic dividend, rests, therefore, on a sometimes rebuttable presumption,[29] and the many modern attempts to exploit a national monopolistic position are not necessarily irrational in the premises on which they are built. The universally valid case for free trade is not as a method for improving the material welfare of any given nation (which it will usually but perhaps not invariably do) but, as a value in itself, as part of the "natural right" of the individual to liberty, on equal terms to all, and as a system conducive to *general* (cosmopolitan) advantage.[30]

The classical and neo-classical writers on international trade were, however, never quite able to bring themselves to a whole-hearted treatment of their subject as trade between individuals (undifferentiated except that they belonged to different national groups between which the flow of factors of production was inhibited) rather than as trade, between nations, each of which was to be regarded as a single business unit. The one treatment called for the attitude of the cos-

[29] This was recognized even in Mill's time since Mill, and his followers, spent much ingenuity in discussing the possibility of national gain, at the expense of other nations, from various forms of restraint on trade.

[30] The American Revolution, as a demand for freedom, was based, in large part, on the asserted right of the individual to buy and sell freely in the best markets available. It is not a little ironical that the government of the republic has so much, and so consistently, invaded the rights for which its founders fought.

mopolite (to whom humanity is above all nations, with every individual an end unto himself and all of equal value in the sight of God or the "impartial observer"), while the other rested on a narrow nationalism in which the fortunes of the denizens of one's own nation were regarded so indulgently that they were to be furthered even at the expense of the world at large. The result is that the classical theory of international trade is, in part, a theory of economics and, in part, a theory of national business enterprise.[31] The former is the way of civilization and the latter that of barbarism which, among other undesirable effects, will certainly impoverish most, and presumptively all, of those concerned.[32] If we are to advance in civilization the present excesses of nationalism, in commerce as elsewhere, will someday run their course and men will turn from them with disgust as, a century and more ago, they turned from the Mercantilism of earlier times.

To mix the principles of trade with those of *Realpolitik* is, in any

[31] "Even the most clearheaded of [the classical] writers . . . seem not to distinguish very sharply the ideas of advantage to the world and to a particular nation" (F. Y. Edgeworth, *op. cit.*, p. 7n).

[32] The pursuit of national interest at the expense of other nations is a more or less ruthless form of piracy and, just as a pirate may sometimes do better for himself than he could do as an honest trader in a non-violent environment, so it is *possible* for any nation, in a position effectively to employ coercive tactics, to improve its economic status over that which it could attain in a freely competitive (i.e. non-violent) world. But piracy can be profitable only when the great majority of mankind does not resort to it and, as it becomes general, inevitably declines in attractiveness. Carried to any considerable lengths it falls of its own weight since the pirates will then be reduced to robbing one another of possessions which steadily dwindle in the absence of productive activity. If other defense against widespread piracy is not, or cannot be, organized, however, the only alternative to the immediate ruin of would-be honest traders is recourse to something like piracy on their own account. The analogy, in the case of nations, is close. If a piratical attitude is at all widespread, even the nations of best intentions are all but forced to retaliation as their sole effective defense. The result is that all nations, not excluding the original offender, suffer impoverishment. Retaliation will probably be as costly to the retaliator as to those against whom the action is taken and, except as a regrettably necessary defense against still worse evils, is never advisable. It is most unlikely to cause the abandonment of the original offense but will frequently result in counter-retaliation and a consequent worsening of the general situation. While it might not be safe, or profitable, for any individual, or single nation, to abandon predatory policies in a stubbornly predatory world, it would obviously be of benefit to all men and nations of reasonably good will to forgo the practice of, or "right" to, predation, provided all others will do the same. It should nevertheless be said that coercive or inhibitory national policies might be pursued by a single nation, to change the terms of international trade to its advantage, without an *inevitable* adverse effect even on world output. This possibility, however, is all but negligible and it disappears when the injured outside-world resorts to retaliation, as all history indicates will be the case.

event, a fruitless conceptual task since they run, in large part, in opposite directions. It is at least comparatively easy, on the assumptions more or less traditional in economics, to assess the results of free enterprise in a free market, but it is all but impossible to comprehend, to say nothing of measuring the effects of, the play of a conflict of infinitely varied predatory power exerted to material ends. When one departs from the non-coercive principles of economics he has nothing on which a science, as distinct from an art, can be built. Once we admit of predatory methods it is only a question of time and expediency as to how far they will be carried. We are then dealing with war rather than economics and, when we are dealing with war, we should take in *all* of the factors that make for military strength or weakness.

There is, of course, a fairly sharp line of distinction between negative coercion (such as partial exclusion from access to markets) and positive predatory action (such as the exaction of tribute by violence or the threat of it). The possible gains and losses, for the coercer and coercee, are typically much more limited in the former than in the latter case. Through merely negative coercion it is possible for any national trading unit to secure for itself no more than the full gains attributable to such international trade as it carries on (leaving no gain to the other party).[33] It can then, at most, render the exploited country no worse off than it would be, without the trade at all, on the nationally self-sufficing basis to which it could turn as an alternative. But, through *positive* coercion, exploitation can go far beyond this point, with war as an ultimate sanction. War as a business enterprise may offer no great prospect of success in modern times.[34] A powerful nation however may, without much immediate risk, use so-called economic weapons to exploit the impotent so greatly that the latter are worse off than they would have been on a self-sufficing independent basis. Recent cases of this sort may not be altogether lacking but, though they may have been profitable for the coercing state, they were rightly damned as uneconomic. As

[33] It is still possible to call these transactions "trade" rather than pillage since action is still volitional on the part of all concerned. This is far from the *ideal* of trade but it is equally far from outright plunder.

[34] The Romans, however, for long seem to have done well out of war, and the raids of the Vikings, according to Thorstein Veblen, were highly successful business undertakings. Some predatory colonial ventures were in the same category, and the designs of the Nazis were partly inspired by the not entirely unwarranted hope of exploitation of the conquered.

business tactics, however, they could be regarded as a profitable extension of a hitherto purely negative coercion.

The potentialities of positive coercion are so much greater than those of mere restriction that they could scarcely be neglected in a theory of national business enterprise. This would of course, on almost any definition, take us out of the field of economics. In dealing with international trade, as an *economic* phenomenon, we must eschew the consideration of purely national interest and put the case on a cosmopolitan basis. If it can be shown that a given trade policy will, as against any other such policy, not only maximize the total satisfactions from a given stock of goods but also, for a given cost, the world *per capita* stock, it is a matter of irrelevance to the economist, *qua* economist, whether any given nation might possibly improve its material welfare by some alternative policy which would cost others more than it would yield to the nation in question. If the world is ever to get on an economic rather than an exploitative basis, it is to an economic theory of this sort rather than to a theory of coercive power that it must turn as a criterion for its action and its policy.

The international immobility of productive factors assumed in the theory of international values is not necessarily, or even presumably, the result of coercion, positive or negative (prohibition). Trade on this basis, though not perfectly competitive, could nevertheless be free, and the *pattern* of trade so developed is applicable to all truly economic international transactions. Any transaction that can make any pretension to being economic must therefore have such a pattern as a *base*. It is clearly of the utmost importance that that base be well and truly laid and, in that conviction, the outline of a new, and, I think, more valid theory of international values is here set forth. This cannot fail to be of interest to peace-minded men in any effort to use international trade, as an invention, to increase the effectiveness of production and enlarge the satisfactions of those who are not so stupid as to refuse its benefits.

"The alternative to freer trade . . . is a resurgence of bilateral trading, quota restrictions, and exchange controls—which in turn will tend to be consolidated in single national trading authorities. Thus nations will seek, if only from defensive necessity, to manipulate foreign trade as a national monopoly-monopsony. Private competitive trading, even with much protectionist restriction, is essentially a peaceful and productive process, serving to promote economic division of labor and generally higher real income. The collectivist trading of national monopolies, on the other hand, is essentially exploitative and essentially a power contest, imperialist in the worst sense, and conducive to lower real income (and militarism) everywhere."[35]

[35] Henry C. Simons, *Economic Policy for a Free Society*, University of Chicago Press, Chicago, 1948, p. 269.

CHAPTER II

TWO-COMMODITY, TWO-COUNTRY, TRADE

In greater measure than perhaps any other branch of economics, the theory of international values has been subject to mortmain. This mortmain derives mainly from John Stuart Mill. In a reformulation of the theory it is, therefore, all but inevitable to begin with Mill.

Mill assumes that the two commodities with which he will deal are capable of being produced in both of two countries at relatively different but, within each country, constant (labor) costs per unit.[1]

[1] Labor cost is a not very clear or easily measurable concept and the concept is not necessary to Mill's argument. All that is necessary is that either of the two assumed commodities be capable of increased production, within the respective countries, at constant cost per unit in terms of forgone production of the other commodity. The argument will, therefore, be put in terms of opportunity cost except when Mill is directly quoted. It should be noted that the postulate merely requires that one commodity be indefinitely substitutable for the other, in either of the two countries, at a given rate in each. This rate must not be assumed to be the same for the two countries and it is not even necessary, in most cases, to posit that *all* of the producers, in either country, should be on the margin of indifference as to whether they produce the one or the other commodity at the ratio prevailing, for representative producers, in the country concerned. It will be sufficient if the number of such producers is adequate to any adjustment of supply, at the designated ratio, that conditions may at one or another time require. So far as pure exchange phenomena (commodity values) are concerned, it is of no consequence that even the representative producers, *within* either country, are of very diverse absolute competence, in both commodities, so long as each of the producers can, without loss, shift from one to the other of them at the posited opportunity cost. *A fortiori,* a contrast between the absolute competence of producers as a whole, in the one and in the other country, is of no relevance whatever for commodity values though it will, of course, make for differences of prosperity (the value relationship between representative labor-time and commodities in general). This is likewise true of divergences in absolute competence among producers *within* either country. When, however, we are dealing with problems of production rather than exchange (and when, as is not unusual, changes in the volume of production, even if appropriately distributed, affect exchange values), it will be convenient to assume that, whatever may be the differences *between* countries, all of the producers of any commodity *within* any country are of substantially equal absolute competence.

The assumption of constant (opportunity) cost is by no means unreal since it involves merely a *transfer* of factors of production, when a change in relative supply is required, and does not necessarily imply any increased, or diminished, draft on any one, or on all, of them. If, as is reasonable, we assume that the total demand for any product is adequate to call forth a number of productive units, each of optimum size, there is small ground for supposing that the expansion of output of one product might not proceed indefinitely at constant cost in the sacrifice of output of another.

The first systematic use of opportunity cost as a replacement for labor cost in the theory of international values was made by Professor Gottfried Haberler

Constant cost is not, of course, the same thing as stable cost (a cost that is stable over time). All that is meant by constant cost is that unit costs do not vary with a change in the volume of output, that is, that supply could have been indefinitely different *at the present moment*, or could now be altered in either direction, without any change in unit cost. Constant unit costs, therefore, are not constant in any temporal sense but merely in the sense that they are the same, at any given moment, regardless of the amount supplied. Under constant cost there can, at any moment, be only one normal value for a commodity whatever the supply (or demand), but, even though constant cost conditions should prevail throughout, that norm would change, over time, with every improvement or deterioration in the processes of production. Contrariwise, unit costs, for any given volume of output, could be stable over time even though the condition of variable costs, whether increasing or decreasing, were prevalent throughout the period under review. When unit costs are not constant, the normal price of the commodity, at any moment, will alter with variations in the amount supplied, but the normal price *for any given supply* would nevertheless remain fixed for an indefinite period during which "the general conditions of life" (that is, of production) did not change.[2] Just as constant costs may be unstable so variable costs may be stable. The distinction between constant and stable costs, and between variable and unstable costs, should be clear when we note the apparent paradox that unit costs of production of a given commodity might, over time, steadily decline despite the fact that the condition of increasing costs for the commodity was operative throughout and, *per contra*, that unit costs of production of the commodity might, over time, steadily advance without departure, at any time, from a condition of decreasing cost.

Transport costs are ignored by Mill though it would be more realistic, equally simple, and just as convenient, to assume that

(*Der Internationale Handel*, Julius Springer, Berlin, 1933). As pioneers in the development of the concept, Haberler (English edition) cites David I. Green ("Pain Cost and Opportunity Cost," *The Quarterly Journal of Economics*, Vol. VIII, 1894, pp. 218-229), Herbert J. Davenport (*Value and Distribution*, University of Chicago Press, Chicago, 1908), and Frank H. Knight (in various writings). The essential idea of opportunity cost is that the real cost of anything is the loss of the opportunity to procure an alternative good (satisfaction, or relief from irksomeness) which conditions the acquisition of the good in question.

[2] It is clear that Marshall, in the passage cited on page 316, completely confused the one with the other type of change in the norm.

either of the commodities could be put on the foreign market at the same cost as would be required to put it on the domestic market. In the one case transport costs are abstracted; in the other they would be included in the data as an invariable. The cost of production must, in any case, be assumed to include all costs necessary to get the goods to market and it is not unreasonable to posit that transport costs are the same whether the goods are sold abroad or at home.

Competition is assumed to be free, under individual enterprise, except that for one reason or another there is no, or at least an inhibited, movement of factors of production across national boundaries. There is, in consequence, no tendency toward equality of value of any given factor of production as between one country and the other (except so far as specialization in production may work to this end), whereas the values of mobile commodities, once international trade is under way and costs of transport are abstracted, will everywhere be the same. Since there are assumed to be no restraints whatever on competition *within* any country, the normal values of the commodities *produced* in either country, would, whether in the absence or presence of international trade, be identical with the relative costs of production there prevailing but the ratio of exchange between the commodities which are, and those which are not, produced in a given country will, under a regime of international trade, deviate from the cost of production ratios obtaining in that country for the two groups of commodities. Full utilization of labor resources is always presumed.

With these expressed or implied assumptions of Mill, modified as suggested, we may suppose with him: ". . . that 10 yards of broadcloth cost in England as much . . . as 15 yards of linen, and in Germany as much as 20. . . . The problem is, what are the causes which determine the proportion in which the cloth of England and the linen of Germany will exchange for each other?"[3] In his analysis of this situation Mill arbitrarily assumes a state of reciprocal demand which will bring about equilibrium on some terms of exchange (such as 17 yards of linen = 10 yards of cloth) well within the limits, set by comparative (labor or opportunity) costs, of 15 to 20 yards of linen for 10 yards of cloth. This in-between ratio he regards as

[3] *Principles of Political Economy*, 5th Edition, D. Appleton and Company, New York, 1906, Book III, chap. XVIII. There would be no harm in paraphrasing Mill's statement to read that 10 yards of broadcloth could always be secured in England by forgoing the output of 15 yards of linen; in Germany, that of 20; and *vice versa*.

typical though he says: "It is even possible to consider an extreme case, in which the whole of the advantage resulting from the interchange would be reaped by one party, the other country gaining nothing at all. There is no absurdity in the hypothesis, that, of some given commodity, a certain quantity is all that is wanted at any price; and that, when that quantity is obtained, no fall in the exchange value would induce other consumers to come forward, or those who are already supplied to take more. Let us suppose that this is the case in Germany with cloth."[4]

Mill then shows that the English demand for linen might be so strong as to force up the price of linen to 10 yards of cloth for only 15 of linen, in which case Germany would gain the whole of the advantage arising from trade and English consumers would be in exactly the same position as before the trade commenced. The reverse of this might also occur, with 10 yards of cloth exchanging for 20 of linen, and English consumers get the whole of the advantage.

So far from either of these being extreme and barely conceivable cases, logic compels the conclusion that, on Mill's assumptions, one or the other is all but inevitable.[5] As a condition precedent to the conclusion that one of the countries will obtain the whole of the gain from the trade, and the other none of it, it is by no means necessary to assume an absolutely inelastic demand for either of the commodities concerned. All that is necessary is that either country be incapable of producing as much of one commodity as it could market, in both, within the limits of the range of potential movement of the ratio of exchange, or that it be incapable of finding a market, within those limits, for all of any such commodity as it could produce. It is evident that the probability is high that its productive capacity will fall in one or the other of these categories. It will certainly do so when a large country trades with a small one in commodities of approximately equal total value or when two countries of approximately equal economic importance trade in commodities the total values of which show a considerable disparity. It will be noted that Mill selected for his exposition countries of approximately equal economic size and that the commodities (in his illustration at least) are of approximately equal total value. Let us see what would

---

[4] *loc. cit.*

[5] The ensuing discussion draws freely upon my article "The Theory of International Values Re-examined," *The Quarterly Journal of Economics,* Vol. xxxviii, 1923, pp. 54-86.

happen (1) if, instead of England and Germany, he had supposed trade between England and Denmark in cloth and linen, or (2) if, instead of cloth and linen, he had supposed trade, between England and Germany, in cloth and matches. The assumption in the one case is that the commodities are of approximately equal total economic importance while the countries are not, and, in the other, that the countries are of approximately equal total economic importance while the commodities are not.

Taking the first case and paraphrasing exactly Mill's assumptions, but with the substitution of Denmark for Germany, let us suppose that trade is initiated at the exchange ratio of 10 yards of cloth for 17 of linen. At that ratio, there are no producers in either country on the margin of indifference as between the two commodities. Such a trade must therefore cause a rapid shifting of English production from linen to cloth, and of Danish production from cloth to linen, and, at any such ratio and on Mill's general assumptions, nothing can stop this shifting until it has completely eliminated either the Danish production of cloth or the English production of linen. Since we are supposing that the total value of linen and cloth is in approximate equality, Denmark, as the smaller country, will be completely specialized in linen production while there are, perhaps, the more inert nine-tenths of the original English linen producers still struggling on in that business, the specialization by the Danes being sufficient to drive only one-tenth of the English linen producers into the making of cloth. In these circumstances the equilibrium ratio of exchange of cloth for linen must move to the extreme most favorable to Denmark, that is to say, 10 of cloth for 15 of linen; for a supply of linen adequate to the demand is not obtainable on any better terms, the terms which the English linen producers ultimately require if they are to continue their operations. At the 10 cloth for 15 linen ratio, however, English producers are on the margin of indifference, as to whether they produce cloth or linen, and linen can then be supplied in indefinite quantities at the expense of cloth.

Let us go now to the second case, in which we shall suppose that England and Germany, countries of approximately equal economic importance, possess a comparative productive advantage in cloth and matches respectively, 10 yards of cloth exchanging for 15 crates of matches in England and for 20 crates in Germany. The opening up of trade on the basis of 10 yards of cloth for 17 crates of matches will quickly put English producers of matches out of that business and into the making of cloth. But the Germans will never be able to find in England a market for matches large enough to pay for the German consumption of cloth, and they must therefore continue to produce cloth at home. Such a situation will mean that the ratio of exchange of cloth for matches will move to the extreme most favorable to England, that is to say, 10 yards of cloth for 20 crates of matches; for a supply of cloth adequate to the demand is not obtainable on any better terms, the terms which the German cloth producers require if they are to continue their operations. At that ratio, however, German producers are on the margin of indifference, as to whether they produce cloth or matches, and cloth can then be supplied in indefinite quantities at the expense of matches.

On Mill's assumptions, the establishment in international trade of any equilibrium other than at one of the extremes of the possible terms of interchange is dependent upon the *simultaneous* elimination, in each of the trading countries, of the industry which is, to it, of comparative disadvantage. The chance of this happening is negligible; this is the extreme, the barely conceivable, case, not, as Mill alleged, the normal one; while that which Mill regarded as abnormal, namely, that the terms of interchange should go to one or other of the points which mark the limits of comparative advantage, must (again on his assumptions) prove all but inevitable. Only if the dice are loaded by assuming trade in two commodities of approximately equal total consumption-value, between two countries of approximately equal economic importance, or by some combination of disparity in these conditions under which inequality under the one head will be cancelled by an opposite inequality under the other, can Mill's intermediate ratio be realized.

Any equilibrium that, under favoring circumstances, might be established at other than one of the extremes set by comparative costs would, moreover, be highly unstable. Indeed, with the volatile nature of desires, it could not be more than momentary and, except under very peculiar conditions of demand, no movement in the ratio of exchange, once under way, would ever stop short of attainment of one of the limits.

The Hidden Consequence of Mill's Assumptions

Mill's supposition of a state of trade, at other than one of the limiting ratios set by cost schedules, involves an immensely important hidden consequence. We have seen that the condition of the establishment of any intermediate ratio is the complete and synchronous specialization of both countries, each in the commodity of its comparative advantage, since neither country will produce both commodities except at its own cost ratio (one of the limits). On the express or implied supposition of unchanged general conditions, and of free competition within each country, this means that the supply of each of the commodities is irrevocably fixed. A shift in the relative desirability of the two commodities to the trading group as a whole is then, of course, the only circumstance that can affect the terms on which they will be exchanged; nor can any change in those terms have any effect on the relative output of the commodities. With no possibility of adjustment of supply to altered schedules of desirability, every shift in relative desires would be registered immediately, definitively, and solely, in the ratio of exchange, and there its effect would cease. Since there could be no response, in supply, to the shift in price there could be no tendency of movement toward any *normal* ratio of exchange. The shifting winds of desire would persistently initiate changes in the ratio, any one of which would be definitive, *for any given shift in the wind*, but would be instantaneously replaced as the wind veered in one direction or the other.

On this grotesque base rests the whole not only of the classical, but also of the neo-classical, theory of (normal) international values. That theory, as Marshall sensed and went to futile pains to deny, is purely a theory of demand (or rather desire) but not so much of demand (or desire) in the marginal sense of the term, which envisages shifts in relative supply, as of demand (or desire) in a generic sense which shuts out any change in supply in response to movements in price. It has already been noted that neo-classical modifications of the two-commodity, two-country, approach typically go not much farther than to the assumption of an exchange of unique *composites* of commodities (representative bales of goods) between a given country and the outside world taken as a whole.[6]

[6] F. W. Taussig, for example, in his chapter "Two Countries Competing in a Third" (*International Trade*, Macmillan, New York, 1927, pp. 97-107) can merely

The supply of one of the composites as against the other is frozen in this as in Mill's approach and, since desires are highly volatile, there can, under this theory, be no possibility of establishing any stability in international values. The "terms of trade" (the ratio at which one of the composites exchanges against the other) would, under any such theory, be in constant motion without any centripetal tendency whatever.

Let us, by contrast, consider trade at one of the "limiting ratios," and ask ourselves what there sets bounds upon the fluctuation in the rate of interchange of the commodities. It is clear that, at either of the limiting ratios, the essential factor is the adjustment of supply, by producers on the margin of indifference, to *any* shift that may occur in the relative desirability of, or total relative demand for, the two commodities. This establishes a tendency to keep the relative marginal utilities of, and the exchange ratio between, units of the two commodities in steady correspondence with their cost ratios in one of the two countries.

With 10 yards of cloth exchanging for 15 yards of linen, the ratio will be unaffected no matter how much, within perhaps very wide limits, the desire for cloth relative to linen may rise, and, also, no matter how much, without limits whatever, the desire for cloth relative to linen may fall. With 10 yards of cloth exchanging for 20 yards of linen, on the other hand, the ratio will be unaffected no matter how much, within perhaps very wide limits, the desire for linen relative to cloth may rise, and, also, no matter how much, without limits whatever, the desire for linen relative to cloth may fall.[7]

At the ratio of 10 cloth to 15 linen, Germany would be specialized in linen and England would be producing both cloth and linen. *Without any change in the ratio of exchange*, as the demand for cloth rose relatively to that for linen, producers in England could

---

say of a simple trade involving two commodities and *three* countries that the ratio of exchange will be somewhere between the limits set by the *maximum* difference in comparative costs, and that the outcome depends on *the state of demand between the countries*. The matter is more adequately treated in the next chapter of this .book.

[7] The statement, of course, abstracts from temporary deviations of market price from the current norm. These will occur in the degree in which suppliers have misjudged the trend of demand and will be eliminated in the degree in which adjustment of supply is effected. It should be emphasized that, unless otherwise expressly stated, this book is concerned only with *normal* values and will commonly ignore the (temporary) aberrations of market values from the norms.

expand the production of cloth at the expense of linen up to the point where England was completely specialized in cloth. If the demand for cloth, even then, continued to be relatively strong, the ratio would shift. It would be unstable and indeterminate (a limbo ratio) so long as there were no producers, anywhere, on the margin of indifference as between cloth and linen. But when it reached 10 cloth = 20 linen, German producers would become indifferent as to which commodity they put out, Germany would produce both commodities, and the yardage of cloth, produced in the two countries together, could, *without any change in the ratio*, then be made many times the yardage of linen. The supply of cloth could, in fact, be increased in any degree at the expense of linen, without further change in the ratio, so that, whatever the extremes of the shift in relative demand, the marginal utility of cloth, in terms of linen, would thenceforth be kept in correspondence with German opportunity costs.

With an original ratio of 10 cloth to 20 linen, on the other hand, England would be specialized in cloth and Germany would produce both commodities. A growth in the demand for linen relative to cloth would then be supplied, without a change in the ratio of exchange, until Germany had completely abandoned the production of cloth and was specialized exclusively in linen. If the demand for linen, even then, continued to be strong, relatively to cloth, the ratio would change since all the producers on the margin of indifference would have been eliminated. A limbo ratio would emerge. When, however, with a persistent urgent demand for linen, the ratio reached 10 cloth = 15 linen, English producers would go in for linen as readily as cloth, and, a new margin of indifference having been established, the total supply of linen, at the expense of cloth, could then be increased without further change in the ratio in whatever degree was necessary to keep the relative marginal utilities of the two commodities in correspondence with opportunity costs in England.

A temporary shift in market values, slightly beyond the "limits," would spur the transfer of resources from linen to cloth in Germany or from cloth to linen in England. This change in market values is not inevitable, however, and might not ever appear. The transfer could take place merely because the market for cloth was good and that for linen slow, or *vice versa*. If, however, any temporary stretching of the ratio *should* occur as a facilitating, but not essential, factor in the shifting of resources, this, it must be stressed, would be a phenomenon of market and not of normal values. If the classical writers had intended to lay down merely a theory of *market* values, the whole apparatus of comparative cost would be irrelevant, superfluous, and vexatious, since the "limiting ratios" set by comparative costs might, at times, be greatly transcended.[8] These ratios set limits on *normal* values or they set them on nothing at all.

As soon as relative supply is flexible (as can be the case only at one of the limiting ratios set by comparative cost) normal values appear. Without this flexibility, ratios of exchange will move, within or outside the limits set by comparative cost, in response to every flutter in capricious desires; but, *with* such flexibility, market values, regardless of shifts in demand, will (1) either not deviate at all from current normal values, or (2) will cluster around these normal values (at one of the limiting ratios—the cost ratio in one of the countries), or (3), with the establishment of a new set of normal values (the cost ratio in the other country), will center on this new norm.

Whenever the total relative demand for linen and cloth is such that the fixed supplies (when each country is completely specialized, with England in cloth and Germany in linen) can be equated at some ratio of exchange between 15 and 20 yards of linen to 10 of cloth (an unusual case), the ratio will be unstable, in response to persistently evolving shifts of relative demand, and for its motion there will be no norm.

At some point which, in systematically traversing the range of possible demand from one extreme to the other, one must momentarily hit, the classical analysis becomes more or less valid. Let us suppose that trade starts at one of the limiting ratios (which would almost inevitably be the actual situation) and let us assume that the desire for cloth relatively to linen when the initial ratio is 15 linen = 10 cloth, or the desire for linen relatively to cloth when the initial ratio is 20 linen = 10 cloth, continues to grow indefinitely. The ratio of exchange of cloth for linen must then, at some point, enter the limbo between 15 and 20 yards of linen to 10 yards of cloth.

[8] The magnitude, and duration, of deviations of market values from *any* norm will be a function solely of the facility of adjustment of supply to an evolving demand of given elasticity.

While it remains anywhere within this range there can be no tendency to change the relative supplies of the two commodities, since any such ratio will be possible only when both countries are fully specialized (with Germany in linen and England in cloth) and, as long as any such intermediate ratio prevails, there will be no inducement to anyone to shift resources from their current employment in either country.

Since supply under these conditions is absolutely fixed, a naked theory of demand is all that is necessary to account for the momentary status of the ratio of exchange and, as already noted, every shift in the relative desirability of the goods will be reflected in the ratio, immediately, in full measure, and without any effect on the relative quantities put on the market. This, it will be recognized, is the classical theory of international values, which has thus advanced not at all beyond Ricardo's statement that the terms of trade would tend to settle *somewhere* between the limits set by the cost ratios, for the products concerned, in the respective trading countries.[9]

The English cost of production ratio (15 linen = 10 cloth) will be the unchanging norm for all situations in which, at that, or any other possible, ratio, the total amount of linen demanded in both countries would be more than Germany could supply or (what is the same thing) the total amount of cloth demanded in both countries would be less than England could supply. The German cost of production ratio (20 linen = 10 cloth) will be the unchanging norm for all situations in which, at that, or any other possible, ratio, the total amount of cloth demanded in both countries would be more than England could supply or (what is the same thing) the total amount of linen demanded in both countries would be less than Germany could supply. Only in the highly unlikely event that the economic size of the two countries is closely correlated with the relative total importance of the two commodities and, at the same time, that the comparative advantage of the larger country lies in the commodity of greater, and that of the smaller country in the commodity of lesser, total economic importance, is there any possibility of any ratio other than at one of the extremes set by the relative cost ratios in the two countries.

[9] Ricardo's examples indicate a split down the middle of the range but he never committed himself to the proposition that this was to be expected and simply left the matter indeterminate.

Importance of the Margin of Indifference

It is perhaps worth while to reiterate that the ratios at one or the other of the extremes set by comparative cost are stable solely because at these points English producers in the one case, and German producers in the other, are on the margin of indifference as to which commodity they shall produce. No matter what may then be the shift in the relative desirability of cloth and linen taken as wholes, the relative *marginal* desirability of units of the two commodities will be kept constant through adjustment of relative supplies. Only when the margin of indifference in production disappears in one country, and is not replaced by its counterpart in the other, could the limbo ratio assumed in the classical theory occur. Except in the case of a limbo ratio no change in *total relative demand* for the respective commodities can have any influence on (normal) *marginal* demand or the (normal) ratio of exchange.

Whenever it so happens that there are no producers on the margin of indifference, and a limbo ratio (indeterminate and without a norm) prevails, an opportunity for strategy in the manipulation of that ratio is always present. Bargaining skill then becomes important. Marshall has shown that, even with given schedules of desire and unchanging supply, the ratio of exchange under conditions similar to those here posited is indeterminate.[10] Marshall believed that this was a consequence of barter, but practically identical results would be reached in pecuniarily processed trade under similar conditions. When no one in either of the trading groups is on the margin of indifference as to whether he produces the one or the other commodity the members of either group may exert a form of monopoly power and, with such a dual monopoly, bargaining skill assumes importance. Bargaining skill, indeed, is of consequence only in the degree that competitive conditions do *not* prevail and in truly competitive markets is wholly irrelevant in the determination of price.[11] Even, however, though the traders in either of the posited groups compete, in a fashion, one of the groups as a whole may, without any necessarily conscious collusion among its members,

[10] Alfred Marshall, *Principles of Economics*, 6th edn., Macmillan, London, 1910, Appendix F, pp. 792-793.
[11] Certainly in ideal, and allegedly in actual, competitive markets, the shrewd and the stupid trader, at any given time, pay, or receive, exactly the same price for any given good.

exploit the other whenever no one, anywhere, is on the margin of indifference as to which good he will produce. If, for instance, the members of one group are merely lazy, relative to those of the other group, the supply of the commodity in which they find it advantageous to specialize may fall relative to the supply of the commodity in which the other group will specialize. The ratio of exchange will, in consequence, tend to move in favor of the lazy group and, since this may promote their lethargy and further reduce supply, it may move so far that the group will get a greater total of goods by being lazy than it could obtain by being industrious.

Collusive action, whether on private initiative or at the instigation of government, has at least equal prospects of success, and is, moreover, somewhat more attractive to an energetic group which can then devote part of its productive powers to goods not subject to trade between the groups. Much of the neo-classical literature on international trade deals with the possibilities of changing the ratio of exchange ("terms of trade")¹² by some such action. The prospects would be good, however, only in the very rare case on which classical theory is erroneously built. Where, at any given ratio, there are producers, somewhere, on the margin of indifference as between commodities (as will nearly always be the case) the slightest shift in the ratio will suffice to transfer productive resources indefinitely from the output of the relatively depreciating to that of the relatively appreciating commodity. There is then no possibility of manipulating the market, or of any but minimal shifts in the ratio of exchange, and lethargic or scheming traders could, under these conditions, never exploit their industrious and candid fellows.

Applications

In the world as it is, we are, of course, seldom likely to encounter trade involving only two countries and two commodities. Something close to it momentarily appeared, however, in the trade between the British and the South Sea Islands, after the explorers' penetration of the latter areas. Let us suppose (what may have been historical fact) that a British sea-captain, with a good stock of Scotch whisky aboard his ship, discovers, in the late eighteenth century, an

¹² The phrase "terms of trade" will usually be put in quotation marks since it ordinarily connotes the rate at which national blocs of commodities exchange against one another. The concept of such national blocs of commodities is persistently under attack, in this book, as unreal.

island in the South Seas where pearls of purest ray can be fished up by expert native divers but not by his own seamen. The chief of the tribe might retain in his own hands all negotiations. The captain plies him, and the tribesmen, with a certain limited amount of free whisky as a preliminary to trade. They find it so good as to rate it very highly in terms of pearls (taking, as a criterion, the standards of the captain who, we will suppose, is a teetotaler). There is evidently here an enormous range within which the terms of any exchange that may be arranged could take place. What the terms will actually be will depend almost exclusively on the relative bargaining shrewdness of the captain and the chief. If, moreover, the chief drives a sufficiently good bargain he may, for a few pearls, get enough whisky to keep him and his subjects persistently drunk. This will, of course, greatly inhibit the on-coming supply of pearls, and thus keep the ratio of exchange of pearls against whisky persistently high and, perhaps, rising.

The British could not produce the pearls themselves, and the islanders could not produce Scotch whisky, so that there is no possibility of any of the producers of either commodity coming to a margin of indifference as between the output of pearls and whisky. In these circumstances the ultimate ratio of exchange might well depend very largely on the terms first established, and these, it will be recalled, would hang on the fortuitous relative bargaining capacity of the captain and the chief. If the captain had been the shrewder of the two, or of more coldly calculating cupidity, he might have obtained his original pearls for so small an amount of whisky as would be sufficient to whet the appetites of the islanders but not to admit of a prolonged orgy, and the natives might then go on assiduously fishing for pearls as a means of acquiring an innocuously small further supply of whisky. In other words, the ratio of exchange would then, in contrast with the preceding assumption, begin, and stay, in the neighborhood of what, from the purely trading point of view, would be a most unfavorable status for the islanders. The fact is, however, that the ratio in such trade is indeterminate, that any ratio momentarily established would probably be unstable, and that movements in the ratio in either direction might, for a lengthy period at least, be self-inflammatory.

As soon, however, as, in the one case, diving equipment enabling the British to match the sub-marine skill and endurance of the islanders was procured or, in the other, the natives learned to make their own whisky, a normal and stable ratio of exchange, based on the (opportunity) costs of those who, in the one or the other case, were on the margin of indifference as between the output of pearls and whisky, would come into being. The islanders, in the one case, could not then gravely exploit the British, and the British, in the other, could not then gravely exploit the islanders.

Although, in the modern world, there is probably no counterpart of the trade just discussed, it sometimes happens that a given country produces for export a single commodity which cannot be obtained anywhere else. Before the development of synthetic nitrate, Chile was, with respect to the natural product, in some approximation to this position. The ratio of exchange between nitrates and the commodities imported by Chile was then primarily determined along the lines of the classical analysis of two-country, two-commodity, trade. Since producers for export in Chile were not on the margin of indifference as between nitrates and other exportable or importable products, and since nitrates could not be produced in substantial quantities in any other country, there was no *normal* ratio of exchange, based on opportunity costs, at any margin of indifference between nitrates and Chilean imports. The actual ratio was, in consequence, determined by the erratic reciprocal demand of the users of nitrates and of the Chileans for their imports.[18] The consequent vicissitudes in the price of nitrates (in a stable money or in other commodities) were a factor in the establishment of the equivalent of a monopoly control of the product, to ensure, among other objectives, a "satisfactory" return to the producers or, at any rate, to Chile.

If the foregoing examples of approximation to the conditions assumed in the classical analysis seem far-fetched, one can but reply that that analysis, which professed to be representative, is in fact appropriate only to conditions so unusual as, in the modern world, to be practically non-existent. The analysis cannot, therefore, serve as a foundation of any theory which we can hope to apply, with legitimate abstractions, to existing phenomena.

18 The Chilean demand for imports was, of course, in a process of interaction, greatly affected by the ratio of exchange of nitrates against other products, and that ratio was itself affected by the demand. It is, on the other hand, unlikely that the demand of the outside world for nitrates was equally influenced by the ratio of exchange between nitrates and Chilean imports (the exports of other countries).

APPENDIX TO CHAPTER II

IN THE CASE of two-country, two-commodity trade, there is no difficulty in deciding, on a mere inspection of comparative costs, where comparative advantage (if any) lies, though, as we shall presently see, the decision is by no means obvious when more complex conditions are under investigation. Comparative advantage is not only a function of comparative costs but also of the ratio of exchange of commodities. The ratio in complex trade is often, in large part, determinative of comparative advantage, even as comparative advantage (or cost) is itself a primary factor in the determination of the ratio. (This interaction will become clear as we proceed.) When the ratio of exchange, in the trade between two countries in but two commodities, is at one or the other of the limits of the range set by comparative costs (the normal case), one of the countries finds no advantage in the production of either of the commodities rather than the other and so will produce both. It may then be said to have no comparative advantage in either commodity though, since the other country *will* have a comparative advantage in the production of one of the commodities, a nice regard for logical elegance, and correlatives to any relative, might require the assertion that the first country had had a conditional comparative advantage in the production of one of the commodities and that this conditional comparative advantage had been rendered void in the process of trade and the establishment of the existing ratio of exchange. At any point short of the, to it, most unfavorable limit of the ratio of exchange, the country in question has a comparative advantage in the production of the commodity which the other country will find it unprofitable to produce but, when the limit is reached, this advantage disappears (as the correlative advantage of the other country reaches a maximum). The question arises as to why, when this happens, the first country should bother with international trade at all, since, at the then established ratio of exchange, it would lose nothing by being on a self-sufficient basis. The answer is that at any point which, within the range of the potential ratio of exchange, falls short of the unfavorable limit, the producers in the said country will find it profitable to specialize in the commodity in which they would then have a comparative advantage. Any further specialization in that commodity would, however, drive its price beyond, and below, the cost ratio in the country in question. This would (if it could occur, which, as a norm, is not the case) make the production of the *other* commodity a superior alternative. The shift to the other commodity could, however, not go far, without *reversing* the preceding movement in the ratio of exchange, and thus make it preferable for the country to continue in the original product. No equilibrium can be established without the country in question producing a quota of both commodities, one of them for export (as well as home consumption) and the other as a supplement to imports. Any attempt, in a given state of demand, to change the relative output of the two commodities, either in a move toward self-sufficiency or toward concentration on the commodity of conditional comparative advantage, would thus immediately be nullified by such a shift in the ratio of exchange, in one direction or the other, as would restore the equilibrium split of output between the two commodities.

While, therefore, there is no advantage to any country in carrying on international trade with another at a ratio of exchange identical with its own cost ratio (the other country getting all of the gain), such a country will, under free trading conditions, nevertheless not move toward a self-sufficient status. (Prohibitive duties on imports would, however, do it no harm whether these were levied by itself or by the other country: the other country, however, would suffer greatly from such duties no matter by whom they were imposed.)

In two-country, two-commodity, trade there are five possible combinations of absolute efficiency or cost (i.e. per capita production per unit of labor time) and relative efficiency or cost. The absolute *per capita* efficiency, or cost, is irrelevant to the ratio of exchange of commodities (except so far as it conditions *total* output) but is a primary factor in prosperity. *Total* national output (a combination of per capita output and the numbers of the population), *does*, however, have a bearing on the international ratio of exchange.

The five possible combinations may be illustrated as follows:

CASE I

In a unit of representative labor time there can be produced:[14]

Commodities	In Country A	In Country B
x	1	1
y	1	1

[14] Labor time per unit of product is here used as an elliptical expression for

In this case absolute and relative per capita powers are the same in both countries. There will be no reason for international trade since the normal price of a unit of x will be a unit of y in both countries (and both will exchange for the same amount of money). Per capita incomes will be the same in both countries.

CASE II

In a unit of representative labor time there can be produced:		
Commodities	*In Country A*	*In Country B*
x	1	10
y	1	10

In this case the absolute labor-time cost of either commodity will be only one-tenth as much in B as in A (B has an absolute advantage in both) but *relative* labor costs of the commodities are identical. Here also there is no reason for international trade since a unit of x will exchange for a unit of y (and each for the same amount of money) in both countries. Per capita wage (and other) incomes (whether expressed in real terms or in a common money such as gold) will be ten times as great in B as in A; the citizens of B will be ten times as prosperous as those of A.

CASE III

In a unit of representative labor time there can be produced:		
Commodities	*In Country A*	*In Country B*
x	1^{15}	10
y	1^{15}	5

In this case the absolute labor cost of either commodity will, as in Case II, be very much less in B than in A (B has an absolute ad-

absolute per capita productivity. While absolute per capita productivity, as just noted, is of practically no consequence to the theory of international values, and was quite unnecessary to the development of the classical theory, some such concept is requisite to comparisons of national per capita incomes under international trade. It seems worth while here to bring out *clearly* the irrelevance of absolute per capita productivity to commodity prices. A concession to the classical method of exposition is therefore, for the moment, expedient even though this requires a generally inadmissible recognition of identity of labor-cost and commodity-value relationships within any country. On this latter point, cf. Edward S. Mason, "The Doctrine of Comparative Cost," *The Quarterly Journal of Economics*, Vol. XLI, pp. 63-93.

[15] It is always possible to keep a 1-to-1 relationship between amounts of the two commodities produced in any one country in a given time since the size of the selected unit of either x or y can, regardless of the actual output per man-hour of either commodity, be taken to be whatever amount of either commodity can be produced, per worker, in one hour or multiple thereof.

vantage in both commodities) but the relative labor costs are not identical. Country B now has a *comparative*, as well as an absolute, advantage in x and a *comparative* disadvantage in y (i.e. it cannot produce y as well as it can x, the situation in A being taken as a criterion) whereas A, though at an absolute disadvantage in both commodities, has a *comparative* advantage in y and a *comparative* disadvantage in x (i.e. it cannot produce x as well as it can y, the situation in B being taken as a criterion).[16] International trade will now be profitable since the price, in A, of a unit of x will, in the absence of international trade, be a unit of y, whereas its price in B will, in the absence of international trade, be only one-half a unit of y (10 : 5 :: 1 : $\frac{1}{2}$). Anyone in A, sending a unit of y to B, can, at the start of trade, obtain two units of x in exchange (instead of the single unit he would receive at home), and anyone in B, sending a unit of x to A, can obtain a unit of y in exchange (instead of the half-unit he would receive at home). Producers in A will therefore tend to specialize in the output of y and those in B in the output of x. After trade has proceeded for some time the exchange relationship between x and y (and the money prices of each) will come to identity in both countries and is likely to be either $x = y$ (in which case the citizens of B will get all of the gain from international trade) or $x = \frac{1}{2}y$ (in which case the citizens of A will get all of the gain from the international trade).

If A should have between five and ten times the population of B (and the commodities, at the ultimately established ratio of exchange, were of approximately equal total economic importance), so that A's low absolute per capita productivity would be compensated in its effect on total supply by the relatively large number of workers in A, it could happen that A could specialize completely in y, and B in x, with the price of the commodities in both countries somewhere within the range $x = \frac{1}{2}$ to $1y$. Each of the countries would then get a smaller or larger share of the gains from the in-

[16] It is sometimes said that a country of low all-round absolute productivity will tend to specialize in the commodity in which its comparative *dis*advantage is at a minimum. This is a misconception. No country, under free international trade, will at any time produce a commodity in which it has a comparative disadvantage, however small, since it cannot have a comparative disadvantage without having a comparative advantage. It will, therefore, always specialize in goods in the latter category. The good of least comparative disadvantage would be that in which, when more than two goods are involved, the *increase* in cost of acquisition, by self-sufficient production, would be a minimum. But it would still pay the country to secure the commodity by import.

ternational trade. (A similar limbo ratio might be established if the economically smaller country should have a comparative advantage in a commodity of something like proportionately minor total economic significance.)

The (approximate) total gain, per unit of labor-cost, attributable to the international trade is easily assessed. In ten units of labor-time (*e.g.*, man-hours), concentrated on the production of y rather than equally split between the two products, A will produce 10 units of y (in lieu of its former output, from the same effort, of 5 units of each product) and B, concentrating on x, will produce, per man-hour, $10x$ in lieu of the $5x$ and $2\frac{1}{2}y$ which it could get in the same time, split equally between the two products, on a basis of national self-sufficiency. The total output under international trade is thus $10x$ plus $10y$ for the same effort that would produce but $10x$ and $7\frac{1}{2}y$ under national self-sufficiency.[17]

[17] That the gain shows up entirely in y is a fortuitous result of the choice of time-units. If, instead of selecting the output of one man-hour in B, that of two man-hours had instead been taken, the result would have shown 20 x, with concentration in B on that product, in lieu of 10 x plus 5 y if the time had been equally split between the two commodities. The total output of a given effort (10 man-hours in A and two man-hours in B) would then be 20 x plus 10 y, under national specialization, in lieu of 15 x plus 10 y when both countries produce both products and split their time equally between them. Under this selection of time-units the gain shows up entirely in x, As a matter of fact the gain will normally be taken partly in one product and partly in the other, the total production and consumption of both being increased. Any specialization along lines of comparative advantage, however limited, always increases total output. It could happen, however, that, with a different ratio of exchange in one or both countries from that prevailing under national self-sufficiency, the amount of the one commodity demanded, relative to the other, may so increase as to lead to an absolute reduction in the taking of the second commodity, with more than the whole of the total increase in output going into the former of them. When the ratio of exchange is at one of the limits set by comparative cost and there are, in consequence, producers on the margin of indifference between the two products, the supply of either commodity can always be increased indefinitely at the expense of the other and at a given opportunity cost. This, however, is not true when any limbo ratio prevails. If, at such a limbo ratio (possible only when each country is completely specialized, the one in the one and the other in the other commodity) the amount of the one commodity demanded should persistently rise relatively to the amount demanded of the other, the limbo ratio (which, in any case, would be a *rarissima avis*) would disappear in a stable ratio corresponding to relative costs of output of the commodities in the country of conditional comparative advantage in the product for which there was a relatively decreasing desire. The relative supply of the two commodities could then be changed in any desired degree.

The indifference-curve analysis of demand originated by Edgeworth and Pareto, and developed by R. G. D. Allen and J. R. Hicks, may here have application though I have been somewhat disappointed (perhaps only with myself) at not seeing elsewhere much opportunity for its fruitful use. Starting with equal amounts of the two commodities available, alternative supplies (with the output of one of the commodi-

Commodity prices under trade will, in all cases, be the same in both countries, and per capita money incomes in B will be anywhere from 5 to 10 times those in A, depending on the degree of specialization in either country and on whether A gets all of the gains from the international trade, or B does, or they split them.

CASE IV

In a unit of representative labor time there can be produced:

Commodities	In Country A	In Country B
x	1	10
y	1	1

In this case, the absolute labor cost of one of the commodities, y, is the same in both countries while that of the other, x, is very different. The *relative* cost of the two commodities is therefore disparate in the two countries. The case is practically on all fours with that just discussed. Country B has a *comparative* advantage in x and a *comparative* disadvantage in y whereas A has a *comparative* disadvantage in x and a *comparative* advantage in y. International trade will be profitable since the price, in A, of a unit of x will, in the absence of international trade, be a unit of y, whereas its price, in B, will, in the absence of international trade, be only 1/10 of a unit of y. Traders in either country could make a profit by buying in the domestic market the commodity which is there relatively cheap and selling it in the other country where it is, *ipso facto*, relatively dear. Producers in A will specialize in y and producers in B will specialize in x. After trade is opened up prices will come to identity in both countries and are likely to be either $x = y$ (in which case the citizens of B will get all the gain from the international trade), or $x = \frac{1}{10}y$ (in which case the citizens of A will engross all the benefits). Under certain very improbable conditions (which can readily be determined on analogy with the case previously discussed) a limbo ratio any-

---

ties increasing at the expense of the other) could be plotted. This could be fitted as a tangent to an indifference curve of total demand (assuming it were possible to show what combinations of amounts of the two commodities were of equal significance to consumers taken as a whole) and the tangential point would show the respective amounts of the two commodities that would actually be produced and consumed. For further suggestions on the expedient employment of indifference curves cf. Wassily W. Leontief, "The Use of Indifference Curves in the Analysis of Foreign Trade," *The Quarterly Journal of Economics*, Vol. XLVII, pp. 493-503; and A. Lerner, "The Diagrammatical Representation of Cost Conditions in International Trade," *Economica*, No. 37, pp. 346-356.

where between $x = \frac{1}{10} y$ and $x = y$ might be established. The gains from international trade would then be (more or less equally) shared by the two countries. The total gains from the trade will be very much greater than was true of Case III from the fact that the spread in comparative costs (advantage) is here greater. Country B will, without trade, be more prosperous than A by an amount dependent upon the relative importance of x and y in total income. Neither country can lose by trade but, under trade, *per capita* money and real incomes in B will range from a mere equality with those in A to ten times those of A according to (1) the relative importance of x and y in total income, (2) whether B gets none, some, or all of the gains from the international trade, and (3) the degree to which *both* countries are specialized.[18]

[18] If B were a small country, and x a specialty in which it had extraordinarily good relative resources (let us say, iron), B would be able to engross the total gains from trade so long as, even when it was fully specialized in x, the demand for that product was so strong as to call for its production, along with y, in A. But if B could not put all of its productive powers into x without depressing the price of x so much as to make it worth while also to produce y in that country, A would engross the total gains from the trade. While, in such simple cases, the terms on which international trade is carried on can make an enormous difference in the relative prosperity of the participating countries it will, for reasons later to be developed, appear that it is highly improbable that there could be any counterparts of this situation in the real world. Yet some of the neo-classical writers have been trapped, by the possibilities in these simple cases, into assertions that will not stand scrutiny. Professor Taussig, for example, attributes the relatively low incomes of India, in comparison with those of Great Britain, to the unfavorable terms on which India carries on its exchange of goods with the British (F. W. Taussig, *International Trade*, The Macmillan Company, New York, 1927, p. 157 *et seq.*). I can perhaps do no better, in comment on this, than to quote from my article ("The Theory of International Values," *The Quarterly Journal of Economics*, Vol. XLVI, 1932, pp. 611ff.).

"The terms of trade are, in fact, rather unfavorable to India. This is shown, not by the relative height of British and Indian incomes, but by the circumstance that India is, in late years, entering more and more into the production of several typically British goods while there is no possibility of Britain's entering into the production of most of the typically Indian goods. . . . This . . . means that England is getting the greater share of the gains from the trade. Great Britain is thus somewhat richer, and India somewhat poorer, than if the terms were more favorable to India. The overwhelming reason for the great difference in incomes, however, is not the ratio of interchange but the disparity in absolute productivity of the workers in the marginal export, and in most of the domestic, commodities of each country. The ratio of interchange is a minor factor which could be of decisive importance only in the case of small countries with a limited number of exports. If India should greatly raise her absolute productivity, per worker, in all agricultural products, the 'terms of trade' with Great Britain [measured in the prices of imports in terms of exports] would, in the absence of other changes, become even more adverse [to India] but the disparity between British and Indian incomes would nevertheless be reduced. The present terms of trade are unfavorable to India, because the *relative* cost of production, in India, of all of the various commodities exchanged in both

CASE V

In a unit of representative labor time there can be produced:

Commodities	In Country A	In Country B	
x	1	12	{a ratio
y	5	3	{of 4:1

In this case, the respective countries each have an absolute advantage in one of the products and an absolute disadvantage in the other. It is in this type of case that, *ceteris paribus*, the greatest comparative advantages appear and the gains from international trade tend to be maximal. It is typical of trade between regions of very diverse climate or other natural resources (e.g. Sweden and Ecuador). Country A has an absolute as well as a comparative advantage in *y*, and B in *x*. International trade will be very profitable since, in its absence, a unit of *x* will exchange for 5 units of *y*, in A, and for only one-quarter of a unit of *y* in B. The range of the ratio (the limits between which international trade will be profitable to both) are therefore $x = \frac{1}{4}y$ to $5y$. The ratio of exchange is likely to be either $x = \frac{1}{4}y$ or $x = 5y$ (the whole gain going to A in the former case and to B in the latter) but, in peculiar conditions of supply and demand, the gain might be shared in a ratio lying somewhere between these extremes. If the ratio is $x = \frac{1}{4}y$, A will get twenty times as much *x*, per unit of cost in labor-time, as it could get if it produced *x* at home, while, if the ratio is $x = 5y$, B will get twenty times as much *y*, per unit of cost in labor-time, as it could get in the domestic production of *y*.

Per capita incomes in the two countries would, in the absence of trade, be not very widely divergent (the difference depending, in considerable degree, on the relative importance for total income, in each of the countries, of *x* and *y*). With, however, an international

directions is closer to their relative cost of production in the world at large than is the case with Great Britain. This is, of course, a more or less fortuitous situation which happens to be unfavorable to India. But the low level of Indian incomes is so much more due to deficiencies in absolute productivity, over a range of products sufficient to employ the whole Indian population, that India need not devote any excessive concern to the terms of trade. In any case, so long as productive conditions in India and in the outside world remain substantially as at present, there is no possibility of changing the ratio of exchange very much. The character of the British demand schedule for imports from India, or of the Indian demand schedule for imports from Britain, is in no way responsible for the situation" (cf. later chapters).

ratio of exchange of $x = \frac{1}{4}y$, per capita incomes in B might be only a fraction of those in A, whereas, with a ratio of $x = 5y$, per capita incomes in B might be many times those in A (depending, in each case, on the factors already listed under Case IV).

Since, at least on the conditions so far assumed, no country could ever be worse off with international trade than without it (but, for a special case, cf. Chapter VIII), the enormous alteration in relative per capita incomes in the two countries attendant upon shifts in the ratio of exchange when, as in this case, the range is wide, is likely to impress the observer with a highly exaggerated notion of the significance of the international ratio of exchange in determining the prosperity of any given country. International trade, and the ratio, are *important*, but usually not *predominant*, in national income. Later chapters will show that, in the more complex trade that is akin to that of the actual world, there is a wholly negligible possibility either that any country would run into the, for it, *pessimum* ratio of exchange (in which it would get no gain from the international trade it carries on) or that, the international ratio of exchange being once established in a complex trading world (at a level at which all of the participating countries share in the gains), any great alteration will occur so long as national cost structures remain unchanged. If, however, (real) cost structures should change, per capita (real) incomes will be likely to change along with them both as a result of the alteration of cost structures and of the consequent shifts in the international ratio of exchange of commodities. Any change in per capita real incomes in a country is, nevertheless, much more likely to be a reflection of a change in the real costs of commodity production in the country in question than of an alteration in the international ratio of exchange relative to those costs.

Prosperity in any country is a function of per capita productivity and of the ratio of exchange of exports for imports. In most, certainly in large, countries, per capita productivity is by far the more important of the two factors. Professor Taussig, in treating the topic discussed in the note to Case IV, was a victim of the illusions nourished by the classical concentration of attention on the two-country, two-commodity, situation and was thus led into the certainly erroneous statement that the relatively high incomes in Great Britain were primarily attributable to favorable terms of trade with the Orient (including India). Taussig still further confused the matter, and involved himself in a complete logical circle, in his implication that the relatively high British (money) incomes are a *cause* of the favorable ratio of exchange (*loc. cit.*, p. 157) which he also cites as a cause of those incomes.[19] The implication, moreover, runs counter to classical doctrines which it was out of character with Taussig to repudiate.

[19] cf. Appendix B.

CHAPTER III

TWO-COMMODITY, TRI- OR MULTI-COUNTRY, TRADE

The Intermediate Cost Ratio

IF the chances are strong that, in two-country two-commodity trade, the international ratio of exchange of the commodities will settle at the cost ratio in one or the other country, it is still more probable that, in trade involving more than two countries, it will settle at the cost ratio in some one of such a larger group of trading entities. It is, in fact, highly probable that it will settle at the cost ratio of a country in an intermediate position in the scale. If, for instance, a third country, France, should enter, along with England and Germany, into our posited trade in cloth and linen, and could produce those commodities at a constant cost ratio of 10 cloth = 18 linen, the ratio of exchange will inevitably settle at 10 cloth = 18 linen unless the demand for cloth relative to that for linen, (for linen relative to that for cloth), should be such as, with a much reduced range of any possible "limbo" ratio, would either permit *complete* specialization in every country, two of them exclusively in cloth, or linen, and the third (either Germany or England) in the other commodity, or would put all of the countries into one of the commodities, the other commodity also being produced in one of them.

At the ratio 10 cloth = 18 linen, France would produce both commodities, with Germany exclusively in linen and England exclusively in cloth. Without a change in that ratio, the French producers could alter the relative world supply of the commodities to correspond with any change in demand not so great as to eliminate the French production of one or the other of the goods.

Only if the total demand for cloth relative to linen were great enough to impel French producers to concentrate exclusively on cloth yet not great enough to induce any output of cloth in Germany, or if the total demand for linen relative to cloth were great enough to impel French producers to concentrate exclusively on linen yet not great enough to induce any output of linen in England, could the ratio of exchange be other than the French cost ratio or the cost ratio of one of the other countries. If, for example, the relative demand for cloth should be so great at the 10 cloth = 18 linen ratio as to exceed the combined cloth capacity of England and France, some "limbo" ratio, between 18 and 20 linen for 10 cloth, could prevail only when, at that ratio, the total relative demand for cloth and linen would, by some rare accident, equate with the respective outputs of France and England (engaged exclusively on cloth) and Germany (engaged exclusively on linen). Otherwise, with an enlarged demand for cloth, it would be necessary to get some of the Germans into the production of that commodity and, to this end, the ratio of exchange must move to 10 cloth = 20 linen (the German cost ratio). It would then stay at that ratio, regardless of the strength of the increase in the relative demand for cloth, since, at that ratio, the world supply of cloth could be augmented, at the expense of linen, until, if necessary, the supply of linen fell to zero.

Similarly, with a strong demand for linen relative to cloth, the ratio of exchange could move away from 10 cloth = 18 linen (the French cost ratio) only if the relative demand for linen were so great, at that ratio, as to exceed the combined linen capacities of Germany and France, and it could continue at a "limbo" ratio, between 18 and 15 linen for 10 cloth, only when the total demand for linen should, by some rare accident, be no stronger than that which, at such a ratio, could be exactly equated, against English production concentrated on cloth, by the combined German and French productive capacity fully specialized in linen. Otherwise, with an enlarged demand for linen, it would be necessary to get some of the English into the production of that commodity and, to this end, the ratio of exchange must move to 10 cloth = 15 linen (the English cost ratio). It would then stay at that ratio regardless of the strength of the increase in the relative demand for linen, since, at that ratio, the world supply of linen could be augmented, at the expense of cloth, until, if necessary, the supply of cloth fell to zero.

No ratio will be stable, or normal, at any time, except such as would correspond with the cost ratios in one country or another, that is to say: (i) 10 cloth = 20 linen (in which case all countries will produce cloth, and Germany, alone, will produce linen); (ii) 10 cloth = 18 linen (in which case England will produce cloth exclusively, Germany will produce linen exclusively, and France, both commodities); or (iii) 10 cloth = 15 linen (in which case all countries will produce linen, and England, alone, will produce cloth). Any other ratio would be in a state of constant flux, with every change in relative desires, since there would then be no producers, anywhere, on the margin of indifference between the two products, and no possibility, therefore, of shifting supply to meet an altered demand situation.

Effects of Enlarging the List of Countries

The greater the number of countries engaged in trade the smaller is likely to be the difference between the cost ratio in any given country and the cost ratio in the country of greatest relative cost propinquity to that of the given country. This has an important bearing on the potential range and permanence of any given "limbo" ratio.

Let us suppose that ten countries (including England, France, and Germany, designated respectively as E, F, and G) are involved in the trade in cloth and linen and that cloth can be substituted for linen or *vice versa*, indefinitely, at the following cost ratios in each country:

					Countries					
	A	B	C	D	E	F	G	H	I	J
Cloth	10	10	10	10	10	10	10	10	10	10
Linen	8	9	11	13	15	18	20	24	28	32

Some of the countries may be large and some small, economically considered, and how large or small any country will be, relative to the others, will be partly the result of the ratio of exchange which comes to be established between the commodities. If, for instance, the terms should be 10 cloth for 8 linen, country J would be several times as large (in productive capacity, measured in value terms, and in consumption) as it would be if the terms were to settle at 10 cloth for 32 linen.

If, regardless of terms, country A were, relative to the others, a very large country economically, either because it was populous or because its per capita productivity was high (or both), or if cloth, at whatever ratio of exchange is established, were of minor total economic importance compared with linen, or if any combination of these factors should enable country A to supply all the other countries with cloth without fully exhausting its productive capacity, the terms of trade would be 10 cloth = 8 linen. Country A would then produce both commodities while all the others would produce linen only, all of them sending some of their linen to A in exchange for cloth, even though producers in A, at this ratio, have no comparative advantage in cloth.[1] No increase whatever in the relative desirability of linen to cloth could cause any long-time deviation from this ratio (since producers in A can shift, in any degree, from cloth to linen until there is no supply of cloth at all) nor could any increase in the relative desirability of cloth to linen affect the ratio until all of the linen producers in A had shifted over to cloth and the country had become fully specialized in that material. At this point the ratio might become indefinite and unstable, between 8 and 9 linen to 10 cloth, but, so soon as the growing relative desirability of cloth had sent the terms to 9 linen for 10 cloth, the ratio would become stable once more, with producers in B now on the margin of indifference. The vagaries of relative desire would then be nullified in their potential effect on the ratio of exchange by shifts in B from linen to cloth or *vice versa*, until, with a still growing relative demand for cloth, B was fully specialized in cloth. The ratio might then move, uncertainly, in the area between 9 and 11 linen for 10 cloth, until, at 11 linen to 10 cloth, country C would come in as a producer of cloth as well as linen. And so on for D, E, F, G, H, I, and J, at ratios of 13, 15, 18, 20, 24, 28, and 32 linen, respectively, for 10 cloth, on the assumption of a steady increase in the demand for cloth relative to linen. With J, eventually, the sole producer of linen, and also producing cloth, the world supply of cloth, relative to linen, could be expanded in infinite degree at the 32 linen = 10 cloth ratio.

If, now, we reverse the original assumptions and suppose that J is the largest country, or that linen is of minor economic importance (or take any combination of the two suppositions), so that J can provide the total required amount of linen without exhausting its productive capacity, the original terms will be 32 linen to 10 cloth. Country J will then produce both commodities and all the others

---

[1] At any other possible ratio, however, country A *would* have such a comparative advantage, and, by specializing, would so enlarge the relative supply of its specialty (cloth) as to drive the value of cloth down to the 10 cloth = 8 linen ratio. Any deviation from the 10 cloth = 8 linen ratio would stimulate the output of cloth in A and, without destroying the trade, the relative specialization in cloth would always set up the 10 cloth = 8 linen ratio. Country A will therefore not tend to be self-sufficient even though, at the ratio eventually established, it gains nothing from the trade.

will specialize in cloth. If we then assume an increasing demand for linen, relative to cloth, the ratio of exchange will move in the direction opposite to that posited above.

Whatever the constellation of demand it is all but certain that one of the countries will, at any given time, produce both commodities and the others only one. Suppose that, at any given moment, the combined productive powers of the countries to the left of F, producing cloth, is in something like the same ratio to the combined productive powers of the countries to the right of F, producing linen, as the total demanded amount of cloth is to the total demanded amount of linen at the 18 linen to 10 cloth ratio. Country F will then be the focal country producing both commodities. The ratio of 18 linen to 10 cloth, as a norm, will thereupon prevail so long as *any* producers of either commodity in F find it worth while to continue as is, rather than go over to the other commodity. Any change in demand inadequate to force complete specialization in F will, in a word, have no effect whatever on the ratio, but only on the composition of F's industry. If F is a large country, with a fairly evenly divided production of cloth and linen at any given time, it will obviously take a very great shift of total demand one way or the other to effect any change in the (normal) terms on which they are exchanged. Similarly, with any other large country, if the terms of trade should be established at *its* cost ratio.

Far from the (normal) "terms of trade" moving coincidently with every shift in desire schedules, as the classical theory posits, it is clear that, in multi-country as in two-country trade on the classical assumptions, they will ordinarily not move at all with any probable shift in such desires, and that, if they *are* shaken from their inertia, the movement is likely to be not in a steady progression, in continuous correspondence with the direction of the shift, but in a sudden jump to the cost ratio of the country next in taxonomic line. They will then remain stable during any further shift of relative desires not so great as to put that country completely out of production of the commodity in which its comparative advantage had hitherto lain.

Since, when trade is expanded to include more than two countries, the spread between the cost ratios of either of the original two and that of the country of greatest cost-ratio propinquity with one or the other cannot be greater, and will in all probability be less, than the spread between the cost ratios of the original pair, the range of any possible "limbo" ratio of exchange can, so long as the original countries continue to produce different goods, never be greater, and will usually be less, when the number of trading countries is enlarged than it would be when the trade is confined to two countries only. The possibility, moreover, of the persistence of any "limbo" ratio, as well as its range, will be greatly reduced with every increase in the number of trading countries since, in the more widely divided total output, it will take a much smaller proportionate shift in the relative desirability of the two commodities than would be necessary in a simpler case to effect a transfer from a "limbo" exchange ratio to a ratio of stable equilibrium. Small as is the probability of a lasting "limbo" exchange ratio when two countries only are involved, it is, therefore, reduced to something not much above zero when there are many countries in the picture. We may, in consequence, conclude that, when there is trade in two commodities between many countries, the ratio of exchange will in practically every case be at the cost ratio in one of the countries concerned. The country whose cost ratio will, at any time, determine the ratio of international exchange will be that one of the group whose production will divide the total (world) supply of the two commodities in proportions which roughly correspond with the total relative demand for them at the focal country's cost ratio (with all the countries to the "left" of the focal country specializing in one of the commodities and all to the "right" in the other). Precision in the adjustment of supply to demand will be reached through shifts in the relative output of the two commodities in the focal country. No movement in the normal ratio of exchange will be necessary to this end. There may be a (temporary) change in *market* ratios but the market for one of the commodities will, of course, quicken, and, for the other slacken, whenever demand moves toward the former, and away from the latter, commodity, and this may well be all that will be required to secure the appropriate shift in supply.

Interdependence of Comparative Advantage and the Ratio

It should be noted that in any country, other than those at one or the other extreme of the taxonomic scale of comparative costs, it is not possible to determine comparative advantage until the ratio of exchange is established. We know that country A will have a comparative advantage in the production of cloth, if in anything, and that J will have a comparative advantage in linen, if in anything. But it is possible that the terms might be such that either country might produce both commodities. In such a case it would have no comparative advantage. Any country from B to I (inclusive) will find it to its advantage to specialize in the one commodity or the other according to where the terms of trade may fall, outside its own cost ratio, within the range of 8 to 32 of linen for 10 cloth. It is therefore not possible to state, in advance of the determination of the ratio of exchange, where such a country's comparative advantage, if any, will prove to lie. The two things are interdependent.

It is clear that the international ratio of exchange between any two commodities is likely to settle at the cost ratio between those commodities in some country, of great economic size, in the middle range of the cost ratios, since specialization by such a country in either of the commodities would so increase the relative supply of the commodity concerned as to drive its value down to the cost ratio in the country in question. Any such country tends, therefore, to become a focal country, producing both commodities, while other countries will specialize in the one or the other of the two commodities according as their cost ratios lie on the one or the other side of those that prevail in the focal country. For this reason there is a presumption against the probability that a large country will gain as much from simple international trade (if, indeed, it gains at all) as will the smaller countries which are much less likely to be the focus of the international ratio of exchange. Later consideration will show that no country, however large, is likely to be excluded from substantial gains in international trade of complex character but the presumption of a greater probable gain for the small countries will still hold. A small country may have opportunity-cost ratios that deviate in any degree from those of the focal country, and the farther they deviate the greater is its gain from specialization and international trade. The cost ratios in large countries, on the other hand, tend, for certain products, to be identical with the international ratio of exchange (which they dominate) and, to the extent that this occurs, international trade produces no gain for such a country.

A large country, with an inevitable variety of output, *makes* the international ratio of exchange in the products it produces. When, as a result of its great productive capacity and specialization, it brings that ratio into correspondence with its own cost ratio, it can gain from international trade only on the (relatively limited) number of products it does not produce. The small country, in contrast, gains on all products other than its own single specialty and, on each of the products in its more varied import list, is likely to gain more than the large country does on its less numerous list of imports. This follows from the fact that the bigger a country, and the more varied its resources, the more likely is its cost structure to approximate the ratio of exchange which will evolve in international trade.

Conjectural Simple Trade

It is difficult to present any actual case of trade in only two commodities among three or more countries but we can imagine a trade of grain for wine, in the Middle Ages, among England, France, the Rhineland, and Hungary. In such a trade it would be likely that France would be the focal country, with the Rhineland specializing in viticulture and Hungary and England in grain. The French cost ratio between grain and wine would then be reflected in the international ratio of exchange between the two commodities which (transport costs being abstracted) would sell, in all the countries, according to their cost ratio in France. If the demand for wine, in the four countries taken together, should grow relative to that for grain, or *vice versa*, some French producers on the margin of indifference as to whether they produced the one or the other commodity would shift from grain to wine, or from wine to grain, in correspondence with the direction of the shift in demand, and, so long as there were any French producers of either commodity, there would, on the assumption of constant (opportunity) costs, be no tendency for the normal international ratio of exchange between the commodities (the French cost ratio) to alter. Only if the French had to abandon grain altogether (in order to meet a surging relative demand for wine) or wine altogether (in order to meet a similar demand for grain) would the (normal) international ratio of exchange tend to move. It might, in the one case, remain for a time in limbo between the French and Hungarian cost ratios, and, in the other, in limbo between the French and Rhenish cost ratios, but would more probably shift immediately, in the one case to the Hungarian cost ratio and, in the other, to the Rhenish cost ratio between the commodities.

In either case the international ratio of exchange would then remain stable for all fluctuations of demand which could be met without a new transfer, or a re-transfer, to some other country, of the current locus of diversified production.

Manipulation of the Ratio

The possibilities of manipulation of the ratio of exchange, by collusion, are high in the simple trade that has been treated in this chapter. If, for instance, the producers of one of the commodities in one of the non-focal countries were impelled, through governmental action in levying a more or less prohibitive duty on imports, to produce, at home, the domestic consumption of the former import, the world supply of what had hitherto been the specialty of the country would be diminished, through the transfer of productive resources to the output of the protected commodity, and the world supply of the protected commodity would be increased. This might, in a given state of demand, change the market ratio of exchange against the protected commodity, and the movement might continue until it was checked, stabilized, and made normal, by the transfer of the locus of the margin of indifference from its former location to the country with cost ratios next in taxonomic line. So far as the levying country, in exchange for its original specialty, continued to import a limited amount of the protected commodity it would then be gaining, relatively to its former situation, *on such international trade as it continued to carry on.* If, moreover, its cost ratio for the commodities were not very divergent from the former international ratio of exchange, its increase in gains from its remaining international trade might more than offset the increase in costs associated with the acquisition of part of the consumption of the protected commodity by domestic production rather than by international trade (at either the new or the old ratio). Other countries producing the original specialty of the country in question would, of course, gain much more than the levying country, and it is conceivable that one or more of them might collude with the levying country to split the increase of gains as a special inducement to the latter to continue the protection. All this, of course, would be at the expense of countries specializing in the commodity against which the protective import duties were levied, and world output, as a whole, would show a net decrease. This follows from the fact that the cost of acquisition of the protected commodity, in sacrificed output of the other commodity in the levying country, would be greater than what would be necessary to acquire the same amount of the protected commodity under international trade.

If, however, protection should be levied *in a focal country* on that one of the two commodities of which it is producing less than its own consumption, the levying country would suffer no immediate loss of any kind nor would world output, as a whole, be diminished. (This follows from the fact that, at the time of levy of the protective duty, it is a matter of indifference to producers in the focal country whether they put out the one or the other commodity since the cost ratio in that country is identical with the current international ratio of exchange.) The countries specializing in the nonprotected commodity produced by the protecting country might eventually however, without any net loss in total world output, attain a gain at the expense of the protecting country, and, still more, of the countries specializing in the protected commodity. Their gain at the expense of the levying country, from any shift in the ratio that might occur as a result of the protection, would develop not because the levying country is put to any increase of unit cost in resources in producing the protected commodity but because its *opportunity* cost in producing the protected commodity would then have risen.[2] Their gain at the expense of the countries producing, at comparative advantage, the protected commodity would, on the other hand, arise from the fact that their *own* opportunity cost of (the potential) production of the protected commodity would have risen.

The relative world consumption of the two commodities would be shifted (in correspondence with the shift in world production) through the change in the ratio of exchange. Provided, however, that this alteration in the ratio does not go beyond limbo limits no change in *resources*-costs will anywhere take place. Some, rather small, presumptive loss in *satisfactions* must be attributed to the protection even if there is no alteration in the ratio of exchange, since not all consumers would be getting precisely the same combination of commodities as they would have had if matters had everywhere been

---

[2] The world output of the protected commodity would be increased and that of the other commodity reduced. If this should cause a shift in the national locus of marginal production, and so in the international ratio of exchange, the protecting country would begin to lose, on its output of the protected commodity, in the failure to utilize what would *then* be a superior opportunity in the other commodity.

left to their own unimpeded choice. But this loss is, in the circumstances, not objectively assessable. It may be, moreover, that the different distribution of consumption would be on an indifference curve passing through both the former and the later combination of products and, in this case, no loss at all would occur.

The chances of national gains from protection have been frequently ventilated in the classical and neo-classical literature where they have been given an importance, in practical application, much beyond their desert. It will later appear that in the complex trade typical of the actual world the possibilities of manipulation of the ratio of exchange are much more limited than in the simple case here discussed. Because the classicists and their followers regarded complex trade as a mere multiplication of simple constituents, and reasoned about it as if it were in fact simple, they were misled into exaggeration of the possibilities of alteration of the "terms of trade" through spontaneous, or induced, collusion in shifting demand out of the channels it would take in the absence of any distortion of the free choice of consumers and producers.[3] The *real* effects of protection are discussed in greater detail in Chapter IX.

[3] It is probable that, even on their own premises, the classicists overdid their argument. cf. Frederic Benham, "The Terms of Trade," *Economica*, Vol. VII (New Series) No. 28, pp. 360-376, especially for a disparagement of the classicists' emphasis on elasticity, or inelasticity, of demand.

CHAPTER IV

TWO-COUNTRY, THREE-OR-MORE-COMMODITY, TRADE

L ET us now look at the trade of but two countries in three or more commodities. When, between two countries, there are three commodities traded, the first thing to be said is that one of the countries must produce at least two of the commodities. This will establish the ratio of exchange between these two commodities at their cost ratio in the producing country. If this country is very large relative to the other, or if the commodity of the other's comparative advantage is of relatively great total value, the first country may produce all three commodities. (The ratio of exchange will then be set by the cost schedule, for the three commodities, in the country in question.) But, if this is not the case, *each* of the countries is, in fact, likely to produce two commodities, one of each pair being produced in common.[1] This situation will fix the exchange ratios (in correspondence with the respective cost ratios) not at the level of the cost ratios prevailing for all three commodities in either country but through the merger of two pairs of cost relatives focused on the product common to both countries.

C. F. Bastable has given some attention to the case of trade between two countries in three commodities and, in doing so, has expanded Mill's original illustrations. Taking over from Bastable let us assume that, without trade, $10x$, $20y$, and $100z$ are indefinitely substitutable for one another in country A, and that, in country B, the corresponding ratios are $10x$, $15y$, and $90z$. It is clear that any export of x will be made by B, and that any export of y will be made by A, but that z could be an export of either A or B according to the terms of interchange of x and y. With the terms $10x$ for $16y$, producers in B could offer $90z$ (in lieu of $10x$) for $16y$ while producers in A could turn out only $80z$ as easily as $16y$. But, with the terms $10x$ for $19y$, producers in A could offer $95z$ (in lieu of $19y$) for $10x$ while producers in B could turn out only $90z$ as easily as $10x$. At anything less than $18y$ to $10x$, commodity z becomes a "B" good, whereas, at anything more than $18y$ to $10x$, commodity z becomes an "A" good. The comparative advantage in z will thus shift

---

[1] Only under very unusual demand conditions would one of the countries produce two and the other specialize in the third of three commodities. In such a case a limbo ratio of exchange would appear.

from one country to the other according to the terms on which x and y are exchanged, and this may be generalized in the assertion that, in the trade between two countries in more than two commodities, any commodity, except it be one of the pair which marks the greatest difference in relative productive power, may be either an export or an import of either country.

Bastable, rather slavishly following Mill's misguided lead, arbitrarily *assumes* that trade has been established between A and B, in x and y, at an exchange ratio of $10x$ for $16y$. He then posits that the parties discover z as a potential object of trade. "B is now able," he says, "to offer to A not x only, but also z, and it will be to A's interest to take some of the commodity z at $17y = 90z$, as there would be a gain of $5z$ by the transaction, since, in A, $1y = 5z$ $\therefore$ $17y = 85z$."[2] Bastable has no idea of what the terms of trade would really be, except that B's position will be improved, and he is satisfied to assume, again quite arbitrarily, that they will settle at $10x = 17y = 90z$. It will presently appear that this is a highly improbable ratio.

It is obvious that, if there had originally been any such nice balance in the trade in x and y as to lead to the simultaneous complete elimination of producers of x in A and of y in B (which is necessary to the establishment of the assumed $10x = 16y$ ratio or, indeed, any other ratio between $10x = 15y$ and $10x = 20y$), the introduction of z as an export of B, and an import of A, would produce not a moderate but a very sharp shift in the terms in favor of B. They would almost certainly go as far as $10x = 18y = 90z$.[3] At that point the movement of the terms would be subject to a sudden check. The ratio $18y$ for $90z$ is the same as $20y$ for $100z$ and, on those terms, country A will begin to replace the production of y with z. By indefinitely reducing the output of y, in expanding that of z, A would keep y from ever falling below the level of $18y$ for $90z$.[4] With both countries producing z, while A also produces y and B produces x, the ratio of exchange cannot be other than $10x = 18y = 90z$. This is a position of extremely stable equilibrium since, without any

[2] C. F. Bastable, *The Theory of International Trade*, Macmillan, London, 1903, p. 36.

[3] The $10x = 90z$ ratio is inevitable if B is to export both x and z; the only question is the ratio of y to the other two commodities.

[4] For similar reasons, associated with the cost ratio in B, $10x$ can never be worth less than $90z$. But while $18y$ can never be worth less than $90z$, and $10x$ can also never be worth less than $90z$, it is possible for $10x$ to be worth less (or more) than $18y$.

change in the ratio, the relative supplies of x, y and z can be altered in almost any degree to correspond with shifts in the relative desirability of given total amounts of the three commodities. Just as, at that ratio, A can shift the supply of y relative to z, so B can shift the supply of x relative to z, and, by either method or a combination of both, the supplies of x and y may be shifted relative to one another with, or without, a concurrent shift in the supply of x or y relative to z. If x should tend to fall in price (that is, in the exchange ratio against y or z or both) B would shift some of its production to z and, if this should cause the price of z to waver, A would shift out of z and into y. Similarly, with any tendency toward a rise in the value of z, or toward a rise or fall in the value of any of the commodities, relative to either or both of the others, supplies could be so adjusted as to preserve the $10x = 18y = 90z$ ratio of exchange so long as both countries produce two commodities.

It may be said, in conclusion on this point, that whatever the respective economic size (total production) of the two countries, and the total economic importance of the several commodities, the only possible stable, and therefore normal, ratios of exchange are:

$$(1) \quad 10x = 20y = 100z^5$$
$$(2) \quad 10x = 15y = 90z^6$$
$$(3) \quad 10x = 18y = 90z^7$$

Whether A will export z to B, or B export z to A, when both countries are producing z at the ratio $10x = 18y = 90z$, will depend upon the degree to which the production of y absorbs A's productive (and, therefore, consuming) power relative to that absorbed in B by the production of x.

Any terms other than one of the three sets above laid down would be unstable, a fleeting transition from one to the other of the stable three, and could by no stretch of the imagination constitute a norm. To maintain any such limbo ratio (e.g. $10x = 17y = 90z$, or

[5] In this case country A would produce all three commodities and could make any adjustments in their relative supply that might be called for by an alteration in desire schedules. Country B would produce x only, to meet its own and part of A's needs in that article, and would import y and z in exchange.

[6] In this case country B would produce all three commodities and could make the necessary adjustments of supply to an alteration in desire schedules. Country A would produce y only, to meet its own and part of B's needs in that article, and would import x and z in exchange.

[7] In this case any requisite adjustments of supply to altered desire schedules would be made in the manner already indicated.

$10x = 19y = 95z$) the demand situation would have to be so nicely adjusted, and so invariable, as to cause, and maintain, a complete and exclusive concentration of producers in A on y, or of those of B on x. This would absolutely fix, in the one case, the supply of y and, in the other, that of x, though the supply of z would, in *every* case, and of one of the other commodities in *either* case, be indefinitely variable. No change in relative demand that did not take the ratio out of limbo, into one of the three stable ratios, could raise or lower the production of the commodity in which one country was completely and exclusively specialized and, with price movements thus quite unchecked on the side of supply of that commodity, any limbo ratio, if ever established, would, in the ceaseless play of demand, be practically certain to disappear and be replaced by one of the stable three.

Quadration of the Ratio of Exchange with Internal Costs

On extending his consideration to include a fourth commodity Bastable gets out of the field of mere improbability into what is flatly impossible. He assumes that the cost ratios in A for the commodities x, y, z, and w are $10x = 20y = 100z = 50w$ and that, in B, they are $10x = 15y = 90z = 40w$. He then goes on to say that if the ratios of exchange, before the introduction of w, are $10x = 17y = 90z$, "it will be A's interest to offer $45w$ for $10x$, since it thus gains $5w$; it is, too, for B's advantage to accept these terms, as it will also gain a similar amount."[8] This would give us an exchange ratio of $10x = 17y = 90z = 45w$, with A allegedly producing y and w and B producing x and z. Bastable's attention is so firmly fixed on demand, in complete neglect of the conditions of supply, that he has forgotten his assumption of free competition *within* each country and does not see that, at the ratio $10x = 17y = 90z = 45w$, no enterpriser in A would produce w since, on the posited ratio of exchange, it would never pay an enterpriser in A to abandon the production of y for w (where for every 17 units of y forgone he will get only $42\frac{1}{2}w[20y : 50w :: 17y : 42\frac{1}{2}w]$) if he has to give up $45w$ for $17y$ (or its equivalent in x or z). The ratio $10x = 17y = 90z = 45w$ is, therefore, impossible and would controvert Bastable's own assertion that commodities produced in either country will exchange on the basis of their cost of production in the country of origin.

[8] *loc. cit.*, p. 36.

With a ratio of $17y$ for $10x$ or $90z$ producers in A would, how-ever, be ready to offer $42\frac{1}{2}w$ as readily as $17y$ and, under the cost conditions, this might well be acceptable to consumers in B who could, by production at home, get only $40w$ for $10x$ or $90z$. At the ratio $10x = 17y = 90z = 42\frac{1}{2}w$ then, with A producing y and w and B producing x and z, it would be feasible to alter the supply of any one of the commodities relative to any one of the others. This ratio would, therefore, seem to promise some stability. With each country producing but two commodities, it would, nevertheless, be impossible to alter the supply of y and w, taken together, relative to x and z, taken together, and, if the desire for the products of one of these groups should alter relative to that for the other, a shift in the ratio must occur. Let us suppose that, when w comes into the picture where $17y$ is exchanging for $10x$ or $90z$, the demand for w is very strong. The price, in x and z, of both y and w would then rise (the two commodities in each group always keep-ing to the ratio of their costs of production in A and B since, otherwise, the production of one of the commodities in either group would be completely abandoned for the other) through, let us say, a ratio of $10x = 16\frac{1}{2}y = 90z = 41\frac{1}{4}w$ to the ratio $10x = 16y = 90z = 40w$. Up to this point the ratio would be in limbo but, at $10x = 16y = 90z = 40w$, the commodity w could be produced in B. The ratio of exchange of w to y would then be fixed, at $16y$ for $40w$, by their relative cost of production in A ($20y : 50w :: 16y : 40w$) which has been producing them all along, and the ratio of exchange of w to x and z would be fixed by their relative cost of production in B ($10x = 90z = 40w$) which now produces w for the first time. This establishes the ratio of each of the products, against all of the others, at $10x = 16y = 90z = 40w$. The commodity w could rise no farther in value since any such tendency would be accompanied by an indefinite increase in B's output of w, at the expense of x or z, or of A's output of w at the expense of y. The commodity y could rise in value (against all of the other commodities) only after B had so ex-panded its initial production of w as not only to be supplying all of its own requirements for w but also to be exporting w to A in an amount sufficient to enable all producers of w in A to go into y. If, even then, the supply of y should, at the $10x = 16y = 90z = 40w$ ratio, be inadequate to an enormously expanded demand for it, the value of

y would rise in all of w, x, and z until, as a limit, B would produce all four commodities at the ratio $10x = 15y = 90z = 40w$ (the cost ratio in B). Country A, producing y only, would then exchange part of its output of that commodity for w, x, and z from B.

Taking the converse case, let us now assume that, at the ratio $10x = 17y = 90z = 42\frac{1}{2}w$, that is, with each country producing two of the commodities (with A in y and w, and B in x and z), the desirability of x or z, or both, so increases relatively to that of y and w as to cause x and z to rise in price against y and w (the terms again will inevitably move in pairs with the ratio between the commodities in either pair remaining constant in correspondence with costs in the country of production). A check on the movement will be inserted when the terms have passed through various limbo ratios (such as, e.g. $10x = 17\frac{1}{2}y = 90z = 43\frac{3}{4}w$) to the ratio $10x = 18y = 90z = 45w$. At the latter point, producers in A will find it just as advantageous to produce z as y or w ($18y : 90z : 45w :: 20y : 100z : 50w$) and no further shift of the terms in the current direction is possible until A is not only producing all of its own consumption of z (at the expense of its output of y and w) but is exporting z to B in volume sufficient to enable all producers of z in that country to go into x. Long before this point is reached the supply of y and w would be so reduced relatively to x and z (as the two countries specialize, the one in x and the other in z, the supply of y and w would approach zero) as to make it very difficult for the price of y and w to fall farther in terms of x and z. The commodity z cannot, indeed, under any circumstances, rise in value above $90z$ for $18y$ or $45w$. It would, however, be possible for x to rise farther if the demand for x were great enough to permit of the concentration of B on that product. The eventual limit is, of course, A's cost ratio for all four products, viz, $10x = 20y = 100z = 50w$.

When we are dealing with the trade between two countries in four commodities it is clear that the stablest, and the most probable, situation is for one of the countries to be producing three of the commodities and the other two, with one commodity, inevitably therefore, common to both. This fixes all four terms of the exchange ratio and permits, within this ratio, so wide a range of accommodation of relative supply, to the shifting relative amounts from time to time demanded, as all but to preclude an alteration.

Importance of the Commodity Produced in Common

The commodity produced in common in the two countries is vital in the determination of international values. The exchange ratios of all the other products against this common product are fixed by the posited cost ratios in one country or the other. They are therefore fixed against each other. Whatever the shifts in relative demand, normal values are then indefinitely maintained by the shift of producers, on the margin of indifference, from one product to another, in one country or the other, in whatever degree is necessary to bring marginal values into correspondence with constant (opportunity) costs, in the two countries, for the commodities produced in each. The norm will change only with a transfer of the locus of the margin of indifference, between two commodities, from one country to the other.

The miscarriage of the classical and neo-classical theory of international values arises from the fact that, far from realizing the vital importance of the common product, the exponents of that theory completely excluded it from their conceptions.[9] The result is that their exchange ratios have no anchor and float around at the mercy of every shift in the wind of desire.

Mill said that, under his assumptions, no country would produce anything that it would not also export, and the classical economists in general, along with their followers, consistently speak of "A's products" and "B's products," or of "representative bales" of "A

[9] The statement is not altogether true of P. J. Stirling, Henry Sidgwick, J. Shield Nicholson, H. von Mangoldt, and F. Y. Edgeworth. These men more or less fully sensed the importance of commodities produced in common by the trading countries but, as a result of their preoccupation with some form of the labor theory of value, were precluded from bringing their insight to fruition. Mangoldt missed the right road only by a hair but a wrong turning eventually led him far astray. Edgeworth, in comment on Sidgwick and Mangoldt, maintains, against adverse critics of their doctrines, that "it is quite *conceivable* that, even on the . . . hypothesis of constant costs of production and no cost of transport, there should be a common product" and says that one might even regard this phenomenon as *normal* (*Papers, op. cit.,* p. 30, italics mine). He fails, however, to make the appropriate use of his contention and is, in fact, disposed to treat it as of minimal significance. Bastable, who had originally thought that the case of a common commodity could arise only under conditions of increasing cost, admits that Edgeworth is justified in his assertion but brushes the matter aside as an unimportant curiosity (*The Theory of International Trade, op. cit.,* p. 179). Both writers thus rejected the stone that they should have made the head of the corner. Viner does likewise in presenting the theoretical possibilities of production in two countries of a given commodity without any recognition of the fact that this is not only normal but actually establishes the norm. *Studies, op. cit.,* pp. 458 *et seq.*

goods" and "B goods," as mutually exclusive collections of immutable ingredients. If, under the assumptions of the classical economists, it were true that no country would make anything for itself that it did not make for other countries the phenomenon of common products would not only be neglected but there would be a specific denial of its possibility. The fact is that it is not only possible, but is all but inevitable, that one of two countries trading in several commodities will produce some commodity which it will not only not export but will not put out enough for its own consumption, and that it will resort to import from the other country (which will be producing that same commodity) to cover the deficiency.

It will later appear that, except under miraculously unlikely conditions of demand and supply, no country will produce a range of exportable products none of which has any counterpart in the output of other countries, and that, even on the most rigid adherence to the assumptions of the classical economists, there is every reason for supposing that each of many competing countries will produce *some* product which is also produced elsewhere. All that is required, however, to fix exchange ratios, more or less permanently, is that, in the range of output of every country, there be but *one* commodity (whether or not it is exported) which is also produced in some other country, while, without this, there can be no schedule of normal international values. All products are in fact linked together, through internal cost ratios and commodities produced in more than one country, in a world-wide system of normal exchange ratios from which, in a given state of the industrial arts and on the assumption of constant (opportunity) costs of production in the several countries, deviation would be a rare event.

Résumé

Before we proceed to the case of trade between several countries in several commodities (truly multilateral multi-commodity trade) it will be well to lay out schematically all the possibilities in the trade between two countries, A and B, in four commodities x, y, z, and w. The (opportunity) cost ratios, it will be recalled, are:

In A	In B
$10x$	$10x$
$20y$	$15y$
$100z$	$90z$
$50w$	$40w$

The possible exchange ratios then are:

(1) $10x = 20y = 100z = 50w$ (stable).

This ratio will be attained whenever (i) country B is economically small relative to country A, or (ii) B's inevitable product, x, is important in total economic value relative to y, z, and w, or (iii) some combination of these conditions occurs, so that, in spite of B's complete specialization in x (with export of x to A in exchange for y, z, and w), the value of x does not fall below the maximum set by the cost ratios in A. Country A will then produce all four of the commodities (as well as import x from B in exchange for z, y, w), and, so long as this is the case, the normal exchange ratio cannot deviate from the posited figures no matter what shifts in demand may occur. Since, at this ratio, producers in A are on the margin of indifference as between any of the products, the relative supply of the several commodities can be indefinitely adjusted, within A, to correspond with any alteration that may occur in desire schedules.

(2) A limbo ratio (unstable) between:

$10x = 20y = 100z = 50w$ and $10x = 18y = 90z = 45w$.

In order that this ratio be established, we may suppose that country B is, or becomes, economically somewhat larger, relative to country A, than is assumed above, or that commodity x is, or becomes, less important relatively to y, z, and w, so that, in A and B combined, the market for x, at the $10x = 20y = 100z = 50w$ ratio, is not quite sufficient to absorb B's full productive powers. The price of x in y, z, and w will fall. If matters are so nicely gauged that, somewhere within a 10 per cent fall in the price of x, country B's full production of x would be taken off the market, the ratio of exchange will move erratically within the limits set by ratios (1) and the next in order, (3).[10] No producer of x is then on the margin of indifference and there will then be no normal ratio of x against y, z, and w, though the latter three will exchange at a constant ratio against each other.

[10] With the fall in the relative value of x, the income of B's citizens will be reduced. They will presumably then take less than before of y, z, and w, and perhaps even of x. The citizens of A, contrariwise, will find their incomes increased and will almost certainly take more of x, and probably also of y, z, and w. The net result of the shifts in demand is problematical and the ratios of exchange and the amounts demanded are, of course, interacting. It should be noted, however, that it is the net shift of the *total* demand for any of the products, relative to that for the others, which is important. How this shift may be distributed between the two countries is of no significance. Contrast this statement with the doctrine of the classical economists that it is the reciprocal demand of the two countries for "each other's products" that is the determinative influence in exchange ratios (terms of trade).

Since the supply of x is absolutely fixed by B's productive capacity, the slightest shift in the relative desirability of x against the other commodities will then be reflected in a price movement (of x against any and all of the others). The supply of any one of y, z, and w, however, can be altered against the others in any degree, and it will always be so altered, in correspondence with shifts in the relative desirability of these commodities against each other, as, whatever the exchange ratio against x, to preserve the price structure of $20y = 100z = 50w$ (e.g. $10x = 19\frac{1}{2}y = 97\frac{1}{2}z = 48\frac{3}{4}w$; $10x = 19y = 95z = 47\frac{1}{2}w$; $10x = 18\frac{1}{2}y = 92\frac{1}{2}z = 46\frac{1}{4}w$).

The supply of z, y, and w, taken together, is, however, rigidly determined by the total productive capacity of A (even though the supply of any one of them, relative to any one of the others, can be changed in any desired degree), and the supply of x is rigidly determined by the productive capacity of B. Any shift in the ratio of exchange between x and the total of the other three can therefore, so long as the limbo ratio obtains, be followed by no adjustment in the relative volume of the two *groups* of output. The essential volatility of desire schedules will therefore keep the ratio of exchange between them in persistent motion until it moves to one of the neighboring stable positions, (1) or (3), in which supply is flexible all round.

(3) $10x = 18y = 90z = 45w$ (stable).

If country B is presumed to be still larger, relative to A, than in the case just discussed, or if commodity x is, or becomes, of still less economic importance relative to y, z, and w (which could come about through a shift in desire schedules) the ratio of exchange will shift to the present position (3). This, as noted earlier, will be a highly stable ratio. Country B will produce z as well as x, and A will produce z as well as y and w. The supply of any of the commodities relative to the others (taken singly or in any group) will, in response to shifts in demand, then be adjustable in any degree short of the complete elimination of the production of z in one of the countries. There are always, in the case here under consideration, producers on the margin of indifference as between any one commodity and any one of the others.

(4) A limbo ratio (unstable) between:
  $10x = 18y = 90z = 45w$ and $10x = 16y = 90z = 40w$.

If, in a process of expansion, country B should grow to about the same economic size as A, and if the total value of x and z, taken together, were not greatly disparate to that of y and w taken together, or if B's economic size relative to A should be so correlated with the total value of x and z, relative to y and w, that B's complete concentration in x and z would, at some ratio within the limits set by ratios (3) and (5) be not more or less than sufficient to supply both markets with those commodities, a limbo ratio (in which y and w together would move, relatively to x and z together, between the range of $18y$ or $45w$ and $16y$ or $40w$ to $10x$ or $90z$) would again appear. Such, e.g., are the already suggested ratios $10x = 17y = 90z = 42\frac{1}{2}w$ or $10x = 17\frac{1}{2}y = 90z = 43\frac{3}{4}w$. The supplies of y and w relative to one another, and of x and z relative to one another, could in this case be changed in any degree, but not the supplies of y and w, taken together, relative to the supplies of x and z, taken together. Commodities x and z would always tend to exchange against one another on the basis of their cost ratio in B, and commodities y and w would always tend to exchange against one another on the basis of their cost ratio in A, but the ratio of exchange between the two pairs of commodities, indeterminate within the prescribed limits, would move erratically with every shift in consumers' caprice (e.g., $10x = 17\frac{1}{4}y = 90z = 43\frac{1}{8}w$, or $10x = 16\frac{3}{8}y = 90z = 40\frac{15}{16}w$, or $10x = 16.1357y = 90z = 40.33925w$). Sooner or later the terms would strike, and tend to settle at, one of the stable ratios.

(5) $10x = 16y = 90z = 40w$ (stable).

Should country B predominate over A in economic size, but y, the inevitable product of A, be not important enough to absorb all of A's productive powers, A will produce y and w, B will produce x, z, and w, and a new stable ratio (5), the counterpart of (3) but with the relative sizes of A and B reversed, would be attained. In (3) country A produces three commodities and country B two, whereas in (5) country A produces two commodities and country B three.

(6) A limbo ratio (unstable) between:
$10x = 16y = 90z = 40w$ and $10x = 15y = 90z = 40w$.

If, following the posited trend, we let country B grow relatively still larger than in the preceding illustration, or the commodity y be, or become, relatively more important, it may happen that A's output of y (in which A is now fully specialized) will be taken off the market at some ratio between 16 and 15 of y to $10x$, $90z$, or $40w$. No one in B will yet find it profitable to produce y at this ratio. The supply is therefore absolutely fixed at A's output, with a consequent high degree of instability in the ratio and with very little likelihood, therefore, of its long remaining in limbo.

(7) $10x = 15y = 90z = 40w$ (stable).

If country A is overshadowed by B in economic size, or if y is a very important commodity, so that A cannot, at any limbo ratio, produce enough of y for both countries, the price of y will rise to the level of ratio (7). Country B, producing all commodities, will then fill any deficiency in y out of its own production at the expense of x, z, or w. Adjustments of supply to shifting desire schedules can then all be made within B without any change in relative values, and the ratio of exchange, identical with B's cost ratios, will persist indefinitely regardless of any further increase in the relative desirability of y.

Summing up, for the trade of two countries in four commodities, we may say that highly stable ratios will prevail when conditions are such that either country produces all of the commodities or when they are such that either produces three and the other two. The ratios will be unstable, however, when either country produces but one commodity and the other the remaining three, or, taking the commodities in pairs, when each country produces two commodities only.

Except by wild accident there would, under conditions of constant cost and costless transport, be no chance that both countries would produce, simultaneously, *more* than one commodity in common. This could not occur unless the opportunity cost ratios of two commodities, in each country, should happen to coincide. With an infinite range of possibility of difference it would certainly be invalid to posit any such coincidence. It may, indeed, here be said that, no matter how many countries are involved in trade in no matter how many commodities, there is no likelihood, under conditions of constant cost and no differential between domestic and international costs of transport, that any country will produce more than one commodity in common with any other single country. One there will almost certainly be, and one only. Yet this one is all-sufficient. Lest this seem strangely unlike the real world we should hasten to note that constant costs are unlikely to be realized indefinitely over the whole range of commodities, and that transport is not without differentials, so that, when we relax these assumptions (as we shall later do), there may be no limits on the number of commodities that may be produced in common in different countries.

The limbo ratios, to which we have in this section drawn attention as exceptions, are the accepted type in classical theory but they are possible only in peculiar conjunctures, are never likely to be realized in fact, and would, if temporarily attained, quickly pass over into one of the stable ratios as a result of the kaleidoscopic play of relative desires. Except when we are dealing with immediate market values (which the classical economists did not profess to do) limbo ratios are unworthy of more than passing interest and cannot furnish norms. Classical theory is, at best therefore, a theory of exceptional and ephemeral cases rather than a basic explanation of the phenomena of international trade.

CHAPTER V

SEVERAL-COUNTRY, SEVERAL-COMMODITY, TRADE

We have now considered trade in two commodities among several countries and trade between two countries in several commodities. The next step is trade among several countries in several commodities. Let us suppose that four countries, A, B, C, and D, trade in three commodities which, to give reality, we may call cloth, linen, and corn. It is by now clear that the relative economic size of the respective countries, coupled with the relative total economic importance of the commodity or commodities that each may produce, will determine that one of the limited number of sets of stable exchange ratios which will prevail. It would be irksome to run completely through the gamut of possibilities. We shall therefore make certain assumptions, as to relative size of the countries and importance of the commodities, and shall refer as occasion requires to the effects under altered data.[1] Let it be assumed, then, that before international trade is opened up each of the countries A, B, C, and D devotes one-third of its productive resources to each of the three products, cloth, linen, and corn, that each increases its consumption of each of the products in proportion to its gains from international trade, and that the total productive power of the respective four countries, *measured in cloth*, is in the ratio 1 : 2 : 3 : 4.[2] Suppose further that, in the respective countries, it is possible to substitute one product for another, at constant (opportunity) cost, according to the following scheme:

In A	*In B*	*In C*	*In D*
10 cloth	10 cloth	10 cloth	10 cloth
19 linen	20 linen	15 linen	28 linen
42 corn	24 corn	30 corn	40 corn

[1] The exposition in the next few pages draws heavily on my article "The Theory of International Values Re-examined," *The Quarterly Journal of Economics*, Vol. xxxviii, pp. 54-86.

[2] Total productive power, it should be noted, is a function not only of per capita general productivity and of the numbers of the working population but of productivity in the specialties in which, under international trade, the country concentrates, as well as of the international ratio of exchange that becomes established. Productivity, of course, cannot be measured accurately in any commodity which, with international trade, a country does not produce. But it will serve the present purpose to use cloth as a measure in all cases, provided we later translate productivity in cloth into the products the various countries in fact turn out.

and that, on a non-specialized basis without international trade, there would be produced in a given time:

In A	In B	In C	In D
10,000 cl. $(10)^3$	20,000 cl. $(10)^3$	30,000 cl. $(10)^3$	40,000 cl. $(10)^3$
19,000 l. (19)	40,000 l. (20)	45,000 l. (15)	112,000 l. (28)
42,000 co. (42)	48,000 co. (24)	90,000 co. (30)	160,000 co. (40)

It is of course impossible to determine, by inspection, where comparative advantage may lie since this will depend on the international ratio of exchange that is ultimately established. What will that ratio be? Let us try A's cost ratio of 10 cloth = 19 linen = 42 corn. At this ratio of exchange, B, C, and D will all want to exchange cloth or linen against A's corn. A, a small country, could not supply them fully and the price of corn must rise in one, or both, of the other products. Suppose it rises to the point where the ratio of exchange is 10 cloth = 19 linen = 30 corn. At these values A will specialize in corn, B in linen, C in cloth and corn, and D in linen (since, on these terms, D has a greater advantage in linen than in corn). With countries B and D specializing in linen the price of that commodity must *fall* since their total production would be 456,000 units of linen (3 x 40,000 plus 3 x 112,000),[4] an amount in excess of the total requirement of linen, by all four countries, at the posited ratio of exchange and on the assumption that each country expands its demand for linen in proportion to its gains from trade. How far will the price of linen fall? Suppose it falls to 10 cloth = 22 linen = 30 corn.[5] At these prices A will specialize in corn, B in cloth, C in cloth and corn, and D in corn (for, at this exchange ratio, producers in D have a greater advantage in corn than in linen). The supply of linen would then have disappeared, since no country finds its comparative advantage in that line.

On the terms 10 cloth = 19 linen = 30 corn, then, too much linen tends to be produced, while, on the terms 10 cloth = 22 linen = 30 corn, there is no tendency to produce linen at all. When, in other

[3] The figures in parentheses, read downward, represent cost relationships in each of the countries.

[4] Without specialization, equal resources are devoted to each of the three products. With full specialization each country can therefore produce three times its production of any one commodity under the non-specialized regime.

[5] It will be well in indicating price changes to keep 10 cloth as a constant base, and to show a rise or fall in cloth relative to linen or corn or both, and of linen and corn relative to each other, by changing the number of units of linen or corn, or both, offered for 10 units of cloth.

words, D specializes in linen, the price of linen falls; but when, as a result of that fall, D specializes in corn, the supply of linen tends to sink to zero, since B, as a result of the fall in the price of linen, is impelled to go out of the production of that commodity in favor of cloth. The price of linen must therefore move upward from the 10 cloth = 22 linen = 30 corn ratio but not to the 10 cloth = 19 linen = 30 corn ratio. No stability can be reached while D specializes exclusively in either linen or corn, and the only solution is to have D produce both of those commodities. The terms of exchange which will accomplish this are 10 cloth = 21 linen = 30 corn; for on those terms D has an equal comparative advantage in linen and corn and will therefore do as well in the one as in the other (21 linen to 30 corn is D's cost ratio since 21 : 30 :: 28 : 40). The ratio of 21 linen to 30 corn, which gives D an equal comparative advantage in linen and corn, could of course be preserved with an exchange ratio for each against cloth very different from that here laid down, but, with any other than the terms 10 cloth = 30 corn, C, a large country, would specialize in either cloth or corn exclusively (according as one or the other sold on better terms) and, along with B's cloth or A's corn, would flood the market with its specialty and impel a readjustment in price. This brings it about that 10 cloth must exchange for 30 corn, and that 21 linen must also exchange for 30 corn. The ratio of exchange 10 cloth = 21 linen = 30 corn is consequently the inevitable ratio. It alone can show any stability, and it is stable because, under it, both C and D, the two large countries of the four, tend to diffuse their productive resources, rather than concentrate them upon a single product, and thus keep a balance of production which is impossible when they devote their full efforts to the production of but one commodity.

It must not be supposed that C and D will divide their productive resources equally between the commodities they now produce even though, in a non-specialized regime, they would have done so. How much of each they will put out, when stabilized conditions are attained, will depend upon the preceding play of prices in the process of adjustment. The play of prices will have encouraged a greater production in one line than in another, in any country producing more than one commodity, according to the relative supplies forthcoming from other centers of production.

When we take the figures of production on a non-specialized basis, and adhere to our supposition that, after international trade is opened up, the gains which each country derives from that trade are spent so as to keep the same proportionate consumption of each of the commodities as prevailed under the non-specialized regime, it is possible to determine precisely what the trade would be.

Method of Determining the Course of Trade

We have seen that the terms of interchange will be 10 cloth = 21 linen = 30 corn, and that, on these terms, A will produce corn, B cloth, C cloth and corn, and D linen and corn.[6] When A specializes exclusively in corn it can produce, in a given period, 126,000 units of corn (3 x 42,000). To preserve the original proportions in A's consumption of cloth, linen, and corn (viz., 10 : 19 : 42), A will retain 53,378— units of this corn, and will export 72,622+ units in exchange for 12,709— units of cloth and 24,147— units of linen.[7]

When country B specializes exclusively in cloth, it can produce in the given period 60,000 units of cloth (3 x 20,000). To preserve the original proportions in B's consumption of cloth, linen, and corn (viz., 10 : 20 : 24) B will retain 21,799+ units of cloth, and will export 38,201— units of cloth in exchange for 43,599— units of linen and 52,318+ units of corn.[8]

Country C produces both cloth and corn. If its whole productive power were concentrated on cloth, it could produce, in the given period, 90,000 units of cloth (3 x 30,000); if on corn, it could pro-

---

[6] The exposition will be followed more easily if reference is made as required to the table on pages 80-81.

[7] The method adopted for obtaining the desired proportions is as follows. Take the proportions in country A, viz. 10:19:42. At the established ratio of exchange (10 cloth = 21 linen = 30 corn)

$$
\begin{array}{rcl}
10 \text{ cloth} &=& 30 \text{ corn} \\
19 \text{ linen} &=& 27 \; 1/7 \text{ corn} \\
42 \text{ corn} &=& 42 \text{ corn} \\
\hline
\end{array}
$$

(By addition) 10 cloth plus 19 linen plus 42 corn = 99 1/7 corn

By concentrating on the production of corn, country A, for the same effort that would, in that country, yield 10 cloth plus 19 linen plus 42 corn, can produce 126 corn. The consumption in A of the respective commodities under a trading regime will therefore be to the consumption under the non-trading regime in the proportion of 126 to 99 1/7 and the income of A will be increased in the ratio of 26 6/7 to 99 1/7, that is, by **27 31/347%**.

[8] B's income is increased through trade by 8 288/289%. This comparatively small gain from international trade, true also of countries C and D, is a consequence of the fact that the arbitrarily designated national cost ratios for the various commodities were not widely different from one another and a fortiori, therefore, from the international ratio of exchange.

COUNTRIES	UNITS OF CLOTH				UN[	
	PRODUCTION	EXPORTS	IMPORTS	CONSUMPTION	PRODUCTION	EXPO[
Country A. (Productive capacity in cloth = 1)	—	—	$12708\frac{324}{347}$	(10)* $12708\frac{324}{347}$	—	—
Country B. (Productive capacity in cloth = 2)	60000	$38200\frac{200}{289}$	—	(10)* $21799\frac{89}{289}$	—	—
Country C. (Productive capacity in cloth = 3)	$51302\frac{10480606}{20959147}$	$18144\frac{12686832}{20959147}$	—	(10)* $33157\frac{17}{19}$	—	—
Country D. (Productive capacity in cloth = 4)	—	—	$43636\frac{4}{11}$	(10)* $43636\frac{4}{11}$	$239664\frac{5245392}{20959147}$	$117482\frac{9?}{20?}$
Totals† (All countries)	$111302\frac{10480606}{20959147}$	$56345\frac{1135}{3817}$	$56345\frac{1135}{3817}$	$111302\frac{10480606}{20959147}$	$239664\frac{5245392}{20959147}$	$117482\frac{9?}{20?}$

Explanation of the Trade

A produces 126,000 corn. It imports 12,709— cloth for which it must export 38,127— corn, an[d] it imports 24,147— linen for which it must export 34,496— corn; a total export of 72,622+ cor[n]

B produces 60,000 cloth. It imports 43,599— linen for which it must export 20,761+ cloth, an[d] it imports 52,318+ corn for which it must export 17,439+ cloth; a total export of 38,201— clot[h]

C produces 51,302+ cloth and 116,092+ corn. It exports 18,145— cloth for which it obtai[ns] 38,104— linen, and it exports 16,618+ corn for which it obtains 11,633+ linen; a total impo[rt] of 49,737— linen.

D produces 239,664+ linen and 137,622+ corn. It imports 43,636+ cloth for which it mu[st]

duce 270,000 units of corn (3 x 90,000). Taking either as a base, it will be found that, to preserve the original proportions in C's consumption of cloth, linen, and corn (viz., 10 : 15 : 30), C must use 33,158— units of cloth, 49,737— units of linen, and 99,474— units of corn.[9]

[9] C's income is increased through trade by 10 10/19%.

		UNITS OF CORN			
PORTS	CONSUMPTION	PRODUCTION	EXPORTS	IMPORTS	CONSUMPTION
$\frac{338}{347}$	(19)* $24146\frac{338}{347}$	126000	$72622\frac{166}{347}$	—	(42)* $53377\frac{181}{347}$
$\frac{178}{289}$	(20)* $43598\frac{178}{289}$	—	—	$52318\frac{98}{289}$	(24)* $52318\frac{98}{289}$
$\frac{16}{19}$	(15)* $49736\frac{16}{19}$	$116092\frac{10476476}{20959147}$	$16618\frac{17095194}{20959147}$	—	(30)* $99473\frac{13}{19}$
—	(28)* $122181\frac{9}{11}$	$137622\frac{10471566}{20959147}$	—	$36922\frac{20014466}{20959147}$	(40)* $174545\frac{5}{11}$
$\frac{9056146}{20959147}$	$239664\frac{5245392}{20959147}$	$379714\frac{20948042}{20959147}$	$89241\frac{6162573}{20959147}$	$89241\frac{6162573}{20959147}$	$379714\frac{20948042}{20959147}$

91,636+ linen, and it imports 36,923— corn for which it must export 25,846+ linen; a total of 117,482+ linen.

exports and imports, and total production and consumption, of each article must of correspond.

figures in parentheses (read crosswise) represent the ratios in which the three commodities onsumed in the several countries before trade was opened up; this ratio of consumption n assumed to have remained constant after the development of trade.

more or less ridiculous fractions shown here, and elsewhere in this table, may seem to a morbid passion for accuracy. But, since a *precise* balancing of the accounts is necessary argument, it seemed best, for the time being at any rate, to sacrifice convenience to per-

Country D is the only country producing linen. Countries A, B, and C must all, therefore, obtain their linen from D. We know how much linen each will consume (24,147—; 43,599—; and 49,737— units respectively), and therefore how much linen will be exported by D (117,482+ units). In the same manner as for C we find that to preserve the original proportions in D's consumption of cloth, linen, and corn (viz., 10 : 28 : 40), D must use its productive power to secure 43,636+ units of cloth, 122,182— units of linen, and 174,545+ units of corn.[10] Having the amount of linen exported by D (117,482+ units), and the amount consumed at home (122,182— units), addition will give us the total production of linen in that country, viz., 239,664+ units. The remainder of D's productive capacity, devoted to corn, will yield 137,622+ units of that product; but as D requires 174,545+ units for its own consumption, it must import, from A or C, 36,923— units of corn.

We have now obtained the figures of production in A, B, and D; country C, it will be remembered, produces cloth and corn. Country B is the only other country producing cloth. We know how much cloth B produces (60,000 units), and how much B itself consumes (21,799+ units). Subtraction will give us how much cloth B exports (38,201— units). We know also how much cloth A and D import (12,709— and 43,636+ units respectively). This is greater than B's export by 18,145— units, and this amount must therefore be obtained from C. Add this to C's own consumption of cloth, 33,158— units, and we get C's production of that commodity, viz., 51,303— units. The remainder of C's productive capacity is devoted to corn, of which it can produce 116,092+ units. Its own consumption of corn is 99,474— units and it thus has for export 16,619— units. These, together with A's export of 72,622+ units of corn, will, of course, be just adequate to meet the demand of B and D for that commodity.[11] The foregoing table shows the whole situation clearly.

Comparison with Classical Conclusions

The results, as we might by now have expected, are quite at variance with the conclusions on international trade drawn by Mill and his followers. Thus, though Mill claimed that, under the conditions we have assumed, no country would make anything for itself that it did not make for other countries, we find country D not only producing corn but importing it; moreover it is absolutely essential that D should do so if any stability is ever to be reached or retained in the trade between A, B, C, and D. For, if D should at any time produce enough corn for its own consumption or even increase its production

---

10 D's income is increased through trade by 9 1/11%.

11 This is, *of course*, the demand of B and D for corn because demand, as distinct from desire, requires a *quid pro quo* and imports must equate with exports.

very slightly, the total supply of corn must be sold at such a (low) price per unit as to make it unprofitable for D to continue in that line; while, if D should go out of corn altogether or even diminish its production of that commodity slightly, and, *pro tanto*, turn its productive powers to the making of linen, the increased supply of linen would so lower the price of that commodity as to make it unprofitable for D to continue to manufacture linen. The play of prices in the process of adjustment will therefore cause D to produce both corn and linen, corn in a supply inadequate for D's own need but linen in a supply sufficient for D's needs and for the needs of the three other countries as well. Similarly, the play of prices will set country C to producing both cloth and corn; but, unlike D, country C will export both of these commodities in exchange for imported linen. There is no *inherent* reason why a country, in the premisses laid down, might not find the terms, and general conditions, of trade such that it would produce exactly its own consumption of any commodity, or all of them, and neither export nor import some, or any, of them, though the chance of this happening is negligible. There is, on the other hand, no reason to suppose that a country will always export, or that it will not import, commodities in which, at the prevailing exchange ratio, it has a comparative advantage. Exports, of course, are always an indication of comparative advantage, or, at least, of no comparative disadvantage, but imports are not necessarily an indication of lack of comparative advantage. Comparative advantage may exist in some import, as well as in export, commodities. Comparative disadvantage can be present only in the import list but imports do not *necessarily* imply comparative disadvantage.

Stability of the Ratio in the Face of Shifts in Demand

The stability of the ratio 10 cloth = 21 linen = 30 corn, in the face of great changes in demand under the posited conditions, will now be tested. Let us suppose, first, that, instead of each country expanding its consumption proportionately to its gains from international trade, it continues, under trade, to put one-third of its productive resources (or what, in the circumstances, amounts to the same thing, one-third of its income) into the acquisition of each of the commodities. On this basis country A will consume 42,000 units of corn and its trading value equivalent in each of cloth and linen, B will consume 20,000 units of cloth and its trading value equivalent in each of linen and corn, C will consume 30,000 units of cloth and its trading value equivalent in each of linen and corn, and D will consume 160,000 units of corn and its trading value equivalent in each of cloth and linen. With the terms at 10 cloth = 21 linen = 30 corn, A will always produce 126,000 corn and B will always produce 60,000 cloth. The necessary adjustments to the shifts in demand will be made by C increasing or decreasing its production of cloth, or D its production of linen, relative to corn in each case.

The following table presents the consumption and production figures on the new assumptions.[12] The ratio of exchange is unaffected by the shift in demand.

Ratio of Exchange: 10 cloth = 21 linen = 30 corn

	CONSUMPTION				PRODUCTION		
	Cloth	Linen	Corn		Cloth	Linen	Corn
A	14,000	29,400	42,000		—	—	126,000
B	20,000	42,000	60,000		60,000	—	—
C	30,000	63,000	90,000		$57,333\frac{1}{3}$	—	98,000
D	$53,333\frac{1}{3}$	112,000	160,000		—	246,400	128,000
	$117,333\frac{1}{3}$	246,400	352,000		$117,333\frac{1}{3}$	246,400	352,000

The above would be the situation when a general increase in income, arising from a shift from national self-sufficiency to international trade, is associated with a *relative* cheapening of corn to most consumers and a demand for corn inelastic relative to that for cloth and linen. Not so much corn is then taken as was the case when demand, in all of the countries for each of the products, increased in proportion to their cheapness. This, nevertheless, has no effect on the normal exchange ratios.

We can, in fact, go much farther in varying demand assumptions without affecting the terms. In the immediately following tables six cases are presented in which the demand for cloth, linen, and corn, respectively, is assumed to vary so that, in each country, the proportion of productive resources, or income, devoted to the acquisition of the several products is in:

Case I: 5/20 to cloth, 8/20 to linen, 7/20 to corn
Case II: 5/20 to cloth, 7/20 to linen, 8/20 to corn
Case III: 7/20 to cloth, 8/20 to linen, 5/20 to corn
Case IV: 7/20 to cloth, 5/20 to linen, 8/20 to corn
Case V: 8/20 to cloth, 7/20 to linen, 5/20 to corn
Case VI: 8/20 to cloth, 5/20 to linen, 7/20 to corn

[12] Exports and imports can be readily ascertained from the figures of the production and consumption of the several countries and are, therefore, omitted.

No change in the ratio of exchange will occur as a result of any of these shifts in demand. The figures of production and consumption, in the several cases, are presented in the following tables.

Case I.

5/20 of income to cloth, 8/20 to linen, 7/20 to corn
Ratio of Exchange: 10 cloth = 21 linen = 30 corn

	CONSUMPTION			PRODUCTION		
	Cloth	Linen	Corn	Cloth	Linen	Corn
A	10,500	35,280	44,100	—	—	126,000
B	15,000	50,400	63,000	60,000	—	—
C	22,500	75,600	94,500	28,000	—	186,000
D	40,000	134,400	168,000	—	295,680	57,600
	88,000	295,680	369,600	88,000	295,680	369,600

Case II.

5/20 of income to cloth, 7/20 to linen, 8/20 to corn
Ratio of Exchange: 10 cloth = 21 linen = 30 corn

	CONSUMPTION			PRODUCTION		
	Cloth	Linen	Corn	Cloth	Linen	Corn
A	10,500	30,870	50,400	—	—	126,000
B	15,000	44,100	72,000	60,000	—	—
C	22,500	66,150	108,000	28,000	—	186,000
D	40,000	117,600	192,000	—	258,720	110,400
	88,000	258,720	422,400	88,000	258,720	422,400

Case III.

7/20 of income to cloth, 8/20 to linen, 5/20 to corn
Ratio of Exchange: 10 cloth = 21 linen = 30 corn

	CONSUMPTION			PRODUCTION		
	Cloth	Linen	Corn	Cloth	Linen	Corn
A	14,700	35,280	31,500	—	—	126,000
B	21,000	50,400	45,000	60,000	—	—
C	31,500	75,600	67,500	63,200	—	80,400
D	56,000	134,400	120,000	—	295,680	57,600
	123,200	295,680	264,000	123,200	295,680	264,000

Case IV.

7/20 of income to cloth, 5/20 to linen, 8/20 to corn
Ratio of Exchange: 10 cloth = 21 linen = 30 corn

	CONSUMPTION			PRODUCTION		
	Cloth	Linen	Corn	Cloth	Linen	Corn
A	14,700	22,050	50,400	—	—	126,000
B	21,000	31,500	72,000	60,000	—	—
C	31,500	47,250	108,000	63,200	—	80,400
D	56,000	84,000	192,000	—	184,800	216,000
	123,200	184,800	422,400	123,200	184,800	422,400

Case V.

8/20 of income to cloth, 7/20 to linen, 5/20 to corn
Ratio of Exchange: 10 cloth = 21 linen = 30 corn

	CONSUMPTION			PRODUCTION		
	Cloth	Linen	Corn	Cloth	Linen	Corn
A	16,800	30,870	31,500	—	—	126,000
B	24,000	44,100	45,000	60,000	—	—
C	36,000	66,150	67,500	80,800	—	27,600
D	64,000	117,600	120,000	—	258,720	110,400
	140,800	258,720	264,000	140,800	258,720	264,000

Case VI.

8/20 of income to cloth, 5/20 to linen, 7/20 to corn
Ratio of Exchange: 10 cloth = 21 linen = 30 corn

	CONSUMPTION			PRODUCTION		
	Cloth	Linen	Corn	Cloth	Linen	Corn
A	16,800	22,050	44,100	—	—	126,000
B	24,000	31,500	63,000	60,000	—	—
C	36,000	47,250	94,500	80,800	—	27,600
D	64,000	84,000	168,000	—	184,800	216,000
	140,800	184,800	369,600	140,800	184,800	369,600

It would seem that, once international trade in staple products is established, the changes in demand would seldom, if ever, go beyond the very wide limits above assumed (and the ratio of exchange will, of course, not shift with any smaller alteration of demand). We may therefore conclude, tentatively, that the *normal* exchange ratios between staple products in this more complex international trade will, regardless of any ordinary shift of demand, stand fast under any given constant cost conditions. (Only some specialty, produced in only one country which produces nothing else, would be likely to show any deviation from the general ratio at any time established, and any such deviation would not affect the ratios of all of the rest of the commodities, each against the others, but only the ratio of all against the specialty).

We shall later see that, in yet more complicated trade, exchange ratios will, perhaps, be not quite so insensitive to large shifts in demand as in the models so far presented, but that, if any change should then occur in the ratio of exchange, it will tend to be of much smaller magnitude, for a given shift in demand, than that which *can* happen, in the less complicated trade here depicted, whenever a truly catastrophic shift in the relative desirability of the several com-

86

modities takes place. In other words, the ratio of exchange will then, perhaps, be slightly less stable with respect to minor, but not nearly so saltatory with respect to major, shifts in demand.

Catastrophic Shifts in Demand

Let us now assume, with the present models, a truly catastrophic shift of demand. We shall contrast what would happen when incomes in each of the countries are split in the proportions of 1/5 to cloth, 3/10 to linen, and 1/2 to corn with the conditions under which 1/2 of the incomes go to cloth, 3/10 to linen, and 1/5 to corn.[13] Under the first of these assumptions the ratio would remain as in Cases I-VI. Consumption and production would be as follows (Case VII):

CASE VII.

1/5 of income to cloth, 3/10 to linen, 1/2 to corn
Ratio of Exchange: 10 cloth = 21 linen = 30 corn

	CONSUMPTION			PRODUCTION		
	Cloth	Linen	Corn	Cloth	Linen	Corn
A	8,400	26,460	63,000	—	—	126,000
B	12,000	37,800	90,000	60,000	—	—
C	18,000	56,700	135,000	10,400	—	238,800
D	32,000	100,800	240,000	—	221,760	163,200
	70,400	221,760	528,000	70,400	221,760	528,000

But, when we reverse the proportions of income devoted to cloth and corn respectively, the demand for cloth at the ratio 10 cloth = 21 linen = 30 corn would require 176,000 units of that commodity. This is beyond the combined productive powers of countries B and C, who have hitherto produced all of the cloth, and the price of cloth will, in consequence, rise in terms of linen and corn. It so happens that the demand cannot be met through any rise in the linen and corn price of cloth short of that which will bring country D into the production of cloth. No limbo ratio will suffice and the terms must therefore shift to D's cost ratios, 10 cloth = 28 linen = 40 corn. Country D will then produce all three commodities, and consumption and production will be as follows (Case VIII):

---

13 Since it is total demand, only, which is of importance, it would make no difference whether or not the demand schedules *in any given country*, at any given time, were similar to those in others, but it would complicate the exposition, to no purpose, to assume that they were not. All that is necessary, however, is that the *total* demand be split between the commodities in the assumed proportions. It need not be *pro rated* to the several countries.

Case VIII.

1/2 of income to cloth, 3/10 to linen, 1/5 to corn
Ratio of Exchange: 10 cloth = 28 linen = 40 corn

	CONSUMPTION			PRODUCTION		
	Cloth	Linen	Corn	Cloth	Linen	Corn
A	15,750	26,460	25,200	—	—	126,000
B	30,000	50,400	48,000	60,000	—	—
C	45,000	75,600	72,000	90,000	—	—
D	60,000	100,800	96,000	750	253,260	115,200
	150,750	253,260	241,200	150,750	253,260	241,200

At a certain point of relative demand between a disbursal of 2/5 and 1/2 of total income on cloth (75/176 to be precise) the consumption of cloth would reach 150,000 units. This is the productive capacity of B and C, together, when their resources are fully concentrated on that commodity. Up to this point, in increasing the demand for cloth, the ratio 10 cloth = 21 linen = 30 corn will persist. Any disposition to acquire cloth beyond this amount will, inevitably, raise its price in linen and corn. If, however, we assume the relative demand for cloth, beyond 75/176 of total income, to grow slowly, rather than at a leap (and if we depart in other ways from the assumptions on demand so far made), the ratio of exchange might not immediately shift from 10 cloth = 21 linen = 30 corn to 10 cloth = 28 linen = 40 corn but might enter a limbo between them. Linen and corn would preserve the same ratio against one another (proportionate to their cost of production in D), and the terms might, for example, move to 10 cloth = 23 linen = $32\frac{6}{7}$ corn. In this situation the classical analysis is partly applicable. As cloth becomes more expensive to the producers of linen and corn (A and D) they can obtain less cloth for the expenditure of a given proportion of their income. They might, moreover, with the increase in the price of cloth reduce the share of their income devoted to the purchase of that commodity. This would prevent the rise in the price of cloth from going very far. But, since their total income will be reduced by the movement of the terms of trade against them, they might even *increase* the share of their income devoted to cloth and still not buy as much cloth as they had hitherto purchased. A limbo ratio would then still prevail. If, however, the increase in the demand for cloth arises from a general determination, shared by consumers in A and D, to have more of that material, the terms will move immediately to 10 cloth = 28 linen = 40 corn, to bring about produc-

88

tion of cloth in D, since it would be scarcely valid to assume that the citizens of B and C, whose incomes will have been *increased* by the movement of the terms, will, merely to accommodate the citizens of A and D, consume less cloth than they had hitherto done.[14]

Objection might be taken to the method of presenting variations in demand in terms of the proportion of income spent for the several commodities. But, with a given group of commodities and, for the most part, an unaltered exchange ratio, this serves well enough to represent different general positions of demand. Refinements in the concept are quite unnecessary to the demonstration that, under constant cost, no shift in demand within the range of reasonable conjecture will have any effect whatever on the (normal) terms of trade. It would be more realistic to regard the altered status of demand treated in the latter part of this chapter as new, rather than revised, data—a different sort of world.

14 It may be noted that, in spite of their determination to get more cloth, A and D do not succeed in securing as much cloth when they spend one-half of their incomes on that product as they had done when they spent, along with B and C, only two-fifths of their incomes for cloth.

CHAPTER VI

COMPLEX TRADE

THE exposition, so far, has enabled us to lay down some general principles, in refutation of accepted theory, but it is still far from furnishing a representative model of conditions in a trading world of many countries and commodities. Let us therefore proceed to the consideration of this more complex trade. In the models that follow, ten countries are assumed to trade in ten commodities. Not much purpose would be served by adding to this number of countries or commodities, or both, though the difficulties would perhaps not rise proportionately with such additions. This very fact, however, is evidence of the adequacy of the sample for the apprehension of all the principles involved.

The Tableau of Costs on the following page sets forth a schedule of the opportunity cost ratios, in various countries, in the production of the commodities z, y, x, w, v, u, t, s, r, and q (that is, the possibility of indefinite substitution, at the stated cost ratios, of units of one commodity for those of any other). The countries are A, B, C, D, E, F, G, H, I, and J.[1] The cost ratios are referred, in each case, to a unit of z, and the countries, from A to J, are ranged in order of their relative total potential productivity in z.[2] Thus if,

[1] The figures in the Tableau were originally set down at random but were later modified, very slightly, in order to avoid unwieldy fractions and yet achieve absolutely accurate results. The random character of the selections was not thereby essentially modified. The figures are representative of cost conditions which will be assumed to remain unchanged for the discussion in this and the following chapter.

[2] It is, of course, arbitrary to take productive capacity in any one commodity as representative of economic size since to do so exaggerates, for listing purposes, the true size of such countries as, under any established set of exchange ratios, happen to have a comparative advantage in that commodity, and correspondingly minimizes the size of the others. According as the ratio of exchange shifts from one position to another the relative total value output of the several countries will alter and, with the countries rated according to their total potential productive capacity in a single commodity (which many will not produce), the alteration in the relationship between the total value of their respective outputs may be so great that the places of some of the countries in the scale of economic size may be inverted. The matter is of no significance to the exposition, and since, without knowing the ratios of exchange (the *quaesitum*) it is impossible to know the relative economic size of the countries (which will appear only when it is found), the procedure here taken is necessary to secure a foothold for an attack on the problem. Furthermore, it simplifies matters, enormously, to have a common denominator. The relative productivity in the several commodities in each country is therefore always referred to a unit of z as the yardstick. Nothing is said about *per capita* efficiency in the production of z, or any other commodity, in any country. This may, no doubt, vary greatly between

by specialization, country A could produce a thousand, a million, or any other number of units of z, country B could produce twice as much of that commodity, C three times as much, and D, E, F, G, H, I, and J, respectively, 4, 5, 8, 12, 20, 30, and 40 times as much.

TABLEAU OF (OPPORTUNITY) COST RATIOS

SIZE OF COUNTRY*	COUNTRY	COMMODITIES									
		z	y	x	w	v	u	t	s	r	q
1	A	1†	10	8	22	80	25	7	44	51	87
2	B	1	12	12	19	54	18	5	29	25	96
3	C	1	14	3	15	21	50	11	31	30	32
4	D	1	16	6	5	96	37	4	23	36	14
5	E	1	28	16	48	12	31	2	13	81	29
8	F	1	36	5	7	45	23	12	38	37	31
12	G	1	18	4	9	63	34	6	60	43	35
20	H	1	17	18	27	33	45	2	14	54	17
30	I	1	32	7	13	43	12	16	80	64	52
40	J	1	21	20	17	64	38	3	34	26	72

* Measured in total productive power if concentrated on the output of commodity z.

† It would be possible, without changing the *real* results, to use a series of single units running horizontally, as well as vertically, from the upper left corner of the Tableau. The Tableau, as it now stands, shows that the opportunity cost in A of a unit of z is 10 units of y, 8 of x, 22 of w, etc. But 10 of the designated units of y, 8 of those of x, 22 of those of w, etc., could be gathered together to make a new unit (of larger size) in each case. Columns y, x, w, etc. would then be divided vertically by 10, 8, 22, etc. (without any but a nominal effect on the cost ratios) to give a series of single units running along the top line, left to right, correlative with those running, "north and south," in column z. This might, formally, be somewhat more elegant than the present scheme but it would introduce awkward fractions into the cost ratio schedules and thus complicate the task of exposition.

Let us now suppose, to get a start, that 1/10 of the productive power and, therefore, of the income of each country, at the ratio of exchange that comes to be established in the course of trade, is devoted to the acquisition of each of the commodities. This assump-

the countries, but, taken alone, is of no relevance to trade or to the ratio of exchange. The (absolute and relative) economic size of the countries will be a function of three variables, viz., the size of the working population, its per capita productivity, and the ratio of exchange of commodities. The relative size of the countries will appear in accordance with the original assumptions (modified by the composition of output under any established exchange ratio) in the later presented tables of production and consumption. These relatives may be multiplied by any constant factor to give any desired range of absolutes. Per capita *prosperity* is, of course, a function both of absolute productivity, per head, in commodities of comparative advantage, and of the ratio of exchange.

tion will later be modified to show the effects (if any), on the ratio of exchange, of other constellations of desire and demand.

It is impossible by mere inspection to do more than guess at the commodity, or commodities, in which the comparative advantage of any given country, at the ratio of exchange which will evolve, may lie. It might seem, for instance, that country A would be likely to produce z, or q, in which it is nearer to the best relative performance in any country than in any commodity except z, or that E would produce r in which it surpasses the relative performance of all other countries. But such does not, in fact, prove to be the case. On the other hand, one would scarcely suppose that country H would produce r in which it is surpassed relatively by two other countries of which one is large. Country H nevertheless finds it to its advantage to produce r. Every country will, of course, produce the commodity, or commodities, in which opportunity cost is at a minimum (the ratio of exchange actually established being used as a referent). This will be that commodity, or those commodities, which, taking the figures in the Tableau of Costs as numerator, commodity by commodity, and the terms of the ratio of exchange as denominator, will give the highest ratio available to the country in question.

The exchange ratio, comparative advantage, and the composition of output in any country react each upon the others. How, then, are we to determine any of them? The first approximation lies in the thesis that the largest countries must produce several commodities since specialization, in one or two only, would result in so great an output of those commodities as to offer no chance of their sale at any price which would not make it profitable to the producing countries to add other commodities to their list. When, however, the ratio of exchange so alters as to impel enterprisers in any country to produce a commodity which had hitherto not been profitable to them, enterprisers in other countries may be induced to shift not only the proportions between, but also the character of, *their* output, and this will have repercussions on the first country. A kaleidoscopic movement of comparative advantage and of resources will then occur. One must be Argus-eyed indeed to foresee all of these shifts. It is, in fact, very difficult, if not impossible, to foretell whether a shift in the exchange ratio which will open up to any given country the opportunity of profitable production of a new commodity, or will impel it to forgo the production of one or more of those that it had hitherto been producing, will not so shift productive relationships in other countries as greatly to modify original, more or less naïve, expectations. Much depends on the size of the country originally affected, the size of the other countries shifting production in response to the alteration in the ratio of exchange, the reaction of the originally affected country, and the pre-existing distribution of output in the several countries. The only practicable course is to try out various possibilities in an effort to find the ratio which will not only quadrate with cost ratios in the various countries, for the commodities they may produce, but, with any given conditions of demand, will also permit the absorption of the full productive powers of the several countries. In the actual world this process occurs, all but imperceptibly, in the private pursuit of profit.

"Mock-Ups"

If, to begin, we assume that J, the largest country, will produce at least four commodities (a trial will readily show that, under the given demand conditions, any lesser number will not suffice to absorb J's productive power along with that of any other country that may find it advantageous to produce the same commodities at a price ratio for the products which will not make it worth while for producers in J to take on a new line) the cost ratios indicate that the commodities are likely to be z, x, v, and q.

Country I is relatively very strong in t and s (see Tableau of Cost Ratios) but it will need other outlets for its productive power. Commodity y seems likely to offer such an outlet. But F, a sizable country, will probably specialize in y, leaving but a small place for I in this product. Country I will therefore have to go into r, as well as y, in addition to t and s.

At any ratio which will permit country J to produce z, x, v, and q, and country I to produce y, t, s, and r, country H will find it advantageous to produce w and u. But w will also be produced in E, and u will be produced in C, so that H, as well as I, will have to find an outlet in r.

There is now no commodity which will not be produced by one of the "Big Three," J, I, and H, so that G, not a small country, will be unable to find an outlet for its full productive powers in any single commodity. It must have at least two strings to its bow. For various reasons, associated with the ratio of exchange in correspondence with cost schedules, it will go into s in addition to z.[3]

Determination of the Ratio

Country J's production of z, x, v, and q fixes the ratio of exchange for these products, in the proportions of $1 : 20 : 64 : 72$ (J's cost ratios). Country I's output of y, t, s, and r must exchange at I's cost ratios for these products of $32 : 16 : 80 : 64$. Country H's products, w, u, and r, must in turn exchange at H's cost ratios for these commodities of $27 : 45 : 54$; while z and s, G's products, will exchange at $z = 60s$ (the cost ratio in G).

These figures determine the complete set of exchange ratios. Commodity z exchanges for $60s$ and also for $20x$, $64v$ or $72q$. But $60s$ exchanges for $24y$, $12t$, or $48r$ (I's cost ratios in these products). Therefore $z = 24y = 20x = 64v = 12t = 60s = 48r = 72q$. But $48r$ will exchange for $24w$ or $40u$ (H's cost ratios in these products). The full set of exchange ratios is, therefore, $z = 24y = 20x = 24w = 64v = 40u = 12t = 60s = 48r = 72q$. This we shall designate the "initial" ratio of international exchange. Under this ratio country F will produce y, E will produce w, D and A will produce v, C will produce u, and B will produce q.[4] The consumption and production of the various commodities are shown, in Tables A_{1c} and A_{1p} (pp. 96 and 97), for the situation in which each country devotes a tenth of income to each product. (Exports and imports are omitted since they can be readily determined from the consumption and production figures). The method of computation of production and consumption is the same as that used in the preceding chapter.[5]

[3] Country G's comparative advantage in z is fairly obvious since one country or another greatly surpasses it, relatively, in every other commodity. But it is the play of prices that puts G also into s rather than, for example, v.

[4] Small countries, as noted above, would, under conditions of constant cost, almost never produce more than one commodity since this would require that they should have the same cost ratios, for two or more commodities, as those prevailing for those commodities in one of the large countries that produced them. This is, to say the least, improbable. No country, in fact, would be likely to have the same cost ratio, for any two commodities, as any other. Large countries, however, are very likely to have a product in common with some other large country and, almost certainly, with some of the smaller. This will never require identity of cost ratios between any two commodities in any two countries.

[5] 1/10 of the income of any country is 1/10 of the potential output of any export provided the country were to specialize exclusively upon the production of that commodity. Whatever, at the established ratio of exchange, this will buy of each of the other commodities will constitute an expenditure of 1/10 of total income on each

It can be said, with some confidence, that the exchange ratio $z = 24y = 20x = 24w = 64v = 40u = 12t = 60s = 48r = 72q$ is the sole ratio that will provide a solution to the problem.[6] There is no other *apparently* feasible solution which will not, with the given status of demand, be found to result in a shortage of some commodities and a corresponding surplus of others. Any but the right ratio inevitably restricts certain countries to lines which will not fully absorb their productive powers whereas the countries producing the remainder of the products cannot supply the full amount demanded. Some idea of the difficulties into which any but the right ratio runs may be obtained when we reflect that anything that tends to lower the (normal) price of z, for instance, in terms of y, w, u, t, or r will inevitably affect equally the normal price of x, v, and q, the other products of J. But, as a result of the production of s as well as z in G, it will also equally affect the price of s. When, however, s is affected, y, t, and r are equally involved through country I; and, when r is affected, w and u will be drawn in through country H. So long as the several countries produce unchanged *lists* of commodities all commodities are thus involved in any shift in the price of z or, in fact, in the price of any other of the goods. Since prices are the ratios of exchange, since it is impossible for all the terms of a ratio to be equally affected without leaving the ratio as it was, and since the normal ratio of exchange of products supplied by any one country cannot deviate from the cost ratios in that country, it is

---

product. Country A, for instance, specializes in v of which it can produce 800 units. It will consume 80 of these, and use the remaining 720, split into nine parts of 80 each, to procure the other nine commodities.

[6] The ratio that will solve the problem can ordinarily be ascertained only through a tedious process of trial and error in which the whole course of trade must be worked out before one can know whether the exchange ratio with which he is experimenting will, in fact, provide a solution. It has been suggested that a mathematical formula should be developed which would provide the solution instanter. This would, surely, be desirable, but mathematicians of great repute, to whom I have submitted the problem, have been unable to furnish any such formula (perhaps because they were not sufficiently interested to devote to it the necessary time). The difficulty is that any shift in the ratio will set in motion kaleidoscopic changes not only in consumption but in production, will immediately take countries completely out of the production of at least one commodity and, perhaps, put them into others, and will change their consumption in varying proportions according to the varying net changes in the total income of each country and the opportunity cost, in trade, of each of the commodities. The data change, unevenly, with every change in the (tentative) solution. If, therefore, anyone thinks that there is more than one solution to any set of data, or that a formula is readily at hand, I can only invite him to try to find them. On the other hand, *some* solution is, of course, always possible.

TABLE A$_{1c}$

Ratio of exchange: $z = 24y = 20x = 24w = 64v = 40u = 12t = 60s = 48r = 72q$

CONSUMPTION

(Thousands, or any other multiple, of the figures below)

1/10 of the income of each country to each of the products

	z	y	x	w	v	u	t	s	r	q
A	$1\frac{1}{4}$	30	25	30	80	50	15	75	60	90
B	$2\frac{2}{3}$	64	$53\frac{1}{3}$	64	$170\frac{2}{3}$	$106\frac{2}{3}$	32	160	128	192
C	$3\frac{3}{4}$	90	75	90	240	150	45	225	180	270
D	6	144	120	144	384	240	72	360	288	432
E	10	240	200	240	640	400	120	600	480	720
F	12	288	240	288	768	480	144	720	576	864
G	12	288	240	288	768	480	144	720	576	864
H	$22\frac{1}{2}$	540	450	540	1440	900	270	1350	1080	1620
I	40	960	800	960	2560	1600	480	2400	1920	2880
J	40	960	800	960	2560	1600	480	2400	1920	2880
Totals	$150\frac{1}{6}$	3604	$3008\frac{1}{3}$	3604	$9610\frac{2}{3}$	$6006\frac{2}{3}$	1802	9010	7208	10812

On a self-sufficient basis, and giving equal effort to each of the commodities, A could produce, in a given time, one unit of $z + 10y + 8x + 22w + 80v + 25u + 80w + 7t + 44s + 51r + 87q$ (cf. Tableau of Cost Ratios, p. 91). By concentrating on v, A can, in the same time, produce 10 times $80 = 800v$, and, at the established ratio of exchange, this will permit the consumption indicated in the table. Take now another country, F. On a self-sufficient basis, and giving equal effort to each of the commodities, F could, in a given time, turn out 8 times as much z as A and its total production would be $8(z + 36y + 5x + 7w + 45v + 23u + 12t + 88s + 37r + 31q)$. By concentrating on y, F can produce, in the same time, 10 times 8 times $36 = 2880y$ and, at the established ratio of exchange, this will permit the indicated consumption. Though country G could, in a given time, produce 12 times as much z as A (50% more than F) its concentration on z and s is not as profitable to it as F's concentration on y, because 12 times as much z as A comes only to parity with that of F. By specialization in z or s, country G could produce 10 times 12 = 120z, or 10 times 12 times 60 = 7200s, and either of these, or any possible combination of the two, is, at the established ratio of exchange, merely equivalent in value to F's production of 2880y. Total incomes in these countries, at the established ratio of exchange, are, therefore, equal. A similar situation develops in the case of countries I and J.

Assuming that, on a nationally self-sufficient basis, 1/10 of the income of each country would have been spent on each of the ten commodities, the *minimum* gains from international trade, that is to say, the percentage by which the consumption of all commodities could be *equally* expanded as a result of such trade, would be, for the various countries, ranged from A to J, 52.5%, 92.1%, 94.1%, 142.6%, 138%, 109.6%, 42%, 57.6%, 49.5%, and 26.7%, respectively. It so happens that the middle-sized countries get the largest gains. This is fortuitous as against the smaller countries (a result of an accidental relatively wide deviation of national cost ratios from the established ratio of exchange). There is, however, a real bias against the probability of the *largest* countries gaining heavily (See

TABLE A$_{1p}$

Ratio of exchange: $z = 24y = 20x = 24w = 64v = 40u = 12t = 60s = 48r = 72q$

PRODUCTION

(Thousands, or any other multiple, of the figures below)

	z	y	x	w	v	u	t	s	r	q
A	—	—	—	—	800	—	—	—	—	—
B	—	—	—	—	—	—	—	—	—	1920
C	—	—	—	—	—	1500	—	—	—	—
D	—	—	—	—	3840	—	—	—	—	—
E	—	—	—	2400	—	—	—	—	—	—
F	—	2880	—	—	—	—	—	—	—	—
G	$101\frac{1}{2}$	—	—	—	—	—	—	1110	—	—
H	—	—	—	1204	—	$4506\frac{2}{3}$	—	—	2984	—
I	—	724	—	—	—	—	1802	7900	4224	—
J	$48\frac{2}{3}$	—	$3003\frac{1}{3}$	—	$4970\frac{2}{3}$	—	—	—	—	8892
Totals	$150\frac{1}{6}$	3604	$3003\frac{1}{3}$	3604	$9610\frac{2}{3}$	$6006\frac{2}{3}$	1802	9010	7208	10812

J produces z, x, v, q
I produces y, t, s, r
H produces w, u, r
G produces z, s
F produces y

E produces w
D produces v
C produces u
B produces q
A produces v

The division of production in any country producing more than one commodity is determined by total consumption in conjunction with the output of countries concentrating on the production of commodities also put out by the country in question.

clear that, except in a limbo situation (that is to say, where there is no link in costs between one, or more, of the commodities and the others), no shift in demand not so great as completely to eliminate the production of some commodity in a country which had hitherto been supplying it, or to establish the production of some commodity in a country which had hitherto not engaged in its output, can have any effect whatever on the normal ratio of exchange. If, however, such a change in the ingredients of any national output occurs, the national focus of opportunity cost ratios is altered and the international ratio of exchange will be affected. In the absence of such a shift of the ingredients in some national output, the relative supplies of the various commodities will, *without alteration in the existing ratio of exchange*, be adjusted to changing demand through shifts in the proportionate output of the several commodities *within* the countries that produce more than one of them. Producers can, under these circumstances, transfer resources from one to another of the commodities, at constant opportunity cost, and no changes in relative *marginal* utilities will occur.

Countries H, I, and J, among them, put out the whole list of commodities. Some one of these countries produces at a minimum (in y) one-fifth of the whole supply of any commodity. Except for y and z, some one of these countries, indeed, produces from one-third to the full (world) supply of one or more of all the traded commodities. The potentialities of shifts, *within* any of the larger countries, are, therefore, great.

Since total demand is equal to total productive power the demand for one or more commodities cannot fall without that for others rising. The rising demand may be for commodities produced in the same country as produces that or those for which the demand is falling but, even if this does not occur, it will *somewhere* draw resources out of the production of the goods of relatively impaired demand and thus make more room for the output of one or more of the products of some large country originally affected by the decline in demand. Since the ratio of exchange is predominately determined by conditions in the largest countries, none but very great shifts in demand will usually, therefore, have any effect upon it.

COMPLEX TRADE
Shifts of Demand

To test this proposition let us suppose that, instead of an expenditure of 1/10 of total income for each of the products, demand so shifts that 2/25 of total income is laid out for each of z, y, x, w, and v while 3/25 of total income is spent for each of u, t, s, r, and q. It so happens that country J produces three of the commodities for which demand is here presumed to have fallen and only one for which demand has risen, that country I produces three commodities for which demand is here presumed to have risen and only one for which it is presumed to have fallen, that H is putting out one of the commodities for which the demand has gone down and two for which it is enhanced, and that G has one commodity in either category. Countries F, E, D, and A are specialized in commodities of diminished, and C and B in those of increased, demand. On classical reasoning J, F, E, D, and A would suffer, and the condition of most of the other countries would be improved.[7] The relative prosperity of the various countries is in fact, however, quite unaffected by the shift in demand since the terms of trade will remain unchanged. Table A_2 (p. 100) shows the new status. (So far as consumption is concerned, totals only are presented.) The shifts in consumption in each of the countries equally reflect the shift in demand since relative national incomes are not altered. On the production side, adjustments are as follows: country J, to compensate for reductions in its output of x and v, which, taken together, are in excess of its expansion in q, increases its output of z. This happens in spite of the fact that the total demand for z is reduced. Country G, the other producer of z, is then impelled to shift a large part of its resources to its alternative product s and produces so much of that commodity that country I is forced to reduce its output of s even though the total demand for that commodity has risen. Producers in I, moreover, all but completely move out of y (in which they had not originally been very heavily involved). Thereby they can expand the output of t and r. Producers in H shift resources from w to u but make no change in r. All of the countries concentrating in one commodity (A, B, C, D, E, and F) continue, of course, to produce their full quota of their specialty.

[7] Classical analysis, however, would be at a loss to know what to say about country G which produces two commodities for one of which the demand has increased and, for the other, diminished.

TABLE A_2

(Compare with A_{1c} and A_{1p})

Ratio of exchange: $z = 24y = 20x = 24w = 64v = 40u = 12t = 60s = 48r = 72q$

CONSUMPTION

(Thousands, or any other multiple, of the figures below)

2/25 of total income to each of z, y, x, w, v;
3/25 of total income to each of u, t, s, r, q.

	z	y	x	w	v	u	t	s	r	q
Totals	$120\frac{2}{15}$	$2883\frac{1}{5}$	$2402\frac{2}{3}$	$2883\frac{1}{5}$	$7688\frac{8}{15}$	7208	$2162\frac{2}{5}$	10812	$8649\frac{3}{5}$	$12974\frac{2}{5}$

PRODUCTION

(Thousands, or any other multiple, of the figures below)

	z	y	x	w	v	u	t	s	r	q
A	—	—	—	—	800	—	—	—	—	—
B	—	—	—	—	—	—	—	—	—	1920
C	—	—	—	—	—	1500	—	—	—	—
D	—	—	—	—	3840	—	—	—	—	—
E	—	—	—	2400	—	—	—	—	—	—
F	—	2880	—	—	—	—	—	—	—	—
G	$41\frac{13}{30}$	—	—	—	—	—	—	4714	—	—
H	—	—	—	$483\frac{1}{5}$	—	5708	—	—	2984	—
I	—	$3\frac{1}{5}$	—	—	—	—	$2162\frac{2}{5}$	6098	$5665\frac{3}{5}$	—
J	$78\frac{7}{10}$	—	$2402\frac{2}{3}$	—	$3048\frac{8}{15}$	—	—	—	—	$11054\frac{2}{5}$
Totals	$120\frac{2}{15}$	$2883\frac{1}{5}$	$2402\frac{2}{3}$	$2883\frac{1}{5}$	$7688\frac{8}{15}$	7208	$2162\frac{2}{5}$	10812	$8649\frac{3}{5}$	$12974\frac{2}{5}$

J produces z, x, v, q
I produces y, t, s, r
H produces w, u, r
G produces z, s
F produces y
E produces w
D produces v
C produces u
B produces q
A produces v

The shift in demand from the conditions shown in Chart A_1 to those shown in Chart A_2 might, of course, produce *temporary* movements in the ratio of exchange and it will always be assumed that these occur in the degree necessary to induce the appropriate adjustments in output. Since these price movements are ephemeral, and we are dealing with normal values, they will hereafter not be noted.

The limit, without a change in the ratio of exchange, on a shift in demand of the character at present under consideration is set by the decline in the demand for y. It is clear that the demand for y, along with that for z, x, w, and v, could not fall much farther, along the lines of the present assumptions, without eliminating the output of y in I and, therefore, the possibility of any further adjustment through a shift of resources from y to those commodities, produced in I, for which demand is increasing.[8] Country F is the only other producer of y, and F is fully specialized in it without any readily available alternatives. So soon as the total demand for y, at the existing ratio of exchange, falls from the present level of $2883\frac{1}{5}$ units to something less than F's output of 2880 units, a change in the ratio must occur. The price of y would then fall in terms of *all* other commodities. Commodity y would be "wild" in a limbo ratio in which F is not only the sole producer of y but produces nothing else. The actual price of y at any moment (measured in its power to command any or all of the other commodities) would be such as would result, in the current state of declining demand (not only for y but also for z, x, w, and v), in the absorption of 2880 units (F's output of y).

A new *stable* ratio would be established whenever the decline in the price of y made it worth while for F to shift part of its resources to another product. It so happens that, with F's cost ratios, this might be either z or t, or both, and the ratio would be $36y = z = 20x$, *etc.* Whether the ratio moves to this point or stays in limbo (at anything from 24 to $36y = z = 20x = 24w = 64v = 40u = 12t = 60s = 48r = 72q$), *all* countries other than F, regardless of the composition of their output, benefit in the same degree from a shift in demand which adversely affects the demand for z, x, w, and v, equally with y, but enlarges the demand for the remaining products. Country J, producing z, x, and v, for all of which the demand is re-

---

[8] Reference to Table A_2 will show that, under the conditions of demand there assumed, country I's production of y has all but disappeared.

duced (as against the increase in the demand for only its q), does just as well as any other country through the fall in the value of y. Country I, though an original producer of y, will be similarly benefited by the fall in the value of y, by the loss of demand for its output of that commodity, and the elimination of its production within the borders of I.[9]

Reversing the Shift

Let us now reverse our assumptions about demand and suppose that the shift is toward rather than away from z, y, x, w, and v, and therefore away from, rather than toward, u, t, s, r, and q. In this event the shift of demand cannot go nearly as far as in the preceding case without producing an alteration in the ratio of exchange.[10] But with, or with not much more than, 21/200 of total demand devoted to each of z, y, x, w, and v, and 19/200 of total demand to u, t, s, r, q, the original ratio will be preserved. Total consumption, and production by countries, are shown in Table A_3.

As compared with the initial situation in which 1/10 of total income was devoted to each of the commodities (cf. Tables A_{1c} and A_{1p}) country J now reduces its output of z (in spite of the increased demand for that commodity) in order to expand its production of x and v by more than the equivalent of the decline in its production of q. Country G thereupon steps into the breach and so expands its output of z as all but to eliminate its production of s. Country I, consequently, increases the production of s (in face of the decline in the total demand for that commodity) and somewhat enlarges its turnout of y (for which demand has risen) at the expense, in each case, of t and r (for which demand has declined). Country H shifts some of its resources from u to w, leaving its output of r unchanged; and all the other countries continue to produce as before.

[9] Since any shift in the total demand for a product implies a correlative opposite shift in the total demand (and supply) of others (which will affect production all round) it will frequently happen that a country may find an opportunity, with equal or greater profit than before, to *expand* its output of some good for which the foreign, and total, demand has declined. Conversely, with equal or greater profit than before, it may find occasion to *contract* its output of some good for which the foreign, and total, demand has risen. All this is quite contrary to the neo-classical analysis which, it will be recalled, runs in terms of reciprocal *national* demands for composite bales of products of mutually exclusive ingredients, and alleges that a country will always be benefited by an enlarged demand for "its" products, and will be injured by any decline in this demand.

[10] The reasons for this will be later explained.

TABLE A_3
(Compare with A_{1c} and A_{1p})

Ratio of exchange: $z = 24y = 20x = 24w = 64v = 40u = 12t = 60s = 48r = 72q$

Consumption

(Thousands, or any other multiple, of the figures below)

21/200 of total income to each of z, y, x, w, v;
19/200 of total income to each of u, t, s, r, q.

	z	y	x	w	v	u	t	s	r	q
Totals	$157\frac{81}{120}$	$3784\frac{1}{5}$	$3153\frac{1}{2}$	$3784\frac{1}{5}$	$10091\frac{1}{5}$	$5706\frac{1}{3}$	$1711\frac{9}{10}$	$8559\frac{1}{2}$	$6847\frac{3}{5}$	$10271\frac{2}{5}$

Production

(Thousands, or any other multiple, of the figures below)

	z	y	x	w	v	u	t	s	r	q
A	—	—	—	—	800	—	—	—	—	—
B	—	—	—	—	—	—	—	—	—	1920
C	—	—	—	—	—	1500	—	—	—	—
D	—	—	—	—	3840	—	—	—	—	—
E	—	—	—	2400	—	—	—	—	—	—
F	—	2880	—	—	—	—	—	—	—	—
G	$116\frac{31}{60}$	—	—	—	—	—	—	209	—	—
H	—	—	—	$1384\frac{1}{5}$	—	$4206\frac{1}{3}$	—	—	2984	—
I	—	$904\frac{1}{5}$	—	—	—	—	$1711\frac{9}{10}$	$8350\frac{1}{2}$	$3863\frac{3}{5}$	—
J	$41\frac{19}{120}$	—	$3153\frac{1}{2}$	—	$5451\frac{1}{5}$	—	—	—	—	$8351\frac{2}{5}$
Totals	$157\frac{81}{120}$	$3784\frac{1}{5}$	$3153\frac{1}{2}$	$3784\frac{1}{5}$	$10091\frac{1}{5}$	$5706\frac{1}{3}$	$1711\frac{9}{10}$	$8559\frac{1}{2}$	$6847\frac{3}{5}$	$10271\frac{2}{5}$

J produces z, x, v, q
I produces y, t, s, r
H produces w, u, r
G produces z, s
F produces y
E produces w
D produces v
C produces u
B produces q
A produces v

The limit on the shift of demand in this direction, without an alteration in the ratio of exchange, is set by the productive capacity of country G. Country J, as noted, is heavily engaged in increasing its output of both x and v and cannot, therefore, also expand in z. It must, in fact, *contract* its production of z. Country G must, in consequence, put out the bulk of the z. But, on the basis of 1/10 of income to each product, country G had already been mainly in z and it is therefore not possible for G greatly to increase the supply of that commodity. The demand could, without alteration in the ratio of exchange, shift a very little farther, until G had transferred to z the slight remainder of its resources still in s, but beyond that point the ratio of exchange must alter to bring other producers into z, and will, for a time, be a limbo ratio. In this, as in other limbo ratios, the classical theories find partial application. The value of the *commodity in limbo* will fall far or but little according to the elasticity of the total demand for it. It should be noted, however, that, in such a limbo ratio, it is only the value of the commodity in limbo that changes, against *all* the others. All other ratios, *inter se*, remain unaltered.

The ratio $z = 24y = 20x = 24w = 64v = 40u = 12t = 60s = 48r = 72q$ covers a demand ranging anywhere from a little less than 16/200 (2/25) to a little more than 21/200 of total income in each of z, y, x, w, and v, and from a little less than 19/200 to a little more than 24/200 (3/25) of total income in u, t, s, r, q.[11] Provided pressure were taken off certain "weak" points, associated with bottle-necks in the supply of y and z, the shifts in demand could, in every case, be carried much beyond the limits so far set forth and still cause no change in the ratio. If for instance, in the one case, the demand for z, x, w, and v, but not y, should continue to fall while that for u, t, s, r, and q should continue to rise, or if, in the other, the demand for y, x, w, and v, but not z, should continue to rise, while that for u, t, s, r, and q should continue to fall, no change would occur in the ratio until the limits suggested above had been far transcended. The ratio $z = 24y = 20x = 24w = 64v = 40u = 12t = 60s = 48r = 72q$ is, in short, highly stable and will prevail

---

[11] The reason that the demand can move farther in one direction than in the other, without a change in the initial ratio, is that the initial assumption of one-tenth of total income devoted to each product happens to bring about a distribution of resources a good deal nearer one shifting point than the other.

throughout very wide random changes in demand more or less centered on that of 1/10 of income to each product.

Concentration of Shifts in Demand on Single Countries

Supporters of the classical and neo-classical position will suspect that it is only because the shifts in demand are not *exclusively* concentrated, in a single direction, on the commodities currently produced in any given country that the ratio of exchange remains stable. That this is far from being the case will be shown if we suppose that the demand for z, x, v, and q (all of the commodities currently produced by J) diminishes, that the demand for w and u remains unchanged, and that the demand for y, t, s, and r (all of the commodities currently produced by I) increases. Table A_4 shows that the demand for each of z, x, v, and q can fall from 1/10 to 67/800 of total income, at the same time that the demand for y, t, s, and r rises from 1/10 to 93/800 of total income, without causing any shift in the ratio of exchange. Country J cuts its output of x, v, and q but it expands its output of z to compensate for the contraction of its other products. Country G, in consequence, all but abandons the production of z in favor of its alternative product s. The large output of s in G impels I to divert resources from s to its other products of increased demand, y, t, and r. Country H's production is not disturbed nor, of course, is that of any of the countries concentrating on a single commodity.

For the same reasons as in the former case the ratio of exchange will alter earlier when we reverse the trend and assume that the relative desirability of z, x, v, and q rises while that of y, t, s, and r falls. In this case the ratio of exchange remains unaffected only so long as the demand does not go much beyond 41/400 of total income for each of z, x, v, and q, and below 39/400 of total income for each of y, t, s, and r (cf. Table A_5).

The range of variation in demand, without any alteration in the ratio of exchange, is thus just a little less, in both directions, when the shifts in demand are exclusively concentrated on the current output of given countries than when a more probable random incidence of such changes is posited. It runs, approximately, in the one case, from an expenditure of 67/800 to 82/800 (41/400) of total income on each of z, x, v, and q and, in the other, from an expenditure of 64/800 (2/25) to 84/800 (21/200) of total income on each of

TABLE A₄
(Compare with A₁c and A₁ₚ)

Ratio of exchange: $z = 24y = 20x = 24w = 64v = 40u = 12t = 60s = 48r = 72q$

CONSUMPTION

(Thousands, or any other multiple, of the figures below)

67/800 of total income to each of z, x, v, q;
1/10 of total income to each of w, u;
93/800 of total income to each of y, t, s, r.

	z	y	x	w	v	u	t	s	r	q
Totals	$125\frac{367}{480}$	$4189\frac{13}{20}$	$2515\frac{7}{24}$	3604	$8048\frac{14}{15}$	$6006\frac{2}{3}$	$2094\frac{33}{40}$	$10474\frac{1}{8}$	$8379\frac{3}{10}$	$9055\frac{1}{20}$

PRODUCTION

(Thousands, or any other multiple, of the figures below)

	z	y	x	w	v	u	t	s	r	q
A	—	—	—	—	800	—	—	—	—	—
B	—	—	—	—	—	—	—	—	—	1920
C	—	—	—	—	—	1500	—	—	—	—
D	—	—	—	—	3840	—	—	—	—	—
E	—	—	—	2400	—	—	—	—	—	—
F	—	2880	—	—	—	—	—	—	—	—
G	$31\frac{107}{120}$	—	—	—	—	—	—	$6966\frac{1}{2}$	—	—
H	—	—	—	1204	—	$4506\frac{2}{3}$	—	—	2984	—
I	—	$1309\frac{13}{20}$	—	—	—	—	$2094\frac{33}{40}$	$3507\frac{5}{8}$	$5395\frac{3}{10}$	—
J	$1211\frac{257}{1440}$	—	$2515\frac{7}{24}$	—	$3408\frac{14}{15}$	—	—	—	—	$7135\frac{1}{20}$
Totals	$125\frac{367}{480}$	$4189\frac{13}{20}$	$2515\frac{7}{24}$	3604	$8048\frac{14}{15}$	$6006\frac{2}{3}$	$2094\frac{33}{40}$	$10474\frac{1}{8}$	$8379\frac{3}{10}$	$9055\frac{1}{20}$

J produces z, x, v, q
I produces y, t, s, r
H produces w, u, r
G produces z, s
F produces y

E produces w
D produces v
C produces u
B produces q
A produces v

TABLE A₅
(Compare with A_{1C} and A_{1D})

Ratio of exchange: $z = 24y = 20x = 24w = 64v = 40u = 12t = 60s = 48r = 72q$

CONSUMPTION
(Thousands, or any other multiple, of the figures below)

41/400 of total income to each of z, x, v, q;
1/10 of total income to each of w, u;
39/400 of total income to each of y, t, s, r.

	z	y	x	w	v	u	t	s	r	q
Totals	$153\frac{221}{240}$	$3518\frac{9}{10}$	$3078\frac{5}{12}$	3604	$9850\frac{14}{15}$	$6006\frac{2}{3}$	$1756\frac{19}{20}$	$8784\frac{3}{4}$	$7027\frac{4}{5}$	$11082\frac{3}{10}$

PRODUCTION
(Thousands, or any other multiple, of the figures below)

	z	y	x	w	v	u	t	s	r	q
A	—	—	—	—	800	—	—	—	—	—
B	—	—	—	—	—	—	—	—	—	1920
C	—	—	—	—	—	1500	—	—	—	—
D	—	—	—	—	3840	—	—	—	—	—
E	—	—	—	2400	—	—	—	—	—	—
F	—	2880	—	—	—	—	—	—	—	—
G	$116\frac{31}{60}$	—	—	—	—	—	—	209	—	—
H	—	—	—	1204	—	$4506\frac{2}{3}$	—	—	2984	—
I	—	$633\frac{9}{10}$	—	—	—	—	$1756\frac{19}{20}$	$8575\frac{3}{4}$	$4043\frac{4}{5}$	—
J	$37\frac{97}{240}$	—	$3078\frac{5}{12}$	—	$5210\frac{14}{15}$	—	—	—	—	$9162\frac{3}{10}$
Totals	$153\frac{221}{240}$	$3513\frac{9}{10}$	$3078\frac{5}{12}$	3604	$9850\frac{14}{15}$	$6006\frac{2}{3}$	$1756\frac{19}{20}$	$8784\frac{3}{4}$	$7027\frac{4}{5}$	$11082\frac{3}{10}$

J produces z, x, v, q
I produces y, t, s, r
H produces w, u, r
G produces z, s
F produces y

E produces w
D produces v
C produces u
B produces q
A produces v

z, y, x, w, v; or, in the one case, from an expenditure of 78/800 to 93/800 of total income on each of y, t, s, and r, and, in the other, from an expenditure of 76/800 (19/200) to 96/800 (3/25) of total income on each of u, t, s, r, and q.

The limiting factor on the range of such shifts in demand as will not involve a change in the ratio, is, at both ends of the scale, the relative smallness of country G. Whether G concentrates exclusively on s or on z its weight is not sufficient to balance more than medium-sized shifts in output in the larger countries. If G were larger, while the assumed changes in demand proceeded farther, or if further shifts, in either direction, should occur in the demand for the commodities x, v, and q but not z, or for y, t, and r but not s, the range could be much wider without any variation in the existing ratio. In the world as it is, where every important commodity is produced in more than one large country of wide diversity of output, the range of shift in demand that could occur without change in the normal ratio of exchange is enormously greater than that of the present model. This is so because any large country could expand or contract its supply of any produced commodity, with compensating contraction or expansion of others, over a very wide range of output. In the world as it is, therefore, the (normal) ratio of exchange, under any given constellation of constant costs, would be practically unalterable irrespective of any shifts in demand that are at all likely to occur.

It should, by now, be obvious that no change in demand that does not affect the ratio has any consequences, even on the composition of output, for countries so small as to be able to specialize in a single commodity elsewhere produced.[12] Like the larger countries their *income* is unaffected but, in addition, they are not called upon to make any adjustments in production. They will continue to produce, and to export, their specialty in unchanged volume. All the necessary adjustments of supply will be made in countries with producers on

[12] Suppose, for instance, that Cuba is exclusively engaged in producing a single commodity, sugar, and that, under free trading conditions and constant opportunity cost, the United States would also produce sugar, along with corn, cotton, steel, and numerous other commodities. If the relative desirability of sugar increases, Cuba cannot increase the supply of that commodity but the United States, at the expense of other commodities, can and will. If, on the other hand, the relative desirability of sugar should diminish, Cuba would also continue as before. The United States has alternatives at constant cost and the adjustments will, therefore, all be made, in that country, without any alteration in the normal ratio of exchange.

the margin of indifference and, therefore, with alternative outlets for their productive resources.

The Case of Intermediate-Size Countries

The changes in demand so far considered are such as primarily affect the two largest countries J and I. Country G is automatically involved, but G is producing commodities which, in every case, are not only produced in one of the two largest countries but have been on opposite sides of equal shifts in demand, so that G's net income position could not be affected. There remains to be considered, at this stage, only country H, which is heavily involved in w and u. These commodities are not produced in J or I and the demand for each, or of the two together, has so far been kept unchanged in terms of the proportion of income expended on them. Since H also produces r, which is common with y, t, and s in I's output, and, since s is common with z in G while z is common with x, v, and q in J, there is plenty of room for adjustment, without a shift in the ratio, even should the demand for w and u be greatly altered.

Let us assume, instead of any of the suppositions so far made, that 1/15 of total income is spent on each of w and u, that 1/10 of total income goes to each of z, x, v, and q, and that the remainder of income is equally shared among y, t, s, and r (7/60 of total income to each).

The results are shown in Table A_6. No alteration in the ratio of exchange occurs. Country H all but abandons the production of w and shifts heavily to r. As compared with the situation in which 1/10 of total income was devoted to each of the products, country I, in response, reduces its output of r to a low level and expands in y and t. The production in other countries remains unchanged.

Reversing the trend of demand for w and u, we find that, without any change in the ratio, at least 3/25 of total income can be spent on each of those products provided the demand for z, x, v, and u is unchanged at 1/10 of total income to each while that for each of y, t, s, and r is cut to 9/100 of total income to permit the heavier expenditures in w and u. The results of this constellation of demand are shown in Table A_7.

The range of demand for w and u, without any disturbance of the existing ratio of exchange, is thus, other things being as posited, from something less than 5/75 (1/15) to something more than 9/75 (3/25) of total income for each of those products. If, however, de-

TABLE A_6

(Compare with A_{1c} and A_{1p})

Ratio of exchange: $z = 24y = 20x = 24w = 64v = 40u = 12t = 60s = 48r = 72q$

CONSUMPTION

(Thousands, or any other multiple, of the figures below)

1/15 of total income to each of w, u;
1/10 of total income to each of z, x, v, q;
7/60 of total income to each of y, t, s, r.

	z	y	x	w	v	u	t	s	r	q
Totals	$150\frac{1}{6}$	$4204\frac{2}{3}$	$3003\frac{1}{3}$	$2402\frac{2}{3}$	$9610\frac{2}{3}$	$4004\frac{4}{9}$	$2102\frac{1}{3}$	$10511\frac{2}{3}$	$8409\frac{1}{3}$	10812

PRODUCTION

(Thousands, or any other multiple, of the figures below)

	z	y	x	w	v	u	t	s	r	q
A	—	—	—	—	800	—	—	—	—	—
B	—	—	—	—	—	—	—	—	—	1920
C	—	—	—	—	—	1500	—	—	—	—
D	—	—	—	—	3840	—	—	—	—	—
E	—	—	—	2400	—	—	—	—	—	—
F	—	2880	—	—	—	—	—	—	—	—
G	$101\frac{1}{2}$	—	—	—	—	—	—	1110	—	—
H	—	$1824\frac{2}{3}$	—	$2\frac{2}{3}$	—	$2504\frac{4}{9}$	—	—	$7789\frac{1}{3}$	—
I	—	—	—	—	—	—	$2102\frac{1}{3}$	$9401\frac{2}{3}$	620	—
J	$48\frac{2}{3}$	—	$3003\frac{1}{3}$	—	$4970\frac{2}{3}$	—	—	—	—	8892
Totals	$150\frac{1}{6}$	$4204\frac{2}{3}$	$3003\frac{1}{3}$	$2402\frac{2}{3}$	$9610\frac{2}{3}$	$4004\frac{4}{9}$	$2102\frac{1}{3}$	$10511\frac{2}{3}$	$8409\frac{1}{3}$	10812

J produces z, x, v, q
I produces y, t, s, r
H produces w, u, r
G produces z, s
F produces y
E produces w
D produces v
C produces u
B produces q
A produces v

(Compare with A_{1c} and A_{1p})

Ratio of exchange: $z = 24y = 20x = 24w = 64v = 40u = 12t = 60s = 48r = 72q$

CONSUMPTION

(Thousands, or any other multiple, of the figures below)

3/25 of total income to each of w, u;
1/10 of total income to each of z, x, v, q;
9/100 of total income to each of y, t, s, r.

	z	y	x	w	v	u	t	s	r	q
Totals	$150\frac{1}{6}$	$3243\frac{3}{5}$	$3003\frac{1}{3}$	$4324\frac{4}{5}$	$9610\frac{2}{3}$	7208	$1621\frac{4}{5}$	8109	$6487\frac{1}{5}$	10812

PRODUCTION

(Thousands, or any other multiple, of the figures below)

	z	y	x	w	v	u	t	s	r	q
A	—	—	—	—	800	—	—	—	—	—
B	—	—	—	—	—	—	—	—	—	1920
C	—	—	—	—	—	1500	—	—	—	—
D	—	—	—	—	3840	—	—	—	—	—
E	—	—	—	2400	—	—	—	—	—	—
F	—	2880	—	—	—	—	—	—	—	—
G	$101\frac{1}{2}$	—	—	—	—	—	—	1110	—	—
H	—	—	—	$1924\frac{4}{5}$	—	5708	—	—	$100\frac{4}{5}$	—
I	—	$363\frac{3}{5}$	—	—	—	—	$1621\frac{4}{5}$	6999	$6386\frac{2}{5}$	—
J	$48\frac{2}{3}$	—	$3003\frac{1}{3}$	—	$4970\frac{2}{3}$	—	—	—	—	8892
Totals	$150\frac{1}{6}$	$3243\frac{3}{5}$	$3003\frac{1}{3}$	$4324\frac{4}{5}$	$9610\frac{2}{3}$	7208	$1621\frac{4}{5}$	8109	$6487\frac{1}{5}$	10812

J produces z, x, v, q
I produces y, t, s, r
H produces w, u, r
G produces z, s
F produces y

E produces w
D produces v
C produces u
B produces q
A produces v

mand for w and u should fall very slightly below 1/15 of total income in each country, E would, at the existing ratio, be more than able to supply the full demand for w. The value of w would, in a limbo ratio, then fall in terms of all the other commodities including u, and country H (which by then would be out of w and in u and r only) would benefit as fully as any other country. We thus have what, from the classical point of view, is the paradoxical result of a fall in the total demand for certain commodities which comprise more than two-thirds of the output of H (not compensated by any equivalent rise in the demand for the remainder of H's output) resulting in an improvement in the income of that country.

If, on the other hand, the demand for w and u should *rise*, beyond 3/25 of total income for each of those commodities, country H would exhaust its possibilities of shifting from r to w and u and, in accordance with orthodox expectation, the value of w and u would rise in terms of all other commodities. For reasons that will later appear this rise in the value of w and u would, however, be checked at 5%, practically regardless of any further increase in the demand for w and u.

If, in considering variations in the demand for w and u, the demand for z, x, v, and q had not been assumed to remain constant but had shared with y, t, s, and r, or had itself fully absorbed, the impact of changes in the demand for w and u, the range of possible variation of demand for w and u, without any shift in the ratio, would have been somewhat reduced. It would, in fact, have been largely determined by the potentialities of G in altering the supply of z, rather than by those of H in altering the supply of w and u, and would thus have been an analogue of the range of variation shown in Tables A_3 and A_4.

Effect of Increasing Complexity of Trade

It would be otiose further to pursue the present type of alterations in the constellation of demand. No alteration, which does not affect the terms, can be of any consequence to the small countries. More can now be learned, therefore, in a study of such catastrophic shifts of demand as would assuredly bring about a change in the ratio. Before turning to these, however, we should note that the more complex the trade the greater will be the permutations in the number of producers on the margin of indifference between differing pairs, triads, or larger aggregations of products, and, once the general lines of trade have been established, the less likely, therefore, is any ordinary shift in demand to alter the normal ratio of exchange. Where, moreover, trade is freely carried on by individuals, and there is, in consequence, no such thing as reciprocal *national* demand, the several national units will not be continuously offering one another unique composites of products. The demand for almost every product transcends all national lines, and the supply of any product will normally cut across more than one of them. The only way, therefore, in which demand could affect the normal ratio of exchange would be through a change in the relationship between the *total* demand for the various products (the division into national sectors is of no relevance) and it could affect it *then* only if, for some reason, the relative supply could not be adjusted to the altered demand without a shift of the national focal point in opportunity cost relationships. When such a shift occurs it may benefit a country for some, and even all, of whose products demand has fallen. The classical allegation that every shift in reciprocal "national demand" will alter the ratio between internationally traded products, favorably when the demand for given "national" products increases relative to the "national" demand for foreign products and unfavorably in the opposite case, is, for normal values, an inference from a tissue of error.

CHAPTER VII

CHANGES IN THE RATIO OF EXCHANGE

W E have seen that, in general, only such great changes in demand as result in the complete elimination of the output of some commodity in some country, or such as cannot be met by any shifts short of the inception in some country of the production of a commodity which it had hitherto not produced at all, will be attended by an alteration in the ratio of exchange.[1] Any such alteration in the ratio may change the comparative advantage of *several* countries in the various commodities and, when this happens, some surprises are likely to occur. A more or less widespread rearrangement of the national composition of industry will be set in motion, and the pursuit of new lines of production which, to some countries, have now become more profitable than those they have hitherto followed, may draw resources so heavily from the output of some of the goods for which demand has declined as to *raise*, rather than lower, the *general* value of these latter goods. Some further illustrations of this phenomenon will be later presented. It is enough, at this point, to say that the form of the new ratio will be quite unpredictable without reference to the interlocking character of cost schedules in the various countries in their relation to this evolving ratio of exchange and, even then, would be veiled to the pre-view of any but an omniscient observer.[2]

Random Great Transformations of Demand

Without more ado we shall suppose a constellation of demand so different from that of 1/10 of income to each product as to be all but certain to shift the national locus of marginal production of some commodities and, therefore, to produce changes in the ratio with which we have hitherto been concerned (the initial ratio). To present,

---

[1] The *chief* possibility of a change in the ratio, apart from this, arises when a country is engaged in the production of a single commodity not produced elsewhere. In the rare case which meets these conditions, a limbo ratio, for this commodity against all the others, will prevail. Such a ratio will be susceptible to every zephyr of demand.

[2] Though I have given myself much practice in the matter and can make some more or less accurate guesses as to the *direction* of changes, when the data are so simple (relative to those of the real world) as in the present models, the degree of experimentation necessary to a *solution* of even so relatively simple a problem is frequently great.

at this point, the effects of *random* great shifts in demand (in the sense that they are not so selected as to correspond, positively or negatively, with the output of any particular country) let us vary the original assumptions so that 1/20 of total income is presumed to be spent for every alternate commodity beginning with z while 3/20 of total income is spent for every alternate commodity beginning with y. Commodities z, x, v, t, and r will then be in greatly diminished, and commodities y, w, u, s, and q in greatly increased, demand. It so happens that this will affect very adversely the demand for three, and very favorably that for one, of the four commodities that J had hitherto been producing, that it will greatly increase the demand for two, and lower that for the other two, of the four commodities that I had been producing, that it will favorably influence the demand for two, and adversely influence that for one, of the three commodities hitherto produced by H, and that it will divide effects between the two commodities in which G has so far been specializing. The smaller countries will be exclusively on one or the other side of the changed demand. Experimentation will show that the unique solution of this combination of demand with cost schedules (See Tableau of Costs, p. 91) is the exchange ratio $z = 24y = 20x = 22\frac{4}{5}w = 64v = 38u = 12t = 60s = 48r = 72q$, with consumption and production as shown in Tables B_c and B_p (pp. 116 and 117). The only change in the ratio resulting from this huge shift of demand, as against the situation in which 1/10 of income is devoted to each of the products, is that the value of w and u rises by 5% in terms of all other commodities.[3] H, E, and C are the only countries that benefit. All the others lose, *including those that produce nothing but commodities of increased demand.*

The commodities y, s, and q, the demand for which has increased equally with that for w and u, do not rise in value against the commodities of reduced demand z, x, v, t, and r, or at all. Even as with the commodities of reduced demand, the value of y, s, and q falls relatively to that of w and u.

It might be imagined that country I, with two commodities in each of the categories of proportionately altered demand, would not suffer at all from the shift, or that, at any rate, it would suffer less than J which is, apparently, in a much worse position. Neither notion

[3] The initial ratio was: $z = 24y = 20x = 24w = 64v = 40u = 12t = 60s = 48r = 72q$. The present ratio is: $z = 24y = 20x = 22\ 4/5w = 64v = 38u = 12t = 60s = 48r = 72q$.

TABLE B$_c$

Ratio of exchange: $z = 24y = 20x = 22\frac{4}{5}w = 64v = 38u = 12t = 60s = 48r = 72q$

CONSUMPTION

(Thousands, or any other multiple, of the figures below)

1/20 of the income of each country to each of z, x, v, t, r;

3/20 of the income of each country to each of y, w, u, s, q.

	z	y	x	w	v	u	t	s	r	q
A	$\frac{5}{8}$	45	$12\frac{1}{2}$	$42\frac{3}{4}$	40	$71\frac{1}{4}$	$7\frac{1}{2}$	$112\frac{1}{2}$	30	135
B	$1\frac{1}{3}$	96	$26\frac{2}{3}$	$91\frac{1}{5}$	$85\frac{1}{5}$	152	16	240	64	288
C	$1\frac{37}{38}$	$142\frac{2}{19}$	$39\frac{9}{19}$	135	$126\frac{6}{19}$	225	$22\frac{13}{19}$	$381\frac{11}{19}$	$94\frac{14}{19}$	$426\frac{6}{19}$
D	3	216	60	$205\frac{1}{5}$	192	342	36	540	144	648
E	$5\frac{5}{19}$	$378\frac{18}{19}$	$105\frac{5}{19}$	360	$336\frac{16}{19}$	600	$63\frac{3}{19}$	$942\frac{2}{19}$	$252\frac{12}{19}$	$1136\frac{16}{19}$
F	6	432	120	$410\frac{2}{5}$	384	684	72	1080	288	1296
G	6	432	120	$410\frac{2}{5}$	384	684	72	1080	288	1296
H	$11\frac{16}{19}$	$852\frac{12}{19}$	$236\frac{16}{19}$	810	$757\frac{17}{19}$	1350	$142\frac{2}{19}$	$2131\frac{11}{19}$	$568\frac{8}{19}$	$2557\frac{17}{19}$
I	20	1440	400	1368	1280	2280	240	3600	960	4320
J	20	1440	400	1368	1280	2280	240	3600	960	4320
Totals	$75\frac{313}{456}$	$5474\frac{13}{19}$	$1520\frac{85}{114}$	$5200\frac{19}{20}$	$4866\frac{22}{57}$	$8668\frac{1}{4}$	$912\frac{17}{38}$	$13707\frac{29}{38}$	$3649\frac{15}{19}$	$16424\frac{1}{19}$

TABLE B$_D$

Ratio of exchange: $z = 24y = 20x = 22\frac{4}{5}w = 64v = 38u = 12t = 60s = 48r = 72q$

PRODUCTION

(Thousands, or any other multiple, of the figures below)

	z	y	x	w	v	u	t	s	r	q
A	—	—	—	—	800	—	—	—	—	—
B	—	—	—	—	—	—	—	—	—	1920
C	—	—	—	—	—	1500	—	—	—	—
D	—	—	—	—	3840	—	—	—	—	—
E	—	—	—	2400	—	—	—	—	—	—
F	—	2880	—	—	—	—	—	—	—	—
G	$31\frac{20}{57}$	—	—	—	—	—	—	$5318\frac{18}{19}$	—	—
H	—	—	—	$2800\frac{19}{20}$	—	—	—	—	—	—
I	—	$2594\frac{13}{19}$	—	—	—	$4331\frac{3}{4}$	$912\frac{17}{38}$	—	$3649\frac{15}{19}$	—
J	$44\frac{153}{456}$	—	$1520\frac{85}{114}$	—	$226\frac{22}{57}$	$2836\frac{1}{2}$	—	$8388\frac{31}{38}$	—	—
Totals	$75\frac{813}{456}$	$5474\frac{13}{19}$	$1520\frac{85}{114}$	$5200\frac{19}{20}$	$4866\frac{22}{57}$	$8668\frac{1}{4}$	$912\frac{17}{38}$	$13707\frac{29}{38}$	$3649\frac{15}{19}$	$16424\frac{1}{19}$

J produces z, x, v, u, q
I produces y, t, s, r
H produces w, u
G produces z, s
F produces y

E produces w
D produces v
C produces u
B produces q
A produces v

is true. Country I suffers equally with J in the increased cost of w and u, and the relative income positions of the two countries are quite unchanged. The incomes in both countries are equal, just as they were when demand was such that 1/10 of total income was devoted to each commodity, though both countries are now on a lower general income level.

It must be even more suprising to adherents of the classical doctrines to note that countries F and B, which produce nothing but commodities of increased demand, suffer, equally with J and I, in an adverse movement of the "terms of trade."

What happens is this:

Neither of the largest countries J and I produces w or u. When the demand (and price) for those products rises, while that for r falls off, country H abandons the production of r and concentrates on w and u. This leaves to I the field in r so that I is not forced greatly to restrict its output of r in spite of the heavy cut in the demand for that commodity. Country I's output of s, on the other hand, cannot be much expanded in response to the rise in the demand for that product, since G, impelled to reduce its output of z, puts the bulk of its resources into s, its alternative product. Country I's potential of expansion in s is, in fact, not sufficient to compensate for even the relatively minor reduction in its output of r. The large cut in t, of which I, the sole producer of that commodity, must bear the full impact, accentuates I's difficulties, but a compensation for most of I's troubles is found in y. Since F had already been fully engaged in y the whole of the expansion in the demand for that product must be supplied by I (which almost quadruples its output of y).

Country H's increase in the output of w and u, made possible by its abandonment of r, is inadequate to meet the enlarged demand for w and u, and no more of those commodities can come from E and C since those countries had already been fully specialized, the one in w and the other in u. The value of w and u therefore rises but the rise is abruptly checked at 5% by the inauguration of production of u in J where the cost ratios, coupled with the rise in the value of u, now make the production of u, at the ratio of $38u$ to z etc., equally advantageous with that of z, x, v, and q. The new product, u, is highly welcome to J by reason of the facts that the production of v in J is reduced almost to zero because the two specialists in that product, A and D, can supply almost the whole of the reduced demand for it and that the full cut in the demand for x falls entirely on J which is the sole producer of that commodity.[4]

The production in A, B, C, D, E, and F remains as before.

Effects of Reversed Transformation of Demand

Let us, now, reverse the shift in demand, and assume that 3/20 of total income goes to each of z, x, v, t, r, with only 1/20 of total income going to each of y, w, u, s, q. The change in the ratio of exchange, as compared with that when 1/10 of total income is spent on each of the commodities, will then assume somewhat larger proportions. The new ratio will be $z = 36y = 20x = 32w = 64v = 45u = 13\frac{1}{2}t = 67\frac{1}{2}s = 54r = 72q$. There is here, too, a considerable alteration in the composition of industry. Country J continues to produce z, x, v, and q, but I drops y, H drops w and enters upon the output of z, G drops s, F adds z, and E, for the first time producing two commodities, adds r. The tables, C_c and C_p, of consumption and production are shown on pp. 120 and 121.

It is perhaps worth while to point out that, though the demand for t and r is greatly increased, their value in all commodities except y is either unchanged or reduced, and that, though the demand for q is greatly reduced, its value does not fall in anything, but, on the contrary, rises in y, w, u, t, s, and r. The country that suffers most is F. The fall in the demand for y reduces the total taking of that commodity so greatly that, though its production is abandoned by I, there is an inadequate outlet in y for F's productive resources even when the price of y, against z, x, v, and q, drops to two-thirds of its former level ($36y$, instead of $24y$, $= z = 20x = 64v = 72q$). But, at $36y = z$ etc., it becomes as advantageous in F to produce z as to produce y, and producers of y in F then shift resources to z in the degree necessary to cut the supply of y to the amount that can be sold at the price $36y = z$ etc.

Similarly, the new demand for w is inadequate, at the old price, to absorb E's output of that commodity, to say nothing of what H had hitherto produced. But when w drops in value from $24w$ to $32w = z$ etc. it becomes as profitable in E to produce r as to produce w (even when r, though in lesser degree, has also fallen in general value).

When the value of y falls heavily the producers of that commodity

---

[4] Without a very drastic fall in the price of v neither A nor D would resort to other commodities and the adjustment in v must, therefore, be solely made by J.

TABLE C_e

Ratio of exchange: $z = 36y = 20x = 32w = 64v = 45u = 18\frac{1}{2}t = 67\frac{1}{2}s = 54r = 72q$

CONSUMPTION

(Thousands, or any other multiple, of the figures below)

3/20 of the income of each country to each of z, x, v, t, r;
1/20 of the income of each country to each of y, w, u, s, q.

	z	y	x	w	v	u	t	s	r	q
A	$1\frac{7}{8}$	$22\frac{1}{2}$	$37\frac{1}{2}$	20	120	$28\frac{1}{8}$	$25\frac{5}{16}$	$42\frac{3}{16}$	$101\frac{1}{4}$	45
B	4	48	80	$42\frac{2}{3}$	256	60	54	90	216	96
C	5	60	100	$53\frac{1}{3}$	320	75	$67\frac{1}{2}$	$112\frac{1}{2}$	270	120
D	9	108	180	96	576	135	$121\frac{1}{2}$	$202\frac{1}{2}$	486	216
E	$11\frac{1}{4}$	135	225	120	720	$168\frac{3}{4}$	$151\frac{7}{8}$	$253\frac{1}{8}$	$607\frac{1}{2}$	270
F	12	144	240	128	768	180	162	270	648	288
G	18	216	360	192	1152	270	243	405	972	432
H	30	360	600	320	1920	450	405	675	1620	720
I	$53\frac{1}{3}$	640	$1066\frac{2}{3}$	$568\frac{8}{9}$	$3413\frac{1}{3}$	800	720	1200	2880	1280
J	60	720	1200	640	3840	900	810	1350	3240	1440
Totals	$204\frac{11}{24}$	$2453\frac{1}{2}$	$4089\frac{1}{6}$	$2180\frac{8}{9}$	$13085\frac{1}{3}$	$3066\frac{7}{8}$	$2760\frac{3}{16}$	$4600\frac{5}{16}$	$11040\frac{3}{4}$	4907

TABLE C_p

Ratio of exchange: $z = 36y = 20x = 32w = 64v = 45u = 18\frac{1}{2}t = 67\frac{1}{2}s = 54r = 72q$

PRODUCTION

(Thousands, or any other multiple, of the figures below)

	z	y	x	w	v	u	t	s	r	q
A	—	—	—	—	800	—	—	—	—	—
B	—	—	—	—	—	—	—	—	—	1920
C	—	—	—	—	—	1500	—	—	—	—
D	—	—	—	—	3840	—	—	—	—	—
E	—	—	—	$2180\frac{8}{9}$	—	—	—	—	$369\frac{3}{4}$	—
F	$11\frac{61}{72}$	$2453\frac{1}{2}$	—	—	—	—	—	—	—	—
G	120	—	—	—	—	—	—	—	—	—
H	$50\frac{111}{216}$	—	—	—	—	$1566\frac{7}{8}$	—	—	6192	—
I	—	—	—	—	—	—	$2760\frac{3}{16}$	$4600\frac{5}{16}$	4479	—
J	$22\frac{7}{72}$	—	$4089\frac{1}{6}$	—	$8445\frac{1}{3}$	—	—	—	—	2987
Totals	$204\frac{11}{24}$	$2453\frac{1}{2}$	$4089\frac{1}{6}$	$2180\frac{8}{9}$	$13085\frac{1}{3}$	$3066\frac{7}{8}$	$2760\frac{3}{16}$	$4600\frac{5}{16}$	$11040\frac{3}{4}$	4907

J produces z, x, v, q
I produces t, s, r
H produces z, u, r
G produces z
F produces z, y

E produces w, r
D produces v
C produces u
B produces q
A produces v

in I quit in favor of t or r (as do also some of the producers of s).
But there is then not enough room for the full productive powers of
I and the prices of t, s, and r therefore decline (though not so far
as the price of y). Any fall in the price of s immediately produces
repercussions in G which shifts, *in toto*, to z, leaving more room for
I in s, and, when r falls sufficiently (along with u) to make it worth
while in H to enter upon the production of z, in lieu of some r, the
pressure on I is entirely removed. The net result is that the group of
products now produced in I falls in price, against the group produced in J, by $11\frac{1}{9}\%$. The product y, however, which I drops from
its list, falls in price, against the group of commodities produced in
J, by $33\frac{1}{3}\%$, while, against those still produced in I, it falls by 20%.
Country I therefore gains, *on the import of y*, as compared with the
cost of its production to I when it was on I's list of output.

A caveat may well be repeated here against the notion that, even
when the demand for most of the goods that a country happens to be
producing drops so far that they fall sharply in value against some
of its imports, the country *must*, in its re-formed international trade,
suffer proportionately or at all. Country H, for instance, which, on
the basis of 1/10 of income to each of the products, was producing
w, u, and r (the demand for two of which declines), no longer maintains that composition of industry but shifts from w to z. Though
w falls in value by 25%, against z, x, v, and q, H's import income is
not thereby reduced in that proportion but falls, in J's products, by
merely $11\frac{1}{9}\%$, does not fall at all in terms of imports from I, and
rises in terms of w. Similarly I's import income, measured in the
products that I continues to make, is not reduced in the degree of
the net fall in the prices of its *original* products.

The net result, for any country, of the change in demand and the
consequent alteration in the ratio of exchange, is not easy to express
in any general terms since it will often be a combination of increased
cost (in terms of its exports) for some of its imports and of reduced
cost of others, with variations in the relative amounts imported. The
matter will be discussed, at a later stage, under the topic "terms of
trade." The point of interest, here, is that the international ratio
of exchange, and especially an alteration in it, does not at all lend
itself to treatment in terms of *national* components such as Marshall's "representative bales."

Great Transformations of Demand Concentrated
on Single Countries

Changing our assumptions once more, let us suppose that a cata-strophic shift in demand is exclusively concentrated on the output of given countries. Thus, instead of 1/10 of income being spent on each of the ten commodities, we shall posit that demand so alters that, regardless of price, only 1/20 of the income of the several countries is spent on each of z, x, v, q (the original products of country J) and that 3/20 of income is spent on y, t, s, r (the original products of country I). This leaves, as in the original model, 1/10 of total income to be spent for each of w and u (the products of country H).

The exchange ratio which will issue from this constellation of de-mand and the existing cost structure is:

$$z = 21y = 20x = 21w = 64v = 38u = 10\tfrac{1}{2}t = 52\tfrac{1}{2}s = 42r = 72q$$

as against the initial ratio:

$$z = 24y = 20x = 24w = 64v = 40u = 12t = 60s = 48r = 72q$$

when 1/10 of total income was devoted to each of the products. Con-sumption and production figures are shown in Tables D_c and D_p on pp. 124 and 125.

To an adherent of the classical or neo-classical theory of inter-national values the comparatively minor magnitude of the shift in the ratio of exchange must, to say the least, be surprising. A huge shift in demand concentrated, on the negative side, on all of the prod-ucts of a given country J, and, on the positive side, on all of the products of another country, I, results in a fall in the value of the products of J, in terms of those of I, of only $12\tfrac{1}{2}\%$. The posited demand schedule for the original products of J is certainly not elastic. On the basis of frequent assertions of classical and neo-classical writers, one might therefore have anticipated a truly devas-tating effect on J's "terms of trade." The adverse effect is, in fact, of very modest dimensions.

The gains of I in the "terms of trade" are exactly paralleled by H, G, F, and E,[5] while J's set-back is paralleled in D, B, and A.

---

[5] The gains (or losses) from *international* trade can, however, not be assumed (as is common among classical and neo-classical theorists) to alter in the same degree for all countries affected by a given shift, in the same direction, in the terms of trade. The reason is that the volume of foreign trade per unit of output may be very different for different countries even though their comparative advantage, at any given ratio of exchange, lies in the same products or in products

TABLE D_c

Ratio of exchange: $z = 21y = 20x = 21w = 64v = 38u = 10\frac{1}{2}t = 52\frac{1}{2}s = 42r = 72q$

Consumption

(Thousands, or any other multiple, of the figures below)
1/20 of total income to each of z, x, v, q;
1/10 of total income to each of w, u;
3/20 of total income to each of y, t, s, r.

	z	y	x	w	v	u	t	s	r	q
A	$\frac{5}{8}$	$39\frac{3}{8}$	$12\frac{1}{2}$	$26\frac{1}{4}$	40	$47\frac{1}{2}$	$19\frac{11}{16}$	$98\frac{7}{16}$	$78\frac{3}{4}$	45
B	$1\frac{1}{3}$	84	$26\frac{2}{3}$	56	$85\frac{1}{8}$	$101\frac{1}{8}$	42	210	168	96
C	$1\frac{37}{38}$	$124\frac{13}{38}$	$89\frac{9}{19}$	$82\frac{17}{19}$	$126\frac{6}{19}$	150	$62\frac{13}{76}$	$310\frac{65}{76}$	$248\frac{13}{19}$	$142\frac{2}{19}$
D	3	189	60	126	192	228	$94\frac{1}{2}$	$472\frac{1}{2}$	378	216
E	$5\frac{5}{7}$	360	$114\frac{2}{7}$	240	$365\frac{5}{7}$	$434\frac{2}{7}$	180	900	720	$411\frac{3}{7}$
F	$6\frac{6}{7}$	432	$187\frac{1}{7}$	288	$438\frac{6}{7}$	$521\frac{1}{7}$	216	1080	864	$493\frac{5}{7}$
G	$6\frac{6}{7}$	432	$187\frac{1}{7}$	288	$438\frac{6}{7}$	$521\frac{1}{7}$	216	1080	864	$493\frac{5}{7}$
H	$12\frac{6}{7}$	810	$257\frac{1}{7}$	540	$822\frac{6}{7}$	$977\frac{1}{7}$	405	2025	1620	$925\frac{5}{7}$
I	$22\frac{6}{7}$	1440	$457\frac{1}{7}$	960	$1462\frac{6}{7}$	$1787\frac{1}{7}$	720	3600	2880	$1645\frac{5}{7}$
J	20	1260	400	840	1280	1520	630	3150	2520	1440
Totals	$82\frac{239}{3192}$	$5170\frac{109}{152}$	$1641\frac{397}{798}$	$3447\frac{11}{76}$	$5252\frac{316}{399}$	$6237\frac{29}{42}$	$2585\frac{109}{304}$	$12926\frac{241}{304}$	$10841\frac{88}{76}$	$5909\frac{52}{133}$

TABLE D$_p$

Ratio of exchange: $z = 21y = 20x = 21w = 64v = 38u = 10\frac{1}{2}t = 52\frac{1}{2}s = 42r = 72q$

PRODUCTION

(Thousands, or any other multiple, of the figures below)

	z	y	x	w	v	u	t	s	r	q
A	—	—	—	—	800	—	—	—	—	—
B	—	—	—	—	—	—	—	—	—	1920
C	—	—	—	—	—	1500	—	—	—	—
D	—	—	—	—	3840	—	—	—	—	—
E	—	—	—	2400	—	—	—	—	—	—
F	—	2880	—	—	—	—	—	—	—	—
G	—	—	—	—	—	—	—	7200	—	—
H	—	—	—	$1047\frac{11}{76}$	—	—	—	—	$8705\frac{27}{88}$	—
I	—	$1320\frac{107}{152}$	—	—	—	—	$2585\frac{109}{304}$	$5726\frac{241}{304}$	$1635\frac{55}{76}$	—
J	$82\frac{239}{8192}$	$970\frac{1}{76}$	$1641\frac{897}{798}$	—	$5252\frac{816}{399}$	$4787\frac{29}{42}$	—	—	—	$3989\frac{52}{133}$
Totals	$82\frac{239}{8192}$	$5170\frac{109}{152}$	$1641\frac{897}{798}$	$8447\frac{11}{76}$	$5252\frac{816}{399}$	$6287\frac{29}{42}$	$2585\frac{109}{304}$	$12926\frac{241}{304}$	$10341\frac{33}{76}$	$5909\frac{52}{133}$

J produces z, y, x, v, u, q
I produces y, t, s, r
H produces w, r
G produces s
F produces y
E produces w
D produces v
C produces u
B produces q
A produces v

Country C gains on its imports of z, x, v, and q, but not to the same extent as do countries I, H, G, F, and E. This is because C produces u exclusively. This commodity rises in value against all of J's former products but not as much as do the former, and present, products of I, or the present products of H. Country C therefore loses, as compared with the situation under the initial ratio, on its imports of y, w, t, s, and r.

The drastic drop in the demand for J's products leaves that country without an adequate market, on the old terms, for its full productive powers. The prices of the products in which J has hitherto specialized therefore fall in terms of the other six commodities on our list. When they fall by 5%, however, it becomes just as profitable in J to produce u as to produce z, x, v, or q, and u is therefore added to J's output. Countries H and C are, however, already in u and, since the share of total income devoted to u has not changed, J gets little relief from its ability now to produce u. The prices of J's products, expressed in other goods, therefore continue to decline or, to put it conversely, the price of other products, in terms of J's output, continue to rise. Since u has become part of J's output its price is now, however, tied to that of z, x, v, and q, at the cost ratios in J. The commodity u, in consequence, drops out of the list of products of advancing price and this makes w and r, the alternatives to u in H (country C has no available alternative to u), more attractive than u to H's enterprisers. The production of u in H is, therefore, abandoned. Country J's position is thereby much alleviated but, even with a sizable production of u, J's full productive powers cannot be engaged. Country J's products z, x, v, q, and now also u, therefore

---

sharing equally in the gains (or losses) from any shift in the ratio of exchange. In the present instance, for example, country G exports 6/7 of its output of s but country I, producing s and other commodities sharing equally with s in the gains from the shift in the ratio of exchange, does not export anything like that proportion of its production. Country I, moreover, *imports* y and r in spite of the fact that it has the same comparative advantage in their production as it has in t and s (which it *exports*, though in lesser proportionate degree, taking the two products together, than G exports s). How much, if any, of its output of goods of comparative advantage any country will export depends on the play of adjustment, at home and in other countries, to every alteration in demand or the ratio of exchange and also on the composition of output, previously built up at home and in these other countries, in response to varying opportunity. What one country, as compared with another exporting and importing similar commodities, fails to gain (or lose) in *international* trade, as a result of a shift in the ratio of exchange, will however (unless the *qualitative* content of its output is altered) be exactly compensated, *within* its borders, in the shift from one to another commodity of equal comparative advantage.

fall farther in terms of the other commodities or, what is the same thing, y, w, t, s, and r rise farther in terms of J's products. Under the cost conditions in J, this presently brings y within the range of profitable production in that country and, with this additional product, J's full productive powers can be engaged in the output of z, y, x, v, u, and q. Since these must exchange at J's cost ratios, J can now gain, by international trade, on only four products, out of the total of ten, whereas any country that can specialize on a single commodity will gain on nine.

Country I has of course found it profitable to stick to its original products, y, t, s, and r, for which the total demand has greatly increased and the price risen, though it is obliged to face thoroughgoing changes in the proportions of its productive resources devoted to the several commodities. In spite of J's entry into the production of y, the output of that commodity in I can be expanded to take care of part of the greatly enlarged demand. The same is true of t in which the producers in I have no competitors in other countries. The expansion in y and t will, of course, necessitate a contraction in I's output of s or r, or both. This contraction is facilitated, and compensated, by G's exclusive concentration on s when G's original alternative, z, falls in price, and also by H's large shift to r consequent upon H's complete abandonment of one of its original alternatives, u. This dropping of u by H comes about, it will be recalled, as the rise in the price of u is stopped, short of that of w and r, after the production of u is taken up by J. The shift to r in H is also furthered by the (slight) reduction in the output of H's other alternative, w.[6]

The composition of output in A, B, C, D, E, and F is unchanged in any respect but the incomes of A, B, and D are reduced, through the shift in the ratio of exchange, in the same degree as that of J. The incomes of E and F, on the other hand, are enhanced in the same degree as those of I, H, and G. Country C, as already noted, is in an intermediate position, gaining on imports of z, x, v, and q but losing (in greater degree) on imports of y, w, t, s, and r.

---

[6] Though the proportion of total income spent on w remains unchanged, at 1/10, the total amount of w demanded at the new ratio of exchange falls slightly owing to the fact that w does not decline in value in terms of any commodity but rises in terms of six of the ten.

Reversal of Concentrated Transformation of Demand

The converse case to that just presented will arise when 3/20 of total income is presumed to be spent for each of J's original products z, x, v, q, with 1/20 of total income spent for each of I's original products, y, t, s, r, and 1/10 of total income for each of w and u. The ratio of exchange which corresponds to this constellation of demand and the existing cost structure is:

$$z = 36y = 19\tfrac{11}{16}x = 27w = 63v = 45u = 16t = 80s = 64r = 70\tfrac{7}{8}q$$

as against the initial ratio:

$$z = 24y = 20x = 24w = 64v = 40u = 12t = 60s = 48r = 72q$$

when 1/10 of total income is devoted to each of the ten commodities. Production and consumption figures are given in Tables E_c and E_p on pp. 130 and 131.

The shift in the ratio of exchange is somewhat greater in this than in the preceding case but, even so, is small as compared with the expectations aroused by classical and neo-classical theory, and it takes a very different form from that posited in those theories. The fall in the value of I's products, in terms of those of J, is slightly in excess of 25%.[7]

Country I takes over from J the bulk of the production of z which J finds it profitable to abandon in spite of a rise in the demand for that commodity. The country that suffers most, however, is again F. The decline in the total demand for y is such that the dropping of the production of y by I is inadequate to reduce supply to the shrunken demand for that product. Country F, the sole country now continuing to produce y (in which it has hitherto specialized to the exclusion of all other commodities), therefore finds its productive powers in that commodity in excess of the posited demand. No fall in the price of y is sufficient to absorb F's production so long as F specializes in y, and not until y falls in value, in terms of z etc., to

---

[7] All such expressions, in percentages, are somewhat misleading since it makes a difference *to the percentage* whether a fall in the value of one product relative to another is computed according to the number of units of the first commodity that must be given for the second, or the number of the second that must be given for the first. The degree of the *spread* between the percentage results of the one method and the other grows with the size of the change calculated by either method. This happens, of course, because of the shift of base on which the percentage change is calculated. The matter has often been mentioned in the literature on international trade and elsewhere, but, even with the possibility of misunderstanding, it is convenient to use percentages for purposes of exposition.

$36y = z$ does F find a supplementary outlet, in z, sufficient fully to absorb its otherwise unexhausted productive resources. The fall in the value of y operates not only to the advantage of the original importers of that commodity but also to the advantage of I which has hitherto produced y but now ceases to do so and becomes an importer thereof. Country I is therefore hurt considerably less than F by the change in the ratio of exchange not only because the prices of its retained exports do not decline so far as does the price of y but also because it receives an advantage on the import side, in y, which is denied to F.

Country F's market for its newly undertaken production of z is in part created by J's abandonment of that product (in the face of a rise in demand for it) and the concentration in J on x, v, and q. The abandonment of z by J comes about through a fall in the value of z *relative* to x, v, and q (but a rise relative to the other commodities), which, partly as cause and partly as effect, is attended by the inception of the production of z in countries I and H as well as in F. Country F's opportunity in z is therefore somewhat exiguous. Producers in F, nevertheless, can shift enough of their productive powers from y to z to reduce F's output of y to the amount which will be absorbed under the new conditions of demand and the new ratio of exchange.

A heavy fall in the value of z, which might perhaps be expected on the entry of the large countries I and H, as well as the somewhat smaller country F, into its production, is precluded by the fact that when z falls, in terms of v, from $64v$ merely to $63v$ per unit of z, country G, hitherto a heavy producer of z, finds it advantageous to shift a large part of its resources to v. Even though G, as a result of the fall in the value of s, ceases to produce s, its output of z is, through the transfer to v, very much decreased (in the face of a greatly enlarged total demand for z). This situation opens up the opportunity for the production of z in I and H as well as F. Country G's dropping of the production of s is a further aid to I which, in consequence, does not have to reduce its output of that product as much as the sharp drop in the demand for it might have led one to expect and, since H abandons the output of r (another of I's products), I is enabled to *expand* its output of that commodity in spite of the fact that the demand for it, in terms of the proportion of total income expended thereon, has, as compared with the initial situation,

TABLE E_c

Ratio of exchange: $z = 36y = 19\frac{11}{21}x = 27w = 63v = 45u = 16t = 80s = 64r = 70\frac{7}{}q$

CONSUMPTION

(Thousands, or any other multiple, of the figures below)

1/20 of total income to each of y, t, s, r;
1/10 of total income to each of w and u;
3/20 of total income to each of z, x, v, q.

	z	y	x	w	v	u	t	s	r	q
A	$1\frac{19}{21}$	$22\frac{6}{63}$	$37\frac{1}{2}$	$34\frac{2}{7}$	120	$57\frac{1}{7}$	$10\frac{10}{63}$	$50\frac{50}{63}$	$40\frac{40}{63}$	135
B	$4\frac{4}{63}$	$48\frac{16}{21}$	80	$73\frac{1}{7}$	256	$121\frac{19}{21}$	$21\frac{127}{189}$	$108\frac{68}{189}$	$86\frac{180}{189}$	288
C	5	60	$98\frac{7}{16}$	90	315	150	$26\frac{2}{3}$	$133\frac{1}{3}$	$106\frac{2}{3}$	$354\frac{3}{8}$
D	$9\frac{1}{7}$	$109\frac{5}{7}$	180	$164\frac{4}{7}$	576	$274\frac{2}{7}$	$48\frac{1}{21}$	$243\frac{17}{21}$	$195\frac{1}{21}$	648
E	$18\frac{1}{3}$	160	$262\frac{1}{2}$	240	840	400	$71\frac{1}{9}$	$355\frac{5}{9}$	$284\frac{4}{9}$	945
F	12	144	$236\frac{1}{4}$	216	756	360	64	320	256	$850\frac{1}{2}$
G	18	216	$354\frac{3}{8}$	324	1134	540	96	480	384	$1275\frac{3}{4}$
H	30	360	$590\frac{5}{8}$	540	1890	900	160	800	640	$2126\frac{1}{4}$
I	45	540	$885\frac{15}{16}$	810	2835	1350	240	1200	960	$3189\frac{3}{8}$
J	$60\frac{20}{21}$	$781\frac{9}{21}$	1200	$1097\frac{1}{7}$	3840	$1828\frac{4}{7}$	$325\frac{5}{63}$	$1625\frac{25}{63}$	$1300\frac{20}{63}$	4320
Totals	$199\frac{25}{63}$	$2392\frac{16}{21}$	$3925\frac{5}{8}$	$3589\frac{1}{7}$	12562	$5981\frac{19}{21}$	$1063\frac{85}{189}$	$5317\frac{47}{189}$	$4253\frac{151}{189}$	$14132\frac{1}{4}$

TABLE E_p

Ratio of exchange: $z = 36y = 19\frac{11}{19}x = 27w = 63v = 45u = 16t = 80s = 64r = 70\frac{1}{7}q$

PRODUCTION

(Thousands, or any other multiple, of the figures below)

	z	y	x	w	v	u	t	s	r	q
A	—	—	—	—	800	—	—	—	—	—
B	—	—	—	—	—	—	—	—	—	1920
C	—	—	—	—	—	1500	—	—	—	—
D	—	—	—	—	3840	—	—	—	—	—
E	—	—	—	2400	—	—	—	—	—	—
F	$13\frac{101}{189}$	$2392\frac{16}{21}$	—	—	—	—	—	—	—	—
G	$281\frac{70}{189}$	—	—	—	$5739\frac{1}{3}$	—	—	—	—	—
H	$56\frac{68}{189}$	—	—	$1189\frac{1}{7}$	—	$4481\frac{19}{21}$	—	—	—	—
I	$100\frac{38}{63}$	—	—	—	—	—	$1063\frac{85}{189}$	$5317\frac{47}{189}$	$4253\frac{151}{189}$	—
J	—	—	$3925\frac{5}{8}$	—	$2182\frac{2}{3}$	—	—	—	—	$12212\frac{1}{4}$
Totals	$1992\frac{25}{63}$	$2392\frac{16}{21}$	$3925\frac{5}{8}$	$3589\frac{1}{7}$	12562	$5981\frac{19}{21}$	$1063\frac{85}{189}$	$5317\frac{47}{189}$	$4253\frac{151}{189}$	$14182\frac{1}{4}$

J produces x, v, q
I produces z, t, s, r
H produces z, w, u
G produces z, v
F produces z, y

E produces w
D produces v
C produces u
B produces q
A produces v

been cut in half.[8] Country H, however, on ceasing to produce r, enters into competition with I in the production of z (which is, to both of them, a new commodity) so that I's relief from H's competition in r is largely nullified.

If it had so happened that H's new comparative advantage had lain in a commodity still produced by J, instead of in one now produced by I, the ratio of exchange (net) might have moved little, or not at all, against I in spite of the great decline in the demand for its original products.

Country G's shift from s to v does not do J any harm since, with the greatly expanded demand for x (of which J is the sole producing country) and for q (in which J has competition only from a small country, B, already fully specialized in q and therefore incapable of expanding its output), J must, in any case, contract its production of v as well as cease the output of z (which falls in price in terms of x, v, and q, the products that J continues to produce).

Great shifting of resources in the large countries J, I, H, G, and F, thus occurs. Not only are the proportions of the output of the several commodities in any one country greatly altered but J abandons the output of z, I that of y, H that of r, and G that of s while I, H, and F take on the production of z and G takes on that of v. The output of the small countries A, B, C, D, and E is not affected.

While, on a shift in demand and the ratio of exchange, some of the large countries may drop certain adversely affected commodities altogether, and take on the production of those favorably affected, it is also true that these or other countries often expand, or take up for the first time, the output of a commodity for which the total demand has *fallen*, or that they contract, or completely forgo, the output of a commodity for which the total demand has *risen*. This latter development is always, of course, a consequence of still greater shifts of output, in other countries, in the opposite direction.

The ramifications and repercussions of an alteration in the ratio of exchange are, it is clear, highly devious, and any one of the repercussions has counter effects on the ratio, so that, in the kaleidoscopic movement of production and prices, each operating on the other,

[8] The total production of r is, of course, cut to not quite one-half of the former level since the reduction in the price of r provides an outlet for more than half of the former volume of sales of that commodity, though only one-half as large a share of total income, relatively to the former situation, is spent upon it.

the eventual outcome of any shift in demand is far from obvious even in direction to say nothing of degree. The character of "reciprocal *national* demand schedules," on which classical and neo-classical theory places exclusive reliance as a determiner of the ratio of exchange (which, in the classical analysis, has no reflex bearing on the composition of industry in the several countries), is always a minor, and is typically a negligible, factor in the outcome—if, indeed, one can give any meaning at all to the concept.

The alteration in national incomes arising from the posited great change in demand concentrated, positively, on the products of country J, and, negatively, on those of I, is interesting. Country J gains substantially in the lower cost (in terms of its export commodities) of all of its former imports, and even gains (slightly) on the import of *z* which it no longer produces but which it had hitherto not only produced but exported. The *trend* is here in accord with the expectation of classical theory which, however, never contemplated the transfer of a commodity from the export to the import list of *any* country to say nothing of a transfer of output from one to the other of the two *largest* countries. It is, nevertheless, the relatively slight degree of the alteration in the ratio of exchange, compared with the anticipations of classical theory, which is again remarkable.

Country I, in the opposite position to J, loses substantially, as compared with the original ratio, in the added cost (in terms of its export commodities) of all of its former and present imports and also of *z* which it formerly imported but now produces and exports. But I, nevertheless, gains on the import of *y* as compared with the cost of *y* to it when it was producing that commodity.

Country H loses (less than I) on the cost, in terms of its exports, of its imports of *v*, *x*, and *q*, and it also loses (though to a still lesser extent) on *z* which it formerly imported but now produces for export. On the other hand, it *gains* very substantially on the cost, in terms of its exports, of its imports of *t*, and *s* and still more on its import of *y*. It also gains on the cost, in terms of its exports, of the commodity *r* which it now imports though it had formerly been an exporter of that product. On the whole H's income is increased, though this is not immediately apparent inasmuch as, like all the other countries, it has enlarged its consumption of those goods with a general tendency, in the situation, toward appreciation in relative value, and reduced its consumption of those with a general tendency toward depreciation in relative value.[9]

Though country G completely loses its market in *s*, and reduces its output of its only other former product, *z*, to not much more than one-fourth of its original level (compensating for both of these losses of output by an expansion in *v* which it had hitherto not paid producers in G to turn out), G's income is increased by only slightly less than that of J, whose gain is at a maximum. The cost to G, in terms of exports, of its imports *x* and *q* is increased, as compared with the original ratio, by less than 2%, and the cost, in terms of resources, of *v*, which it now produces rather than imports, is raised by the same slight amount. But far more than offsetting these losses are the gains on G's imports of *t*, *s*, *r*, and, especially, *y*, with lesser, but still substantial, gains on its imports of *w* and *u*.

The cost of every one of F's imports, on the other hand, rises markedly (though in different degrees) in terms of its original sole specialty *y*, and the cost to F of *z* also, which F now produces in an amount very slightly more than adequate for its own consumption, is greater (in expended resources) than it had been when that commodity was imported.

The gains of countries A, B, and D parallel those of J whereas countries C and E gain in substantially the same degree as H.

Tentative Conclusions

The (tentative) general conclusions from the models presented in this chapter are that even catastrophic changes in demand concentrated on specific countries occasion nothing but modest changes in the (normal) ratio of exchange and that the incidence of the changes that do occur in the ratio of exchange is likely to be very different from the naïve expectations of classical and neo-classical theory. A decline in the demand for goods exported from any given country may, in conjunction with its logically necessary correlative effects, actually increase the country's income and its gains from trade. When, in a later chapter, we come to examine attempts at a conscious manipulation of the "terms of trade" we shall find that a faithful reliance on classical and neo-classical theory would be likely

[9] It is, of course, the general enhancement of the desire for the one class of goods which causes a shift to new focal cost ratios, raises the prices of these goods, and yet enlarges their consumption. Conversely, with the other class of goods.

to result only in the failure of the manipulators to obtain the objectives which that theory promises.

Even with the extreme vicissitudes in demand above assumed, the general pattern of ratios of exchange, though affected, is still comparatively stable. Contrasted with the initial ratio, reproduced as (1), the various evolved ratios are as follows:

$$(1)\ z = 24y = 20x\quad = 24w\ = 64v = 40u = 12t\ = 60s\ = 48r = 72q$$
$$(2)\ z = 24y = 20x\quad = 22\tfrac{4}{5}w = 64v = 38u = 12t\ = 60s\ = 48r = 72q$$
$$(3)\ z = 36y = 20x\quad = 32w\ = 64v = 45u = 13\tfrac{1}{2}t = 67\tfrac{1}{2}s = 54r = 72q$$
$$(4)\ z = 21y = 20x\quad = 21w\ = 64v = 38u = 10\tfrac{1}{2}t = 52\tfrac{1}{2}s = 42r = 72q$$
$$(5)\ z = 36y = 19\tfrac{11}{16}x = 27w\ = 63v = 45u = 16t\ = 80s\ = 64r = 70\tfrac{7}{8}q$$

The changes that occur, moreover, are not at all correlated, *en bloc*, with national outputs, and not only in degree, but often in direction, shifts in national income fail to correspond with shifts in demand.

We may now affirm, more certainly than before, that, once a trade between many countries in many commodities has been established even if only under a fairly remote approximation to perfectly free conditions, the existing norm in the ratio of exchange is unlikely to be altered much, if at all, by any change in demand that would ordinarily occur. No such revolutions, in the relative desirability of commodities, as those assumed in this chapter are within the range of sober expectation. The degree of complexity, and consequent closeness of gradation in opportunity cost, is, moreover, so much greater in actual trade than in the models here presented that the magnitude of any alterations in the ratio of exchange attributable to even such great shifts in the demand as are sufficient to transfer the national locus of the margin of indifference (without which a change in the ratio, except it be in limbo, cannot occur), is much less, in fact, than the models imply.

Large countries with a necessarily diversified actual, and a still more diversified potential, output are, of course, much less affected by vicissitudes in the ratio of exchange, favorable or otherwise, than are those of small size. Aside from transitional adjustments, however, only a country so small, and also with such a unique scale of comparative costs, as to find it profitable to concentrate exclusively on a commodity not produced in any large country (or at least not produced in substantial volume in any such country) is likely to be greatly affected by a shift in the demand for internationally traded products. Country F, in the models here presented, is in such position and, as repeatedly demonstrated, is subject to much greater vicissitudes than other countries. Even if a sizable or large country is more or less exclusively specialized in a certain *line* of products as, e.g., foodstuffs, raw materials, or finished manufactures, there will be, in the world as it is, other large countries where output straddles all such lines. Any tendency for total demand to shift from one of these groups to another would, therefore, tend to be compensated by corresponding shifts in supply from these "straddling" countries and, on the assumption of constant (opportunity) costs within any such country, there would then be little, if any, change in the normal world ratio of exchange of products.[10]

It is, moreover, only shifts in the *world* demand for certain commodities relative to others that could have any effect on the ratio of exchange. Reciprocal *national* demands could have no significance apart from their reflection in this total demand (if they can be traced). It is, moreover, all but inconceivable that a shift in total demand would be exclusively concentrated in one direction on the exports of any given large country and, in the other, on its imports, and that, in addition, other countries would have a list of exports and imports which did not anywhere traverse those of the given country.[11] This being so, no change in the ratio of exchange which may occur is likely to cut exclusively, or even largely, along national lines. It will thus not operate exclusively, or even largely, to the good of some, and the harm of other, nations.

These (still tentative) conclusions will, with some slight modifications, be confirmed when, in the next chapter, the rigidity of our assumptions up to this point is relaxed in a greater approximation to reality.

The *immediate*, as opposed to the ultimate, effects even of much smaller shifts in demand than those assumed in the present chapter might of course be (temporarily) devastating. Deviations from the current norm will, moreover, tend to be greater, both in scope

[10] It would be only some exotic specialties that would be at all likely to be smitten (favorably or otherwise) since it would be these only that would be newly brought in, or would be forced out, of production in any country. Aside from these commodities, relative to all the rest, the ratio of exchange would remain as before.

[11] That is to say a list of exports and imports which did not, in the one case, include goods which were also exports, and, in the other, goods which were also imports, of the given country.

and duration, in the degree in which mobility of adjustment is naturally, or artificially, inhibited.

The (opportunity) cost structure is, of course, always in process of unpredictable change, and any given norms, whether for constant or variable costs, are norms only so long as the cost conditions remain as given. Costs, whether constant or variable, that are unstable over time will always be setting up new constellations of cost ratios, and the norm of each of these would have to be worked out on the basis of the then relevant data. No norm could of course be discovered, for any great length of time, in a situation where costs, over time, are changing in a wholly unpredictable way.

CHAPTER VIII

RELAXATION OF ASSUMPTIONS IN THE APPROACH
TO REALITY

The trend of the argument and of the demonstration, so far, is clearly toward the inference that the greater the number of countries and of commodities in any trading situation the less is the magnitude and the smoother is the course of any movement which, as the result of a given impetus in shift of demand, may occur in the ratio of exchange. It may, indeed, be true that, with multi-country multi-commodity trade, any given ratio of exchange will be somewhat less stable, in the sense that it will remain quite unchanged in the face of extensive, if not catastrophic, shifts in demand, than would be the case with fewer countries and commodities.[1] It will, however, be much more stable in the sense that such movements in the ratio as may occur will not be in the great leaps that might characterize the few-countries few-commodities situation but will, at any one time, be of modest dimensions. In multi-country trade involving hundreds, or even thousands, of commodities, no alteration in the ratio can be of more than strictly limited dimensions without changing, qualitatively, the composition of production in those countries in which cost ratios, as between the commodities of relatively rising and those of relatively falling value, are closest to the terms of the pre-existing ratio of exchange. Any shift in demand that eventually brings about an alteration in the ratio of exchange will already moreover, as a precedent to that alteration, have caused a quantitative shift in supply through the virtual elimination of the output of the relatively less desired commodities (with a correlative expansion of the output of the relatively more desired) in all countries in which the composition of output straddles goods of increasing and goods of diminishing relative desirability. The additional shift in supply, as certain countries in consequence of an alteration in the ratio of exchange shift their output, qualitatively, by taking up for the first time the production of the relatively more desired commodities

---

[1] This is because, when many countries and commodities are involved, a smaller proportionate volume of resources is likely to be devoted to the production of a given commodity, in the country focal for it, than would be true of any commodity in trade involving only a few goods and countries. The probability that the focus will shift from one country to another is therefore greater in the former than in the latter case.

(correlatively restricting output of those in the other category), will negate the movement in the ratio at terms which are in line with the (national) cost ratios in greatest propinquity with those which had hitherto conditioned the then current (normal) ratio of exchange.[2] So extensive and readily induced an adjustment of supply, in response to changing demand, greatly narrows the potential spread between any two stable ratios of exchange and sets a general pattern for the ratio from which deviations, issuing out of any shift in demand however great, must be of only minor magnitude. We shall see that a closer approach to reality, as we relax our assumptions, operates, on the whole, to fortify this tendency.

Relaxation of the Assumption of Costless Transport

Let us first abandon the postulate of costless transportation, or of equal cost of transportation whether goods are sold on the domestic market or to any one of a number of foreign markets. With costless transportation, and free trade, the prices of all mobile goods would, of course, everywhere be the same. This will obviously not be true when the assumption of costless transport is relaxed. The ratio of exchange between any two of an indefinite number of commodities may then differ in any one country from that currently prevailing in any other by not more than the equivalent of the cost of outward transport of the commodity relatively undervalued in the given country plus the cost of inward transport of the commodity relatively undervalued in the other.[3] But it by no means follows that the differences in the national commodity exchange ratios will reach these limits. It may happen, for instance, that each country will find in other parts of the world a better market for its relatively undervalued product, and a better source of supply of that which is relatively overvalued, than that which is offered by the other of the two compared countries. In this case the potential difference in the ex-

[2] The magnitude of the potential shift in supply may be gauged from the fact that, with a slight shift in the ratio of exchange, there is nothing to prevent a country from diverting its entire productive resources (or, at least, all of them hitherto devoted to commodities of relatively declining desirability) to a single commodity, of relatively increasing desirability, which it had not previously produced at all. The possibilities of adjustment, *without* any alteration in the ratio of exchange, are not very much less, since any large country will be able to divert very large resources from one to another of its *current* lines of production in response to a shift in the relative desirability of the commodities concerned.

[3] For an exposition of the two-country two-commodity case (with diagrammatic illustration) cf. Viner, *Studies, op. cit.,* pp. 467-470.

change ratios in the two markets will be narrowed. The ratios of exchange will be linked through those of third countries on the basis of a net cost of imports in terms of exports (transport costs included) which, for this (or any other) pair of countries, will permit in them a difference which cannot be greater and will, in all probability, be less, than would be potential if they were directly exchanging the commodities in question.[4]

It will, moreover, frequently be the case that, in a given country, the cost ratios between any currently "domestic" commodity (that is, a commodity which, under prevailing conditions, it does not pay to export or import), and those which it is currently exporting will deviate from the cost ratios prevailing in any other part of the world by an amount less than sufficient to cover reciprocal costs of transport (direct or indirect). When this occurs, the country will normally produce the full amount of its consumption of the commodity in question.[5] Transport costs are thus a principal factor in extending the variety of output within any national unit. Without such costs it would, as already noted, be very unlikely that any country would, under constant returns, produce *more* than one commodity in common with any other single country though it would almost certainly produce *one*. But, in the presence of such costs, any two countries can have an indefinite number of common products. The commodities will, in each country, exchange against exports at the cost ratios there prevailing.

[4] The use of an internationally exchangeable money, such as gold, makes it seem as if the (gold) price of any imported commodity could, under the assumed conditions, not exceed its price in the market of origin by more than the simple cost of transport of the commodity concerned. But this is because the cost of transport of gold (for which the non-monetary commodity is bartered) is so small as to escape casual observation. If we measure the value of gold in the export good we should find that gold is more valuable in the country *to* which, than in that *from* which, it moves by an amount sufficient to cover not only the cost of transport of the non-monetary commodity but also the cost of transport of the gold in the opposite direction. The ratio of exchange between the non-monetary commodity and gold may vary in the two countries by an amount adequate to cover the cost of transport of both.

[5] This follows from the fact that it would be unprofitable to import any of the commodity at the assumed ratio of exchange unless transport costs from some foreign center of computation of exchange ratios were so much less, to *peripheral* consumers in the country in question, than the transport costs to those consumers from the domestic center of computation of cost ratios as to nullify the ability of the domestic producers to compete with the foreign supply in the peripheral areas of their own country. (It might well be that producers with a comparative disadvantage in the output of any given commodity, at exchange ratios computed at the points of production, could supply peripheral areas in a given foreign country more cheaply than the domestic producers could.)

In order to pursue more fully the effect of transport costs it will be convenient to shift from the barter ratios, in which we have hitherto conducted our analysis, to an investigation in monetary terms.[6]

When the monetary costs of output of any commodity, at two centers of production in different countries, differ by an amount less than the cost of transport of the commodity from one center to the other, the dividing line between the markets "tributary" to each center will be drawn not on national lines but will be a "transport cost hyperbola" curving around the center of higher cost of output.[7] At any point on this line the difference between transport costs from the two centers of production will be precisely equal to the difference between the costs of output at the respective centers. The whole area "inside" the curve can then be more cheaply supplied from the center of higher cost of output while the whole area outside the curve can be more cheaply supplied from the center of lower cost of output. If, to elucidate, the supply price of any given product is $1.00 per unit in A and $1.08 per unit in B, while the cost of transport of the commodity from A to B is 10¢ per unit, the line separating the market tributary to B from that tributary to A would curve hyperbolically around B with its apex, Z, at the point which would divide the cost of transport to Z, from A and B respectively, at 9¢ and 1¢ per unit of the commodity transported (a difference of 8¢, to equal the difference in production costs). The appended figure (p. 142) will clarify the matter. At any other point on the curve YZS the difference between the transport costs from A and B will likewise be 8¢, that is to say it will equate the delivered price of the product from A with that from B. Thus, at point Y, the cost of transport, from A, will be 15¢ per unit and, from B, 7¢. The difference, 8¢, is the difference in costs of production at A and B.

---

[6] There are excellent reasons for avoiding an analysis of *fundamental* relationships in pecuniary terms. But, on the assumption that, as a result of trade, a common money such as gold does not change in its *relative* value in the several countries, the process of analysis is greatly simplified, for some purposes, by its use. Such an assumption, though logically objectionable in dealing with the *fundamentals*, is permissible when the basic ratio of exchange has been established. For the matter in hand the very small cost of transporting money will, therefore, be assumed to be negligible. Computations in inconvertible paper money would not alter the case and would, in fact, be subject to no *doctrinal* objections of any sort. But they would complicate the task of exposition.

[7] For a detailed exposition of this matter cf. "The Economic Law of Market Areas," Frank A. Fetter, *The Quarterly Journal of Economics*, Vol. xxxviii, 1924, pp. 520-529.

At any point within the downward shaded area the cost of transport from A exceeds that from B by more than 8¢ per unit. Within this area A can, therefore, not compete with B. At any point in the unshaded (or in the upward shaded) area, on the other hand, the

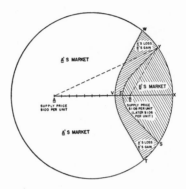

cost of transport from A is less than 8¢ per unit in excess of that from B (if, indeed, it is in excess at all) and, within this area, B can, therefore, not compete with A.[8]

If the supply price at B were $1.10, with the cost of transport, from A to B, 10¢ per unit and everything else unchanged, B's market "area" would be confined to the straight line BX, running away from A, and all the rest of the world would, in the absence of other competitors, "belong" to A. Producers in B would not then in fact have *any* market where they could sell quite free of competition from A and would have no market, outside an infinitesimal area along the line BX, where they could even meet the competition from A.

If, on the other hand, the unit supply price at B were $1.06, with everything else unchanged, the area of B's market would be greatly enlarged. It would then include the whole area within the hyperbola W V T, the upward shaded part being added to B's, and subtracted from A's, market. Within this area the cost of transport, from B to V, is 2¢ per unit of the commodity while that from A to V is 8¢ per unit. The difference, (6¢), is equal to the difference in the (amended)

8 If transport costs always varied proportionately with physical distance the "transport cost hyperbola" would be geographically "true," but, since they do not, the relevant "hyperbola" may take a very contorted physical form. The diagram should represent distance not in physical terms but in terms of transport costs.

price of output at A and B. Similarly the cost of transport from B to any other point on the new hyperbolic curve is 6¢ less than the cost to that point from A, and this just compensates the difference in production costs in A and B.[9]

If there are several centers of output with different unit costs the market area "tributary" to any one of them will be that area which, when appropriate hyperbolic curves are drawn from the given center of output relative to all of the others, is uncut by a curve based on any other center. The various parts of any area intersected by two or more hyperbolic curves drawn around centers of production will, of course, be "tributary" to the center which can set the commodity down at the lowest delivered price.

While it is highly improbable that any two countries should have identical opportunity cost ratios between two or more commodities it is, on the other hand, extremely likely that there will be many cases in which these ratios will not differ by an amount sufficient to cover reciprocal transport costs. Transport costs, relative to the value (at point of origin) of the product transported, will, in fact, vary upward from a negligible fraction of the cost of output to indefinite, even infinite, limits.[10] The "standard" international ratio of exchange, the ratio, *i.e.*, with transport costs abstracted, will be the more nearly duplicated in prices in any given country according as transport costs are low, relative to the value of the product concerned, or the cost ratios in the country concerned happen to be close to the standard ratio. In the former case the assimilation to the standard ratio is achieved through international trade and, in the latter case, is inherent in the situation. With trade free, the price structure in every country would center around the international ratio of exchange (computed on the basis of costless transport) as a norm from which there would be practically no deviations on the side of exports and, with other commodities, no deviations greater than the cost of transport from the center of origin of the imported product to the point of consumption.

No impulse, from a shift in demand, which would not alter the

---

[9] A change in the cost of transport will have effects similar to that of a change in production costs in the respective centers of production. Any lowering of transport costs would increase the area "tributary" to A (the low-cost producer) at the expense of B. *Vice versa*, with any increase in transport costs.

[10] There are some commodities, and services, which cannot be transported at all but can render their utilities only at the point of production.

standard ratio of exchange when transport costs are abstracted will, under conditions of constant cost, have any effect on the several ratios in the different countries when costs of transport are taken into consideration since the differences between the various (national) exchange ratios, arising from costs of transport or from production cost ratios which do not in one country deviate from those in another by an amount equivalent to such transport costs, will clearly remain unaltered by any such shift in demand as does not affect the national locus of the margin of indifference in output. But, if the shift in demand should be great enough to cause an alteration in the national locus of margins of indifference and, therefore, in the international ratio of exchange computed in abstraction of costs of transport, the relationship between the various national exchange ratios may alter, as a result of transport costs, in a manner which is not a mere reflection of the alteration in the standard ratio. The alteration in the standard ratio can take place *only* with a shift in the national location of some focal point establishing margins of indifference in the production of one good or another and any such shift of focal points will entail a responsive shift (which may be greater or less) in the distance from the point of production of some part of the supply of the affected commodities to their various markets. The exchange ratio (prices) in any given country may then deviate from the international exchange ratio (which is computed in abstraction of costs of transport) in greater or less degree than it had formerly deviated from the international exchange ratio then current.

The questions of the effect of transport costs on the international ratio of exchange ("terms of trade"), and of the division of the costs of transport between the (national) parties to trade, have been much discussed in classical literature. Mill asserted that the division of transport costs would be made on precisely the same principles as were, in his judgment, decisive of the "terms of trade," that the division is, in fact, dependent on "the play of international demand."[11] Sidgwick, however, exalted transport costs to the level of a primary factor in the ratio of exchange.

Viner's comment is as follows: "In an obscure and patently confused argument, Sidgwick attempted to show that the existence of transportation costs of commodities provided the sole basis for a

[11] *Principles, op. cit.*, Vol. II, pp. 144-145.

theory of international values different from the theory of domestic values. (Henry Sidgwick, *The Principles of Political Economy*, 1st edn., 1883, pp. 214-30; 2nd edn., 1887, pp. 202-16) . . . Sidgwick refuses to go behind money costs of production, and his argument, I believe, reduces itself to the proposition that the prices in any country of the products of any two (or more) countries, after allowances for transportation costs, are proportional to their money costs of production in their countries of origin, a proposition which no one would deny, and which is embodied, implicitly when not explicitly, in the classical doctrine of comparative costs instead of, as Sidgwick supposed, constituting a correction thereof."[12]

In this statement I fully concur, but Viner then proceeds to a complete endorsement of *Mill's* position. Since this runs in terms of the play of reciprocal national demand (which has been persistently under attack in this book) the reader will not be surprised if Mill's doctrine is here viewed with something more than skepticism.

The fact is that international transport costs will, almost always, be borne *solely* by the importer. The international ratio of exchange (computed in abstraction of costs of transport) is the referent. Importers will be compelled to assume transport charges since producers in the country of origin of the export would otherwise find it advantageous to devote their resources to the output of alternative products. At the international ratio of exchange these producers will be on the margin of indifference as between the production of the export in question and other articles some of which will not be exported. The importers, on the other hand, are on no such margin of indifference as between the good in question and other commodities. If the cost ratios, in their own countries, between any of their exports and the good in question did not deviate from the international ratio of exchange (with transport costs abstracted) by more than enough to cover the costs of transport of the (potential) import they would produce the good at home. But, whenever the cost ratios diverge from the international ratio of exchange by something more than this, they will have no profitable alternative to import even when they are bearing transport charges in full. Since the buyers of imports can afford to bear transport costs, rather than go without the imports or produce them at home, they will, in the presence of readily available productive alternatives in the exporting

12 Viner, *Studies, op. cit.*, p. 470n.

country, be compelled to assume them. The gains from trade will thus, in practically every case, be diminished for the importing country by the amount of the carrying charges.

The carrying trade, as such, should, of course, be regarded as an export of the carrier in all cases in which the carrying is done for foreign interests, and the international ratio of exchange of all commodities will be as much determined by the comparative advantage of certain countries in the transport as in any other industry.

Relaxation of the Assumption of Constant Costs

Let us now abandon the assumption of constant costs of output at any given center of production. Since we are measuring costs in terms of forgone opportunity, any rise or fall in the unit opportunity cost of any commodity is *ipso facto* a converse movement in the unit opportunity cost of some other commodity. If one unit of z could originally have been obtained by the sacrifice of 20 units of x, or *vice versa*, but if, as the output of z is expanded at the expense of x, it becomes necessary to give up 21 units of x for each additional unit of z, then the opportunity cost of a unit of x has fallen, from $1/20$ to $1/21$ of a unit of z, *pari passu* with the rise in the opportunity cost of a unit of z from 20 to 21 units of x. Increasing and decreasing opportunity costs are necessarily correlative.

Provided the optimum-size plant has been attained at any given center of production, an increase in the total output of any one commodity can never, in the absence of variable external economies, involve the sacrifice of *fewer* units of other goods than had been necessary to the attainment of a unit of the good in question before the expansion in its output took place.[13] As the concentration in any one country on any commodity of relatively low (opportunity) cost eventually operates to raise the relevant opportunity cost of that commodity in that country the tendency is for (marginal) cost

[13] If, for instance, the supply of wheat is expanded, at the expense of the supply of Indian corn, it may happen that, for a considerable shift, constant costs will prevail, that is to say that there will be a sizable acreage of land and a sizable group of farmers on the margin of indifference, at the existing exchange ratio, in the production of wheat and corn. But, if the movement goes far enough, this margin will be transcended, and corn-lands and corn-farmers, relatively good in that line (and, therefore, relatively bad in wheat) as compared with those originally transferred to wheat, will have to be drawn into wheat production. The average and marginal unit cost of wheat (in terms of corn) will then rise.

ratios in the several countries to converge and for *international* trade, in consequence, to cease to expand. International trade is, under these conditions, self-limiting, and national diversity of production is, to a very considerable degree, maintained. This is of great significance in the case of national economic entities of large and varied resources. After a certain degree of specialization has been attained a large country is likely to develop marginal opportunity cost ratios which are a simulacrum, over a wide range of products, of the international ratio of exchange.[14] Any such country tends, in the qualitative composition of its output, to become a microcosm of the world at large.

The shift in (marginal) cost ratios attendant upon the expansion, under increasing opportunity costs, in the output of any good, in any given national area, would ordinarily be greatest in those countries which make their adjustment by transfer of resources from a single commodity (rather than from a group of commodities) of relatively declining output to that, or those, in which output is increasing. This shift in cost ratios would then, however, immediately transmit part of the adjustment to other countries and, thenceforward, back and forth in see-saw fashion so as to induce, and keep, an identity in the (marginal) cost ratios of the several countries in the commodities in question.[15] Under conditions of increasing cost for any national specialty there is, in fact, a strong probability that any given country will develop (marginal) opportunity cost ratios substantially the same as those of some other country in certain commodities, and as those of third, fourth, fifth, and nth countries in others, with the production of any commodity in any country being carried up to that point, and no farther, at which the marginal unit cost ratios, between the commodity in question and other products, is similar to that of some of the other countries collectively sharing the output of the commodities concerned. This does not mean, of course, that any one country is ever likely, over the whole range of output, to reach identity of (marginal) cost ratios with

[14] This happens not only because marginal costs, on an increasing cost basis, move toward the relationship expressed in the international ratio of exchange but also because the international ratio of exchange, in the specialties put out by any large (and therefore focal) country, tends, as a result of the great production of that country, to come into line with the cost ratios there prevailing.

[15] This phase of theory is well handled by R. F. Harrod in the early chapters of *International Economics*, Harcourt, Brace, New York, 1933.

any other, and produce exactly the same commodities—albeit in different proportions—as are produced in that other country, but that every country of any size will tend to produce a much wider variety of commodities than it would produce under constant costs of output. Some of these it will share with certain foreign countries, and others with others, with a very considerable number of commodities being produced in each of the great majority of large countries.

In the somewhat special case in which the general-resources cost of a commodity *diminishes* as the national output of that commodity is expanded, the tendency would be toward the supply of the whole world from a given center of production of the good in question.[16] This might or might not engage the whole population of the country of output of the commodity. If it does, the ratio of exchange between this and other products will be a limbo ratio dependent on the shifting of demand. If it does not, the exchange ratio with other commodities produced within the country will depend on cost levels for the current output of the commodities in question, and these will be linked, through common products, with the cost ratios of all other commodities in the countries of their production. The expansion, under decreasing general-resources cost, of the output of any commodity in any one country will, of course, be attended by an automatic increase of opportunity in other countries in other commodities.

It should be noted that, in the theory of international trade, we are concerned only with the effect on unit opportunity, or general-resources, costs of the expansion, or contraction, of the *national* output of given commodities. The problem is not that of the size, or more or less complete utilization, of a given producing plant but

[16] Decreasing general-resources cost as output is expanded will tend to occur only when external economies are available or the optimum-size plant or industry, for the production of the commodity concerned, has not been attained in any country. *Every* commodity, of course, at some time, runs through a condition of decreasing general-resources cost. It would, for instance, cost much more, per unit, to raise ten bushels of wheat than a thousand. With some products, of course, the best proportions in the utilization of resources can be attained only with a very large plant. The factors making for decreasing general-resources unit cost are, however, ephemeral while those making for increasing general-resources unit cost are eternal. Increasing general-resources cost is always latent if not currently operative. Decreasing general-resources costs occur, on the other hand, only when the ever-present tendency to increasing cost is temporarily more than compensated by some adventitious, and ephemeral, circumstance.

148

of the effects of expansion or contraction of the *number* of such plants in any country. (Each of these plants in any one country may be assumed to be of optimum size; all, presumably, have similar cost curves; and the minimum unit costs of all are, presumably, at the same level.) What would happen to unit costs (provided the effect were everywhere the same) with an expansion or contraction of *world* output, is largely irrelevant to the national distribution of production. It is the size of the *national* industry in any commodity, and the differential effects of changes in the composition, but not the total sum, of the *national* outputs, that is significant. Under certain conditions something may be said (even from a cosmopolitan point of view) for fostering (by protective tariffs or otherwise) the national output of goods of decreasing general-resources unit cost, at the expense of goods where the opposite cost conditions prevail, and, in certain circumstances, a case can be made for even more extended interferences with free competition, but all these would seem to be of slight practical importance.[17]

If, to return to conditions of *increasing* general-resources cost, we suppose that the relative demand for commodities is shifting, it may be worth while to reiterate that the relative marginal unit cost of the commodities of increasing demand will rise, and that for the commodities of diminishing demand will fall, *pari passu* in all producing countries, since, if the rate of change in costs is different in the different countries, expansion of the supply of the relatively desired commodities will be carried out in such different proportions in the several centers supplying any common group of products as to keep marginal cost ratios in all countries in line. The exchange ratio will then shift slowly and steadily in correspondence with this assimilated shift in cost ratios. It should be noted, however, that it is only so far as *supply* (cost) conditions are affected by this alteration that a movement in the ratio of exchange will occur. The altered

---

[17] cf. Frank D. Graham, "Some Aspects of Protection Further Considered," *The Quarterly Journal of Economics*, Vol. xxxvii, 1923, pp. 199-227; Viner's comment thereon in *Studies, op. cit.*, pp. 475-482; and Frank D. Graham, *Protective Tariffs*, Princeton University Press, Princeton, 1942, pp. 104-106. J. Tinbergen, in an appendix, "Professor Graham's Case for Protection," to his *International Economic Cooperation* (Elsevier, Amsterdam, 1945), ably reviews the discussion.

It should be kept in mind that what is said, elsewhere, on the effect, or lack of effect, of protective tariffs on the international ratio of exchange, proceeds on the assumption of constant costs. There is, however, little reason to suppose that different assumptions on costs would affect the typical constancy of *relationship* between international ratios of exchange and the cost structures currently evolving.

demand changes the cost *data* of the problem so that the comparative cost structure, *within* the several countries, is no longer that on which the exposition was begun. The ratio of exchange continues to be a derivative of cost ratios, and not of demand schedules, but the Tableau of Cost Ratios is then in persistent, though predictable, change. (Cost *schedules*, however, are not altered.) The (normal) ratio of exchange would alter with every shift in the relationship between marginal costs and would have to be computed, *de novo*, for every alteration in the relative volume of demand with its consequent effect on (marginal) costs. The norm would still be tied to costs as the stable (predictable) element in the situation but there would be interaction between costs (or the ratio of exchange) and the volume of demand for the several commodities. The problem would still be analyzable; generalization is still possible; we remain on a given cost *curve* and the matter is therefore amenable to theoretic treatment. This, in my judgment, is not the case with those truly dynamic situations which cannot, as in the present case, be resolved into a succession of somewhat differing "stills" each of which may be frozen for consideration and then combined in an imaginative panorama showing what the whole situation would be with a range of "varying," yet not "unstable," cost conditions. Such a panorama presents a series of momentary equilibria combined into a moving equilibrium. Shifts in *demand* always mean a transfer to a *new* demand curve but it is only in the case of unstable, not in that of merely variable, costs, that this is true of supply. With variable costs, the international ratio of exchange could be computed, for varying demands, on the basis of a three-dimensional Tableau of Costs which would show, *in depth*, the relevant unit opportunity costs for any given volume of output of any given commodity.

Any rising unit opportunity cost, and exchange value, of commodities of increased demand, with the correlative fall in the unit opportunity cost and exchange value of other commodities, will operate to check the rise in the volume of demand in the one group of commodities, and to limit the fall in the volume of demand for the other, so that the occasional jumps in the exchange ratio more or less characteristic of changes in demand under constant cost conditions, and the shifts to new focal points establishing new margins of indifference, will, to a great extent, be precluded. The shift in relative costs will, instead, take place in slow continuity, indeed in all but imperceptible degrees, and will be so reflected in the evolving international ratio of exchange. The focal "points," in fact, will then constitute a practically unbroken line. The diversity of national production, the result both of costs of transport and of rising unit costs with expansion of output at any one center of production, facilitates a smooth adjustment of supply to shifts in demand, and occasions an orderly progress in (normal) exchange ratio relationships in correspondence with the coordinated shifts in the cost structure in the various producing centers. This diversity thus practically eliminates not only the possibility of any large or sudden alteration in normal exchange ratio relationships but also the appearance of a limbo ratio. Whenever a shift in demand is so persistent as to lead to an expectation of a protracted deviation of the market ratio of exchange from the relationships corresponding to current cost conditions, the adjustments of supply which will be undertaken in many countries in response to the altered demand will, in the several countries, affect a more or less completely different set of commodities, so that the new normal ratio of exchange, coinciding with the current (marginal) opportunity cost for the various commodities, will not be very greatly different from the old.

The Introduction of Money

The next step in the approach to reality is the introduction of money. Where a single commodity is universally or all but universally employed as money (as, for instance, in the heyday of the international gold standard), any one of the commodities $z \ldots q$ might be supposed to be the money material. It would be convenient so to regard z, which has been used as the pivot on which all exchange relationships have turned.[18] The money material z will then, in ordinary trading processes, be distributed among the various nations in such a way as, apart from costs of transfer, to bring about identity of (opportunity) cost ratios, for the various commodities which any country is exporting, with the ratios in the basic ratio of exchange. This is the condition of equilibrium, and money will tend to move internationally, in payment for goods, until this equilibrium is achieved.

The older classical economists asserted that the introduction of

[18] A unit of z might, for instance, be an oz. (troy), or any other weight, of gold.

(metallic or any other) money did not affect the ratio of exchange of commodities. This is an obvious error where a commodity money is in question, since, if we were to eliminate z (which we are now regarding as the common money material) from the list of produced and traded commodities, the ratio of exchange between the remaining commodities would differ from that which, all other things being equal, would prevail in the presence of z.[19] It is only in the case of independent monetary systems (with debt, fiat or other non-commodity monies not used in any but the jurisdiction of issue) that the introduction of money makes no difference to the normal ratio of exchange.[20] A money which has no use in the arts, and does not circulate in any country but the country of origin, is "purer," in the sense that it serves simply as a *numeraire* and does not disturb the commodity exchange relationships that would evolve under a frictionless form of barter of commodities not including the money material, than any commodity money could possibly be.

When, moreover, a commodity of all but infinite durability is more or less universally employed as money, it is not likely at any time to exchange against all other commodities at anything like a precise correspondence with current cost ratios. The accumulated stock of such a money (gold, for instance) eventually becomes so large relative to the annual output that no probable alteration in the rate of that output is likely to affect the total supply adequately to insure any close correspondence, even over a fairly lengthy period, between the ratio at which it exchanges against other commodities and the current cost ratios, especially since these, over time, are always changing. The total supply in existence at any given moment would, in fact, not be *reduced* even if production were completely forgone. Relative demand, rather than supply, conditions (i.e. what, in a loose way, we would call "short-run" considerations) will therefore be preeminent in determining the value of a commodity

---

[19] Mill seems to have been aware of the fact that international trade involving a money material will not, except as it covers a mere flux and reflux of the money material to and from any country, be carried out on precisely the same terms as would trade in which a money *material* was absent (*Principles, op. cit.*, Book III, Chap. XIX). But his statement as to the irrelevance of money stood unchanged.

[20] The rate of exchange between the several independent currencies would then move to whatever point was necessary to adjust national prices (measured in any of the currencies) to the position corresponding to the (barter) ratio of exchange of commodities evolved along the lines already propounded. Independent currencies, when exchanged, must be considered to be bartered against each other since neither of them is a money in *both* of the concerned jurisdictions.

money (in other commodities) though it will of course not affect the normal exchange relationships of these latter commodities against each other. All of these latter ratios, in the degree of the celerity of adjustment of supply to current demand relationships, will persistently move into correspondence with current opportunity costs. The cost of production of the money commodity, on the other hand, may, with reference to the existing exchange ratio, always be out of line with the costs of other commodities.

Since, however, the production of a metallic monetary material is almost certain to be on an increasing resources-cost basis, marginal costs in the production of money are brought more closely into line with the marginal costs of other materials than might, at first blush, seem probable.[21] The adjustment typically occurs, however, in a movement of marginal costs (through expansion or contraction of output) toward the current exchange ratio rather than in a movement of the exchange ratio toward the current marginal costs.

Where a debt money is used, the cost of production is practically zero and, so long as issue is so restricted as to keep the value of the monetary unit high, there can, of course, be no correspondence of the cost with the exchange ratio of the money against commodities.[22] The supply of money under these conditions is in no way affected by cost but is arbitrarily determined by the issuing authorities. The value of the money, in other commodities, is still a function of supply but, since the supply is not a function of cost, the connection between cost and value is disrupted.

In general, it may be said that the value of money, in terms of commodities, is little, if at all, associated with relative costs but that, however remotely the value of money is associated with cost, the discrepancy affects only the relationship between money and all other commodities. It has no bearing on the linkage of the exchange ratio between the various non-monetary commodities with relative costs, whether these costs are measured in terms of money or opportunity. The fact that gold money may have, in its relationships against non-monetary commodities, no normal ratio of exchange based

[21] When the cost is below the current exchange value, output is indefinitely expanded until the marginal cost rises to bring the two into correspondence, whereas it is contracted when the cost is above that value. In short, the margin is, in this case, determined by costs rather than costs by the margin.

[22] This, of course, is a phenomenon of monopoly and is, perhaps, somewhat irrelevant in a discussion of exchange relationships under competition.

on costs will not affect the composition of production in any but gold-mining countries. The composition of production in all other countries, except so far as a certain amount of more or less specialized production is used to buy gold from abroad, will be the same as if gold were not in the picture.

Money *qua* money, national price levels, and national per capita pecuniary incomes, play no role in the determination of normal barter ratios or normal price relationships of commodities. Money is often a factor initiating, or prolonging, disturbances of equilibrium in international, as in domestic, transactions but it is of no significance for the norms.

Since it was not until the last decades of the 19th century that the concept of price *levels*, as we now understand the term, received any serious attention from economists, the classical writers cannot be supposed to have cherished the notion that, whether as cause or effect, price levels had anything to do with the "terms of trade." Ricardo even denied that the general value of money could anywhere be ascertained and, therefore, that national price levels could be compared. The typical classical position, as stated for example by Henry Thornton, was that "bullion necessarily bears that value, or nearly that value, in each country, in exchange for goods, which it bears in all, allowance being made for the expence of their transmission, inclusive of export and import duties, ordinary profit of the merchant, freight, insurance, and other customary charges."[23] We may, in consequence, assume that the classicists, so far as they considered the matter, held to the (sound) view that national price levels, other than for factors of production, had a strong tendency toward equality. (The expenses of transmission of goods would, in every country, cut both ways, the exports of any country being lower in price than in the countries of destination and the imports higher in price than in the countries of origin.) None of the classicists imagined that the prices of goods not internationally traded would have any causal influence on the ratio of exchange of those that were, and they could not, therefore, presume that any inequality between national price levels that might stem from such goods had any significance for the "terms of trade."

It was Mill who seems first to have supposed that a high national

[23] *An Enquiry into the Nature and Effects of the Paper Credit of Great Britain,* Hatchard and Rivington, London, 1802, p. 299.

price level would be an *effect* of favorable "terms of trade," and it is Bastable who is, perhaps, responsible for the notion that it would be a *cause*.[24] Neither view has much, if any, validity. The "terms" (ratio of international exchange of commodities) could vary in indefinite degree within a context of equality of national price levels and, whatever the "terms of trade" might be, the *tendency* toward such equality of national price levels (measured in any given money) would always be present.[25] Such deviations from equality of national price levels as may occur will have little or no connection with the "terms of trade."

If a country could, at will, develop a relatively high price level,[26] and was (momentarily) quoting its exports on dearer terms, measured in imports, than those which would derive from a barter analysis on the basis of opportunity costs, it would soon find itself in the position, described by Hume, in which an excess of commodity imports over exports would drain it of much of any commodity money material it might have, or, if it were operating under an inconvertible paper money, would lower the exchange value of its currency. In either case its price level would "come into line" at a ratio of exchange of exports against imports identical with that which would issue from a barter analysis.

Except, possibly, in the case of artificial barriers to trade (discussed in the next chapter where the assumption of freedom of trade is relaxed), any inequality between national price *levels* is determined by factors mainly extraneous to the "terms of trade" (which are a matter of individual, or group, commodity price relationships within any given level of national prices). Barriers to commodity transactions may, on occasion, improve the "terms of trade" for

---

24 J. S. Mill, *Principles, op. cit.*, Book III, Chap. XIX, §2, and C. F. Bastable, *Theory, op. cit.*, p. 71. The matter is more fully discussed in Chapter XII of this book. I am not at all sure about the priority of the attributions here made but since both of the doctrines are, in my view, erroneous, it would not seem to make much difference.

25 If two countries exchange shoes at $10.00 a pair for wheat at $2.00 a bushel (a pair of shoes for five bushels of wheat), the goods will sell at identical prices in the two countries (cost of transport abstracted) but, merely from these or any other such data, it would be impossible to say which good was high or low, what either country was getting out of the transaction, or how the countries were sharing the gains from the trade.

26 It should be noted that the relationship in question is that between countries, at a given time, not as between one time and another in a given country, and that it must be measured in some one currency converted, for one side of the transaction, into another in a free market and, for the establishment of norms, at an equilibrium rate of exchange.

the levying country (though this is usually formal rather than real)[27] and will, in any case, raise its relative general level of prices by making the prices of otherwise freely importable goods dear.

Other factors in raising the general price level of any country relative to others, though not, in general, altering the basic international ratio of exchange of commodities, would be:

1. a narrow list of exports and numerous imports (usually, but not necessarily, associated with favorable terms) ;
2. high transport costs on imports;
3. low efficiency in a *majority* of domestic goods' industries relative to efficiency in exportables (the ratio in other countries serving as a standard) ;
4. an export industry in the money material;
5. the presence of national monopolies, especially if accompanied by dumping in foreign markets;[28]
6. the presence of a large net income from services (including the provision of capital) rendered to foreigners.

The last of these items will lead to a wider range of commodity imports, relative to exports, than would otherwise be the case and might also change the basic "terms of trade" from those that would prevail in its absence. Logically considered such services should be included, as exports, within the complex of traded commodities and opportunity costs.

International trade, though fundamentally a matter of barter, is *proximately* a matter of price. Its principles can be grasped on a price basis, however, only if it is thoroughly understood that equilibrium price *relationships* are a consequence, and never a cause, of (normal) barter ratios, and that the latter, in general, are neither a cause nor result of differences in national price *levels*.[29] We cannot make spatial comparisons of national price levels except by conversion through exchange rates between currencies and these also, in equilibrium, fall into the relationship which will identify price ratios, expressed in any one currency, with barter ratios of exchange.

[27] cf. the following chapter.

[28] The effect of monopolies on the "terms of trade" is a moot question, to which this book pays only casual attention.

[29] In whatever money they may be expressed, national price levels tend to move in consonance with one another. The movements are basically a reflection of the supply of the several monies relative to the supply of goods they circulate. For a further discussion of this matter see Appendix B.

CHAPTER IX

"RECIPROCAL NATIONAL DEMANDS"
AND THEIR MANIPULATION: PROTECTIVE TARIFFS:
INTERNATIONAL TRANSFERS OF CAPITAL

In the cosmopolitan, humanistic, philosophy which the classical economists more or less overtly professed (but from which they frequently departed) the phrase "terms of trade" would be synonymous with the general ratio of exchange of products and could have no other connotation. The nationalistic sentiment of the classical writers, however, gave to "terms of trade" the connotation of the rate at which the exports of any given nation, taken as a whole, exchange against its imports taken as a whole. This, as already noted, was associated with the concept of "national demands" as if the trade the classicists were talking about were trade between national entities, in national bales of goods, rather than between individuals buying and selling, as traders nationally indistinguished, individual commodities in a market competitive in every respect except in the mobility of factors of production across national boundaries.

Even the *market*, to say nothing of the normal, ratio of exchange between internationally traded (as all other) commodities is a function of *total* reciprocal individual demand (supply), for the various products, and not of the supposititious reciprocal demands (supply) of segregated national units; but national specialization, and temporary immobility of factors of production *within* the several nations, may bring it about that market values of internationally traded goods may behave, *temporarily*, as if the goods were being bid for, and offered, as national composites. This, however, is never true of *normal* values.

International trade is but one phase of the total trade in any given market. The trade of any given market, even when it seems to be almost purely domestic, is, on the other hand, but a phase of a larger (international) whole of which it is an interacting part. The repercussions of international on domestic transactions, and *vice versa*, are so numerous and intricate as to make any segregation of the one from the other a logical impossibility. Every trading connection, like every road, leads to the end of the earth, and every bit of commercial traffic both modifies, and is modified by, all the rest. All

157

trade is part of a network of world-wide scope. In any freely organized market, for any given internationally traded commodity,
demand will be partly from residents of the country of the market
in question and partly from residents of other countries. The
influence of either is indistinguishable from that of the other. The
nationality of the buyer is, economically, a matter of complete indifference to the seller or to the market as a whole. Conversely, the
nationality of the seller is, economically, of no concern to the buyer,
and the total supply may, or may not, come from the citizens of one
nation only. The price of any freely traded good is unaffected by the
national origin of sellers or buyers and there is, in consequence, no
occasion for grouping buyers or sellers into more or less antagonistic
national sectors. In a system of mutual interdependence, not only
of prices but of reciprocal demand (supply), the foreign as part of
the total demand for, or supply of, any given product has repercussions on what are regarded as purely domestic markets (of other
goods). The demand for, and the supply of, these domestic goods,
as well as the use of factors of production in their output, affect, in
turn, the volume and prices of internationally traded commodities.
The attempt of the classical theorists to formulate a complete and
systematic theory of domestic values without reference to external
trade, and then to superpose upon this a quite different theory of
international transactions on the factually implied, but expressly
repudiated, assumption that the several nations were trading with
each other as entities, has therefore produced nothing but confusion.

It is of major importance to note not only that no adequate theory
of *domestic* values can be developed in exclusion of international
trade but that no valid theory of international values can be developed without regard for the interdependence, in both prices and
production, of the various national economies. All trade is a unity
in which every change in price relationships, compared with costs,
leads to kaleidoscopic shifts in supply that are likely to run through
all parts of the structure. A theory of normal international values
built on the premise of a fixed composition of industry in a given
area is, of necessity therefore, unworthy of support.

When, instead of discussing the *total* reciprocal demand (supply)
for the various products in an integrated trading system, the classicists split demand (supply) into irrelevant national parts, with
assumed "reciprocal national demands" for fixed sets of commodities

of mutually exclusive composition (supposed, qualitatively, to represent the unalterable output of each of the several trading countries), they were indulging in pure fantasy. With this (unwarranted) construct (vitiating the whole of their subsequent doctrine) it was logical enough to go on to the deduction that, with any change whatever in "reciprocal national demands," the equilibrium prices of all the exports of any one country would rise or fall, as a unit, in terms of all its imports (the exports of other countries). It is obvious, however, that, except possibly in the case of a small country specializing in one or two commodities not produced elsewhere, this does not correspond with fact. No large country has a unique list of exports and, if ever the values of all of the exports of any such country should fall, relative to other goods, that fall would not only be represented in a considerable, but varying, like sector of the exports of most, if not all, other countries but would also lead to a shift in output in all countries at, or at all close to, the margin of indifference between the output of any of the commodities that had fallen, and any of those that had risen, in price. This, in turn, would have counter repercussions on prices.

The *imports* of any large country, like its exports, are represented, more or less fully, in the (import) lists of many other countries. The net result of any shift that might occur in the ratio of exchange between the exports and imports of any given national area would thus be more or less fully shared, by many other countries, in the degree in which their export and import lists happened to correspond with the lists of the country in question. But this would be only the immediate effect. Since any such alteration in the ratio of exchange would forthwith set in motion complex shifts in supply, in all countries of diverse production, it is, as we have seen, far from unlikely that the eventually resulting ratio of exchange might, on the whole, prove favorable to a country to which the initial alteration in demand, or in the ratio, had been adverse, or unfavorable to one to which the initial alteration had been advantageous.

No *spontaneous* shift in demand is likely to affect, in a given direction, the prices of *all* of the exports, in terms of the imports, of any large, and, therefore, diversified, country, and no such shift would have any long-run effect, whatever, on the ratio of exchange unless cost and supply conditions were thereby changed. If these latter should be changed, there is no certain presumption, *from demand,* as to the nature, or direction, of any alteration in the ratio of exchange that may, in consequence, occur.

Alleged Effects of Improvements in Production or of Taxes

The classical vice of thinking in terms of reciprocal national demand, of supposing that the ratio of international exchange ("terms of trade") is a resultant of the status of demand thus envisaged, and, of necessity, disregarding shifts in output, has provoked numerous illusory speculations on what might happen to the "terms of trade" if an alteration in "reciprocal national demands" should spontaneously develop or should be induced by national political action. Mill led off with a discussion of the possible effects of an improvement in productivity in the output of a given commodity.[1] This, of course, changes cost ratios. Provided that only the two-country, two-commodity situation, is involved, such an improvement will, almost inevitably, lead to an increase in the total supply of the commodity affected, and will tend, in consequence, to lower its exchange value to correspond with the new status of costs. The classicists, however, were of the opinion that it might do less, or more, than this, and were especially concerned with the latter possibility. The country in which the improvement in production is made would then, so far at least as its international trade is concerned, suffer from the improvement, and might even find that its *general* income was reduced as compared with the situation that had formerly prevailed.

Mill, it is true, does not commit himself to the view that a country can be worse off *all round*, as a result of an improvement in production, but merely asserts that its gain on international trade may be cut. "Suppose," he says, . . . "that by a mechanical improvement made in Germany, and not capable of being transferred to England, the same quantity of labour and capital which produced twenty yards of linen, is enabled to produce thirty. Linen falls one-third in value in the German market, as compared with other commodities produced in Germany. Will it also fall one-third as compared with English cloth, thus giving to England, in common with Germany, the full benefit of the improvement? Or (ought we not rather to say),

[1] Mill's first assumption was of the output of a *new* commodity: with this case we are not at present concerned. He then went on to discuss a lowering in the unit cost of production of a commodity already traded: it is this case, and Mill's treatment of it, that will here be considered.

since the cost to England of obtaining linen was not regulated by the cost to Germany of producing it, and since England, accordingly, did not get the entire benefit even of the twenty yards which Germany could have given for ten yards of cloth, but only obtained seventeen—why should she now obtain more, merely because this theoretical limit is removed ten degrees further off?

"It is evident that in the outset, the improvement will lower the value of linen in Germany, in relation to all other commodities in the German market, including, among the rest, even the imported commodity, cloth. If 10 yards of cloth previously exchanged for 17 yards of linen, they will now exchange for half as much more, or 25½ yards. But whether they will continue to do so, will depend on the effect which this increased cheapness of linen produces on the international demand. The demand for linen in England could scarcely fail to be increased. But it might be increased either in proportion to the cheapness, or in a greater proportion than the cheapness, or in a less proportion.

"If the demand was increased in the same proportion with the cheapness, England would take as many times 25½ yards of linen, as the number of times 17 yards which she took previously. She would expend in linen exactly as much of cloth, or of the equivalents of cloth, as much in short of the collective income of her people, as she did before. Germany, on her part, would probably require, at that rate of interchange, the same quantity of cloth as before, because it would in reality cost her exactly as much; 25½ yards of linen being now of the same value in her market, as 17 yards were before. In this case, therefore, 10 yards of cloth for 25½ of linen is the rate of interchange which under these new conditions would restore the equation of international demand; and England would obtain linen one-third cheaper than before, being the same advantage as was obtained by Germany.

"It might happen, however, that this great cheapening of linen would increase the demand for it in England in a greater ratio than the increase of cheapness; and that if she before wanted 1000 times 17 yards, she would now require more than 1000 times 25½ yards to satisfy her demand. If so, the equation of international demand cannot establish itself at that rate of interchange; to pay for the linen England must offer cloth on more advantageous terms: say, for example, 10 yards for 21 of linen; so that England will not have the full benefit of the improvement in the production of linen, while Germany, in addition to that benefit, will also pay less for cloth. But again, it is possible that England might not desire to increase her consumption of linen in even so great a proportion as that of the increased cheapness; she might not desire so great a quantity as 1000 times 25½ yards: and in that case Germany must force a demand, by offering more than 25½ yards of linen for 10 of cloth; linen will be cheapened in England in a still greater degree than in Germany; while Germany will obtain cloth on more unfavorable terms, and at a higher exchange value than before."

Mill then proceeds to discuss as follows the relative probability of occurrence of each of the respective contingencies:

"Of the three possible varieties in the influence of cheapness on demand, which is the more probable—that the demand would be increased more than the cheapness, as much as the cheapness, or less than the cheapness? This depends on the nature of the particular commodity, and on the tastes of purchasers. When the commodity is one in general request, and the fall of its price brings it within the reach of a much larger class of incomes than before, the demand is often increased in a greater ratio than the fall of price, and a larger sum of money is on the whole expended in the article. . . . But it more frequently happens that when a commodity falls in price, less money is spent in it than before: a greater quantity is consumed, but not so great a value. The consumer who saves money by the cheapness of the article, will be likely to expend part of the saving in increasing his consumption of other things: and unless the low price attracts a large class of new purchasers who were either not consumers of the article at all, or only in small quantity and occasionally, a less aggregate sum will be expended on it. Speaking generally, therefore, the third of our three cases is the most probable: and an improvement in an exportable article is likely to be as beneficial (if not more beneficial) to foreign countries, as to the country where the article is produced."[2]

On the point made in the last sentence of the above quotation Edgeworth remarks that, if we assume that linen is not an article of German consumption, the exporting country (Germany) is clearly *damnified* by the improvement.[3] But, if the general validity of Mill's,

[2] Mill, *Principles, op. cit.*, Book III, Chapter XVIII, §5.
[3] *Papers, op. cit.*, Vol. II, p. 10.

and Edgeworth's, argument should be granted, Germany might be damnified whether or not it is a consumer of linen. All that would be necessary is that its consumption of that commodity be not large relative to output. The fact is that, if the locus of diversified production had originally been in Germany, the ratio of exchange will move from 20 to 30 linen for 10 cloth. If, however, it had been in England, and stays there, the ratio will remain at 15 linen to 10 cloth. But, if it is shifted to Germany, the ratio will be 30 linen = 10 cloth, with Germany damnified.

Mill later plays with similar ideas in his discussion of the possible effects, on the "terms of trade," of taxes on international commercial transactions. Of these he says:

"Every tax on a commodity tends to raise its price, and consequently to lessen the demand for it in the market in which it is sold. All taxes on international trade tend, therefore, to produce a disturbance and a re-adjustment of what we have termed the Equation of International Demand. This consideration leads to some rather curious consequences. . . .

"Taxes on foreign trade are of two kinds—taxes on imports, and on exports. On the first aspect of the matter it would seem that both these taxes are paid by the consumers of the commodity; that taxes on exports consequently fall entirely on foreigners, taxes on imports wholly on the home consumer. The true state of the case, however, is much more complicated.

"By taxing exports, we may, in certain circumstances, produce a division of the advantage of the trade more favourable to ourselves. In some cases we may draw into our coffers, at the expense of foreigners, not only the whole tax, but more than the tax; in other cases, we should gain exactly the tax; in others, less than the tax. In this last case, a part of the tax is borne by ourselves; possibly the whole, possibly even, as we shall show, more than the whole.

"Reverting to the supposititious case . . . of a trade between Germany and England in broadcloth and linen, suppose that England taxes her export of cloth, the tax not being supposed high enough to induce Germany to produce cloth for herself. The price at which cloth can be sold in Germany is augmented by the tax. This will probably diminish the quantity consumed. It may diminish it so much that, even at the increased price, there will not be required so great a money value as before. Or it may not diminish it at all, or so little, that in consequence of the higher price, a greater money value will be purchased than before. In this last case, England will gain, at the expense of Germany, not only the whole amount of the duty, but more; for, the money value of her exports to Germany being increased, while her imports remain the same, money will flow into England from Germany. The price of cloth will rise in England, and consequently in Germany; but the price of linen will fall in Germany, and consequently in England. We shall export less cloth, and import more linen, till the equilibrium is restored. It thus appears (what is at first sight somewhat remarkable) that by taxing her exports, England would, in some conceivable circumstances, not only gain from her foreign customers the whole amount of the tax, but would also get her imports cheaper. She would get them cheaper in two ways; for she would obtain them for less money, and would have more money to purchase them with. Germany, on the other hand, would suffer doubly: she would have to pay for her cloth a price increased not only by the duty, but by the influx of money into England, while the same change in the distribution of the circulating medium would leave her less money to purchase it with."

This however, Mill goes on to say, is only one of three possible cases.

"If after the imposition of the duty, Germany requires so diminished a quantity of cloth, that its total value is exactly the same as before, the balance of trade would be undisturbed; England will gain the duty, Germany will lose it, and nothing more. If, again, the imposition of the duty occasions such a falling off in the demand that Germany requires a less pecuniary value than before, our exports will no longer pay for our imports; money must pass from England into Germany; and Germany's share of the advantage of the trade will be increased. By the change in the distribution of money, cloth will fall in England; and therefore it will, of course, fall in Germany. Thus Germany will not pay the whole of the tax. From the same cause, linen will rise in Germany, and consequently in England. When this alteration of prices has so adjusted the demand, that the cloth and the linen again pay for one another, the result is that Germany has paid only a part of the tax, and the remainder of what has been received into our treasury has come indirectly out of the pockets of our own consumers of linen, who pay a higher price for that imported commodity in consequence of the tax on our exports, while at the same time they, in consequence of the efflux of money and the fall of prices, have smaller money incomes wherewith to pay for the linen at that advanced price.

"It is not an impossible supposition that by taxing our exports we might not only gain nothing from the foreigner, the tax being paid out of our own pockets, but might even compel our own people to pay a second tax to the foreigner. Suppose, as before, that the demand of Germany for cloth falls off so much on the imposition of the duty, that she requires a smaller money value than before, but that the case is so different with linen in England, that when the price rises the demand either does not fall off at all, or so little that the money value required is greater than before. The first effect of laying on the duty is, as before, that the cloth exported will no longer pay for the linen imported. Money will therefore flow out of England into Germany. One effect is to raise the price of linen in Germany, and consequently in England. But this, by the supposition, instead of stopping the efflux of money, only makes it greater, because the higher the price, the greater the money value of the linen consumed. The balance, therefore, can only be restored by the other effect, which is going on at the same time, namely, the fall of cloth in the English and consequently in the German market. Even when cloth has fallen so low that its price with the duty is only equal to what its price without the duty was at first, it is not a necessary consequence that the fall will stop; for the same amount of exportation as before will not now suffice to pay the increased money value of the imports; and although the German consumers have now not only cloth at the old price, but likewise increased money incomes, it is not certain that they will be inclined to employ the increase of their incomes in increasing their purchases of cloth. The price of cloth, therefore, must perhaps fall, to restore the equilibrium, more than the whole amount of the duty; Germany may be enabled to import cloth at a lower price when it is taxed, than when it was untaxed: and this gain she will acquire at the expense of the English consumers of linen, who, in addition, will be the real payers of the whole of what is received at their own custom-house under the name of duties on the export of cloth.

"It is almost unnecessary to remark that cloth and linen are here merely representatives of exports and imports in general; and that the effect which a tax on exports might have in increasing the cost of imports, would affect the imports from all countries, and not peculiarly the articles which might be imported from the particular country to which the taxed exports were sent.

"Such are the extremely various effects which may result to ourselves and to our customers from the imposition of taxes on our exports; and the determining circumstances are of a nature so imperfectly ascertainable, that it must be almost impossible to decide with any certainty, even after the tax has been imposed, whether we have been gainers by it or losers. In general however there could be little doubt that a country which imposed such taxes would succeed in making foreign countries contribute something to its revenue; but unless the taxed article be one for which their demand is extremely urgent, they will seldom pay the whole of the amount which the tax brings in."[4]

Duties on imports, in the modern world at any rate, are of greater quantitative significance than duties on exports. Mill, in the ensuing quoted passage, was disposed to treat them symmetrically with his discussion of duties on exports:

"Thus far of duties on exports. We now proceed to the more ordinary case of duties on imports. We have had an example of a tax on exports, that is on foreigners, falling in part on ourselves. We shall therefore not be surprised if we find a tax on imports, that is, on ourselves, partly falling upon foreigners.

"Instead of taxing the cloth which we export, suppose that we tax the linen which we import. The duty which we are now supposing must not be what is termed a protecting duty, that is, a duty sufficiently high to induce us to produce the article at home. If it had this effect, it would destroy entirely the trade both in cloth and in linen, and both countries would lose the whole of the advantage which they previously gained by exchanging those commodities with one another. We suppose a duty which might diminish the consumption of the article, but which would not prevent us from continuing to import, as before, whatever linen we did consume.

"The equilibrium of trade would be disturbed if the imposition of the tax diminished, in the slightest degree, the quantity of linen consumed. For, as the tax is levied at our own custom-house, the German exporter only receives the same price as formerly, though the English consumer pays a higher one. If, therefore, there be any

---

4 Mill, *Principles, op. cit.*, Book v, Chapter iv, §6.

diminution of the quantity bought, although a larger sum of money may be actually laid out in the article, a smaller one will be due from England to Germany; this sum will no longer be an equivalent for the sum due from Germany to England for cloth, the balance therefore must be paid in money. Prices will fall in Germany and rise in England; linen will fall in the German market; cloth will rise in the English. The Germans will pay a higher price for cloth, and will have smaller incomes to buy it with; while the English will obtain linen cheaper, that is, its price will exceed what it previously was by less than the amount of the duty, while their means of purchasing it will be increased by the increase of their money incomes.

"If the imposition of the tax does not diminish the demand, it will leave the trade exactly as it was before. We shall import as much, and export as much; the whole of the tax will be paid out of our own pockets.

"But the imposition of a tax on a commodity almost always diminishes the demand more or less; and it can never, or scarcely ever, increase the demand. It may, therefore, be laid down as a principle, that a tax on imported commodities, when it really operates as a tax, and not as a prohibition either total or partial, almost always falls, in part upon the foreigners who consume our goods; and that this is a mode in which a nation may appropriate to itself, at the expense of foreigners, a larger share than would otherwise belong to it of the increase in the general productiveness of the labour and capital of the world, which results from the interchange of commodities among nations.

"Those are, therefore, in the right who maintain that taxes on imports are partly paid by foreigners; but they are mistaken when they say, that it is by the foreign producer. It is not on the person from whom we buy, but on all those who buy from us, that a portion of our custom duties spontaneously falls. It is the foreign consumer of our exported commodities, who is obliged to pay a higher price for them because we maintain revenue duties on foreign goods. . . .

"Duties on importation may, then, be divided into two classes: those which have the effect of encouraging some particular branch of domestic industry, and those which have not. The former are purely mischievous, both to the country imposing them, and to those with whom it trades. They prevent a saving of labour and capital, which, if permitted to be made, would be divided in some proportion or other between the importing country and the countries which buy what that country does or might export."[4]

The doctrines here expounded have, in general, been accepted by neo-classical writers, though Mill's distinction between the possible "virtue," in this respect, of revenue and protective import duties has not been widely accepted.[5] Protective duties, it is true, normally

[5] The effects of duties on the "terms of trade" have been discussed all but *ad nauseam* but, even so, without definitive result. In an article on "The Burden of Import Duties" (*The American Economic Review*, Vol. xxxvi, No. 5, pp. 788 *et seq.*), Earl R. Rolph, using the classical concepts, denies the validity of classical and neo-classical doctrines. Rolph says:

"Mill developed his conclusions concerning the burden and effects of import duties with the concept of reciprocal demand. This technique of analysis was taken over, improved, and made more definite by the neo-classical school, including Edgeworth, Marshall, and Pigou. These outstanding thinkers in the field greatly refined the reciprocal demand technique without, however, reaching conclusions concerning the burden of import duties differing substantially from those laid down by Mill. Edgeworth . . . examines the implications of the concept of reciprocal demand . . . [and places] himself on the side of Mill in opposition to the critics who claim import duties are borne by consumers of taxed imports.

"Marshall likewise endorses the Mill view of the incidence of import duties. . . . Pigou differs only slightly from Marshall . . . [and] comes out unequivocally for the position that import duties . . . 'will . . . always exact *some* contribution from foreigners. . . .'

"Not only is it argued that import duties fall in part upon foreign consumers, but the burden of import duties is shown to be symmetrical with export duties, if it is assumed that the tax is levied in export goods, or if levied in money, the 'proceeds' are spent upon export goods. [A. P. Lerner in his article 'The Symmetry between Export and Import Taxes' (*Economica*, N. S. 3, pp. 306-313) refutes Edgeworth's doubts to the contrary and also develops a formal technique for showing the burden of import and export taxes, however the taxing government 'spends the tax receipts.' The symmetry argument is also presented by Marshall . . . and by Pigou.]

"Yet with all due respect to the brilliance of Mill's arguments and the careful analytical support they have received at the hands of Edgeworth, Marshall, Pigou, and others, one may properly doubt the conclusion that foreign consumers . . . bear part of the burden of . . . import taxes. . . ."

In place of the neo-classical view Rolph goes on to assert, first, "that the burden of import duties *always* rests upon a certain economic segment of the country levying the import duties and *not upon foreigners*, and second that this segment is *not* the consumers of taxed imports. It is, on the contrary, those who own resources, both human and non-human, in the export industries and those who own resources competitive with resources located in export industries. . . . This position differs . . . not only from the neo-classical view of the burden of import duties, but also from the theory developed with the use of partial equilibrium technique . . . that domestic consumers of the country imposing import duties bear such taxes. [Such is the argument of Professor Lionel Robbins and Mr. G. L. Schwartz . . . in . . . William H. Beveridge and others, *Tariffs: The Case Examined*, . . . p. 173.]" (The passages in square brackets appear, in the original article, as notes.)

In comment on this article, James N. Morgan in *The American Economic Review*, Vol. xxxvii, pp. 407-409, avers that, while Rolph is saying something valid, he is not really controverting the classicists. Whether the latter assertion is, or is not, true is of no great consequence since all the arguments (those of the classicists and Rolph's as well) proceed on faulty premisses.

involve a loss, in the uneconomic use of resources, which is not present in the case of revenue duties, but this loss might be more than compensated to the levying country, by a shift in the "terms of trade," which, at least as much as revenue duties, the protective duties would tend to promote.[6]

All this classical and neo-classical reasoning, however, whether on the effects of export or import duties (revenue or protective), improvements in production, or any other influence on demand or supply, runs in terms of reciprocal national demands for unchanged composites of goods and is tainted with the basic defect of excluding the possibility of adjustments of supply through a shift, by producers on the margin of indifference, from one to some other product. To show how far astray this reasoning goes it will suffice, perhaps, to take up, at some length, the case of protective import duties. The effects (if any), on the "terms of trade," of the imposition of such duties will not differ, in essence, from those of many other like "disturbances" of an existing situation.

Real Effects of Protective Import Duties

We may well start with the admission that the imposition of protective import duties in any country increases the world supply of the protected commodity, at least temporarily, and since, in the posited premises, resources must be diverted from other lines to permit of the production of the protected article in the levying country, reduces the world supply of other articles. The protected article has, by definition, hitherto been an import of the country imposing the duty while the commodities from which resources are withdrawn are very probably, if not inevitably, on its current export list. Any shift in the ratio of exchange which may then occur is likely therefore (if not certain) to favor the levying country through an increase in the value of its exports (the world supply of which is reduced) relative to its imports (the world supply of which is augmented). It may, indeed, favor it to such an extent as to more than offset, for that country, the loss from what is, on a cosmopolitan view, an uneconomic use of resources. The levying country

---

[6] cf. Frank D. Graham, "The Theory of International Values Re-examined," *The Quarterly Journal of Economics*, Vol. xxxviii, p. 65n., where it is shown that the case in point, if valid at all, is *stronger* for protective than for revenue duties.

will then get a so much larger share of a reduced world output as to give it a net access of income at the expense of other nations.[7]

Any single tariff, however, even when specifically intended to influence the "terms of trade," will, under constant cost conditions in the various countries, ordinarily have no effect at all on the international ratio of exchange of commodities. If, for instance, we refer again to our initial set of cost conditions (p. 91), and distribution of demand in ten countries, and assume that, all other things being the same, a prohibitive tariff is levied by country H on the import of x, the ratio of exchange $z = 24y = 20x = 24w = 64v = 40u = 12t = 60s = 48r = 72q$ will remain unchanged for all *internationally traded* products.[8] With 1/10 of income devoted to each product, country H will now have its consumption of x reduced from 450 to 360 units (the amount of x that it can produce with 1/10 of its productive power) and will cut its output of r by 1080 units (from 2984 to 1904 units) to permit of the production of these 360 units of x.[9] Country I will then expand its output of r by 1080 units (from 4224 to 5304 units) to make up for the reduction in H's supply of that commodity, and will correspondingly cut its output of s by 1350 units (from 7900 to 6550 units).[10] Country G supplies the consequent deficiency of 1350 units of s by raising its output of that commodity, from 1110 to 2460 units, at the expense of its production of z (which falls, in consequence, from $101\frac{1}{2}$ to 79 units). Country J, in turn, supplies the ensuing deficiency of $22\frac{1}{2}$ units of z by raising its output of z from $48\frac{2}{3}$ to $71\frac{1}{6}$ units. To secure

[7] The classical economists in reaching, on their own premises, this same conclusion were somewhat discomfited since, from the nationalist point of view at least, it rendered rebuttable the presumption in favor of their cherished freedom of trade. They could have avoided the dilemma by a strict adherence to a cosmopolitan attitude since there is no difficulty in showing that there is no gain in *world* income arising from the tariff. But they preferred to take a nationalist attitude and, with their predilection for free trade, this led them to disparage the practical importance of the theoretical possibility of increasing the levying country's income at the expense of the rest of the world. Inconsistently with their cosmopolitan philosophy, but consistently with their national loyalty, they had no objection to increasing the national income at the expense of other nations but some of them were disposed to deny that it was more than *theoretically* possible to accomplish this end. Marshall was strongly of this opinion. In this he was largely right, but for wrong reasons.

[8] The ratio of exchange of x against all other products will, of course, be altered in H, which is now producing its own supply of x at relatively high cost, but no other price, or consumption, change will anywhere take place.

[9] The cost ratio of x and r in H is as 1 : 3 (18 : 54) so that the production of 360 units of x in H cost the output of 1080 units of r.

[10] The expansion of I's output of r by 1080 units requires the contraction of its output of s by 1350 units since the cost ratio of r and s in I is as 4 : 5 (64 : 80).

this supply of 22½ units of z, country J cuts its production of x by 450 units which is at once the equivalent of 22½ units of z and of the x which it had sold to H before country H inaugurated the protection of that commodity. All other production, and all consumption, except H's consumption of its protected commodity, x, remains *in statu quo ante* as equilibrium is thus achieved.

Let us suppose now that protection becomes fashionable and that, in addition to H's protection of x, country I puts up prohibitive barriers against the import of q, and that country J takes similar action against the import of u. The ratio of international exchange is still unaffected. The figures on consumption and production are given in Tables F_c and F_p. So far as production goes, country J substitutes the output of u for the q which country I had formerly imported from it, country I reduces its output of r to produce its own consumption of q, while country H steps into the breach with an increase in its output of r in compensation for the loss of a market for an equivalent part of its u in country J.

The international extension of protection increases, rather than reduces, the probability that the ratio of exchange of those products that continue to be internationally traded will remain unaltered because the imports of one country are the exports of others, and *vice versa*, so that, in a general extension of protection, the increase in the world supply of a formerly imported commodity, and the concomitant reduction in the world supply of the exported commodities of any country levying protective duties, is likely to be compensated by opposite movements of supply in other countries taking contemporaneous protective action.

A world-wide trend toward an increase in the production of a certain type of output, and a concomitant decrease in another type, might, of course, be initiated by a *group* of protectionist countries currently producing similar products, and, when this occurs, a movement in the ratio of exchange, involving these commodities as groups, would not improbably take place.

Even widespread indulgence in a given type of protection is nevertheless not likely to affect the ratio unless the countries levying protection are large and in a strategic position. The protection of any commodity or commodities by countries A, B, C, D, E, or F, would, for instance, be deprived of effect on the ratio through adjust-

TABLE F$_c$

Ratio of exchange: $z = 24y = 20x = 24w = 64v = 40u = 12t = 60s = 48r = 72q$

Each country devotes 1/10 of its income to the acquisition of each of the products. H protects x; I protects q; and J protects u.

(Compare with Table A$_{1c}$, p. 96)

CONSUMPTION

	z	y	x	w	v	u	t	s	r	q
A	$1\frac{1}{4}$	30	25	30	80	50	15	75	60	90
B	$2\frac{2}{3}$	64	$53\frac{1}{3}$	64	$170\frac{2}{3}$	$106\frac{2}{3}$	32	160	128	192
C	$3\frac{3}{4}$	90	75	90	240	150	45	225	180	270
D	6	144	120	144	384	240	72	360	288	432
E	10	240	200	240	640	400	120	600	480	720
F	12	288	240	288	768	480	144	720	576	864
G	12	288	240	288	768	480	144	720	576	864
H	$22\frac{1}{2}$	540	360	540	1440	900	270	1350	1080	1620
I	40	960	800	960	2560	1600	480	2400	1920	1560
J	40	960	800	960	2560	1520	480	2400	1920	2880
Totals	$150\frac{1}{6}$	3604	$2913\frac{1}{3}$	3604	$9610\frac{2}{3}$	$5926\frac{2}{3}$	1802	9010	7208	9492

TABLE F$_p$

Ratio of exchange: $z = 24y = 20x = 24w = 64v = 40u = 12t = 60s = 48r = 72q$

H protects x; I protects q; and J protects u

(Compare with Table A$_{1P}$ p. 97)

PRODUCTION

	z	y	x	w	v	u	t	s	r	q
A	—	—	—	—	800	—	—	—	—	—
B	—	—	—	—	—	—	—	—	—	1920
C	—	—	—	—	—	1500	—	—	—	—
D	—	—	—	—	3840	—	—	—	—	—
E	—	—	—	2400	—	—	—	—	—	—
F	—	2880	—	—	—	—	—	—	—	—
G	79	—	—	—	—	—	—	2460	—	—
H	—	—	360	1204	—	$2906\frac{2}{3}$	—	—	3824	—
I	—	724	—	—	—	—	1802	6550	3384	1560
J	$71\frac{1}{6}$	—	$2553\frac{1}{3}$	—	$4970\frac{2}{3}$	1520	—	—	—	6012
Totals	$150\frac{1}{6}$	3604	$2913\frac{1}{3}$	3604	$9610\frac{2}{3}$	$5926\frac{2}{3}$	1802	9010	7208	9492

J produces z, x, v, u, q.
I produces y, t, s, r, q.
H produces x, w, u, r.
G produces z, s.
F produces y.

E produces w.
D produces v.
C produces u.
B produces q.
A produces v.

ments in supply in G, H, I, or J which, between them, are substantial producers of all of the goods in the trading system.

A comparatively small country producing all, or nearly all, of the world supply of any given commodity may, on the other hand, be very vulnerable to protectionist action by other countries though it does not follow that its vulnerability can be made to redound to the advantage of the country which imposes an import duty on the small country's specialty. If, for instance, in the initial status of demand, country I should decide to levy even a minimal duty on the import of commodity y (which it already produces in an amount less than its own consumption), country F would be unable to find a market, at the existing exchange ratio, for its output of y. This would hurt F but be of no use to I. Since there is no other product to which producers in F can profitably turn until the value of y falls very far indeed, a limbo ratio will develop in which y will be "wild" as against all other commodities. The classical analysis will then apply to y, and the elasticity of world demand for y will determine the degree of its fall in value. If the elasticity of *total* (not merely foreign) demand for y is great, the fall in value will be small; if it is small, the fall in value will be great.[11] If we assume that elasticity of demand for y is unity, so that each country spends, as before, 1/10 of its income on each of the products,[12] the new ratio of exchange will be: $z = 26.4y$[13] $= 20x = 24w = 64v = 40u = 12t = 60s = 48r = 72q$.

The result of I's protection of y is therefore to reduce the inter-

[11] Since I's production of y will be stimulated by only 236 units which is the difference between its former production and its former, and present, consumption of y (consumption will be unchanged because no alteration in I's incomes or prices will occur) it might pay F to subsidize its own consumption of y to prevent an overloading of the foreign market.

[12] The additional assumption will be made that the elasticity of demand of consumers of other products, in F, is unity.

[13] Approximate. The exact ratio of y to the other products would be determined readily enough, in practice, by the process of higgling, but, as a limbo ratio, it is difficult to compute with precision. The change in the international value of y increases the consumption of y in all countries except F and I, the producers. The consumption of all other products is reduced in F and nowhere else. The total of consumption must, of course, be equal to total productivity. When I produces y it must cut down on t, s, or r, or two, or all three of them. The production of other countries is not greatly affected since H can readily shift from w or u to r, G from z to s, and J from x, v, or q to z. To devise a formula, however, to cover these concurrent kaleidoscopic changes in their effect on the ratio has proved to be beyond my capacity and it was necessary to proceed by trial and error, with the use of converging limits, to a close approximation to the equilibrium ratio. To get the *exact* figure would involve computations in intolerably complex fractions.

national value of that commodity by approximately 10%, in terms of all other goods. Rates of duty at, or above, that level would now be necessary in I to exclude competition from F even though enterprisers in I were originally able to compete freely with those in F and there has been no change anywhere in the cost structure. Protection is often thus self-vindicating (to those who favor it) and, conversely, the abandonment of protection of any given commodity might remove the apparent "need" for it in the country in which it had hitherto been employed.

Country I's protection of y has injured F but it has done I, itself, neither good nor harm.[14] All countries other than F and I, however, are benefited by the protective duty levied by I, since they obtain y on better terms, and all other commodities on the same terms as before.

In this case the conclusions of the classical theorists on the effects of protection are almost completely reversed. The "terms of trade" are not improved for the levying country but shift to the advantage of all but one of the other countries. The failure of the levying country to obtain any advantage in its "terms of trade" is nevertheless not attended by the more or less fully, or excessively, compensating loss which, in classical theory, it was assumed that the protectionist country would suffer (through what, from a cosmopolitan point of view, is an uneconomic use of resources) as an offset to any gain arising from a presumptively favorable shift in the ratio of exchange.

Country I is similarly impotent to gain from any other single protective duty which it might levy against the specialties of H, J, or any of the smaller countries. If, for instance, country I should impose prohibitive duties on the import of w or u, producers of those commodities in H would shift to their alternative r, and thus enhance the competition with I's own producers of that commodity. It would be from the output of r in I that resources would therefore be drawn to produce the protected commodity. Country H would then produce still less w or u, but more r, *pari passu* with I's contraction of the supply of that commodity in I's effort to provide at home for its own consumption of w or u. The ratio of international

---

[14] Country I obtains all commodities, including the protected commodity y, on the original terms: its real income is not affected. This is because it was at no original comparative disadvantage in y, even though it was importing part of its consumption of that commodity.

exchange would then be unaffected and, since the production and consumption in all the countries not above mentioned would be untouched, the protection would injure none but the levying country which would now obtain less w or u than it could have had with trade free.

If, furthermore, country I should decide to protect the output of any specialty of J, that is, z, x, v, or q, the net result would, in every case, be merely a shift of production in G, from z to G's alternative product s, to compensate a corresponding reduction in the supply of s in I to provide resources there for the production of the protected commodity.[15] The international ratio of exchange, and production and consumption in all countries other than those above mentioned, would be untouched. Country I would again, therefore, be the *sole* loser from its protective duties in the reduced supply of the protected commodity which it would now obtain at increased unit cost as compared with what it could have had with trade free.

Countries H and G are in no better position than I to affect the ratio of exchange by any protective duties they might levy, and the smaller countries are, as already noted, also impotent in the matter.

The economic weight of country J, in the status of demand we have been assuming, is no greater than that of I but its strategic position for the manipulation of the ratio of exchange in its own favor is much superior to that of I. This superiority arises from the accidental fact that, in the status of demand initially assumed, G is not only a merely medium-size country (whose production traverses that of I and J) but its productive resources are much more fully devoted to J's commodity z than to I's commodity s. Country G can therefore, as we have noted, shift heavily from z to s when occasion demands; but it cannot move far in the contrary direction before it runs out of transferable resources. If, therefore, J should prohibitively protect s, any of the other products of I (y, t, and r), or even w and u (which in H are linked with r and therefore, through I, with y, t and s), the possibilities of adjustment through G would be inadequate to compensate for the elimination of J's import demand for the protected product. The ratio of exchange would then move in J's favor. Any such result will always depend on the possibility of

[15] If z were the protected commodity, production in J would be wholly unaffected. If I's protection were applied to x, v, or q (or any combination of them) the production of the affected commodity (or commodities) in J would be reduced and that of z increased. In all of these cases producers of z in G would shift to s.

somewhere shifting the national locus of the margin of indifference in output.

Suppose, for example, that J imposes a prohibitive duty on the import of u. Producers in H will seek to adjust for the decline in the demand for their output of that commodity by moving into H's remaining specialties w and r. As H expands the output of r, producers of r in I will transfer resources to y, t and s and, as the pressure falls on s, producers of s in G will go more heavily into z. There will be ample room, at the existing ratio of exchange, for more z from G in consequence of the transfer of resources from z to u in J. There will, in fact, be more room than G can fill even by the complete abandonment of s. The value of z will accordingly rise. As z rises in value, however, producers in J will favor the output of that commodity at the expense of x, v, and q until these also show a rise in value equal to that of z. The (approximate) ratio of exchange which will produce equilibrium, on the assumption of 1/10 of the income of each country to each product, is: $z = 25.55y = 20x = 25.55w = 64v = 42.58u = 12.775t = 63.875s = 51.1r = 72q$ as compared with the initial ratio: $z = 24y = 20x = 24w = 64v = 40u = 12t = 60s = 48r = 72q$. Country J thus obtains, in exchange for its exports, approximately $6\frac{1}{2}\%$ more of y, w, t, s, and r than had formerly been the case, and since, under the initial ratio of exchange, it was not far below the line of comparative advantage in the production of u, it secures, at a given cost, 95% as much of that now protected product as in the former situation. The consumption of z, x, v, and q, in J, is unchanged so that, on balance, the protection of u has been of distinct advantage to its citizens. Countries G, D, B and A share all the benefits that accrue to J, without any of the extra cost which J incurs in the acquisition of u, or, with the exception of G, without the necessity of transferring any resources from one commodity to another. Countries F, E and C, on the other hand, sustain losses proportionately equal to those of I and H since they share with those countries the production of commodities of relatively reduced value.

Whether a country, by protective duties, can or cannot alter the ratio of exchange to its advantage and, if so, whether it can alter it sufficiently to offset, or more than offset, the (usual) direct loss from the protection, is thus dependent not only upon its size but upon the fortuitous circumstance of a currently strategic, or non-strategic, position. In the world as it is, with many countries producing commodities in common, and with most or all commodities *somewhere* on the margin of producers' indifference as regards various other commodities, the chance of shifting the normal international ratio of exchange through the imposition of protective duties is always small. Any country desirous of playing this game effectively would be obliged to assess its international position with great care and, if it should discover favorable possibilities, must exploit them by imposing duties specifically devised to hit highly vulnerable spots in the world's system of production. No such duties have ever been levied except by accident.

The chance in any country of securing a net gain by additional protective duties diminishes rapidly with every extension of its own protective system. This is true because the area in which, regardless of a favorable shift in the international ratio of exchange, no gain is possible, and loss is all but certain (the protected area), becomes a progressively larger part of the whole. But there is the further fact that any anterior shifts in the ratio of exchange in favor of the levying country will have brought about a transfer of resources in other countries, from the production of what were formerly, and remain, the imports of the levying country, to the production of the goods it exports. If, then, the protectionist country cuts down still further on its imports it will be faced with an expansion in foreign countries of the output of its own *ex*ports. This will preclude any improvement in the relative value of those commodities.

Limits of the Change in the Ratio

The limits on the movement in the international ratio of exchange consequent upon protective import duties levied by any country will be apparent if we assume complete self-sufficiency on the part of some country with possibilities in that line. If country J should thus withdraw from the world economic system the international ratio of exchange (between the remaining countries), on the assumption of 1/10 of income spent for each commodity, would be approximately: $z = 28.6y = 18x = 27w = 63v = 45u = 14.05t = 70.25s = 56.2r = 45.6625q$ with I producing t, s, r, and q; H producing z, x, w, and u; G producing z and v; and F, E, D, C, B, and A specializing, respectively, in y, w, v, u, q, and q. (See Table G_c for figures on consumption.)

TABLE G$_c$

Ratio of exchange: $z = 28.6y = 18x = 27w = 68v = 45u = 14.05t = 70.25s = 56.2r = 45.6625q$

CONSUMPTION (approximate)

(Thousands, or any other multiple, of the figures below)

1/10 of the income of each country to each of the products

	z	y	x	w	v	u	t	s	r	q
A	1.95	55.77	35.10	52.65	122.85	87.75	26.77	133.85	107.08	87.00
B	4.20	120.12	75.60	113.40	264.60	189.00	59.01	295.05	236.04	192.00
C	3.33	95.33	60.00	90.00	210.00	150.00	46.83	234.15	187.32	152.20
D	6.10	174.46	109.80	164.70	384.00	274.50	85.70	428.53	342.82	278.54
E	8.89	254.22	160.00	240.00	560.00	400.00	124.90	624.50	499.60	405.92
F	10.07	288.00	181.26	271.89	634.41	453.15	141.48	707.40	565.92	459.81
G	12.00	343.20	216.00	324.00	756.00	540.00	168.60	843.00	674.40	547.95
H	20.00	572.00	360.00	540.00	1260.00	900.00	281.00	1405.00	1124.00	913.25
I	34.16	976.98	614.88	922.32	2152.08	1537.20	480.00	2400.00	1920.00	1560.00
Totals	100.70	2880.08	1812.64	2718.96	6343.94	4531.60	1414.29	7071.48	5657.18	4596.67

Country J has withdrawn from international trade and produces all commodities at home.

Country I produces t, s, r, q; H produces z, x, w, u; G produces z, v; F produces y; E produces w; D produces v; C produces u; B produces q; A produces q.

The ratio of exchange between y and all other commodities, and between t, s, r and q, together, and z, x, w, u and v, together, is unstable with changes in demand since the number of trading countries has been reduced below the minimum necessary to a complete interlocking of commodity production.

As compared with the initial ratio $z = 24y = 20x = 24w = 64v = 40u = 12t = 60s = 48r = 72q$, and the initial consumption when J was trading internationally (cf. Table A_{1c}, p. 96), it is apparent that all of I's imports except y (of which it has abandoned production) now cost it more, in terms of I's exports, than they formerly did; and that q (which it now produces) would also cost I more. Country H, on the other hand, obtains not only y but also t, s and r more cheaply than before (in terms of H's continuing specialties w and u) though z and x (which it now produces) and v and q (which it continues to import) cost H more than they formerly did. Country G is impelled to drop the production of s in favor of v but nevertheless gains on the whole, with increases in the consumption of y, w, u, t, s and r, no change in z, a small drop in v, and a sizable drop in q. Countries A and B are much better off, all round, than they had formerly been and B even surpasses C in total income. Country D gains on all of its imports except x and q. Countries C and E show a sprinkling of gains and losses, with a balance toward loss, and F loses all round. It is apparent that the conclusions of classical theory on the international repercussions of protection in any country are, to say the least, naïve.

All of these tendencies would be more or less inherent, though not necessarily realized, in anything short of a complete withdrawal from international trade on the part of J. But it is probable that no country could be hurt more by a partial than by a complete withdrawal of J, that is, by a partial rather than complete protective system in that country. The citizens of J can, of course, get no gain from an international trade in which they do not participate and, when J is completely self-sufficient, the ratio of exchange of products will be, for them, the cost ratio in J, viz., $z = 21y = 20x = 17w = 64v = 38u = 3t = 34s = 26r = 72q$, with a necessary drop in total consumption. Short of complete national self-sufficiency, J's citizens will however, with the extension of protection in J, be making increasing gains *on such international trade as they continue to carry on*. At a fairly early stage in the extension of protection these gains in the more favorable ratio of exchange would nevertheless be more than offset by the heavy (opportunity) cost of the home production of the commodities in which J, on the basis of the evolving international ratio of exchange, is least efficient. Country J's net income would then begin a progressive decline which would be accelerated with every expansion in the coverage of its protective schedule.

That there can be no indefinite general tendency of protection to improve the position of the levying country is shown by the fact that self-sufficiency in any country might, on the one hand, result from self-imposed prohibitive duties laid on all imports or, on the other, from prohibitive import duties levied by other countries on all of the exportable products of the country in question. If the situation could be supposed to change, indefinitely, in favor of the countries imposing protection, that is to say, in our illustrations, in favor of J in the one case, and adverse to J in the other, we would reach the absurd result of a given ratio of exchange (that prevailing when the given country had cut off, or been eliminated from, international trade) evolving, from a given initial status, out of continuous, and diametrically opposed, movements in price relationships!

The fact is that the progressive segregation of a country from the rest of the world, however it may be achieved, disrupts any integration of prices and sets up two more or less completely divorced price structures (segregated ratios of exchange) with price relationships moving in opposite directions in the two areas. From the point of view of either area, prices *in the other* are moving in favor of the viewer and his country. (The relative desirability of what, under international trade, would be the exports of any given area will, in that area, fall as national self-sufficiency comes to pass, and the relative desirability of what, under international trade, would be imports, will rise.) But the "gain" is progressively illusory since the movement in prices occurs only insofar as trade is restricted, and the restriction of trade prevents either area from taking advantage of the price situation in the other.

Formal, but not Real, Changes in the Ratio

When any country producing and importing a wide range of commodities restricts international trade by protective import duties it is likely to select for protection those commodities in which its current comparative disadvantage is small. The consequent restriction of its *ex*ports is certain, moreover, to be concentrated in lines where the country is most vulnerable, that is to say where, at the existing or a very slightly changed ratio of exchange, other countries can most easily compete. The result is to remove from the

181

international field the sector of the country's trade in which the difference between the domestic cost structure and the hitherto prevailing international ratio of exchange is at a minimum. The change leaves intact, on the other hand, the sector in which that difference is at a maximum. The *rate* of gain on such international trade as the country continues to carry on always, therefore, tends to rise with an extension of the scope of its protective import duties. This is true even when there is no change in the international ratio of exchange. In spite of this rise in the *rate* of gain, the net absolute gain of the country will normally fall, though it must be conceded that such a fall might be prevented (and even, in certain circumstances of restricted application, turned into a rise) through a favorable movement in the international ratio of exchange, the absence of any *great* exclusion of imports, and the concentration of the protection in lines in which the country is at but a slight comparative disadvantage.

It is fallacious to take the current international price relationships of a fixed list of putative exports and imports of any given protection-levying country as a criterion of its gain, or loss, from protection, since neither the list nor, perhaps, the prices would be the same if the country should enter freely into international trade.

Conclusion on the Effects of Protection

We may summarize as follows. The "terms of trade" of any country at any given moment depend upon the degree of correspondence between the cost ratio schedule, for the various products, in the country in question and the current international ratio of exchange. This, as we have seen, is an almost completely fortuitous matter, though any large country, which must of necessity produce a variety of products, is certain to show an identity (allowance being made for costs of transfer of commodities) in a sector of its cost ratio with the same sector of the international exchange ratio. The possibility, by national protective action, of effecting an alteration in the international ratio of exchange is almost never present to any but some such large country which happens to hold a strategic position. If such a change can be effected it will, at least formally, always be favorable to the protecting country, though any gain it may thus obtain will ordinarily be more or less fully compensated in the higher cost, to it, of the protected commodities. This increase in cost will always tend to override any conceivable gain in the terms of trade as the levying country extends the scope of its protective impositions and thus narrows its trade. Other countries will gain or lose, net, by any such induced change in the ratio of exchange, according to the similarity, or dissimilarity, of their exports and imports with those of the levying country. Some of them may gain when the protecting country suffers a net loss, or they may gain more than the protecting country gains when the net result, to the protecting country, is favorable.

The more closely the cost ratios in any country parallel the current international exchange ratio the less does it gain from international trade and the smaller is the possibility, through protection, of altering the "terms of trade" much in its favor since full self-sufficiency would merely set up an (internal) ratio of exchange not very different from that currently prevailing under international trade. The greater, on the other hand, the divergence between the cost ratios in any country and the current international exchange ratio, the more favorable, to it, are the current "terms of trade." But they are then approaching their limit and the less is the probability, therefore, of making a further improvement through protection. (Marked divergence in the ratios will, moreover, be present only in the case of small countries which can concentrate on a single commodity of high comparative advantage and such countries can ordinarily not affect the ratio by any action within their competence.) The best chance of markedly successful manipulation of the international ratio of exchange lies, in consequence, with large countries in the middle range of divergence of domestic costs from that ratio. Such countries may exploit to their own advantage any fortuitous situation rendering the ratio vulnerable to action specifically devised for the purpose.

Any country, large or small, with a territorial monopoly of a certain product, may, of course, be able to raise the relative value of that product through restriction of its supply. The total value of the export of the reduced supply may readily surpass that of the formerly greater export. The disposition of the withdrawn resources then, however, comes into question. If these resources are put into other exports the result may be a fall in their value which will more than compensate the (national) gain from the enhanced price of the monopolized product. It could thus happen that the best national business result for any country in this position would issue from the failure to make any use of the resources withdrawn from the production of the monopolized commodity or any use, at least, which would in any way tend to promote the output of other exportable goods.

So far as the classical economists took a nationalist position—as, in spite of their cosmopolite professions, they almost invariably did —their case for freedom of trade is (as they, themselves, were disposed reluctantly to admit) thus not *always* tenable. It is scarcely open to doubt, of course, that most, if not all, countries would be much better off with trade free than with trade restricted, and there is no great opportunity open to *any* country, even in an otherwise freely trading world, to increase its income by protection. The opportunity is, in fact, not nearly as good as the classicists supposed. The path of virtue is, on a short view however, not *invariably* profitable. Nations, nevertheless, would do well to remember that, with respect to commerce that could be lastingly recurrent, there is little wisdom in acting as if they were casual horse-traders who need never count on any further business with their current victims. Horse-trading is not easily monopolized.

Effect, on the Ratio, of International Loans or Tribute

Manipulation of the ratio of exchange might be attempted not only by way of tariffs but also through international transfers of capital as loans or tribute, though these, in distinction from protective tariffs, do not necessarily anywhere affect costs. The effects, if any, of capital movements on the "terms of trade" would, of course, be the same whether such effects were, or were not, consciously sought. The postulates of classical theory assume an at least inhibited transfer of the factors of production including capital, from country to country, but the *case* for freedom of international movement of capital resources would, *prima facie*, seem to be on all fours with that for freedom of trade.[16] This *prima facie* view is, in general, valid, and the classicists, in treating innovations in international capital movements (loans or tribute) in the same terms as those employed to assess any other disturbance of an existing inter-

---

[16] This is, however, not true of international freedom of movement of labor resources (workers). cf. Frank D. Graham, *Protective Tariffs*, Princeton University Press, Princeton, N.J., p. 52n.

national trading situation, were doubtless as right, or wrong, in the one case as in the others. We shall see that international capital movements, like tariffs, have no general tendency to alter the "terms of trade" and that, if they do affect them, there is no presumption that the movement will take the direction posited by the classicists.

Viner denies that, on some important points in the general treatment of transfers of loans or of tribute, there is any one doctrine which can properly be labeled *the* classical doctrine but he nevertheless asserts that the theory of the (pecuniary) mechanism, as developed from Hume to J. S. Mill, is still the predominant theory to which no convincing alternative has been suggested.[17] The pecuniary mechanism of international trade moreover is, in spite of the well-justified classical assertion of the essential irrelevance, or even obstreperousness, of money in the general theory, vital to their explanation of adjustments to disturbances of equilibrium in international transactions.[18] We shall, therefore, have to deal with the matter in monetary terms.

Hume is the undoubted originator of what is ordinarily regarded as the classical doctrine on the mechanism of adjustment. This is, in essence, that a disturbance of equilibrium in the international accounts will result in a movement of (metallic) money from any country with a current debit balance in the international accounts to countries with a current credit balance, or will impel a fall in the exchange value of the debtor country's currency against those of creditor countries, or will do both.[19] Any one of these results, it is alleged, or any combination of them, will, in the debtor country, operate to lower the general price level (expressed in any given *numeraire*) in relation to that in creditor countries (expressed in the same *numeraire*), will thus promote the exports and retard the imports of the debtor country (with opposite effects in the creditor

[17] *Studies, op. cit.*, p. 291. Viner also says (*ibid.*, p. 319) that "from Hume on, there was general agreement that some or all types of disturbances in international balances would result in changes in the terms of trade."

[18] Bastable, for instance, following the classicists, implies that, unless there is a counter force compensating any disruption of a previously existing equilibrium, a new equilibrium could be established *only* by an alteration of (national) prices produced by the passage of money or by a change in the ratio of exchange of the currencies in question. (*Theory of International Trade, op. cit.*, p. 78.) Viner supports this contention.

[19] It should be noted that a lending country is, so far as the loan is concerned, a current debtor in the international accounts in that it has, *in the present*, payments to make to the borrower.

countries), and will, in consequence, restore balance in the international accounts *on altered terms of trade.*

Viner cites several passages in which various nineteenth-century writers indicated that they conceived that this doctrine was not fully adequate to the case of a disruption of equilibrium by way of international loans or tribute. These writers asserted that relative shifts in the amounts of (national) means of payment or incomes (the consequence of the international loans or tribute) would exercise, quite independently of any changes in the relationship between national price levels, an equilibrating role in the mechanism of adjustment of international balances.

There were, however, "important divergences of doctrine between these writers. It was common doctrine for all of them that a change in relative money incomes resulting, say, from loans would contribute to the adjustment of the balance of payments to the loans through its influence on the relative demands of the two countries for each other's commodities. But one group (i.e. Ricardo, Longfield, J. S. Mill, Cairnes) either explained this shift in relative incomes as resulting from a prior transfer of money or conceded that a transfer of money would result from it, whereas another group (Wheatley, Bastable, and Nicholson, and, at one point, Cairnes) denied that any transfer of money need take place. One group (Longfield, Joplin, Cairnes, J. S. Mill) left an important place in the mechanism for relative price changes, whereas another group (Wheatley, Ricardo, Bastable, Nicholson) denied, or questioned, the necessity of relative price changes for the restoration of equilibrium.

"In the later literature there continue to be presented explanations of the mechanism of adjustment which do and others which do not assign an equilibrating role to the relative shift in demands, and some writers who at one time take pains to point out its significance at other times permit it to drop out of their exposition and revert to an explanation in terms solely of relative price changes. Mainly owing to Ohlin, however, there has been a growing awareness of the issue. . . ."[20]

The issue to be discussed in this section is not primarily whether, or when, there will be an international movement of money, or of exchange rates, but whether, following an innovation in international

[20] Viner, *Studies, op. cit.*, p. 303.

transfers, equilibrium will be disrupted and can be restored only after an alteration in the "terms of trade" in favor of the recipient country.

Ohlin's original contribution to the topic was made in an article which led to a discussion with Keynes on the probable effects of the transfer of German reparations, after World War I, from Germany to the recipient countries.[21] The source of Ohlin's views was doubtless a paper by Taussig, written in 1917,[22] and Wicksell's reply to it.[23] Taussig's article had broken new ground in the theory of adjustment to disturbance under an inconvertible paper currency, but Taussig rigidly (and, in my view, wrongly) adhered to what he conceived to be orthodoxy in his attitude toward adjustments under metallic currency conditions. Wicksell asserted (I believe rightly) that Taussig's theory applied to metallic as well as to inconvertible paper monetary conditions and Ohlin, in his later articles, not only supported but developed Wicksell's view.[24] The burden of their argument is that adjustment is reached through a shift in the relationship between the prices of *domestic* and internationally traded commodities in general rather than in the relationship between the prices of the exports and imports of the paying and recipient countries.

I could not but welcome what seemed to me a clear refutation by Ohlin of the rather surprisingly orthodox position of Keynes, the more so because three years earlier, in treating the same question, I had myself put in print, as follows, the essence of Ohlin's argument:

"The motivating force . . . will be the transfer of exchange to the creditor countries. This exchange will be sold to merchants importing from Germany. The purchasing power thus transferred, being derived in the first instance from the taxation of German citizens, will reduce their demand for all the commodities normally consumed in Germany, and being presented to the Allied and Associated governments will enable those governments to lift part of the present tax burden from their citizens and thus give those citizens additional

21 *Index*, Svenska Handelsbanken, Stockholm, April, 1928.
22 F. W. Taussig, "International Trade Under Depreciated Paper," *The Quarterly Journal of Economics*, Vol. xxxi, 1917, pp. 380-403.
23 Knut Wicksell, "International Freights and Prices," *The Quarterly Journal of Economics*, Vol. xxxii, 1918, pp. 404-410.
24 cf. *Index*, April, 1928, pp. 2-33; *Economic Journal*, Vol. xxxix, pp. 172-178 and 400-404. cf. also Bertil Ohlin, *Interregional and International Trade*, Harvard University Press, Cambridge, (Mass.), 1933, *passim*, and Carl Iversen, *Aspects of the Theory of International Capital Movements*, Humphrey Milford, London, 1935.

purchasing power with which they will bid for all the commodities which they normally consume.

"Through the diminution of purchasing power in Germany, the German general price level will sink but the prices of export and import commodities, being affected by the foreign monetary situation, will be relatively high. The volume of imports will therefore show a comparative decline, and the exporting industries, being relatively prosperous, will draw labor and capital away from those industries whose product is marketed in Germany. The German industrial system will thus become adapted to the new adjustment made necessary by the reparation payments. In the creditor countries, on the other hand, the general price level will rise, but the prices of export and import commodities, so far as they are obtained from or go to Germany, . . . will be relatively low. The volume of imports will therefore show a comparative increase, and the exporting industries, being relatively unprosperous, will be outbidden for labor and capital by the industries whose product is marketed at home. The industrial system of these countries will thus be adjusted to the necessary new equilibrium in international trade."[25]

Neither Ohlin nor Keynes, apparently, was acquainted with the article from which the quotation just given is taken but the similarity with Ohlin's views is striking.[26] Ohlin says, for example, that a transfer of buying power "sets in motion a mechanism which indirectly calls forth an excess of imports in A [the recipient country] of about the same magnitude. Just as the loss of this buying power indirectly creates an export surplus in B [the paying country]; or, rather, these changes in buying power bring about at the same time an excess of imports in A and of exports in B.

"The increased demand for home market goods in A will lead to an increased output of these goods. In a progressive country this means that labour and capital, that would otherwise have passed to export industries and industries producing goods which compete

---

[25] Frank D. Graham, "Germany's Capacity to Pay and the Reparation Plan," *American Economic Review*, Vol. xv, No. 2, 1925, p. 213.

[26] This is not very surprising since Ohlin studied under Taussig, a little later than I, and both of us, drawing on Wicksell, realized that Taussig's doctrines on international trade under inconvertible paper monetary conditions were, in spite of Taussig's view to the contrary, applicable also to a gold, or any other such, standard. B. M. Anderson Jr. had presented similar views in an article "Procedure in Paying the German Indemnity," *Chase Economic Bulletin*, Vol. i, No. 4, New York, 1921.

directly with import goods, now go to the home market industries instead. Output of these 'import-competing' goods and of export goods increases less than it would otherwise have done. Thus, there is a relative decline in exports and increase of imports and an excess of imports is created.

"A corresponding adjustment takes place in B. Home market industries grow less as a result of reduced demand for their products, and the labour and capital turns in greater proportion to export industries and industries manufacturing goods which compete directly with import goods. The outcome is an excess of exports. B finds a widened market for its goods in A as a result of the adaptation of production which takes place in that country. Thus, the readjustment of production is the consequence of the change in buying power in the two countries."[27]

Ohlin returned to the topic, in 1933, in his *Interregional and International Trade*[28] and, in several cogent chapters, effectively disposed of the classical contentions so far, at any rate, as Hume, Taussig, and Keynes can be regarded as representative. Roland Wilson, in his *Capital Imports and the Terms of Trade*[29] had already presented an acute discussion of the issue and, as Viner notes in his comment, had concluded "that relative price changes will ordinarily be necessary for restoration of equilibrium, but that the type of change will depend on the particular circumstances. . . . He believes that he demonstrates that the changes in export and import prices, *relative to each other,* make no direct contribution to bringing about a transfer of the loan in the form of goods instead of in money, but that the role of these changes is solely to determine for each country to what extent the transfer shall take place through a change in exports or a change in imports, and to bring the two countries to a uniform decision, and that *it is the relative changes in prices between domestic and international commodities which, together with the shift in demands resulting from the transfer of means of payment from lender to borrower, brings about the transfer of the loan in the form of goods.*"[30]

Viner concedes that Wilson's account "marks a distinct advance"

[27] Bertil Ohlin, "The Reparation Problem: A Discussion," *Economic Journal,* Vol. xxxix, p. 174.
[28] *op. cit.,* Part v.
[29] Melbourne University Press, Melbourne, 1931.
[30] Viner, *Studies, op. cit.,* p. 327. (Latter italics mine.)

but alleges that some defects in Wilson's mode of analysis "seriously detract from the significance of the concrete results that he obtains." He grants that "a unilateral transfer of means of payment may shift the commodity terms of trade in *either* direction" though, in something short of enthusiastic allegiance to the more typical classical position, he thinks that it is *much more likely* to shift them against than in favor of the paying country.[31]

There is, however, no presumption that a unilateral transfer of means of payment is more likely to shift the "terms of trade" in one direction rather than the other or, indeed, that it will shift them at all. Let us take the simplest case of pecuniarily processed transactions and suppose that all goods move, one way or the other, in international trade between two countries A and B which use, as their sole money, an identical gold coin which we shall call ₱ (pondus). Suppose further that when, as a result of international loans or tribute, from A to B, the spendable (gold coin) income of the citizens of A is reduced by ₱ one million and that of the citizens of B is correspondingly increased, other conditions (velocity of circulation *etc.*) remain unchanged. In these circumstances it will ordinarily come about that, *regardless of the manner in which any one may spend his (curtailed or expanded) income*, the balance of payments between the countries will, without any change in commodity prices, be automatically altered in precisely the degree necessary to cover the loan or tribute.

Assume that, before the loans or tribute, the annual (value) output of both A and B amounts to ₱ 20 million, that each country consumes ₱12 million of its own production, and that it exports, to the other, goods to a volume of ₱ 8 million. After the loan or tribute is inaugurated, and on the assumption of unchanged output, the citizens of A will, in a year, be able to buy goods to a value of only ₱ 19 million while the citizens of B will be able to buy goods to a value of ₱ 21 million. Suppose that, in the new context of general demand, the citizens of A, taken as a group, cut the consumption of their own products to ₱ 11¾ million and, in consequence, leave ₱ 8¼ million of these goods for export to meet the requirements of the citizens of B, taken as a group, who will step up the consumption of their own

31 *ibid.*, p. 360. The question whether, under gold standard conditions, gold will move, and in what direction, and whether, under an inconvertible paper money, there will be a movement of exchange rates, is discussed in Chapter XII.

products to ₱ 12¾ million (21 million minus the 8¼ million spent on imports from A). The citizens of B, out of their production of ₱ 20 million, will then have goods to the value of ₱ 7¼ million left for export to A. The expenditures by citizens of A of the balance of their incomes (₱ 19 million minus ₱ 11¾ million) will just cover the purchase of these goods. The ₱ 8½ million exports from A will, moreover, exactly balance the ₱ 7½ million from B plus the loan, or tribute, of ₱ 1 million.

The same discrepancy of ₱ 1 million in the commodity exports of A and B (a discrepancy corresponding precisely to the amount of the loan or tribute) would appear with any other split of the citizens' purchases, between their own products and imports, provided money incomes are fully used to buy commodities, that is to say, are not hoarded.[32]

[32] The illustration just given was suggested by a passage from Wilson (*Capital Exports and the Terms of Trade, op. cit.*, Chap. IV) who, however, did not fully realize its implications. Viner, in his discussion of *Wilson's* example, says of it that "it is to be noted that one of the countries spends a substantially larger amount on foreign than on domestic commodities" and goes on to the assertion that "given the assumption that in the absence of price changes the international loan or tribute will not cause either country to desire a change in the proportions in which it had hitherto distributed its expenditures between native and imported commodities, the transfer of the loan or tribute will necessarily result in a movement of the terms of trade unfavorable to the paying country unless before reparations the unweighted average ratio of expenditures on native to expenditures on foreign commodities for the two countries combined is unity or less. . . ." (*Studies, op. cit.*, p. 329.)

It is perhaps worth stating that, on Viner's reasoning, the terms of trade would not remain unchanged, but would move in *favor* of the paying country, whenever the posited ratio was lower than unity. The matter is, however, of no consequence since the whole argument is based on impossible premises. However much the countries, after the change in relative incomes, might *desire* to preserve in unchanged proportions their expenditures on native and imported commodities it is, in the absence of hoarding, price changes, or output, mathematically out of the question that they could simultaneously accomplish this aim and clear the markets.

If, for instance, the citizens of B should spend their (increased) incomes, as between native and imported commodities, in the same proportions as they had formerly spent them, they would buy ₱ 12 3/5 million of native commodities and, out of their production of ₱ 20 million, have ₱ 7 2/5 million of their products left for export. But these products, the imports of A, are not sufficient to permit A to spend on imports the same proportion of its income as it had hitherto disbursed. Conversely, if we suppose that the citizens of A should spend their (reduced) incomes in the same proportions as they had formerly spent them, they would buy ₱ 11 2/5 million of native commodities and, out of their production of ₱ 20 million, have ₱ 8 3/5 of their products left for export. But these products, the imports of B, could not be bought by the citizens of B without raising the ratio of purchases of imports to that of native commodities above the proportion which had hitherto prevailed.

Neither of two countries, with changed relative incomes in an unchanged total,

The situation would not be materially different if we should assume that each of the countries was producing a group of commodities which did not enter into international trade. Let us suppose that, before the initiation of the loan or tribute, production and consumption in the two countries, in millions of ₱, is as follows:

	IN A		IN B	
	Produc-tion	Consump-tion	Produc-tion	Consump-tion
Domestic commodities	8	8	8	8
Exportables	12	4	12	4
Imports	—	8	—	8
Totals	20	20	20	20

and that, after the inauguration of the loan or tribute, it is:

	IN A		IN B	
	Produc-tion	Consump-tion	Produc-tion	Consump-tion
Domestic commodities	$7\frac{1}{2}$	$7\frac{1}{2}$	$8\frac{1}{4}$	$8\frac{1}{4}$
Exportables	$12\frac{1}{2}$	$3\frac{7}{8}$	$11\frac{3}{4}$	$4\frac{1}{8}$
Imports	—	$7\frac{5}{8}$	—	$8\frac{5}{8}$
Totals	20	19	20	21

The disparity between the exports of A and B is still ₱ 1 million and any other distribution of demand, in the two countries, as between domestic commodities, exportables, and imports would have yielded the same disparity of ₱ 1 million, between the exports of A and B, which just covers the loan or tribute. The distribution of

can spend the former proportion of its income on imports without taking such amounts of the output of the other country as to leave the retained production of that other country disproportionate with the former situation.

It is scarcely surprising that, in positing an impossibility, without disruption, Viner finds that the balance is disrupted, with the alleged result of a shift in the terms of trade. In the illustration that I have presented, I have met Viner's condition that neither of the countries spends more on foreign than on domestic commodities but the added condition unwarrantably loads the case in his favor and would preclude the clearing of the market. There is, in fact, no reason to expect any change in the "terms of trade," in either direction, under any probable distribution of expenditures, but to insist that the original proportions between expenditures for native and imported commodities be preserved by *both* countries is, in all cases in which data were originally other than Viner excepts, tantamount to injecting, *by hypothesis*, disequilibrium into the international accounts. This, Viner then presumes, will lead to a shift in the "terms of trade."

purchases between the various commodities is, of course, a resultant of the *total* relative demand for each of them, with citizens of either country bidding both for its exportables and its imports (which are the exportables of the other). The more the citizens of any one country take of imports the less will they have to spend on exportables, and the greater therefore, with a given output, will be their exports. The very fact that they take more imports means that the citizens of the other country have bidden relatively strongly for the first country's exportables.

In the illustration just given the consumption of domestic, as of other, commodities in each country is presumed to have changed after the transfer of the loan or tribute. This, of course, would require a shift in production, in each country, as between domestic commodities and exportables. Such a shift, however, would not occasion any necessary, or probable, disruption of the international balance of payments or any change in the price ratio of imports to exports in either country. The contention that an equilibrium in the balance of payments will, under any distribution of expenditures, tend to be automatic will perhaps be fortified, nevertheless, by an illustration which presupposes that expenditure for domestic commodities (and therefore the composition of production) is unchanged in either country from one situation to the other whereas that for exportables and for imports is greatly altered in both. The following table presents such a phenomenon, in millions of ₱, after the passage of the loan or tribute.

| | IN A | | IN B | |
	Production	Consumption	Production	Consumption
Domestic commodities	8	8	8	8
Exportables	12	9	12	10
Imports	—	2	—	3
Totals	20	19	20	21

The illustration is deliberately made extreme but the disparity, between the exports of A and B, still remains at ₱ 1 million.

A transfer of income from one group of persons to another in a different country may not at all affect the relative *world* demand for the various commodities but, if the relative demand for the various goods *does* alter, there is no ground for supposing that the change

193

will move along lines corresponding, in opposite directions, with the pre-existing, and, in the classical analysis, presumptively unique, national outputs of the transferring and recipient countries. If one might hazard a guess it would be that the country of increased income would consume both an absolutely and a relatively larger amount of luxuries or semi-luxuries, and a slightly larger absolute amount of "necessaries," than was previously the case, while the country of reduced income, in cutting its consumption in both categories, would reduce the relative consumption of the former below that of the latter type of goods. This result, however, would obviously vary according as we were dealing with a loan or with tribute, as well as with the pre-existing incomes in the affected countries, and there is, in any case, nothing to show how the *production* of these types of goods is split between the countries. The net outcome on the relative demand for the various goods, and the national incidence of that demand, is thus not only indeterminate but would by nothing but an infinitesimal chance affect all of the products of the one country in a given direction and all of those of the other (assuming that the two had no goods in common) in the contrary way.

A shift in incomes, from the citizens of a lending, or indemnity-paying, country to the citizens of a borrowing, or indemnity-receiving, country, would obviously have no effect whatever on the relative demand for goods provided the recipients of increased incomes spent it exactly as the contributors of the increase would, in the absence of the transfer, have done and, conversely, the contributors forwent the same goods that the recipients, in the absence of the transfer, would have forgone. This, though a conceivable, is, of course, an improbable case. The transfer of incomes is obviously likely to result in *some* change in the pattern of expenditures. But there is no basis for assuming that the world demand schedules for all of the goods hitherto produced in the recipient country would rise (move to the right), rather than fall, relative to the world demand schedules for all of the goods hitherto produced in the contributing country. There is, in consequence, no reason for the inference that there will be even a temporary rise in the relative value (prices) of the recipient country's set of goods as against those of the contributing country. On the contrary, it would be nothing short of amazing if any shift in the relative demand for goods were not so split as to increase the (world) demand for some of the goods produced in the one country and for some of those produced in the other, and correspondingly to reduce the (world) demand for other goods the production of which is divided, indeterminately, between the two countries. The shifts in demand are obviously more or less fortuitous and might temporarily so affect the price structure, compared with that formerly prevailing, as to render equally probable a temporary net gain, or loss, to either country. A losing country would then change the structure of its supply of the several commodities, enlarging the output of those of "its" goods that had risen in value, contracting the output of those of "its" goods that had fallen, and perhaps taking up the production of some good, or goods, hitherto exclusively produced abroad with the likelihood that, before long, with counter movements of production in countries favorably affected, the original ratio of exchange would be restored.

The modification of representative classical theory presented by Wilson, and others, still runs in terms of demand and pays no, or at best very inadequate, attention to costs.[33] It is essentially "short-run" doctrine. If, as is maintained in this book, costs are the only possible criteria of normal prices, then, since costs will not be affected, any shift in demand that, as a result of the mere process of transfer of loans or tribute from one country to another, may occur, will be attended by a corresponding alteration of supply without any necessary change in the normal price relationships of internationally traded commodities. No such change is essential to equilibrium and, even if it occurs as a facilitating mechanism, it will probably be of very short duration. This, moreover, is true not only of price relationships between "the" exports and imports of any given country (where there is no strong ground for expecting even a temporary change) but also of the normal price relationships between international goods as a whole and the purely domestic commodities of any country.[34] Some temporary shift in the latter relationship may be expected as an incentive to such alteration in the quantitative composition of production as may (but *need* not) be an accompaniment

[33] This is much less true of Ohlin, however, than of most other writers since Ohlin dwells on the effects of alleged, or possible, relative shifts in the prices of factors of production.

[34] The classicists, in abstracting from transport costs, left no room for "domestic" commodities (those that are neither imports nor exports). The presence of these goods somewhat complicates the situation but probably increases the likelihood of adjustment without *substantial* change, even temporarily, in price relationships.

of the alteration in the volume-ratio of exports to imports in countries on the paying or receiving side of some newly introduced unilateral transfer. But, if the intra-national cost ratios are not persistently to be traversed in prices, the prices of domestic goods in every country must, under constant and stable costs, soon return to the original price relationship against exports, while, under variable and unstable costs (for goods in either category), price changes would show a dispersal which could not be subsumed under any of the usual generalizations. Since any given country has exports in common with other countries, no shift in the normal price structure of one country, relative to that of another, can occur unless or until the linking commodities are altered.

If the shift in relative world demand, which may be a consequence of an international transfer of purchasing power, should be great enough to affect the (normal) international ratio of exchange of commodities (which is most unlikely) the movement in the ratio will be a function of a new constellation of opportunity costs consequent upon a shift in the national locus of producers on the margin of indifference in the production of the various commodities. This, as we have seen, will have diverse, more or less completely unforeseeable, effects on the fortunes of any given country.

Under any *ordinary* circumstances, then, disturbances in the international balance of payments will be adjusted not by an alteration in any normal price relationships but by an expansion, in the paying country, of the emission to foreign countries of a given output of exportable goods, and a contraction of imports (with, possibly, an expansion of output of export lines or of lines competing with imports, in either case at the expense of domestic commodities). Temporary price changes to facilitate the matter must be cancelled, even before the adjustment has been fully made, if overcompensation in the balance of payments is to be prevented. The statements just made apply, in reverse, to the recipient country.

Under *extraordinary* circumstances it may be necessary for a debtor country to change the qualitative as well as quantitative composition of its exports or imports by adding, as the case may require, items which formerly did not appear in its export list or subtracting from those which had formerly been found among its imports. It might even shift items from the import to the export category. None of these changes can occur, however, until the price of such items so alters, in relationship to the prices of all the commodities hitherto exported, imported, or domestically produced in the country in question, as to shift the national locus of producers on the margin of indifference as between these and other commodities. This would bring about *some* change in the relationships between individual commodity prices of goods internationally traded (to accord with altered opportunity costs and barter ratios), but the net effects on the fortunes of individual countries would be very diverse.

Where international transport costs are heavy, adjustments may be reached by an expansion in the area served, for any commodity, from any one (national) center of production (at the expense of another). When the margin of competition in sales from competing centers of production is thus shifted, the price of the product to consumers *at or near the former margin of competition* will be somewhat altered. This will not necessarily, or probably, effect a shift in the composition of production in any such consuming areas.

It is a matter of some interest that, in the case of international transfers of capital, most of the classicists couched their argument in terms of *supply* of goods rather than demand for them, and that, in the course of the argument, they resorted to a *money-cost* explanation of price relationships. They said, for instance, that the country making the loan, or paying the tribute, must, in order to consummate the transaction, *offer* "its" goods on better terms than before. Since it was obvious, in the type of trade under review, that *countries* did not, in fact, offer their goods to one another and, since most of the classicists did not explore what, in the circumstances, might happen to *individual* demands (or supply), there was need for an answer as to why the international exchange of goods took place *as if* individual citizens felt in their own transactions the (national) obligation of a country under the necessity of transferring loans or paying tribute. This was the occasion for the recourse to the international-specie-flow analysis (without which it was usually presumed, and not infrequently stated, the transfer of loan or tribute could not be effected) and, in consequence, to a (money) *cost* explanation of the "terms of trade."

The classicists concealed any embarrassment they might well have felt at this forced recourse to monetary movements, as a *determinant* of the terms of trade, in the face of their general denial that money was anything other than a lubricant and their specific statement that the "terms of trade" would not be at all altered by its use. If, moreover, they had stuck to their practice of exposition in terms of demand, rather than have shifted to an inadequate, because unilaterally-conceived, supply, they would have reached the conclusion that the "terms of trade" would probably be altered to the *advantage*, rather than to the disadvantage, of a country making loans or paying tribute, since the (monetary) demand of the citizens of the country receiving the loans or tribute, for the payer's products, would thereby be increased and that of the citizens of the disbursing country for the recipient country's products would be reduced. On classical demand-analysis this would certainly operate to move the "terms of trade" in *favor* of the disbursing country, though none of the classicists ever alleged that this would occur. They shifted between a "reciprocal national demand" explanation of the terms and a "necessity for balance" explanation, and their conclusions from one or the other (neither of which was relevant) were frequently in conflict.

The international ratio of exchange is much less likely to be affected by innovations in loans or tribute than as a consequence of tariff changes (and even there, as we have seen, the likelihood of a shift in the ratio of exchange is not great) since, in the case of protective tariff innovations, the immediate effect is that, in addition to the shift in demand, the relative *supply* of the various goods is automatically altered *in the opposite direction from the change in demand* whereas there is no such effect in the case of loans or tribute. The persistent effect of tariffs, moreover, is to bring about a permanent alteration of costs though not, usually, in the *effective* costs (those in the focal country).

It should be stressed that, in the manner noted above, the mechanism of (temporary) price adjustment (if any) of the international accounts to innovations in loans, tribute, tariffs, or such similar disturbance of international equilibrium, is not in the price ratio between the exports and imports of the various countries but in that between the prices of domestic commodities in each country and those of internationally traded goods taken as a group. The price relationships between internationally traded goods are, in any given cost situation, presumptively stable, and neither these relationships nor the price level of international goods as a whole is likely to be at all altered by any of the posited innovations.

Let us now review the whole situation. Opposite changes in national spendable income, probably accompanied by a comparatively small international movement of gold or shift in exchange rates, in countries respectively disbursing and receiving new tribute, loans, or the like,[35] will, as a first effect, lead to a diminution of all purchases (even with relatively low prices for purely domestic goods) in the disbursing country, and an augmentation of all purchases (even with relatively high prices for purely domestic goods) in the recipient country. This will increase the volume of goods immediately available for export, and will diminish the imports, of the disbursing country, whereas it will diminish the volume of goods immediately available for export, and will increase the imports, of the recipient country. The shift in the price relationships between the international goods sector and the domestic goods sector in the respective countries concerned (which is a consequence of the movement of gold or of exchange rates) will be temporarily exaggerated by the fact that the supply of domestic goods in any affected country is, for the moment, fixed, whereas the domestic (that is to say, the *sole*) monetary demand for those goods is altered. Neither the *total* supply, nor the *total* demand for international goods, however, is necessarily changed. The price situation, moreover, will furnish strong encouragement to producers of domestic goods in the disbursing country to shift to export commodities, or to commodities competing with imports, and it will have the opposite effect in the recipient country. This stimulus to an enlargement of the ratio of exports to imports in the disbursing country, and to a contraction of that ratio in the recipient country, will, without any probable changes in the price relationships between different sectors of internationally traded goods or in their general price level (measured in any international money such as gold), nearly always bring about the changes in the international trading situation necessary to consummate the transfer of any loans or tribute and to the restoration of equilibrium in the international accounts. Any disturbance in the price relationship of international to domestic goods that *may* occur will, however, be cancelled in the course of time even if the "disturbance" of the original equilibrium is persistent. Such a price shift

---

[35] The movement of gold, or of exchange rates between currencies, would be a consequence of the current abstention of the recipients of increased income from spending for goods, *anywhere*, the full access to their buying power.

may well be requisite to induce, but it will not be requisite to maintain, the appropriate ratio of exports to imports and, if this is the case, it is likely to be attended by a small but temporary movement of gold (or fall in the exchange value of the currency) from the paying to the recipient country.

Equilibrium in the international accounts will be automatically maintained, without a shift in the price relationships between internationally traded commodities, provided the money incomes of various countries are kept proportionate to the relative shares of world output that, on the basis of real output, the current ratio of exchange, and current unilateral international transactions, they are entitled to consume. This may, or may not, at any time require a movement of money, or of exchange rates between independent currencies, and, if it does, the movement may be in either direction.

If, moreover, world demand were so transformed by a mere transfer of purchasing power as to necessitate a change in the national locus of producers on the margin of indifference as between two or more commodities (a most unlikely event) the consequent shift in the ratio of exchange of goods might alter, in either direction, the net "terms of trade" of either of the countries concerned (or any other country). But this would come about, if at all, only through a rise, or fall, in the relative demand for individual commodities by the collective demanders in both countries. Neither national group demands "the products of the other," but all demanders are in the market for products in general. What prices will rise or fall, as a result of shifts in marginal costs following changes in the relative amounts of the various commodities demanded, and the final incidence of any altered ratio of exchange, is, as the models in previous chapters have shown, an all but completely fortuitous matter—depending on the interrelationship of cost structures in the various national entities. Without a shift in relative marginal opportunity costs there can be no alteration in normal values.

Cost-Changing Capital Movements

Let us now turn to some of the effects of such international capital movements as alter costs *per se*. While there is no reason to believe that there is any validity in the classical notion that the (normal) "terms of trade" will, as a mere result of the transfer, move against a lending, or tribute-paying, country, or at all, it is nevertheless likely that international investment will have eventual significant effects, either adverse or favorable to the lending country, when it is directed into lines which, in the one case, lower the opportunity cost of production, in foreign countries, of the lending country's current exports and, in the other, lower the opportunity cost of its imports. Any foreign investment which results in a greater disparity between the cost ratios in the lending and in the borrowing countries will tend to improve the situation of both countries so far as gains from trade are concerned.[36] Any foreign investment, on the other hand, which results in a reduction in the disparity between these cost ratios, or in its elimination, is likely to impair the situation of the lending country and may, moreover, be of no value to the borrowing country. These conclusions follow from the fact that an increasing disparity in cost ratios will tend to promote, at lower opportunity cost, the production in the borrowing country of commodities that are on the current import list of the lending country, and that the elimination of that disparity will, on the other hand, tend to promote the production in the borrowing country of commodities on the lending country's current export list. The shift in the cost structure will, in the one case, operate to lower the relative prices of the lending country's imports and, in the other, to lower the relative prices of its exports, that is to say, to improve, or impair, for it, the "terms of trade." (There will, presumably, have been no change in relative costs in the lending country.) In either case it could happen that the *borrowing* country's position was unimproved.

Even if foreign investment in any given case is applied, in the borrowing country, to the production of commodities which are neither exported nor imported by the lending country it may, in an expansion of the production to which the capital is applied, draw (labor) resources away from lines in which the lending country is concerned as an exporter or importer. The result, for the lending country, may be much the same, conversely reflected, as if the capital had gone, in the borrowing country, directly into the latter lines.

Where an importation of capital increases productivity in the borrowing country, in lines which the lending country is importing, the lending country stands to gain both because its imports are put out at lower opportunity cost to the producer and because an increase in their supply may *possibly* lower their price, in terms of the

---

[36] For a discussion of the logic of this occurrence cf. Chap. XI.

lending country's exports, by more than the equivalent of the reduction in their cost. This could occur through a shift in the national locus of the margin of indifference in production.

So far as the borrowing country is concerned, investment is wasted if it is so applied as to bring cost ratios in the borrowing country into approximation or identity with those in the lending country. For this would mean only that the borrowing country would now produce, at home, commodities which it had formerly acquired by international exchange at an opportunity cost less, by the use-value of the imported capital, than that now prevailing. The lending country, also, will tend to lose from such a use of its capital. If, on the other hand, the capital is applied so as to *increase* the spread between national cost ratios, the borrowing country will gain or lose according as the reduction in the opportunity cost of its exports is less or more than fully compensated by any adverse shift in the ratio of exchange attendant upon the enlarged relative supply of the commodities to which the imported capital is applied. For such a shift, an alteration in the national locus of the margin of indifference in production would be a necessary condition.

It is clear that international transfers of capital, according to their application and any resulting shift in the ratio of exchange, may be useless to both the lending and the borrowing country, injurious to one of them, or beneficial all round. From the national point of view they require scrutiny and it cannot be assumed that what may here be good business for the contracting individuals is at all necessarily of mutual, or even unilateral, national advantage. The effects both on cost ratios and on ratios of exchange of commodities must be watched. Cost ratios may be so affected as to make the investment disadvantageous to *both* of the countries, and exchange ratios may be so affected as to bring injury to one of them.

The case just made is even stronger when the investment is put into industries of comparative disadvantage in such a way as to diminish the disparity between cost ratios but by not enough to permit the investee country to dispense with tariffs on the products of the new investment. Such an investment could not possibly be of advantage in any cosmopolitan sense.[37]

[37] For a pioneering article on the matters just discussed, cf. Charles R. Whittlesey, "Foreign Investment and the Terms of Trade," *The Quarterly Journal of Economics*, Vol. XLVI, pp. 444-464.

CHAPTER X

EFFECTS OF THE ENTRY OF NEW COUNTRIES INTO
THE INTERNATIONAL TRADING SYSTEM

THE classical habit of thinking of international trade as an exchange of irrevocable composites of unique national outputs has, among other errors, led to the unwarranted conclusion that a country *must*, even in the long run, suffer from a movement in the ratio of exchange in which the commodities it has hitherto been importing rise in value in terms of the commodities it has hitherto been exporting. This conclusion has already been attacked, but the fallacy involved will be more obvious on examination of the effects of the entry of new countries into an already established international trading system. The classicists implied that the advent into international trade of a country producing no new commodity must impair the position of some, at least, of those already engaged.[1] That this is not necessarily true will appear in the sequel.

Let us suppose that two countries, A and B, are trading freely in three commodities, z, y, and x, that these commodities are of approximately equal total value at the eventually established ratio of exchange, and that A's productive capacity is considerably greater than, yet less than twice as much as, that of B. Let the opportunity cost ratios, in A, be $z = 1\frac{1}{2}y = 4x$, and, in B, $z = 1\frac{1}{3}y = 2x$. Country A, by virtue of its size, must produce the bulk of at least two of the commodities, but B will also produce two since its size is such that it would not find a market for its output of a single commodity without driving the price of that commodity down to the point at which an alternative product would

---

[1] I have, however, not been able to find a forthright assertion on this point. It is implicit in Mill's §4 of his chapter on international values (*Principles, op. cit.*, Book III, Ch. XVIII) where one of two originally trading countries is benefited by an alteration in the "terms of trade," attendant on the entry of a third country, and the other (which, in Mill's analysis, keeps the qualitative composition of its production unchanged) must, therefore, be injured. Bastable (*Theory of International Trade, op. cit.*, 4th edn., p. 40) affirms the probability of injury of one of the two original trading entities but he does not allege its inevitability. *On classical principles*, however, it is certain that the entry of a new country producing no new commodity must either have no effect whatever on the prosperity of *either* of the original trading groups or must injure the prosperity of one of them. This does not mean, of course, that the latter country would be better off without, than with, international trade but merely that it does not gain as much from such trade in the later as in the earlier situation.

become equally profitable to its enterprisers. Country A will, therefore, produce y and x, and B will produce y and z, at an exchange
ratio of $z = 1\frac{1}{3}y = 3\frac{5}{9}x$.[2] Country A will then obviously produce
the bulk of the y since it is so much larger than B as to have a much
greater productive power undevoted to x than B has undevoted to
z. Country B will import some y, as well as all of its x, from A in
exchange for z. If it be assumed that each country assigns one-third
of its productive power to the acquisition of each of the commodities,
A's gains from trade, as compared with a former state of self-sufficiency, work out at $12\frac{1}{2}\%$ of its original output of z (with its consumption of x and y unchanged) while B's gains from trade come
to $77\frac{7}{9}\%$ of its original output of x (with its consumption of y
and z unchanged). This gain, in either case, might, under different
conditions, be distributed, in any proportions, over the consumption
of all three commodities.

Let us now assume that a third country, C, with cost ratios at
$z = \frac{5}{8}y = x$, enters the trade. Country C, we will suppose, is approximately as large as A. Both A and C must therefore produce at
least two products, with B now specializing in only one. Inspection
will show that C will produce z and y, that A will continue to produce
some y and all of the x, and that B will shift completely out of z
(hitherto its principal product) into y, at an exchange ratio of
$z = \frac{5}{8}y = 1\frac{2}{3}x$.[3]

The position of both A and B is improved by the entry of C, and
C, of course, also gains as compared with self-sufficiency. Instead
of an expansion of $12\frac{1}{2}\%$ in its consumption of z, country A can
now, relative to the situation under self-sufficiency, increase its intake of that commodity by 140% (without curtailing its consumption of x and y), whereas B, instead of a single expansion equivalent
to $77\frac{7}{9}\%$ of its consumption of x, can now maintain unchanged
its consumption of that commodity, and of y, and obtain, in addition,
an increase of $113\frac{1}{3}\%$ in its intake of z. Country C can, in turn,
relative to the situation under self-sufficiency, expand its consumption of x by $66\frac{2}{3}\%$ without any curtailment in its consumption
of y or z.

Up to the time of entry of country C the commodity z was the sole

[2] $Z = 1\,1/3y$ (B's cost ratio between y and z), and $1\,1/3y = 3\,5/9x$ (A's cost ratio
between y and x).

[3] $Z = 5/8y$ at C's cost ratio between z and y, and $5/8y = 1\,2/3x$ at A's cost ratio
between y and x).

export of B. (This follows from B's comparatively small production of y.) The competition of C forces the relative value of z down far in terms of both y and x, that is to say, the "terms of trade," *on the basis of original output*, move strongly against B. But B, in fact, is now much better off (in importing its full consumption of z, as well as x, in exchange for part of a greatly expanded output of y) than it had been when it was an exporter of z.

Such an enormous shift in the ratio of exchange as that involved in the preceding illustration is scarcely conceivable in a world of well-established trade involving many countries and commodities. The illustration, nevertheless, is not without a certain practical importance. Not so long ago the exports of the United States were predominantly foodstuffs and raw materials and its imports manufactured goods. The situation has been in process of reversal (following a similar trend that occurred much earlier in Great Britain). The change is, at least in part, attributable to the entry of new countries, into the world trading situation, as exporters of foodstuffs and raw materials. The process of transition has, of course, been prolonged, is possibly not yet complete, and the effects have been mixed, but there is no justification for the conclusion that what, on classical reasoning, was an adverse alteration in the "terms of trade" (without which this evolution would not have taken place) was, on the whole, unfavorable to the United States.[4] This country passed from a comparative advantage in foodstuffs and raw materials into a regime of natural, though incomplete, self-sufficiency, and finally emerged, on the other side, with a comparative advantage in manufactured goods. Exports and imports had been, in part, reversed. The shift of production in *any* country, in response to an alteration in the ratio of exchange, may thus bring about a long-term gain even from what is, at first blush, an adverse movement in its "terms of trade."[5]

[4] The case is complicated by dynamic factors but, whatever may have been the actual course of events, it *could* have occurred under completely static conditions in the United States.

[5] The entry of Japan, in the latter half of the 19th century, into the international trading system, probably operated to the ultimate national advantage of the older trading countries, with their progressive relative abandonment of many of the commodities in which the Japanese were specializing, and it would have been still more productive of gain to them if they had not resorted to partial protection of the output of the commodities which the Japanese began to export.

The More Usual Case

Though, as has just been shown, it is theoretically possible that, without the introduction of any new commodities, both of two trading countries may benefit by the advent of a third (which will also gain), it is nevertheless more than equally likely that (as the classicists supposed would always be the case) the position of one of the originally trading countries will be impaired. It is only because country C, at the original ratio, had a very low comparative cost in the production of z (which A did not produce and from which B found it profitable to withdraw) that all of the countries benefited from C's advent to the trade.[6] But with a different cost structure, country C would have increased the supply, relative to the demand, of products of either A or B from which the thus affected country could not profitably withdraw. The position of one of the latter countries would then have been worsened.

The advent to international trade of any large country specializ-

---

[6] In the illustration above given, B, the small country, is in a strategic position. When C comes into the picture B is producing y and z and, with the advent of C, will be able to devote its full productive powers to either. It is, in the circumstances, impossible for both y and z to fall simultaneously in terms of x, since A, a large country, must produce either y or z in addition to x. This means that either z must be worth $4x$ or that $1\ 1/2y$ must be worth $4x$ (the cost ratios in A). Neither ratio is worse for B than the exchange ratio prevailing before the advent of C ($z = 1\ 1/3y = 3\ 5/9x$). This is the same ratio as $1\ 1/2y = 4x$ but is not so good for B as $z = 4x$. Country C could, of course, drive the producers of x in A out of business, as might well be the case if the producers in C should have a low relative cost of x. This must, however, redound to the advantage of B, an importer of x, since A would not give up the production of x unless the price of x should fall in terms of y or z, or both. Since B can specialize in either y or z, as the price situation warrants, it cannot, therefore, possibly lose by the entry of C.

A's position is not nearly so strong as B's but it is nevertheless impossible for A to lose *much* through the advent of C since, in the circumstances posited, the ratio of exchange in the absence of C ($z = 1\ 1/3y = 3\ 5/9x$), is already close to A's cost ratio ($z = 1\ 1/2y = 4x$). Country A is not then, in any case, getting much gain from the international trade and so cannot lose much by anything that can happen to the ratio (which is already close to pessimum point for A). Nevertheless, if the cost ratios in C should, for instance, be $z = 2y = 5x$, the exchange ratio which would emerge is $z = 1\ 3/5y = 4x$, with C producing y and x, A shifting from y to z but continuing in x, and B abandoning y for specialization in z. Country A would then be somewhat worse off, i.e. still nearer to the (for it) pessimum ratio, than it had been before C came into the picture.

If, however, the original exchange ratio had happened to be more favorable to A, the probability of loss to A from the advent of C, and the extent of any loss it might suffer, would be great. No matter what the cost ratios might be in C the exchange ratio would then almost certainly move strongly against A. This follows from the fact that A and C, by reason of their size, must have a common product and that B can specialize in either of the other commodities as the ratio of exchange may impel it.

ing in anything but completely new commodities will, in fact, in the world as it is, ordinarily be harmful to some of those already engaged. Others will be favorably affected. Neither the gains nor the losses (to others) from the entry of a country into complex trade will, however, be of anything like the magnitude of those possible in the simple trade so far treated in this chapter. The entry into complex trade of any country large enough to affect the ratio of exchange will operate to shift the ratio adversely to those already participating countries whose exports parallel those of the newcomer. Such a shift in the ratio will, of course, be favorable to countries *im*porting those commodities. Most countries, of course, will have had some exports and some imports among the commodities now exported by the incoming country and, in this case, their net *immediate* gain or loss will depend on the number and importance of the commodities on the one side or the other. Their *ultimate* gain or loss, under the newly established equilibrium, will depend upon their possibilities of adjustment to the new exchange ratio, that is to say on the degree to which their cost ratios will permit them to expand any immediate gain, or reduce, negate, or convert to profit, any immediate loss, that may accrue to them from the alteration in the ratio of exchange.

Effects and Causes of Diversification of Output

The more diversified the production of any country the less likely is it to suffer greatly from any alteration in the ratio of exchange whether or not this occurs as a result of the advent of a new country to international trade. This follows from the fact that its diversity of production will enable it readily to expand its output of such items on its list as are favorably, or at worst not very unfavorably, affected by the change in the ratio, while it withdraws from those to which the change is strongly adverse.

Even if a country is merely *potentially* diversified, that is with cost ratios which, at the current international exchange ratio, lead to specialization but would induce a considerable diversity of output if the ratio of exchange should move but slightly in an adverse direction, it will be protected against severe loss from any such movement.

The classical economists recognized this fact in their (more than dubious) assertion that a variety of exports is a cause of a favorable ratio of exchange ("terms of trade") for the country concerned.[7] The doctrine issued from their convictions on the primacy of reciprocal demand in determining the "terms of trade" since, in their view, a variety of exports meant that there was a strong foreign demand for the home products relative to the home demand for foreign products.[8] The fact is, however, that a variety of exports, while a safeguard against further deterioration, is an effect of *un*favorable rather than a cause of favorable terms of trade. The presence of many exports, or the potentiality of a large variety of exports at terms not much worse for the country in question than those currently prevailing, will prevent any sharp adverse movement in those terms. To posit this, however, is a very different thing from saying that a variety of exports, as such, makes for a favorable ratio. A movement of the terms of trade away from the ratio most favorable to any given country will always operate to increase the number of its exports and reduce the number of its imports. It may, in certain cases, take but a small adverse movement of the terms of trade to bring in a number of new exports, or exclude a number of old imports, sufficient to establish equilibrium. But in other cases it might take a rather heavy adverse movement to do so. A multiplicity of exports in any given case may therefore mean either that many commodities became exportable before the terms of trade had moved far away from the most favorable possible position for the country in question or that the terms of trade had moved so far away from that position as to bring a large number of commodities into the export list. Every new commodity which enters the export list will, of course, exert its influence in checking the adverse movement in the terms, but one might as well say that the large number of buyers who come into the market when the price of any commodity falls sharply is the cause of the "high" price at which that commodity is selling as that a large number of exports is the cause of the "favorable" ratio at which they are being exchanged. It is true that a multiplicity of exports prevents the ratio

[7] cf. C. F. Bastable, *Theory, op. cit.*, p. 36. The initiation of export of a marginal commodity does not so much improve the terms of trade for the exporting country as keep them from getting worse. If the (temporary) export of such a commodity should actually improve the "terms of trade" for the exporting country it would no longer be able to sell the commodity, in foreign markets, at a profit.

[8] cf., e.g., Alfred Marshall, *Money Credit and Commerce*, Macmillan & Co., Ltd., London, 1923, Appendix J.

of interchange from being as bad as it might otherwise be, but it does not, *per se*, make it good.[9]

The most favorable possible terms of trade for a given country could be attained only when exports were confined to a single commodity. The least favorable terms possible, on the other hand, would surely obtain when the export list comprised all but one of the articles consumed. The larger the number of exports of any given country, relative to the total number of commodities consumed in that country, the more certain, therefore, is it that the terms of trade are tending toward the position most unfavorable to it. A wide variety of exports from any given country is thus always evidence that the terms are *worse* for it than they would be if, under the same conditions of production, the export list were more limited. Similarly a narrow list of exports is always evidence that the terms are *better* for the country concerned than they would be if, under the same conditions of production, the number of exports were larger. The statement that a variety of exports is a cause of favorable terms of trade can scarcely be reconciled with these facts.

Concentration of potential exports near the optimum ratio for any country (a wide divergence between the exchange ratio against imports and its own cost ratios for the two groups) will prevent the actual ratio of international exchange of products from becoming very unfavorable to that country until, at least, the list of its exports is extended beyond the range of this concentrated group. It is, however, not the variety of actually existing exports but this concentration of commodities about what, with a given ratio of international exchange, is the upper rung of the scale of comparative cost (as against an even dispersion or a concentration at the lower end) that has any causal force in making the terms of trade favorable for the country concerned. The greater the concentration of potential exports about this upper rung the greater is the assurance that the "terms of trade" will, on the whole, be favorable, whether or not the existing export list is wide. But even here a narrow list of exports will mean more favorable terms than will a wide one. The less the concentration of potential exports about the upper rung of the existing scale of comparative cost, on the other hand, the

[9] The discussion at this point is a paraphrase of part of my article on "The Theory of International Values," *The Quarterly Journal of Economics*, Vol. xlvi, No. 4, pp. 581-616.

more likely are the "terms of trade" to be unfavorable,[10] though here again a small number of exports will mean more favorable terms than will a varied list. It is true that a great variety of exports may not only coincide with fairly favorable as well as with unfavorable terms but also that, though the most favorable terms possible can be secured only when the export list is highly limited, a limited list is no *guarantee* that the terms will, in fact, be favorable. These modifications, however, are very far from lending any real support to the view that a variety of exports and favorable terms of trade go hand in hand.

It is, of course, futile to attempt sharply to distinguish cause and effect in cases of interaction. If it be granted, however, that the variety of exports from any country tends to be increased by an adverse movement in the "terms of trade," and that, though every increase in the number of exports acts to prevent a further fall in the ratio, the tendency toward a movement in the ratio unfavorable to any given country is quickly counteracted only in the exceptional case of a concentration of exports about the upper end of the scale of existing comparative advantage, we shall not be likely to follow the orthodox school in associating a variety of exports with favorable "terms of trade." We shall rather hold to the contrary view knowing, however, that, according to circumstances, both a varied and a narrow list of exports may coincide with favorable or with unfavorable terms. Of any given country with a varied export list we can hold both that, under a given set of conditions of production, the terms will be less favorable than they would be if the export list were more limited, and that, if diversity of export had not been possible, the terms might be much worse than they are owing to the failure of a multiplicity of exports to develop and thus set an early check upon an adverse movement in the ratio.

The fact is, however, that a sharp movement in the "terms of trade" against any given country is not so much inhibited by the nature of the given country's cost structure, or list of exports, as by a close gradation in cost ratios in other countries and in the (nationally segregated) world as a whole. When new countries break into

[10] The terms of trade *for such a country* might shift from the favorable ratio which it would obtain when its export list was very limited to a quite unfavorable ratio without bringing any great change in the *general scheme* of international values. The only goods which would be much affected would be those few in the export of which the country had formerly been concentrating to the exclusion of other countries.

such a system, both on the export and the import side, the possibilities of adjustment without substantial changes in cost relationships are so great that no "old" country is likely to be much affected unless the new-comer should concentrate heavily in an "old" country's sole export.

Except when it goes so far as to bring the cost ratios in any country into practical identity with the international ratio of exchange, "natural" diversification, or potential "natural" diversification, of output is more effective as a protection against the loss arising from an alteration in the ratio of exchange than as a preventive of gain. It is true not only that the more diversified a country's output the less likely is an, on balance, adverse alteration in the ratio of exchange to cut all one way, or go far, but also that, when the net balance is favorable to any such country, there is no inherent obstacle to the gain being large unless, as a result of the change in the ratio, other countries shift from the production of the imports to the production of the exports of the country so favored. This will, of course, depend on the structure of the cost ratios of these other countries.

Prospects on the Advent of "New" Countries

There is nowadays small possibility of any economically important, or potentially important, country entering, for the first time, into international trade (as Japan did, in the nineteenth century, after hundreds of years of isolation) but, if the industrialization of Russia, India, China, or all three, should proceed apace, and they should come to play a large role in international trade, the effects on the international ratio of exchange might be analogous to those of the entry of a new and important country into the international trading system. The pressure of population on the land is so great in India and China that it would seem almost inevitable that the output of manufactured goods would offer comparative advantages to them. If this should prove to be the case, and they should specialize in manufacturing, the international ratio of exchange would tend to alter in favor of foodstuffs and raw materials as against manufactured goods. Countries now highly specialized in manufactured goods, and without good alternatives, could not fail to be somewhat injured by any such development.[11] Diversified

[11] This does not necessarily mean that their prosperity would *inevitably* decline since their per capita productivity might contemporaneously rise, but it does mean

countries on the other hand might, by shifting the composition of their output, lose little, not at all, or even, after adjustments had been made, show a gain from this phenomenon, and countries already specialized, and remaining, in non-manufacturing lines would gain heavily.

Divergences in the Prosperity of Countries

Where migration is not free, and were it not greater than it has ever been whether free or not, there is no validity in the contention that the prosperity of any one country is dependent upon the prosperity of others. The classicists, of course, never said that it was.[12] National prosperity is a function of two variables (1) the per capita physical productivity of the citizens and (2) the "terms of trade." The first of these variables is unaffected by conditions in other countries while the second may be affected *in either direction* by the entry of new countries into trade or by any change, whether for better or worse, in economic conditions abroad. The *prima facie* "terms of trade" may, in fact, move adversely to any given country as a result of an increase in productivity abroad (which has the same effect as the entry of a new country with a comparative advantage in the commodities concerned) just as they may so move in response to an increase in productivity at home. Any movement in the "terms" which increases the prosperity of some countries is, so far as it is independent of a change in costs and merely reflects a shift in the national locus of marginal production, almost certain to reduce that of others.

The principal recipe for prosperity is high per capita productivity, and the general rule is that an increase in per capita productivity will redound to the more or less exclusive benefit of the citizens of the country in which it occurs. It is nevertheless true that an increase in per capita productivity in (economically small) countries devoted to one or two products not widely consumed at home is, when those countries are without alternatives at any ratio of exchange at all close to that hitherto prevailing, not unlikely to impoverish rather than enrich the nation in which it takes place. The whole value of the improvement, and more, might accrue to

---

that, *ceteris paribus*, it would fall. Such a fall might, or might not, be compensated by other factors.

[12] Short-run considerations are, of course, not in question.

other countries. Such a result will eventuate, however, only if it should happen that no country of diversified output is producing the commodities to which the small country is fully committed. For, otherwise, the country of diversified output would abandon the commodities in question for some alternatives readily at hand. By so doing it would leave room for the expansion of their production, in the small country, on, at worst, nothing more than a minor recession in the exchange value of the affected commodities beyond the point which would correspond with the reduction in their unit cost.

No country of even very partially diversified output is likely to suffer much from an alteration in the international ratio of exchange. International trade, and *a fortiori* the international ratio of exchange, will not, in any case, be of pre-eminent importance to such a country and, even if, by some strange chance, a movement in the international ratio of exchange should adversely affect the whole range of its current exports, to which it had no readily available alternatives, a transfer of resources, in other countries of a different diversity of output, to lines favorably affected by the shift in the ratio of exchange would certainly be inaugurated. This would not only hold to small dimensions the movement in the ratio but would remove competitors in the supply of the commodities produced in the country to which the movement had been generally unfavorable.

If the entry of a country into an international trading system may conceivably improve the situation of all those hitherto engaged, or may hurt some of them and benefit others, the (partial or complete) withdrawal of any country from such a system could be expected to hurt all of them or to improve the status of some and injure that of others. This expectation is corroborated in the effects, shown in the preceding chapter, of the withdrawal of country J from the ten-country, ten-commodity, system of which it had originally been a member.

CHAPTER XI

THE GAINS FROM INTERNATIONAL TRADE:
CONCEPT, MEASUREMENT, AND DIVISION

With every individual free to produce and to trade as he pleases, and with all individuals, whatever their nationality, held to be of equal worth, it would be tedious, purposeless, and practically impossible to trace the gains from international trade or their division among the individuals involved.[1] A lively nationalist feeling, however, impelled the classical writers to regard the interest of the citizens of their own state as of much greater moment, to them, than that of the citizens of any other, and this led them to speculate on the gains from trade in nationalist terms. These are difficult, but perhaps not impossible, to measure.[2]

Professor Viner, in his review of the doctrines of international trade, notes that the classical economists followed three different methods of dealing with the question of national gains from trade.[3] They did not, he says, clearly separate these methods, and shifted freely from one to the other, but their criteria of gains were either (1) economy in the cost of obtaining a given (national) income, (2) an increase in (national) income, or (3) a shift in the "terms of trade" (the ratio at which a unit of exports in general exchanges against a unit of imports in general).

---

[1] To do so would require information, on every individual, as to his productive versatility, or the lack of it, and, therefore, his gains from territorial specialization.

[2] It is worthy of note, however, that so soon as we think of international trade in terms of national, rather than individual-cosmopolitan, interest, the case for freedom of trade is seriously weakened. Freedom of trade will, in all probability, be in the national economic interest (as well as a matter of concern to the individual) but, as we have already noted, the presumption is by no means absolute. Any nation in a position to exert, exclusively, some form of monopoly power may, by appropriate restraints on trade, gain so much at the expense of other nations as to be materially better off than it would be under free trading conditions. The case is on all fours with that of a single monopolist in domestic trade otherwise freely competitive. Freedom of trade is in the interest of all but not necessarily in the interest of each. The classical economists should either have taken their stand for individual freedom, in which case they would not have been concerned with *national* terms of trade, or they should have been frank nationalists, in which case they would not have been uncompromising advocates of freedom of trade. Their cosmopolitanism and their nationalism were in conflict. Though the *spread* of restraints on trade is disastrous to every nation, it is futile to deny the theoretical possibility of national business success to a country exploiting a monopolistic or quasi-monopolistic position (either on the buying or the selling side) provided it is not subject to effective retaliation.

[3] Jacob Viner, *Studies, op. cit.*, p. 437.

There would, at first blush, seem to be little difference between the three methods, and especially between (1) and (2), if by (2) is meant an increase in (national) income at a given cost. Any specific gain might be stated either as a reduction in cost per unit of income or as an increase in income per unit of cost. So long as we confine our attention to a given moment the identity of meaning must hold but, as will presently appear, we get into difficulties when, as is necessary to give any meaning at all to method (3), we extend the comparison over time. In the one case we are dealing with a given cost structure and are contrasting the national income currently obtainable at a given cost or the current cost of a given national income, in a regime of international trade, with that which could at the time be obtained, or would cost, in a regime of national self-sufficiency.[4] When, on the other hand, we view incomes over time, we are dealing with a changing cost (and price) structure and may then make such contrasts as that of:

1. the ratio of increase in income, or reduction in cost, attributable to international trade under the original cost (and price) structure with the comparable ratio under the cost (and price) structure that has evolved during the period under consideration;

2. the unit cost of imports, in terms of exports, of the original in comparison with that of the later period;

3. the unit cost of imports, in terms of the labor-time, resources (human and material), or factors of production necessary to the output of the exports with which a given volume and composition of imports could be obtained at the original with that which could be obtained at the later period.

The first of these contrasts is alone valid for measuring the gains from the *policy* of international trade since it alone reflects the results of such a policy. The second and the third contrasts do not show the gains from trade, or even shifts in such gains, because, in the one case, no clew is given as to (changing) real or opportunity costs, or as to incomes, at either period, and because, in the other, nothing is shown, at either period, as to what it would cost to produce at home the given imports. Both contrasts are also defective because

---

[4] This contrast will have to be put in terms of the ratio between the two incomes (of a given composition) obtainable for a given cost, or of that between the costs of identical commodity incomes, under the respective regimes of international trade and national self-sufficiency.

any given volume and composition of imports (or exports) would usually be irrelevant to one or the other of the periods.

Changing Costs and the Calculation of Gains

Suppose that, in the interval between two contrasted periods, a change in cost conditions has occurred in a given country so that it would now cost more than would formerly have been the case to produce, at home, an unchanged volume and composition of imports but that these imports are in fact acquired in exchange for an unchanged volume and composition of exports produced at unchanged cost (in terms of labor-time, resources, or factors of production).[5] It is then correct to say that the policy of international trade (as compared with national self-sufficiency) is providing a greater access of income, or reduction in cost, in the later than in the earlier situation despite the fact that the actual income of the country, and the actual resources-cost of acquisition of that income, remain unaltered.

The best way to measure the gains from trade, and trade alone, is to compute the loss which would be incurred in its absence. This loss would be greater in the later than in the earlier of the two periods just compared. The gain from the *presence* of trade must, *ipso facto*, then be greater. That the income of the country, the price ratio between its exports and imports, and the cost of production of its exports remain unchanged is irrelevant to the determination of the trend in the gains from (the policy of) international trade since, under national self-sufficiency, the national income would not have remained constant but would have been *reduced*, per unit of cost (however measured), in the later as compared with the earlier period.

Since the gains from international trade cannot be computed without reference to what it would cost to produce, in a given country, things which are, in fact, not there produced, computations which rely solely on costs of actual production, and on actual prices, (*a fortiori*, those which rely solely on the latter) fall beside the mark. When we use opportunity as a measurer of cost the appropriate comparison is inevitable. When, however, we use labor-time, resources, or factors of production, as measurers of cost, it is all

[5] In terms of opportunity the exports would cost *less* than they formerly had since a given volume of exports could now be attained by forgoing the output of a reduced volume of (potential) replacements of imports.

too easy to slip into irrelevancies, even though, if care is taken, the appropriate comparison can still be made.

An increase in national income attendant upon the acquisition of imports of given composition at historically declining unit cost (in labor-time, resources, or factors of production devoted to the output of the exports for which they are exchanged) may often be logically attributable to an improvement in productive efficiency in exports rather than to (the policy of) international trade. If the improvement of efficiency should equally apply to the (potential) domestic production of imported goods, as well as to exports, the realizable gains *from international trade*, expressed as a percentage of the national income either with or without such trade, would be unaffected. If, moreover, it should so happen that the improvement in efficiency applied in greater degree to the (potential) domestic production of imported goods than to exports, the realizable gains *from international trade* would be diminished, percentage-wise and perhaps even absolutely, in spite of the fact that the commodity income of the country, including that from its imports, would be in process of expansion per unit of labor-time, resources, or factoral cost. For, in the event cited, the renunciation of trade would cost the country less, percentage-wise or even absolutely, after the improvement had occurred than would originally have been the case. The gains from the trade *per se* are therefore reduced.

Meaning of "Gains"

When we speak of a country's gains from international trade, and of changes in those gains, it clearly makes a difference whether we mean (as we should) the gains attributable to international trade as a policy (opposed to national self-sufficiency) or are referring to the respective volumes of imports of a given composition obtainable, at one time and another, either for a given volume and composition of exports or for a given cost, in labor-time, resources, or factors of production, incurred in the output of such exports.

The classical and neo-classical writers necessarily adverted to the (potential) cost of the domestic production of imports in assessing the *actual* gains from trade at any moment but, in their calculation of *trends*, they quite generally omitted the practice. This would be less objectionable if it could be assumed that the cost structure, everywhere, were subject to no alteration in the interval between two contrasted periods. There might then, with a comparatively small change in the price ratio of exports to imports, be little reason to expect any change in the character, or composition, of international trade, and the shifts in the ratio of the price index of any country's exports to the price index of its imports (cost of acquisition of imports in terms of exports) would be all that would be required to reflect the trend in the gains from trade.[6] An improvement in the gains of one country would, in these circumstances, mean a deterioration for others—Paul's gain would be Peter's loss. With changing costs, on the other hand, *reciprocal* increases, or diminutions, in the gains from trade are possible. This, however, is a matter reserved for later treatment.

If, for the moment, we suppose that the composition of the exports and imports of any country remains unaltered while the prices of its exports rise, or fall, relative to the prices of its imports, the change in price relationships may be an accurate reflection of synchronous changes in the relationship between the cost of exports and what it would cost to produce, at home, the imports for which they are exchanged. The country's gains from international trade, or the losses from its renunciation, are then not affected in any way whatever. This is obvious on opportunity-cost considerations but, even if we think in classical terms, it is clear that when exports cost more or less (in labor-time, resources, or factors of production), and exchange, per unit, for a correspondingly larger or smaller amount of imports, the gains from the trade may (and, conceived in terms of resources-cost, will) remain unaltered.

Whether a country's gains from international trade are rising or falling, when any change in the price relationships between an unchanged composition of exports and imports occurs, depends upon the character of the relationship between the movement in prices and the movement in costs. Export prices in any country may rise, fall, or remain unchanged relative to import prices, and the gains from trade will, in all cases, be enlarged provided, with other things equal, the cost of exports rises less, or falls more (either in terms of resources or in what it would cost to produce, at home, the

---

[6] The cost of imports in exports was dubbed by the classicists "the terms of trade." But the *gains* from trade are a function not only of the terms of trade (ratio of exchange of exports for imports) but of the cost of exports relative to the (potential) cost of the domestic production of imports.

imports for which they are exchanged) than in strict proportion to the alteration in the relationship between the prices of exports and imports. In the converse situation the gains from trade would be reduced.

The classical school saw no reason for questioning the idea of an alteration in the international ratio of exchange in the absence of a change in cost structures (and the consequent composition of exports and imports),[7] but it is clear from our earlier exposition that, except for highly limited shifts in the rare case of a limbo ratio or when the margin of indifference changes its national locus, this phenomenon will not occur. When, on the other hand, costs and cost relationships and, as a consequence, the composition of exports and imports, alter from one period to another, a comparison between the former and present price indices of exports and imports of any given country is useless as a criterion even of a *trend* in the gains from trade. Unless there is a fully compensating prior change in relative costs, everywhere, any substantial change in the ratio of exchange is almost certain to bring about a shift in the composition of the exports and imports of any reasonably diversified country. Even if costs are taken into account, it is then futile to attempt to assess the extent of the trend in the country's gains from international trade in terms of the shift in price relationships between what were once, but are no longer, its lists of exports and imports. Yet this is common practice in neo-classical treatises.[8]

An increase in the *number* of a country's exports, relative to its imports, is *prima facie*, but possibly refutable, evidence of a deterioration in its gains from international trade, and the opposite is

[7] This was the outcome of their emphasis on demand as the sole significant factor in the "terms of trade."

[8] Viner, (*Studies in International Trade, op. cit.,* p. 554), attempts to defend this practice on the ground that perfect homogeneity, over time, in the commodities used in the construction of price indices, is an impossible standard of perfection and that the point made above would preclude the use of *any* index number for *any* purpose. This is by no means the case. The *ideal* in the construction of index numbers is to have perfect homogeneity, over time, in each of the elements of which the indices are composed, but indices do not become useless merely because a bushel of wheat this year is not *precisely* the same as a bushel of the same grade of wheat the year before or after. The lapse from perfection is regrettable but not devastating. Professor Viner is maintaining, however, that there is no difference between this sort of imperfection and the replacement, in the index, of a bushel of wheat by a yard of cloth, and so on with other commodities. It is, to say the least, surprising that he would thus maintain that an index number of one group of commodities could be compared with a later index of a different group with any idea of ascertaining what had happened to the prices, of either group, in the intervening period.

true of its converse.[9] But a comparison of export with import price indices, even with costs taken into consideration, can never then serve as a *measure* of such a shift in the gains from trade since the prices must refer to "bales" of exports or imports which, *by definition*, have altered in composition during the period under review and are, therefore, incomparable as to price.

The point just made is of special significance in connection with the measurement of the effect of protective import tariffs on the "terms of trade" of the levying country. Such tariffs are typically laid on commodities which the levying country can produce, relative to exports, at a not great disparity of opportunity cost with the exchange ratio currently prevailing and, to the extent that the tariffs are prohibitive, the ultimate effect will be to exclude from international trade not only the protected commodities but also so much of the exports of the levying country as would otherwise have been sent out in payment for the now excluded imports. These will be the most vulnerable exports of the country in question, which is to say that, in these goods also, the difference between opportunity costs and the current ratio of exchange will be at a minimum. The upshot of the matter is the elimination of that sector of the international exchange of goods which contributes the least, or, at any rate, much less than the average, to the given country's gains from trade, and this, as already noted, means that, in the absence of any change in costs or in the international ratio of exchange of the goods in the remaining sector, the gains from such trade as is still carried on will be *proportionately* greater than before the imposition of the protection. Though there be no change in the actual terms at which the international trade common to the two periods has been transacted, and though there is no compensation whatever for the losses involved in the diversion of productive powers occasioned by the duties, an "improvement" in the country's "terms of trade" will nevertheless then appear.

Importance of Potential *Costs*

It should now be clear that we cannot know anything about even the *trend* in the gains from trade except from data which reveal

[9] In the absence of a change in cost relationships the *prima facie* case becomes well-nigh absolute but, otherwise, it is no more than a probability.

costs (including the potential cost of the home production of imports) as well as the ratio of exchange. The relevant costs are:

1. the cost of exports actually sent out in the respective periods under review;

2. the (potential) domestic production cost of the imports actually received in the respective periods under review.[10] Even in estimates somewhat more sophisticated than those just censured it is common practice to ignore this second group of costs, to assess the labor-time, resources, or factoral cost of exports in the respective periods under review, and to compare this with the volume of imports received in exchange, or even with the real costs of these imports in their countries of origin.

If the imports happened to be, to all intents and purposes, of identical composition in the two periods it might perhaps be assumed that their unit value to the recipient country was a constant. If this were true, the trend in the subjective "gains from trade" could be more or less closely derived from a comparison of the unit cost of imports in terms of the (changing) labor-time, resources, or factoral cost of the exports for which they were exchanged at contrasted periods. This would, in fact, show the varying cost of unvarying units of imported commodity income of presumptively unvarying unit ophelimity and, if we wish to construe "gains from trade" in this fashion, doubtless has its uses.

The presumption of unvarying unit ophelimity of imports is somewhat strained, however, especially if there has been a change in what it would cost to produce them at home, and we shall, therefore, revert to the practice of measuring gains from international trade by the cost of a policy which would renounce such trade. Such cost can more or less indifferently be measured either in terms of opportunity or labor-time, resources, or factors of production, provided, in the latter cases, we do not, as is impossible in the former, fail to include the (potential) cost of the home production of imports.[11]

---

[10] Opportunity cost (in the narrow sense which excludes leisure as an opportunity) combines these costs in a single expression but does not show anything about absolute productivity. Labor-time cost (or cost in terms of resources or factors of production) does not combine them though they can, of course, be compared. Such costs also show absolute productivity.

[11] One great advantage of the use of opportunity cost is its comparative precision. The other measurers of cost are slippery. But, as noted above, they are necessary (unless we construe opportunity cost to include potential leisure) if we desire something in the nature of an *absolute* cost criterion.

Calculation of Minimum and Maximum Gains

It must be granted that there is no *perfectly* satisfactory measuring rod of (subjective) gains since we have no means of gauging precisely the net loss in *satisfactions* attendant upon national self-sufficiency or the net subjective gains from international trade. It is impossible to assess the relationship between the satisfactions accruing, under self-sufficiency, from the domestic consumption of the goods produced in lieu of exports, with the satisfactions which could be obtained from the imported value-equivalent of the exports under a regime of international trade. Even if we assume that every type of potentially imported good could, and would, be produced, at relatively high cost, in a given self-sufficient national area, total consumption must necessarily be lowered, and the various goods would, in all probability, not be produced and consumed in the same relative proportions as under the very different price structure that would prevail in the presence of international trade. The (subjective) loss from the renunciation of international trade will not then be as great as it would be if the various goods should be consumed in the same proportions as under an international trading regime. The gains from international trade, on the other hand, include not only the possibility of having more of *every* good, in equal proportions, than would be possible under self-sufficiency but also those gains which accrue from the shift in the proportionate consumption of goods when, under international trade, price relationships are so altered as to cheapen the goods which give relatively large (and enhance the value of those that give only relatively small) marginal satisfactions per unit of cost.

In some cases, of course, it would be quite impossible to produce, within the home area, a commodity obtained through international trade. The labor-time cost of obtaining it would then be infinite. The real cost of the failure to obtain such a commodity could, of course, never be greater than the net loss in satisfactions which would attend its absence and, even in the complete failure of international trade, this net loss would be reduced to the difference between the satisfactions which the commodity would afford and the satisfactions derived from the goods accruing from the use, to *some end*, of the resources that must otherwise be devoted to the production of the exports with which the good in question could be acquired.

On the assumption, however, that the same, or substantially the same, classes of goods could be produced and would be consumed under national self-sufficiency as under international trade (albeit in different absolute amounts but, perhaps, the same proportions) the gains from international trade can, with constant costs, be approximated by means of a comparison of the total potential national consumption, under national self-sufficiency, with the total national consumption of similar character that would be possible in the presence of international trade. This will in fact establish, in objective terms, the *minimum* subjective gains from international trade. (The increase in satisfactions derivable from shifts in the proportions of the various products consumed under international trade, as compared with a regime of national self-sufficiency, would be an addendum incapable of exact measurement.)

The calculation is best made in terms of a comparison of the cost (in some single commodity which, under international trade, would inevitably be exported) of the composite of goods which would be consumed under national sufficiency with the cost, similarly computed, of the same composite of goods in the presence of international trade. The thus measured lower cost of a given composite of goods obtained through international trade will provide an index of the amount by which, under international trade, consumption could at a given cost be increased, in equal degree in every commodity, provided the community were minded to take its enlarged real income in this fashion.[12] (If the community should prefer some other fashion in the distribution of its income it will obviously not be gaining less, subjectively, than the subjective equivalent of the potential increase in income thus objectively measured.)

While we thus have a means of determining, for any country, the minimum gains from international trade, it is possible, also, to determine the *maximum* gains. The minimum gains are synonymous with the increase in income (or reduction in cost) which would accompany international trade in the acquisition of the same goods, in the same proportions, as would in fact be consumed in a regime of national self-sufficiency. The maximum gains are the obverse of the increase in cost (or reduction of income) which would accompany

---

[12] Wherever the gains from international trade are stated in this book this is the method of calculation that has been employed.

the attempt to produce at home the same goods, in the same proportions, as would in fact be consumed under international trade.

The *actual* gains from international trade will always be less than the maximum because, under national self-sufficiency, consumption would take a form comparatively well adapted to that system of production, and they will always be more than the minimum because, under international trade, consumption will take a form comparatively well adapted to the system of national specialization.

Factors in the Gains from Trade

Forgoing, perforce, the search for absolute precision we may say that changes, over time, in any country's returns from international trade can arise from (1) a shift in the international ratio of exchange, (2) a shift in the real cost of production of its exports, (3) a shift in what it would cost, at home, to produce its imports, or (4) any combination of these elements.[13] These changes may be such as more or less fully to cancel out, or they may reinforce one another, in their influence on the gains from trade. It is however, as already noted, only a shift in the ratio between the cost of exports and the (potential) cost of the domestic production of imports, *relative to any simultaneous shift in the ratio of exchange*, which will involve an alteration in the gains from trade *per se* (expressed as a percentage of total income).

If the cost of production of exports and the potential domestic cost of production of imports should, in any country, fall, or rise, together and in equal degree, the absolute (but not the relative) returns from trade would, in the absence of any change in the ratio of exchange, of course be affected. That this change, however, is properly attributable to an alteration in general productive power, rather than to international trade as such, is shown by the fact that similar gains, or losses, of income would appear in a nationally self-sufficient regime. They are thus not appropriately designated "gains from trade."

It is here that labor-time, resources, factoral, or any other such measure of cost, serves a purpose (albeit not that of assessing the gains from trade) which opportunity cost, in the narrow sense, will not cover. Opportunity cost, if expressed in terms of commodities

---

[13] Elements (2) and (3) would be merged if we deal in opportunity costs.

only, gives no hint of absolute productivity. When, in any country, the labor-time, resources, or factoral cost of a given group of exports rises, or falls, in equal degree with the (potential) cost in labor-time, resources, or factors, of the domestic production of the imports received in exchange, opportunity costs (narrowly construed so as to exclude the relationship between goods and leisure) will remain as before. In the absence of a shift in the international ratio of exchange this stability in opportunity costs reflects the lack of change in the *relative* importance of international trade (or its renunciation) to the country's economy. But the absolute access of goods, attainable through trade as against national self-sufficiency, will of course, be greater, or less, than before the change took place. If this point, then, is in question, we shall need an absolute measure of costs.

The variety of results from the use of different measurers may be further demonstrated if we assume that, from one date to another, the labor-time, resources, or factoral cost of production of the original exports and the similarly measured (potential) domestic cost of the original imports of any given country are reduced, though in very unequal degree, so that the domestic production cost ratios of the two classes of goods come into all but complete identity with an international exchange ratio which we have no compelling reason to suppose will not remain constant throughout. Let us assume, further, that there remains just enough margin of advantage in the import of the various goods to preserve the original volume and composition of exports and imports. At the end of the period, the country will be getting an increased amount of imports, per unit of labor-time, resources, or factors of production devoted to the output of the exports with which the imports are acquired; it will, however, be getting only the same amount of imports per unit of exported commodities; while its gains from trade (as compared with national self-sufficiency) will have fallen from a high level to something not much above zero.[14]

If, on the other hand, the labor-time, resources, or factoral costs of production of all goods should in any country rise in unequal degree so that the (potential) relative cost of the home production of imports should show a relative as well as absolute increase from

[14] The opportunity cost involved in national self-sufficiency would, in the posited circumstances, be all but negligible.

one period to another, the country, in the absence of other changes, would be getting a diminished volume of imports per unit of labor-time, resources, or factors of production devoted to the output of the exports with which the imports were acquired but would be obtaining the same amount of imports per unit of exports and would have experienced a marked increase in the gains from trade over the income available under national self-sufficiency.

It might be that, for one purpose or another, one would want to know the changes in the ratio of the prices of a given group of export goods to those of a given group of import goods, or the changes in the cost of a given group of imports in terms of the labor-time, resources, or factors of production devoted to the production of the export *quid pro quo*, but we should not confuse either of these with changes in the gains from trade as such. The looseness with which the expression "gains from trade" has been employed, even by highly reputable writers, has led to great confusion. It is, for instance, widely believed than an "improvement" in the ratio of exchange between the exports and imports of any country (a rise in the price index of exports relative to that of its imports) must involve losses to other countries in compensation of the "gains" to the country in question. This would be true only if absolute costs, all round, remained unchanged. But if, without any change in the real costs of the exports of the various countries, the (potential) real costs of the home production of imports should simultaneously rise in every country (as is quite possible), the gains of all countries from international trade would, in the absence of an alteration in the ratio of exchange, be simultaneously enhanced. This might happen, even in the *presence* of alterations in the ratio of exchange if the latter were insufficient, in the case of any country, to nullify the effects of the shift in cost ratios.[15]

Division of the Gains

The classical economists often concerned themselves not only with

[15] It is wholly probable that, from one time to another, all countries might secure their imports at declining real costs. This would occur, in the absence of a shift in the ratio of exchange, as a result of the historical increase in productivity which has now come to be regarded as normal. It might occur even in the presence of such a shift. But, if the (potential) cost of the home production of imports should drop farther than the cost of production of exports, the opportunity cost of national self-sufficiency would, in the absence of a shift in the ratio of exchange, be diminished and, along with it, the (percentage) gains from international trade.

the gains from trade accruing to any given country but with the division of the (total) gains between the trading nations. If only two countries are involved it is clear that, under unchanged cost conditions, any access of gain to one of the countries, over time, must be at the expense of the other, that is to say that, if one of the two countries gets a larger share of an unchanged total gain from trade, as the period under review wears on, the other must, correlatively, be getting a smaller share. This would show up in an alteration of the ratio of exchange in favor of the exports of the former country as against the exports of the latter (the exports of each country being the imports of the other). In these circumstances, any alteration in the ratio of exchange is inevitably invidious. It has already been shown, however, that it need not be invidious to either of the original participants (or, of course, to the newcomer) when a third country enters trade.

When more than two countries are involved in trade it will usually happen that any given country will be obtaining any given import from a nationally varied group of suppliers all of whom deliver the import at the same price. Whatever gain the importing country is making on this commodity will be the same no matter what the source of its supply. Yet the respective total gains in the trade between the importing country and its several suppliers, taken singly, may greatly differ. The importing country will then be getting a widely varying proportion of the several bilateral gains. The total bilateral gains, in each case, will vary in the degree of the disparity between the opportunity cost structures of the importing country and those of its several suppliers, and the national division of each of these gains will depend upon the relative propinquity of the cost structures of the importing and each of the supplying countries to the international ratio of exchange in the products they barter. It is quite possible, however, that what we have called the "importing" country may send none of its own products to some of its suppliers but may pay for its imports from them by transferring to any given exporter the claims against other countries issuing out of an excess in the value of the "importing" country's exports, to those other countries, over the imports it receives from them. This is a commonplace of multilateral trade and is equivalent to the purchase of foreign goods, by the "importing" country, for the purpose of transmitting them as payment to a supplier to whom it exports nothing directly.

This means that any country, in payment for any import, can use any good whatever, since, whether or not it produces any given good, it can acquire that good, in exchange for its own production, and pass it along.[16] The division of the gains from the direct trade between any two countries is, therefore, of negligible significance to either. In few, if any, cases will there be anything like an approximation to equality of gains in various bilateral transactions involving the same goods and, as just noted, there may be no direct exchange of goods at all between any two countries but simply a one-way movement of goods in direct trade with an accumulation of pecuniary claims by the exporter against the importing country. When these claims are used by the acquiring country to buy goods, where it will, the claimee country can make good on them by having shipped goods, where it best can, to acquire the (pecuniary) resources with which to meet the claims as they are presented. The world market for the purchase and sale of claims (the currencies of the various countries) facilitates, but does not alter, the fundamental transactions.

It is clearly of no economic concern whatever to any given nation whether it buys goods from, or sells them to, some country with which the total bilateral gains from such balanced exchanges as are carried on is great, and the division heavily weighted in favor of the nation in question, rather than deal with some other country where the converse is the case.[17] The only occasion for any nation's concern is for the gains on its international trade taken as a whole and, possibly, for the gains of the rest of the world, taken as a unit, in trade with the nation in question. Bi-national comparisons are not only invidious but they are completely futile. Venezuela may export oil to the United States in exchange for wheat, and the United States may, in turn, export an equivalent value of oil to Canada in exchange for Canadian wheat. It would require only a

[16] The process would normally take place through the acquisition and sale of foreign currencies (which tends to conceal the underlying exchange of goods) but the more fundamental exchange has been directly carried on in recent decades under various forms of trade agreements.

[17] It is, of course, impossible to say *which* of the exports of any given country to another with which it has a "favorable" balance are used to pay for its imports from that other country.

perhaps infinitesimal shift in the relationship between the costs of sea and rail transport to divert Venezuelan oil to Canada in exchange for Canadian wheat, with the United States eliminated as both exporter and importer of those commodities. It is certain that this would involve very little change in the economic status of any of the three countries but the gains from the international trade and their division, if assessed on a bi-national basis against the national cost ratios, would almost certainly appear to be greatly changed for both Venezuela and for Canada.[18] For the United States the (slight) original gains from the trade would, of course, vanish along with the trade itself, and there could, for the United States, then be no question of their division.

For any given country the gains from international trade will be a function of the degree of deviation of its internal cost structure from the ratio of exchange of products which becomes established for the world as a whole. No country can do much to shift this ratio and the internal cost relationships are also a matter over which policy can exert only a very slight influence. The extent of the gains of any country from international trade is therefore in large measure fortuitous, depending on the accident of the similarity or difference of its internal cost structure to or from a world ratio of exchange which is at once the resultant of the interplay of the internal cost structures of the various trading countries and, along with them, the determinant of the comparative advantage of each. Any country's gains from trade will, in the absence of a change in costs, be increased (or reduced) by any movement in the ratio of exchange which, on balance, enhances (or impairs) the prices of its previous and present exports relative to the prices of its previous and present imports, but they will also be increased (or reduced) by any change in relative costs which, without a fully compensating change in the ratio of exchange, lowers (or raises) the cost of its previous and present exports relative to the (potential) cost of the production at home of its imports. The total gains from international trade of each of a group of trading countries may expand or contract simultaneously according as national cost ratios, on the

[18] United States producers are on the margin of indifference as between wheat and oil but this is not true of either Canada or Venezuela. The *ostensible* gain is, therefore, much larger when Canada and Venezuela directly exchange their specialties than when they trade with the United States (which is not *specialized* in either commodity).

whole, deviate from or approach the world ratio of exchange, while the *division* of the total gains in the trade between any country and the rest of the world depends on the degree in which its opportunity cost ratios for the traded goods deviate from the prevailing world ratio of exchange for such goods. The gain of any one country, and its share of the total, may be increased, over time, merely because the relative cost of producing at home the goods that it does not in fact produce is rising. This can scarcely be of much concern to any other country and, with the maintenance of its international trade, is not of any concern even to the country in which it occurs.

There is perhaps even less nationalistic reason for comparing the labor-time, resources, or factoral cost of the imports of any given country (as measured in the exports with which they are bought) with the corresponding cost of production of the latter goods in the country of their origin. Ricardo pointed out that it was a matter of indifference to England what it was costing foreigners to turn out the goods that England was importing. England's sole interest lay in what it was costing the English to produce the exports, with which a given volume and composition of imports were purchased, compared with what it would cost to produce these imports in England. This is what Professor Viner, if I rightly conceive him, means by "the single factoral terms of trade," i.e. the cost, in factors of production of England's exports, relative to the (potential) cost, in English factors of production, of producing in England the imports received in exchange.

Interest in the relationship between the cost to the actual producers of the *quid pro quos* in an exchange was, in part, excited by the now discredited labor theory of value. The comparison which attracted attention was not the relevant comparison between two methods available to the citizens of any nation of obtaining commodity income (national self-sufficiency or international trade) but an invidious comparison between the labor-time, resources, or factoral cost of the exports of any nation and the labor-time, resources, or factoral cost, to the foreign producers, of the goods received in exchange. This latter comparison Professor Viner calls the "double factoral terms of trade." Since such a comparison is unconcerned with any data on what it would cost either of the national parties to produce the goods they *im*port it has little or nothing to do with the gains from international trade or the losses incurred in its renunciation.

Provided cost *ratios* for the various goods in the various countries remain unchanged it makes no difference to the (unit) gains from trade what the absolute cost of any or all goods in any given country, or what the relationship between these absolute costs in the various countries, may be or become. Absolute costs, however measured, will go far to determine the general prosperity of a nation, and the relative prosperity of various national units will largely hinge on the relationship between their real costs of production, but a country's unit gain, from international trade, is not a function of general productivity, or cost, either in the country in question or in any other country. However slight, or immense, in labor-time, resources, or factors of production, the cost of the exports of any country relative to the similar cost, to the foreign producers, of an equivalent value of the given country's imports may be or become, the (unit) gains from international trade will remain untouched in the absence of changes in other relationships. A country can nearly always improve its prosperity by lowering the real costs of production of its own output but there is no presumption that it will be affected one way or the other, and certainly none that it will be affected one way *rather* than the other, through any change, up or down, in the general real costs of production in other countries.

Except, therefore, as a matter of xenophobia, or international altruism, it makes no difference to any country whether it obtains its imports cheaply (i.e. at a lower real or opportunity cost than they could be put out at home) because the foreign producers receive low wages (i.e. have high real costs) or because they are highly productive (i.e. have low real costs). Parts of the supply of any given import may, in fact, be produced under either condition. Suppose that without any changes in opportunity cost conditions in a given country, or in the ratio of exchange, the suppliers of its imports (who may also share in supplying other countries with the given country's export commodities) improve their productive efficiency either in general or in export lines only. A given amount of the labor-time, resources, or factors of production of the country in question, embodied in its exports, will, in the absence of other changes, then exchange for a reduced amount of the labor-time, resources, or factors of production of other countries (embodied in its imports). The "double factoral terms of trade" would then have altered in its "disfavor." Conversely, if the efficiency of its foreign suppliers should decline, other things being as posited, the "double factoral terms of trade" would have moved in the given country's "favor." Its income, however, would in neither case be altered. The income of the foreign suppliers would, of course, be affected, but it would be affected not so much by the trade, as such, as by the general results of the change in productive efficiency.

It may, as noted above, well happen that a given group of imports of any given country is obtained partly from a country of low wages (high real cost) and partly from a country of high wages (low real cost). If, without any other change in the given country, the proportions of the total of these imports from these respective suppliers should for some reason alter, the "double factoral terms of trade" would be affected. This would, however, be a matter of no consequence whatever to the country in question, and might well be of none to either of the supplying countries.[19]

It is, to repeat, only when we measure any country's gains from trade in terms of what it would cost, at home, to produce its imports that we are on solid ground. This is, therefore, the only sense in which the phrase "gains from trade" is likely to have much significance and for this measurement there is no need of the concept of "double factoral terms of trade."

Despite the fact that imports produced under low-wage conditions tend to maximize for the importing nation the gains in the "double factoral terms of trade" there is a persistent political bias against them. This particular bias is, if anything, more irrational than the notion that the "double factoral terms of trade" are of any significance for a given country's prosperity. The self-interest of any country would lead it to desire imports at as little cost, to itself, as they could anyhow be obtained and, as already noted, the *reasons* why its imports are cheap are, on nationalist grounds, to it a matter of no concern. We have already noted that there is no warrant for the widely prevalent belief that the permanent prosperity of any one nation is dependent on a similar prosperity in others. It is true that short-run alternations of prosperity and depression spread from one country to others but the modal (long-run) economic con-

---

[19] These countries might readily make the adjustments in each case from, and to, alternative products which are, to them, on the margin of indifference in production.

dition of any country may vary in any degree, and for any length of time, from that of other countries. History, as well as logic, abundantly supports this assertion.[20] There is no reason to suppose that, under the freest of trade, the economic penury of any country has any unfavorable effects on the rest of the world, nor any ground for the belief that an improvement in the *per capita* production and prosperity of economically backward nations would have any generally favorable repercussions in other areas.[21] The prosperity of any country is, to repeat, a function of two variables only: per capita general productivity and the ratio of exchange between its exports and its imports. For the vast majority of countries the first of these is overwhelmingly important and any general improvement in production in any given country is likely to redound almost exclusively to its own advantage. The only way in which other countries not sharing the improvement could conceivably capture any of the gain would be through a shift in the ratio of exchange as a consequence of the improved productivity in the backward areas being concentrated in certain (exportable) lines of output with a resulting fall in the value of the commodities of expanded supply. Any such shift is as likely to injure as to benefit any other country. If, for instance, such a country happens to be an exporter of the goods in which the hitherto backward country concentrates production it will probably suffer from the relative fall in the prices of these goods but, if it is an importer of such goods, it will probably benefit.

The possible shift in the ratio of exchange will, in any event, be strictly limited by changes in the composition of production in all countries in a position to move out of the goods of declining relative value and into those whose relative value is rising. This will minimize the effects on all other countries, for good or ill, of the productive advance in the hitherto backward nation and, by the same token, will concentrate the good effects on the nation in which the advance oc-

20 The logical ground for the assertion is that the lack of international mobility of factors of production (including labor) is the basis of a (special) theory of international values.

21 The International Labor Office has, for decades, striven to raise labor standards in backward areas on the ground that further advances in more favored countries would otherwise be retarded. This is an illusion. The idea is that the competition of low-wage countries is particularly keen and generally reprehensible. This is not true. Wages and working conditions in low-wage countries could be improved only by improvements in the efficiency of their output. The one change would cancel the other in its effect on competitive capacity.

curs. These, however, will be solely the result of its increased productivity. So far as its gains from international trade are concerned they will *diminish* (as a percentage of its total income) in the degree in which, without an alteration in the international ratio of exchange, the improvements in production apply more fully to goods hitherto imported than to those hitherto exported. This will, at any rate, be true until the character of its trade is completely changed. It has already been hinted that such a change took place in Britain in the period climaxed by the industrial revolution. Until comparatively modern times Britain had been predominantly an exporter of foodstuffs and raw materials and an importer of manufactured goods but, after power machinery was introduced, the situation was transformed. The transition period was no doubt marked by a reduction in the gains from trade. The gains were restored only by a concentration of production for export in lines which had formerly been imported, with a corresponding reduction of production in lines formerly exported. Though the United States, in recent decades, has more or less duplicated this transition the United States is in a position, as Britain is not, to reverse the process if the specialization in manufactured goods of hitherto backward, and highly populous, areas should unfavorably affect the ratio of exchange between such goods and raw materials or foodstuffs. This is because the United States is on the margin of indifference in the production of many goods in both categories and can readily shift the emphasis of its production from one category to another in response to actual, or threatened, alterations in the ratio of exchange. This shift would reduce the losses of Great Britain and other countries similarly situated.

Aside from passive adaptation there is not much to be done about an alteration in the international ratio of exchange since no country is in a position greatly to affect that ratio. The obsession of the classical writers with the division of the gains from trade is explicable in their erroneous notions about the determination of the international ratio of exchange and the possibility of facile change in it. The plain fact is that, if the cost ratios in any country closely approximate the rather solidly based international exchange ratio, the country cannot possibly gain very much from international trade, but that, when they widely diverge from it, it cannot fail to gain greatly. Whether the one or the other situation prevails is largely a matter of accident or, at any rate, of conditions, such as the distribution of natural resources, which are beyond human control. No country is responsible for its situation and none, by taking thought or action, can much change its status in this respect. If, in any country, the distribution of relative resources, and relative skills, parallels that of the world at large, if the country is, in this matter, a microcosm, its gains from international trade, and its share of the total of such gains will be small, since cost ratios in such a country cannot be far from the international ratio of exchange in a trading world. If, on the other hand, the distribution of relative resources, and relative skills, happens to be greatly different in a given country from that of the world at large, its gains from the appropriate specialization, and trade, will usually be large, and so will be its share of the total gains of its trade with the outside world.

Further Considerations on the Special Gains of Small Countries

We have seen that the greatest gains from international trade are likely to accrue to comparatively small countries both because the distribution of resources in them will probably not be anything approaching a simulacrum of that in the world as a whole and because no large sector of the world ratio of exchange will, by the sheer mass of production of any such country, be brought into conformity with its own cost ratios. A large country, on the other hand, cannot completely specialize in any one commodity, however economically important, without lowering its value to the point at which that commodity would exchange against some former import at the cost ratio prevalent in the large country. Specialization in these two commodities, moreover, would lower their values, together, until they would exchange against some further former import at the cost ratios of the country in question. And so on in the degree of the country's economic size. This means that, over a considerable range of products, the cost ratios in a large country will be the same as the exchange ratio in the world at large and will, in fact, determine it. This reduces the scope of the country's possible gains from international trade to perhaps a minor fraction of the total of internationally traded commodities. A typical small country, however, can specialize in a single export commodity, without much, if at all, lowering its exchange value, and will gain on all the rest as imports. Economically small countries, almost universally therefore, have a narrow range of exports and a wide range of imports whereas an economically preponderant country like the United States has a great variety of exports, with the great bulk of its imports concentrated in relatively few items. The greater the variety of a country's *imports* the greater, *ceteris paribus*, will be its gains from international trade. The converse is true of its exports.[22]

The classical writers held, on the whole, to the view that the lion's share of the gains from international trade will accrue to the lambs (the small countries) but they usually gave wrong reasons for their (in this case, sound) conviction. Bastable, drawing on J. S. Nicholson, adumbrates valid conclusions, then throws irrelevant doubt upon them, yet finally asserts, somewhat hesitantly, that "the probability is that a small country gains by opening up trade with a large one."[23] Mill alleged that "the richest [i.e. other things equal, the economically largest] countries . . . [tend to] gain the least by a given amount of foreign commerce: since, having a greater demand for commodities generally, they are likely to have a greater demand for foreign commodities, and thus modify the terms of trade to their own disadvantage."[24] Quite apart from the facts, to be expected from Mill and the whole of the orthodox school, that this completely ignores relative costs and that it uses the unwarranted concept of nationally segregatable demands, there is no reason for supposing that the national demand of any large country for foreign commodities will overbalance the demand (whatever these phrases may mean) of the whole of the foreign world for the given country's exports. Marshall citing, with approval, the passage just quoted from Mill, and with the apparent intention of supporting Mill's conclusion, advances the argument that because a small country depends on foreign supplies for many things which a country with more varied resources can produce for herself, its (the small country's) demand for foreign goods is therefore very eager while the large and rich country can attract foreign purchasers (that is to say, can increase the demand of foreign consumers for its goods) by a great

---

[22] This is almost the exact opposite of the classicists' assertion.

[23] C. F. Bastable, *Theory, op. cit.*, p. 43. Put in this fashion Bastable's statement is vapid since *any* new entrant, however large, will inevitably gain by opening up international trade.

[24] *Principles of Political Economy, op. cit.*, Book III, Chap. XVIII, §8.

variety of goods offered for sale.[25] On Marshall's own principles, this would *improve* the terms on which the large country would carry on its trade though, from the context, Marshall seems to be arguing for the contrary view. Finally, Marshall says that the statement he had just made needs to be balanced by others which make for the opposite conclusion. His *prior* conclusion he has never clearly stated, but that it is that large and rich countries *tend* to have unfavorable "terms of trade" would appear to follow from the sequel in which Marshall asserts that large and rich countries have opportunities for developing *new* products of which the sale abroad would operate to improve the terms on which their total trade is carried on (and so to counteract what would otherwise be a very unfavorable ratio of exchange of products).[26] Marshall can scarcely be said to be decisive.

The probability that an economically small country will secure a greater share of the benefits from international trade than will accrue to the larger nations arises *solely* from the fact that such a country may concentrate on the output of a single commodity in which it possesses a very great comparative advantage and exchange it for other goods at the very divergent cost ratios prevailing in some large national entity which also produces, as one of many commodities, the specialty of the small country.[27] A large country, on the other hand, will bring the international ratio of exchange for a large number of products into conformity with its own cost ratios.

It is clear that, if a country is, in hypothetical illustrations, assumed to become all but infinitesimally small, its *rate* of gain from international trade would rise. It would normally then give up the production of many of the commodities it had formerly found it worth while to export and would secure them, as imports, on terms probably unchanged, from those areas, formerly included within its own polity, which had now become foreign nations. Whenever, on the other hand, a country, by hypothesis, grows in size indefinitely, it

25 Charles P. Kindleberger ("Flexibility of Demand in International Trade," *The Quarterly Journal of Economics*, Vol. LI, pp. 352-361) shows the confusion, and contradictions, in the classical treatment of "eagerness," "urgency," and "elasticity" of "international demand."

26 cf. Alfred Marshall, *Money Credit and Commerce*, *op. cit.*, p. 169. In his next two or three pages Marshall pays more attention to *supply* but only in a few *obiter dicta* which he did not see fit to develop. The whole discussion is rambling.

27 The ensuing pages reproduce, with slight changes, some passages from my article, "The Theory of International Values," already cited.

will approach nearer and nearer to the scope of a world state. At a point just before such a hypothetical state had engrossed the whole world it could obviously not be obtaining any great gains from *international* trade, since the terms on which practically all goods (including that or those of the small state still outside its orbit) would be exchanged against one another could not possibly be much different from those which would prevail were the large country's trade purely domestic. Every increase in the size of a trading unit, through a process of annexation, would tend to bring internal cost of production ratios nearer to the ratios of exchange which had prevailed in the world as a whole before the increase in the size of the given state had occurred (and would still prevail), and so make any gain from *international* trade impossible. From this it follows that the tendency of any political unit to secure the larger formal share of the gains from international trade must vary inversely with size. The larger countries will, of course, obtain in *domestic* exchanges many advantages similar to those which international trade gives to the smaller. When a country, without any change in the volume of trade, or its direction, or in the ratio of exchange of commodities, grows larger by annexation of another state, or becomes smaller by scission, it would tend respectively to suffer a loss, or register a gain, in its *international* trade merely by reason of the fact that a converse movement would have taken place in its domestic trade. The *national* terms on which international trade was being carried on would then have formally moved, in one direction or the other, but there would have been no change in the barter or price ratio between the various commodities and no real loss or gain to anyone. So far as conditions of this sort are operative it is somewhat misleading therefore, though it is formally correct, to say that small countries tend to secure the greater part of the gains from international trade.

A favorable formal ratio for any one country, moreover, frequently issues out of the fact that the country in question would be relatively very inefficient in the production of the goods it imports. Suppose that such a country, small and generally inefficient, were wiped out. It might well happen that this would not affect at all the world price ratios between the goods it had formerly exported and those it had imported since resources would, at constant cost, be diverted in other countries toward greater output of the former exports, and smaller production of the former imports, of the vanished country. One could, however, say that, while the small country was in existence, all the other countries of the world were trading with the small country on terms very favorable to it, and therefore unfavorable to them, and that, when it had disappeared, the trade of no country was being carried on at quite so unfavorable a ratio against the world in general as had formerly been the case. The favorable formal ratio at which small countries tend to carry on their foreign trade is often attributable to considerations of this character. When this is the case the unfavorable "terms of trade" of the larger countries, as against these smaller countries only, are a matter of no consequence to such larger countries. As has already been pointed out the significant thing for any given country is not the ratio as against any single foreign political unit (said ratio being determined by the relative powers of the *foreign* national entity, in the production of the commodities exchanged, as much as by its own) but the ratios against a series of countries. It is an error to suppose that, because a small country trades with a large one on what are to the small country very favorable terms, the larger land is carrying on its foreign trade as a ratio which leans toward the unfavorable side. As against third countries, with which it presumably trades in identical commodities on exactly the same terms as with the designated small country, the large country may be securing the major share of the gains. The error lies in taking different bases of comparison. In the one case the basis of comparison covers a large part or the whole of the international trade of the (small) country concerned, and therefore gives a good picture of the advantage of international trade to that country. In the other case the basis of comparison covers only a very small part of the total international trade of the (large) country concerned, or even only a small part of the trade in a single commodity, and therefore gives a very distorted picture of the relative advantage to the large country of its total foreign trade or of the trade in the single commodity the supply of which it obtains in part from the small country above considered.

It is not, however, with such merely formal phenomena but with the real status of small *vis-à-vis* large countries in their international trading that we may more appropriately be concerned. In developing alleged vindications of the orthodox view, some writers violate their own conditions of *ceteris paribus* and their arguments, in consequence, are completely vitiated. This is true of a discussion of the

matter by Otto Frhr. von Mering which is otherwise acute.[28] In varying, by hypothesis, the size of the country with which he is experimenting, von Mering always changes, both absolutely and relatively
to other commodities, the total world supply of the commodities in
which that country specializes. Now every increase or diminution in
the world supply of any commodity or group of commodities, all else
remaining as before, will of course effect a respectively adverse or
favorable alteration in the ratios at which the given commodity, or
group of commodities, will exchange against other articles. Under
these conditions von Mering has no difficulty in showing, *prima
facie*, that the size of a country and the favorableness of its trade
ratio are negatively correlated. But really to prove the point one
must show that a variation in size alone, everything else except the
inevitable accompaniments of such a variation being kept unchanged, will be correlated with favorable terms of trade. To do this
one should revert to the case of a country becoming smaller, by
scission, or larger by consolidation with other countries. Let us deal
with these cases in order. If a country should become smaller by
scission, with both of the severed parts continuing to produce, in the
same volume as they had formerly done, all of the commodities which
had been produced in the original unit,[29] there would be no change
in the terms on which either of the severed parts would trade with the
outside world or in the world ratio of exchange of commodities.
Similarly, a large country trading freely with a number of small
countries would, if the small countries should be consolidated into a
single political unit, obtain no better, nor they a worse, ratio of
exchange from the mere fact that it happened to be dealing with the
citizens of what had become a large country instead of with those
of a number of small constituents.[30] The same result would follow
if, when the size, and the supply of commodities, of any given country should show a change, the size, and the supply of commodities, of

---

[28] "Ist die Theorie der internationalen Werte widerlegt?", *Archiv für Sozialwissen-
schaft und Sozialpolitik*, Vol. LXV, 1931, pp. 251 *et seq.*

[29] This would occur if neither of the parts had had any comparative advantage with
respect to the other.

[30] It should be noted, however, that the newly consolidated state might secure a
worse ratio on its *international* trade than had any of its several parts on *their*
international trade while they had remained independent nations. Much of the gains
from international trade would simply have been transferred to the domestic account.
This is an illustration of a formal (but not a real) adverse movement in the trade
ratio to which attention has already been drawn.

one or a group of other countries producing similar articles should alter in equal degree in the opposite direction. All these would be changes in the absolute and relative size of the several trading countries, all else remaining so far as possible as before, and they are much nearer the essential conditions for the test in question than are von Mering's assumptions. Since such changes in relative size of the trading countries would not alter the terms on which any of them traded, this is evidence that national size, *per se,* whatever its influence in determining the character of "reciprocal national demand schedules," is not *necessarily* a factor in the distribution of the real gains from trade, and that reciprocal "national demand schedules" *per se,* are of no significance.

Small countries, without much effect on the ratio of international exchange, simply contribute to, and draw from, a general pool of products which are traded against one another on the basis of the total reciprocal supply (demand) and not on the supply (demand) from any particular source (national reciprocal supply or demand). The alleged tendency for small countries, *solely by reason of their small demand,* to secure the larger real gains from international trade is therefore non-existent. If a small country happens to have opportunity costs of production which, for most commodities, reflect a fairly close approximation to the current exchange relationships between the various commodities in the world at large, it can gain little from international trade.[31] A large country, such as Britain or Brazil, may, on the other hand, export manufactured commodities in exchange for raw materials and foodstuffs, or raw materials and foodstuffs in exchange for manufactures, on terms which are very greatly more favorable to it than those which would prevail if it had no international trade, and more favorable than those which many small countries obtain. A jack-of-all-trades gains little by trading while "natural" specialists may gain much. Whether the jack-of-all-trades is big or little is, in itself, irrelevant.

The Gains of Rich Countries

The question whether the terms on which *rich* countries carry on international trade tend to lean toward the side unfavorable to them,

[31] Compare the gains of country A (Table A_{1e}) with those of much bigger countries, especially those which are still not so large as to preclude concentration on a single commodity. "Reciprocal national demand" has no bearing on the case.

as the neo-classical writers usually maintained was the fact, is, in the main, a special case of the question of size since per capita incomes are a principal factor in the economic size of any country. A sparsely populated rich country would have precisely the same effect on the international ratio of exchange as a densely populated poor country of equal total output and the same cost ratios. It should be pointed out, however, that a country may be rich not only because it is highly productive but because it actually exchanges its goods against foreign products on terms that are, to it, favorable. If the favorable ratio of exchange were the cause of the riches, it would obviously be untenable to assert that the riches were causal with respect to the ratio, and that, in addition, they tended to make it *dis*advantageous to the rich country. But this contradictory position can be found in classical or neo-classical writings.[32]

National riches may be the result of great general productivity, without any pronounced measure of specialization, or they may be a consequence of concentration in a few lines of output where absolute efficiency is high though in other lines it would be low. In the one case the "terms of trade" will not be very favorable to the country in question, and the riches (so far as they reflect *absolute* economic size) would depress them. In the other case, the "terms of trade" will almost certainly be good. Per capita incomes have no special bearing on the matter but a *populous* rich country can scarcely hope to do as well out of international trade as some of its

[32] We may refer again to Professor Taussig's discussion of the trade between Great Britain and India in his *International Trade* (New York, The Macmillan Company, 1928). On page 18 of that book Taussig says that the key to the apportionment of advantage in international trade is found in the money incomes of the people of the exchanging countries. Since money incomes are high in Great Britain, relatively to money incomes in India, he draws the conclusion that the terms of the trade between the two countries are very favorable to Britain. (This is more specifically stated on page 157.) Developing the idea farther he remarks that it is "conceivable that money incomes in the two regions should be the same, and the gain thus shared equally." I must dissent from the views that equal money incomes in Great Britain and India would furnish any evidence that the gains from the trade between the two countries were being shared equally, that the actual relative incomes provide any criterion of the actual division of the gains from the trade, or that there is any proportionate connection between relative money incomes and the ratio of interchange of products. But I am now concerned merely to point out that Professor Taussig here regards the relative riches of Great Britain as an *effect* of favorable terms and presumably abandons the equally false idea that it will be a *cause* of *un*favorable terms. His erroneous views in this matter issued out of his ill-founded assumption that high-money-income countries are also high-price countries, and the perhaps even more questionable dogma that high-price countries will, *ipso facto*, secure favorable terms of trade.

smaller neighbors (whether rich or poor). That is to say, its gains, per unit of total production, will tend to be small principally because it will, in many products, dominate the international ratio of exchange.

Varying Gains from Different Sectors of a Country's Trade

The composition of a country's *output* ranges from products of low to those of high cost relative to the cost structure of any other single country. What products will be exported or imported, in the absence of restrictions on trade, will be determined by the relationship between the cost structure of the country in question and the international ratio of exchange as modified by costs of international transport. Marginal cost ratios between all exports, however, will be identical with that (unmodified) ratio. The international ratio of exchange is, in turn, interdependent with the cost structures of the various trading countries.

Under the assumption of free internal competition, any one export is as good as any other as a means of payment for imports. Not only the marginal cost ratios but also the marginal utilities of the exports of any country correspond with the international ratio of exchange of the products concerned. The marginal utilities of the various imports, however, deviate in diverse measure from what it would cost, in the importing country, to produce the several commodities. Some imports are therefore much more important than others in the sense that the cost of the domestic production of some would be much greater than that of others, relative to their cost of acquisition as imports. The denial to any country of certain selected imports might do it very little harm whereas the denial of certain others might, to the potential importer, be a matter of grave concern. Similarly, a given amount of protection of domestic industry in any country is of small or great adverse influence on the country's general prosperity according as protective import duties are imposed upon the one or the other group of products.

At one extreme in the range of commodities are those which cannot, or are very unlikely to, move in international trade. These include articles with a heavy cost of transport per unit of value, and those that *must* be consumed *in situ*, together with the numerous services that can be rendered only when the producer and consumer are in close physical contact with one another. Domestic production is here inevitable. At the other extreme are those commodities which either cannot be domestically produced under any circumstances or cannot be domestically produced except at prohibitive opportunity cost. These are the products that a country must, of course, import if it is to have them in any substantial amount or at all. Against such commodities protective tariffs are not usually laid, and from these products the major share of gain in international trade accrues.

Between these two extremes lies a great variety of products which could more or less readily move, in either direction, in international trade. Comparatively slight changes in the relation between the domestic cost structure and the world ratio of exchange might shift some of these products into or out of the export or import category of any given country. Many of them, moreover, may, at a given moment, be neither exported nor imported in any given country since the difference in their opportunity costs in that country and in some exporting area will often not be sufficient to cover the cost of international transportation. The gain, to any such country, from the import of these products is, in any event, small. It is, in consequence, on the import of these products that protective tariffs are most frequently imposed, and international trade, in these products, thereby more or less completely eliminated, with a resulting great increase in the relative weight of other items in the gains from import trade.

It has been estimated that, in 1927, approximately 35% of the imports of the United States consisted of products impossible, or virtually impossible, to produce in this country; that 15% of the imports was of special quality products with characteristics not found in domestic commodities; and that 90% of the remaining half of the imports were articles of which there was an inevitable deficiency of domestic production at a cost even remotely competitive with that of the exporting areas.[33]

The products in the first category were crude natural rubber, coffee, tin, certain fertilizers, diamonds, certain ferro-alloys, nickel, various chemical products, cocoa, tea, and certain tropical fruits,

[33] Commission of Inquiry into National Policy in International Economic Relations, Report on *International Economic Relations*, University of Minnesota Press. Minneapolis, 1934, pp. 135 *et seq.*, and *passim*.

vegetables, and fibers. It is doubtful whether we should include natural silk or jute within the list since it is *possible* to produce them here. In both cases, however, the requirements for very large amounts of (cheap) labor make domestic production out of question. Raw silk, in consequence, is admitted duty free while on jute fabrics only a slight duty is imposed. Since 1927 there have, of course, been significant changes attendant upon the development of synthetic products, notably rubber and rayon. In 1937 crude natural rubber and silk still represented 10 per cent of the value of all our imports, but it is, in the foreseeable future, not unlikely that they may be largely replaced in American consumption by the synthetic products. The imputable gain from the import of these products has, in any case, been much reduced by the development of actual or potential domestic production of the synthetics.

In the second category of imports, viz., specialty products that *could*, perhaps, be produced in the United States, but at very high opportunity cost, the principal types of imports are:

a. Fine goods made entirely, or largely, by hand;

b. Machine-made but not mass-produced goods requiring great care in manufacture and the employment of specially trained and skilled labor;

c. Certain agricultural products requiring assiduous attention in cultivation.

Many of these products possess advantages of superiority in quality, style, or reputation, often because of the assiduous hand-labor required. Fine precision instruments, laces and other textiles (e.g. English woolens), fine chinaware, toys, high grade iron and steel products (e.g. Swedish razor steel), are representative of this group. It is likely that similar considerations apply to French liqueurs and perfumes, extra-long-staple cotton, Turkish tobaccos, cigar wrappers and related products, which, apart from special soils or climate, require the intensive application of labor that, with high wage-rates and no special skill, it would be highly uneconomical in this country to apply.

The third category of United States imports comprises those with domestic production a good deal less than domestic consumption and, for the marginal part of the output of some of them at least, at such high cost that, in spite of tariff limitations, it is commercially profitable to import a sizable fraction of the whole. Some of the articles in this category, however, would probably be produced domestically in part, and in part imported, under perfectly free trading conditions. Such products as mercury, bauxite, tungsten, manganese, olive oil, newsprint, wool, hides, and sugar are representative of this group. With increased depletion of American natural resources it is not unlikely that additional natural resource products will enter the category.

There are, finally, certain commodities which are both imported into, and exported from, the United States. Copper, petroleum and its derivatives, sawmill products, and some fruits, are in this group. Some 90% of American imports of copper are destined for refining and export in the refined state. With increased depletion of American copper resources, however, much larger imports for domestic consumption may develop. In 1937 the United States imported 27 million barrels of crude petroleum while exporting 67 million barrels of crude and 41 million barrels of refined petroleum products. Much of the import was for the purpose of refining and export in the refined state. These imports, at present, represent no great gain to this country but, in the future, this country may move away from the margin in some of them and the gain will then be greater. It may be pointed out that, even in 1929, the money cost of a barrel of domestic crude petroleum was alleged to be 40 cents higher than that of Venezuela crude including the transportation cost in Venezuela to the seaboard.[34] United States imports of sawmill products were approximately 50% of the exports in 1937. For these products also, with an increased depletion of forest resources, the gains from import are likely to become progressively greater as time goes on and, even now, are by no means negligible in special cases.[35]

It is clear that, while the gains to the United States from international trade are not specially great, the gains on most of such imports as it permits are relatively good. The gains diminish as we move from the earlier to the later listed categories of imports and,

[34] cf. United States Tariff Commission Report, *Production Costs of Crude Petroleum and of Refined Petroleum Products*, House Document, No. 195, U.S. Government Printing Office, Washington, 1932, p. 55.

[35] Much of the comment here presented on the foreign trade of the United States is based on an unpublished manuscript of one of my students, George Rosen, concerning the probable effects of the industrialization of the Far East on the prosperity of the United States.

for the bulk of the goods in the group last cited, are very small. This does not mean that any one American import is of any greater significance, as a want satisfier, than any other (of the same value at the existing international ratio of exchange), or that we ought to concentrate our imports in the lines where the (total) gains from international trade are greatest. The proper determinant is that of equal value per unit of cost, at the margin, in the utility schedules. But it *does* mean that, in the final category of imports, the citizens of the United States do not obtain any great "consumers rent," that they could, with much less cost, dispense with imports in this than forgo those in the earlier categories, and produce practically the same goods at home in lieu of the exports by means of which they are now acquired. It also means that any extension of the protective system in the imposition of new, or heavier, duties on the *earlier* categories of imports would run into rapidly rising losses of real income.

With the limitation on the number of goods a large country imports (a consequence of the inevitable wide variety of its exports) its gains from international trade are restricted in the only place where gains occur, viz., in the acquisition, by import, of goods at less cost (in terms of the exports by which the imported goods are obtained) than would be incurred in producing them at home. On the goods it *does* import, however, it may be gaining more, per unit, than many small countries gain on any of their greater variety of imports.

CHAPTER XII

GENERAL CRITIQUE OF CLASSICAL DOCTRINES

The internal contradictions of the classical doctrines on international values can be readily demonstrated as soon as we move out of the simple context on which they are based. The classical analysis posits mobility in the relationship between the prices of national composites of exports and imports as the mechanism through which equilibrium in international trade is acquired and maintained.[1] Normal price relationships, within each composite, are, however, tied to domestic costs and, in a given constellation of constant costs, are therefore fixed. When, under these conditions, a change occurs in the price relationships between the composites, or blocs, of goods, every price within one of the composites must, if we are to have equilibrium, be presumed to move in the same degree and direction against every price in the other. Such a movement is conceivable when no country is producing any commodity produced in any other. But, so soon as this highly improbable condition is lacking, any shift in the price relationships between the products of two countries, taken *en bloc*, will, even though the blocs themselves contain no common commodity, traverse the production of some third country. This will make it impossible to quadrate the terms of the international ratio of exchange of certain products with their domestic costs of production in that country.

Let us suppose that countries A, B, and C are trading with one another in the commodities z, y, x, and w, with A exporting z and y, B exporting x and w, and C exporting z and x. Let the cost ratios on the relevant items be as follows:

	A	B	C
z	2 (1)	–	1 (2)
y	3 ($1\frac{1}{2}$)	–	–
x	–	4 (2)	2 (4)
w	–	5 ($2\frac{1}{2}$)	–

[1] A country with an (assumed) adverse balance in the international accounts is supposed to offer "its" exports at lower exchange values against "its" imports until the total values of exports and imports come into equilibrium through a more than proportionate expansion in the physical volume of its exports, or contraction in the physical volume of its imports, or both. This raises the whole matter of the "elasticity of international demand" to which reference will later be made.

Let the original ratio of exchange, in consonance with costs of production in each of the countries, be $2z = 3y = 4x = 5w$ ($z = 1\frac{1}{2}y = 2x = 2\frac{1}{2}w$). Let us suppose further that, for some reason, the total value of A's exports begins to fall short of that of its imports and that the reverse is true of B and C. On classical analysis, the ratio of exchange should move adversely to A's exports and in favor of those of B and C. Since C is exporting one product in common with A, and another in common with B, this is, to say the least, difficult of attainment though, as a *net result*, it is perhaps not inconceivable. But, even if it could be attained, it must violate the condition that the ratio of exchange will, as a condition of equilibrium, reflect relative costs in the producing countries. Let us assume, for the sake of argument only, that the ratio moves to $2z = 3y = 3.6x = 4.5w$. This is in line with cost ratios in A and B but not in C. C's exports are no longer exchanging against one another on the basis of their relative costs of production in that country. On these terms, then, no equilibrium is possible. There is, in fact, no ratio, other than the original, that will at once secure equilibrium and permit the several countries to retain their respective lists of products. Country C may, of course, completely abandon the production of z provided that a tentative shift in the ratio, adverse to that product, persists indefinitely in face of the induced curtailment of its output in C. But this is adjustment along the lines suggested in the present book, not along those of the classical doctrines.

Since only one ratio of exchange will quadrate with given lists of exports and with given cost structures in the several trading countries, the whole of the classical analysis, which relies on *flexibility* in that ratio, with fixity in the qualitative composition of the several countries' exports and imports, falls to the ground. The notion that national export price structures change, *en bloc*, in their relationship to one another while, within each sector, price relationships remain undisturbed, is obviously fantastic for any trade involving more than two countries with commodities produced in common. The older classicists partly avoided this, to them, unpleasant fact in an exegesis which, expressly or by unwarranted assimilation, assumed that international trade took place between two countries only and in but two commodities, while their followers, even in their most elaborate analyses, expound their doctrines in terms of the trade between any one country and the rest of the world, *taken as a unit,* on the (tacit) assumption that there is no product common to the two sectors. This, in effect, is no departure at all from the inadequate constructs of the older writers and does not have even the virtue of simplicity. It is, moreover, impossible *by definition* to gather, for this purpose, all countries but one into a hypothetically unified "outside world." The very *concept* of international trade segregates the several countries, each as a unit, between each of which and each of the others the flow of factors of production is inhibited. To group them is to merge varying cost structures into a single whole which could be attained in fact only if the posited and, in some cases, inevitable immobility of the factors of production were *not* present.

Sweeping conclusions, affecting practice and policy, have been drawn from acceptance of the fallacious doctrines here under attack. Thus, in inaugurating the discussion on reparations to which reference has been made, the late Lord Keynes assailed the reparations clauses of the Treaty of Versailles on the ground that the payment of "tribute" on the scale laid down would force the Germans to offer their goods on so favorable terms to the buyers as to depress the prices of German exports, relative to the prices of German imports, to a point which would bring about the complete ruin of that nation. This dictum was perhaps sufficiently controverted by Ohlin but it may be worth while to add that, if the relative prices of German exports had been lowered in the manner suggested by Keynes, his jeremiads, for very different reasons than those he alleged, would not have been without justification. Any such fall in the prices of German exports would have carried down with them the prices of many almost identical goods in the export lists of the nations which were the largest creditors on reparations account. This would not only have bedeviled the process of adjustment, along classical lines, which the posited relative fall in German export prices would be supposed to induce, but it would also have disrupted the relationship between international prices and the cost structures not only of Germany but of practically all non-German countries. No real equilibrium would have been possible under those conditions. This does not mean that the payment of reparations was impossible since the conditions imagined could never, in fact, occur.[2]

---

[2] I would contend that equilibrium *would* have been possible, under the payment of reparations, without any probable shift whatever in the price relationships between German exports and imports. For a general attack on Keynes' views cf. Etienne Mantoux, *The Carthaginian Peace*, Oxford University Press, London, 1946.

The truth is that there is little ground, in either logic or experience, for supposing that adjustment would take place in the way that Keynes, following the classicists, averred. There is no *a priori* reason for supposing that the *world* demand for, or supply of, the various goods would have been at all changed by the payment of reparations, and no reason, therefore, for supposing any change in prices, or even in the composition of production in the various countries. *At a given price structure* the Germans, with reduced incomes, would import less, export more, and consume less than if reparations had not been imposed, while the recipient countries, with increased incomes, would, on the contrary, import more, export less, and consume more. In this way, alone, the international accounts could have been adjusted to take care of the payments.[3] If, however, as is not unlikely, relative demand had been, in fact, somewhat altered, there is no way of telling how the change would have impinged upon the former national outputs. With an appropriately shifted relative supply there would, in any event, be small reason to expect an alteration in the international ratio of exchange and no reason at all to expect a change along the lines laid down by the classicists. Specific export industries in Germany might have expanded at the expense of those producing exclusively for domestic consumption, and specific export industries in other countries might have contracted to permit the growth of those serving the home market, but all this, under constant costs, could occur without any disturbance of (normal) international price relationships. Under *variable* costs, moreover, a shift of demand would promote changes in normal price relationships which would not split along national lines and would thus be quite alien to the expectations of classical theory.

There is much inductive evidence, both positive and negative, in support of the foregoing analysis, and some neo-classical writers have been disturbed by it. They have, however, clung to orthodoxy and resorted to mysticism. Professor Taussig for instance, in comment on the international trade of the United States after World War I, says: "To put it in the fewest words, things just *happened* so . . . these ups and downs [in trade] cannot be related to any gen-

[3] The monetary arrangements of the Dawes Plan (1924), if imposed by some malevolent genius, could scarcely have been better devised to *prevent* the required adjustments.

eral price movements of the kind contemplated in the [classical] theoretical analysis. . . . To repeat, it all just happened. One can make out nothing in the nature of an ordered sequence, of conformity to rule or to reasoning."[4]

Taussig's "explanation" is somewhat thaumaturgic and the phenomena are not, in fact, unamenable to rule or to reasoning. The relevant rules and reasoning, however, are not those of the classical theory. No satisfactory explanation can be developed without close attention to relative supplies and costs. The matter will be more fully discussed at a later point.

The Missing Link

The pre-eminent, the fatal, defect of the classical theory lies in the

[4] F. W. Taussig, *International Trade*, Macmillan, New York, 1927, p. 332. The episode under Taussig's consideration was marked by disequilibria of every sort, and deviations from the presumptive norms for the period are not very surprising. But Taussig, with his accustomed candor, confesses that the trade phenomena not only departed from, but seem to *refute*, the classical doctrines to which he nevertheless continued to cling in something akin to desperation.

James W. Angell, in a puzzled article on the same episode ("Equilibrium in International Trade: The United States, 1919-1926," *The Quarterly Journal of Economics*, Vol. XLII, pp. 388-433), says that "Both the gross and the net items in the American balance of payments have shown very large changes, and even outright reversals of movement; yet these changes seem to have produced no material effect whatsoever on the general levels of domestic prices. . . ."

Arthur I. Bloomfield ("The Mechanism of Adjustment of the American Balance of Payments: 1919-1929," *The Quarterly Journal of Economics*, Vol. LVII, pp. 333-377), in reviewing the results of many inductive investigations of episodes in many countries, says (p. 336) that "the studies of the adjustment process have generally yielded rather negative results" (i.e. in verification of the classical doctrines). The only apparent exceptions were the cases of Canada between 1900 and 1913 (investigated by Jacob Viner in *Canada's Balance of International Indebtedness*, Harvard University Press, Cambridge, Mass., 1924) and, *perhaps*, that of the United States in the greenback period. The latter is reviewed in my study "International Trade Under Depreciated Paper: The United States 1862-1879" (*The Quarterly Journal of Economics*, Vol. XXXVI, pp. 220-273). But Robert M. Carr has questioned Viner's conclusions ("The Role of Price in the International Trade Mechanism," *The Quarterly Journal of Economics*, Vol. XLV, pp. 710-719) and I regard my own study as by no means a verification of the standard classical theories but rather of the special theory of Taussig, then newly advanced, of adjustments under inconvertible paper currencies. With this theory I have no quarrel.

A. G. Silverman in an article "Some International Trade Factors for Great Britain, 1880-1913," (*The Review of Economic Statistics*, Vol. XIII, pp. 114-124) shows that, for most of the period he studied, the "terms of trade" of Great Britain appeared to move in the *opposite* direction to that posited in the classical theory, and Harry D. White (*The French International Accounts 1880-1913*, Harvard University Press, Cambridge, Mass., 1933, p. 306) says that, in his opinion, "nothing in the experience of France, the United States, or Canada verifies the claim that the specie-flow-price mechanism of the neo-classical theory is the all-important means of adjustment."

failure of its authors to recognize the crucial importance, or for the most part even the existence, of commodities produced in common either in each of two internationally trading countries or in some two or more of many such trading countries. Except in situations so rare as to find no counterpart in the actual world there will always be such commodities as the necessary condition of the establishment of normal values and of any but the most evanescent "equilibrium." It is impossible to exaggerate the significance of the common commodity since its presence permits of adjustments of supply to changing demand without a change in normal values; correlates the cost structures of the trading countries; in consonance therewith, fixes the (normal) terms of the international ratio of exchange; and facilitates the restoration of equilibrium after a disruption of balance in the international accounts. The international ratio of exchange will always tend to move into the position which will make production in common possible and, once there, will tend to congeal. Normal prices of international goods will, regardless of demand, then remain unaltered, for any given constellation of intra-national costs under constant cost conditions, until some focal commodity ceases to be produced, in common, by the original pair of countries.[5] When this happens a different pair of countries may come to produce the original commodity or it may be replaced, as a link, by some other commodity in the original or in some other pair of countries. Any of these processes will tie national cost structures together at a different, but equally stable, ratio.

Every country producing any mobile commodity also produced elsewhere has its *whole* cost structure linked with that of some other country. Some countries, moreover, will have such direct linkage with two or more national entities. Directly or indirectly the cost structures of all will thus be tied together. If India produces for export, tea, jute, and cotton while the United States produces cotton, cars, and coal, and Britain, coal, whisky, and textiles, the cost structure in the United States will be directly correlated, through common export articles, with that of both India and Britain. The cost structures of the two latter countries will then be correlated with each other through that of the United States.

---

5 The same rule holds for *variable* costs in the sense that the normal international price structure will correspond with costs which will then run on *given* curves rather than on horizontal lines.

Given free competition internally, the normal exchange relationships (prices) between tea, jute, and cotton must be consonant with their relative (opportunity) cost in India. But lots of a given grade of cotton will, at any given time, sell in free import markets at the same price whether they were produced in India or the United States, and the exchange relationships between cotton, cars, and coal will, on the assumption of free competition within the United States, correlate with the (opportunity) cost relationships there prevailing. This links, via cotton, the (normal) prices of tea and jute with those of cars and coal, and ties together the whole of the cost and price structures of India and the United States. But coal is assumed to be an export of Britain, as well as of the United States, and British and American coal of a given grade will, at any given time, sell for the same price in any free market. The (normal) ratio of exchange between coal, whisky, and textiles is established by the (opportunity) cost structure in Britain. The prices of whisky and textiles are thus linked, via coal, with those of cars and cotton, and, via cotton, with those of tea and jute. In fact, the entire price structures of the three countries are, in this manner, brought into alignment. And so for all other countries.

The world integration of prices is also an integration of national relative cost structures. That sector of its cost structure comprised in the exports of every economically large and varied country sets the (normal) international price ratio for the commodities concerned. The price relationships between these several sectors ·are fixed by the commodity the output of which any two sectors may share, and (normal) price relationships in international trade cannot deviate from the pattern thus established unless there be a shift in cost relationships within one or more of the trading countries, or the "link" commodity between any pair of them is altered.

The significance of the common commodity as the key to a valid theory of international price relationships, to the integration of national cost structures with international prices, and to an assimilation of the theories of domestic and international values, was, as we have noted, sensed by P. J. Stirling, Henry Sidgwick, and J. S. Nicholson though none of them was very successful in developing the notion. Sidgwick and Nicholson aimed wildly, and Stirling scored not much more than an "outer" on his target when he said that, in exchange of commodities between any two countries, the terms are regulated not by the relative efficiency of the labor of the two countries in the production of all commodities but by their efficiency in the production of that commodity in which their efficiency is most nearly equal. Professor Viner summarizes Stirling's argument as follows:

"He [Stirling] presented the following case:

1,000 days' labor will produce in

England	*Mexico*
50 iron	50 iron
25 tin	400 silver
50 wheat	100 wheat
150 cloth	75 cloth

"Tin and silver are commodities peculiar to England and Mexico, respectively, and iron has identical [labor] costs in both countries. England will export cloth and import wheat, in the ratio of 150 units cloth to 100 units wheat, or the reciprocal of the ratio of their costs of production in the countries where they can be respectively produced [allegedly] at a comparative advantage. Although he [Stirling] does not expressly say so, silver and tin will also presumably exchange in the reciprocal of the ratio of their costs of production, or 400 units silver for 25 units tin, and iron will not move in trade. He says that if the English output of iron should increase to 55 units per 1,000 days labor, other things remaining the same, then the rate at which English cloth would exchange for Mexican wheat would be 150 units cloth for 110 units wheat, which, it will be noted, makes the double factoral terms of trade with respect to these two commodities conform to the reciprocal of the ratio between the costs in the two countries of the commodity, iron, in which these costs approach most closely to equality."[6]

Viner asserts, correctly, that Stirling offers a purely arbitrary solution of his problem. It is worse than arbitrary—it is wrong. Stirling had a promising clew but he faltered in his conception of what was relevant in costs and in supposing that a commodity produced in common at identical labor-time cost in each of two countries could not be the subject of trade between them.

[6] Jacob Viner, *Studies in the Theory of International Trade, op. cit.*, p. 458. The discussion from here on will run in terms of Viner's treatment of the topics under consideration. This is so far the best available as to be *sui generis*. I should, however, mention as helpful, a book by Chi-Yuen Wu, *An Outline of International Price Theories*, London School of Economics and Political Science, Monograph No. 7, Routledge, London, 1939.

The major classical writers were clear, and correct, on the point that a comparison of absolute (labor-time) costs has nothing to do with the ratio at which commodities produced in different countries are exchanged or the possibility of exchanging them.[7] This conviction, in fact, was responsible for their (reluctant and unfortunate) abandonment of any sort of cost, and their exclusive resort to demand, in explication of international values. Stirling did nothing to shake their position. But if, instead of heading his table of costs with the words "1000 days labor" (will produce stated outputs in England, and Mexico, respectively), Stirling had said that a given amount of labor will produce, in England, 50 iron, or 25 tin, or 50 wheat, or 150 cloth, and that another given amount of labor (probably very different from that taken for England) will produce, in Mexico, 50 iron, or 400 silver, or 100 wheat, or 75 cloth, he would have been on his way to seeing that it is opportunity cost, rather than any kind of absolute cost, that is the means to a satisfactory solution of his problem.

It does *not* follow, on Stirling's data, that iron will be produced in both countries and will not be exchanged between them. The variety of production in the respective countries will be a function of their relative total economic importance and the relative total value of each of the several goods produced. It could be that Mexico would find it advantageous to concentrate exclusively on silver, and import iron, and even wheat, as well as cloth and tin, or that England would find it advantageous to specialize in tin and import cloth, as well as iron, wheat, and tin. One might, perhaps, hazard the guess that wheat, rather than iron, would be the commodity produced in common in Mexico and England, with Mexico producing silver, in addition to wheat, and England producing wheat as well as tin, iron, and cloth. In that case the cost ratios in England between these four latter commodities would set their exchange value each against the other, while their international exchange ratio against silver, in consonance with the cost ratios between Mexico's products (wheat and silver), would be 400 silver = 100 wheat = 50 tin = 100 iron = 300 cloth rather than 400 silver = 100 wheat = 25 tin = 50 iron = 150 cloth.

If, *following Stirling*, we assume that the *given* amount of labor,

[7] The reason, of course, is that, by definition, there is not free movement of workers from one country to another.

in each of the countries, is also the *same* amount, the produce of 2000 days' labor in England would, under the corrected ratio, be exchanging against that of 1000 days' labor in Mexico, and it would be the relative labor efficiencies in the two countries in the production of the common product, wheat (where they are not close), rather than in iron (where they are identical), which would determine not the ratio of exchange (which is nevertheless determined by the fact that wheat is the common product) but the incomes of the two countries so far as these were dependent on international trade. The *per capita* income in Mexico, insofar as it is determined by productivity in the internationally traded commodities, would be twice that of England, and the price (in money or such commodities) of labor-time in Mexico would also be twice what it would be in England.[8]

The amount of the labor of any one country which will exchange for a given amount of labor of another (and, therefore, the relative real incomes of the two countries so far as these are dependent on the productivity of labor in internationally traded commodities) is dependent on the relative efficiency in the output of certain commodities which, on the basis of opportunity cost, both countries find it advantageous to produce for export. Opportunity cost as a criterion of international values is applicable only to commodities (and not to labor) just because, on the very assumptions of international trade theory, labor is not internationally mobile. The cost of commodities, in forgone leisure, is therefore relatively high in countries of relatively low productivity in any exportable commodity which these countries find it advantageous to produce in common with any other, and the cost of leisure, in forgone commodities, is relatively high where the opposite conditions of productivity prevail.

Since nothing is to be gained, in the determination of international values, from a direct comparison of labor-time costs per unit of value output in the various countries, it is the merit of the opportunity cost approach that it does not require the use of any such absolute measure of cost and therefore makes inevitable the appropriate comparison. If 100 units of iron can be obtained by forgoing the output of 100 units of wheat or 300 units of cloth, the cost of 100 units of iron is 100 units of wheat, or 300 units of cloth, whether it takes one day in one country or a thousand in another to

---

[8] This result, needless to say, follows from Stirling's unrealistic assumptions of productivity.

produce them. The normal prices of the products in terms of any one of them, or in silver, will not be affected by the general efficiency or inefficiency of production. These will affect only the value (price) of labor.

The "Terms of Trade" and the Composition of National Output

Even if Stirling had grasped the notion of opportunity cost he could not have reached a solution of the problem of international values without reference to the economic size of the trading countries (with its effect on the composition of their output) and the relative *total* value of the several traded commodities. His omission here is, of course, typical of the classicists. This is, in fact, the second great deficiency in classical theory.[9]

Stirling's contribution was made not in a direct attempt to solve the problem of the "terms of trade" (though, if his thesis had been valid, he would have done so) but rather in an effort to set forth the conditions of the distribution of production between two countries trading in a number of commodities. Longfield had made the first stumbling essay in elucidation of this matter but it was von Mangoldt who furnished what Viner accepts as a "satisfactory" solution.[10] Mangoldt, he notes, shows that "cost of production being regarded as constant, each country will specialize in the production of a group of . . . commodities, that the commodities within each of these groups will exchange for each other in proportion to their real costs of production, and that *the terms on which the commodities belonging to the two different groups will exchange for each other will be determined by the effect of the reciprocal demand of the two countries for each other's export commodities on the relative money rates of remuneration of the productive factors in the two countries.*"[11] In comment on this Viner says that "to find a basis for determining which country will export any particular commodity, Mangoldt posits the existence of a commodity such that, when its

[9] Nicholson, however, was aware of the importance of this omission. cf. J. Shield Nicholson, *Principles of Political Economy*, Macmillan, New York, 1897, Vol. II, p. 302 *et seq.*

[10] Viner, *Studies, op. cit.*, pp. 454, 458, *et seq.*

[11] Viner, *loc. cit.*, pp. 458, 459. Italics mine. It is worth remarking, perhaps, that the only demand which would be relevant would be reciprocal demand at *equilibrium* (which is synonymous with cost) but it is obvious that normal values cannot be *determined* by a demand which is present only when they are already established.

real [i.e. labor-time] costs in each of the respective countries are multiplied by the [money] rates of remuneration prevailing there, there will result a money cost which is equal in both countries."[12]

This is perhaps as close to a lifting of the veil as is possible in the absence of opportunity cost analysis the lack of which necessitates resort to demand rather than costs as the determinant of normal values. Mangoldt, in seeking to determine not only the composition of output in each of the trading countries but also the terms on which they will exchange their products, attempts to bring in costs as a necessary supplement to his data on demand. But the costs on which he relies are not real, or opportunity, but money costs (money rates of remuneration of the factors of production). This is alien to the classical tradition since the classicists rightly felt that, in laying down the basic theory of international values, there was no need to resort to money costs and that to do so would confuse rather than clarify their doctrine. The use of money costs is expressly and convincingly repudiated by Marshall, a much later writer than Mangoldt and the most authoritative of the neo-classicists, who says that "money, even when firmly based on gold, does not afford a good measure of international values, and it does not help to explain the changes in those values, which are caused by broad variations in international demand: but on the contrary it disguises and conceals them. For it measures changes in values by standards which are *automatically modified by the very variations in international demand, the effects of which are to be measured.*"[13] The "complexities . . . become wholly unmanageable if the attempt is made to proceed far into the pure theory of foreign trade on the plan of measuring exports and imports in terms of money."[14]

Even if this objection be disregarded, Mangoldt is in difficulties since he makes money costs (money rates of remuneration) a *resultant* of the reciprocal demand of the two countries for "each other's" export commodities. But whether a (marginal) commodity will be exported by one rather than the other country (and also, the reciprocal demand of the two countries for "each other's commodities"), will, on Mangoldt's analysis, clearly *depend* upon the relative rates of monetary remuneration. Such rates, again on Mangoldt's analy-

12 *loc. cit.*, p. 459.
13 *Money Credit and Commerce*, Macmillan, London, 1923, p. 157.
14 *The Pure Theory of Foreign Trade*, The London School of Economics and Political Science, London, 1930, p. 3.

sis, are, therefore, cause rather than result. It would seem to be no exaggeration to say that Mangoldt is going round in circles though it is due him to point out that he is, by comparison with most of the classicists, clear-headed, that he recognized problems which his predecessors had ignored, and that he made a valiant, even if unsuccessful, essay at their solution.[15]

Money costs are, in fact, a resultant not of reciprocal national demand but of real costs and international (monetary) values. They cannot, therefore, be used to explain those values nor the composition of national output. The level of money incomes in any country and, what is the same thing, of money costs of the factors of production, is in no way a determinant of the commodities that the country exports but, on the contrary, is an outcome of productivity in these commodities and the barter ratio of exchange.

Most of the classical economists "did not deal at all with the problem of what determines relative levels of money incomes in different countries"[16] or they accepted what Viner declares to be an unsatisfactory solution offered by Senior. It seems to me, however, that, on *this* point, Senior was essentially right and there is no difficulty in fitting his explanation into what I conceive to be the valid theory of international values offered in this book. Viner's criticism of Senior is as follows:

"Senior argued that within any country the level of money wages in all occupations—proper allowance being made for differences in the attractiveness of different occupations—was determined by the wages which labor could earn in the export industries,

[15] Mangoldt, indeed, failed by no great margin (the little less, but what worlds away!) to perceive the true determinant of international values. He sensed the importance of a linking commodity, produced in common by trading countries, but, instead of uncovering such an actual commodity based on equal opportunity costs, he was led by his obsession with labor costs, and their differences in the various countries, to posit an *imaginary* commodity which, at the going rate of remuneration of the factors of production in the respective countries, could be (but, in fact, was not) put out by either of them at a given monetary supply-price. There was nothing in this to lock together the several national cost ratios. Within sight of the solution Mangoldt thus resorted to a thoroughgoing *petitio principii* and so missed the bus. An *imaginary* commodity could obviously never serve to tie cost structures to one another since no one could be on the margin of indifference as to whether he would produce some real or this wholly unreal commodity. That Mangoldt was still in the morass, along with the classicists in general, is most readily apparent in the phrase "the demand for each other's exports." Each country is conceived of as having exclusive title to a *given* bloc of exports, though it was Mangoldt's problem to show what the ingredients of these blocs would be.

[16] Viner, *op. cit.*, p. 456.

and that the comparative levels of wages in the export industries of different countries were determined by the comparative prices which the export products of the different countries could command in the world markets. This became standard doctrine, although it left unanswered the question, given more than two commodities, as to how it was determined what would be the export industries. The prevailing level of wages would obviously be a factor in determining which industries could find export markets for their products. But to explain the determination of which industries should be export industries by reference to the general wage level, and to explain the general level of wages by reference to the level of wages prevailing in the export industries, would obviously be reasoning in a circle. Senior's argument sufficed to show that under equilibrium conditions wages in the non-export industries must be equal to wages in the export industries and that wages in different countries must be proportional to the value productivities of labor in the export industries of the respective countries. Senior failed to show, however, that wages in the non-export industries were determined by wages in the export industries instead of both sets of wages being the common product of a number of factors."[17]

Though Senior failed to demonstrate what would determine the export industries of any country he did not, so far at least as Viner's exposition shows, assert that these were determined by the "prevailing" wage level. It is Viner's assertion, not Senior's, that the prevailing level of wages would obviously be a factor in determining which industries could find export markets for their products. It could be answered, on behalf of Senior, that the level of wages in any country settles at such a point as will reflect productivity in, and permit the export of, as many products as will be sufficient to pay for the goods that will, in consonance with opportunity costs, be imported at that level.[18] Such a statement would exempt Senior from the charge of reasoning in a circle.

[17] Viner, *op. cit.*, pp. 456-457.
[18] The money wage-level in any country is a function of the international price level and of the efficiency of the country's producers in export industries. The international monetary price level depends upon the relationship between the supply of the money in which it is measured, the supply of other monies, the rates of exchange between all of them, and the world supply of commodities. The prevailing level of money wages in any country is not, as Viner asserts, an obvious factor in determining which industries in that country could find export markets. On the contrary, it is the industries that, on the principles laid down in this book, can find export

The composition of the exports of any country is determined by opportunity costs in that country in interaction with the evolving ratio of international exchange of products. Whatever be the money that is used as the *numeraire* for this ratio will establish the current international price *level* in that money, with *relative* prices on this level identical with the terms of the ratio of exchange of products established on a barter analysis. The so-established money prices of the opportunity-cost-induced exports of any country, together with the efficiency of production in the export industries, determine incomes in that money in those industries. Neither the exports themselves nor their prices are in any sense a resultant of money wages, but, along with the efficiency of production, are always a cause thereof. The export industries of any country are determined by opportunity costs; the prices that exports obtain in world markets, together with the efficiency of the workers, determine money wages in the export industries; and free competition within the country transmits the wage level for any given grade of labor from the export to all other industries.[19] This, in its latter aspects, is almost precisely what Senior had alleged and there would seem to be no basis for Viner's assertion, in criticism of Senior, that both sets of wages (those in the export and in the non-export industries) are the common product of a number of factors (which Viner does not specify).

Senior's exposition of the factors determining money wages in any country, and his implication that money wages are a consequence and not a cause of the course of international trade, can thus

---

markets which determine the level of money wages in the country. cf. Frank D. Graham, *Protective Tariffs*, Princeton University Press, Princeton, N.J., Appendix I, pp. 134-149.

[19] Whether the workers in non-export industries are efficient or inefficient (that is more or less efficient, relative to export-commodity workers, than are their confrères in other countries relative to workers in those countries producing the same type of exports) will not affect their money wages one iota. The prices of the products they put out will, however, be high (relative to the prices of those products in other countries) when they are inefficient (as thus defined), and low when they are efficient.

Provided exchange rates between currencies are not free to move, or goods are not, wages in any given national money may of course, regardless of productivity, change in any degree either absolutely or in relation to the wages of other countries. International wage (and price) comparisons must, however, be measured in the *same* money for all the countries concerned and, if there is no free market in currencies, or the movement of goods is not at the discretion of private traders, accurate comparisons are practically impossible.

be validated, but Viner's second criticism, that Senior left unanswered the question of what the country's export industries would be, is justly taken. Senior was, in fact, no more successful than any of the other classicists in determining that list. Edgeworth, who points out that "it is not in general possible to determine *a priori*, from a mere observation of the [real] costs of production in the respective countries before the opening of trade, which commodities will be exported and which produced at home," said that the line between the exports and imports of any country "depends not only on the cost of production in each country, but also on the law of demand *in each country* for the different commodities."[20] Had Edgeworth omitted the words italicized in this quotation, the statement, as it would then stand, would have had some validity though it would merely have concealed the true determinants. The role of total relative demand for the various commodities is to determine *how much* of each will be produced in the world as a whole. The *total* demand for any commodity will establish the margin of its supply in some (ordinarily large) country which may or may not export, and might even import, the commodity in question and will certainly be producing other commodities for export. Shifts in the international demand situation will determine whether, and in what volume, that country will, with a given international price structure, export or import the commodity in question. If the shift in demand is sufficiently great the country may cease to be the marginal national producer of the commodity either because, with complete concentration upon it, a supply of the commodity from some new national producer is nevertheless called into being by a rise in the world demand for it or because it is advantageous for that country to abandon the production of the commodity when its price falls relatively to alternative output.[21]

The total world demand for the various products, in conjunction with the supply issuing out of the opportunity cost structures in the various countries, thus determines the line between the exports and imports of any given country. The line traverses that commodity which, with the existing structure of (domestic) opportunity costs together with the current international ratio of exchange, may

---

[20] F. Y. Edgeworth, *Papers, op. cit.,* Vol. II, p. 55. Italics mine.
[21] Any shift in price relationships is thus dependent on an alteration in marginal opportunity costs.

become either an export or import (though still produced, at home, for some part of the domestic consumption).

Where the world demand for any commodity is insufficient to absorb the full productive powers of any producing country, without lowering the value of the commodity (against some other product) below the prevailing ratio between the commodities in the opportunity cost structure of the country in question, it will pay producers in that country to distribute their output over both commodities. If, when this is done, the productive powers of the country are still so great as to lead to a volume of exports sufficient to force down the value of both commodities (in terms of other products) to a level which corresponds with the opportunity cost ratio with some third commodity in the country in question, producers will take up the output and export of this third commodity along with the other two. And so on with a fourth, fifth, and up to an nth commodity.

The country forms part of the world demand for its imports as well as part of the world supply of its exports. The nth export is that which, when added to the list of the country's preceding exports (and subtracted from the imports) will bring the total values of its exports and imports into balance, with one or more commodities being produced in common with other countries of varied production.[22] The citizens of the country in question will not bid for foreign products beyond this point since to do so would raise the cost of marginal imports in terms of marginal exports (the margin being established by the commodities produced in common with other countries) above the domestic opportunity cost of obtaining them. They will on the other hand, with trade free, always bid this much since the opportunity cost of imports, up to this point, is less than that of their production at home.[23]

Comparative advantage, and the extent of any country's export list, is thus not only a function of opportunity cost *and* the international ratio of exchange but the ratio is brought, through exports,

[22] No matter how much the relative demand for, and the prices of, various commodities may alter, this is the mechanism of adjustment. There is, in consequence, never any question of absolute lack of demand for any country's exports. If, at any time, this demand falters, relative to the country's demand for its current imports, a shift of some commodities from the import toward the export side (or merely to domestic production) will reverse "national elasticities of demand" and bring equilibrium.

[23] There is, of course, no reason for rejecting, for any country at any given time, a monetary expression of opportunity costs.

into so much conformity with the country's cost structure as is necessary to promote the volume and variety of exports that will equate in value with the imports that will be demanded at the ratio in question. Once equilibrium has been established, with one or another country on the margin of indifference between the production of a given commodity and any one of the whole range of other products, world demand can shift widely without disruption either of the pre-existing normal ratio of exchange or of equilibrium in the international accounts. Any but the most extreme changes in the world demand for the various products will be met not by a shift in the (normal) price ratios but by an expansion, at the margin of indifference, in the output of the currently more desired products at the expense of those currently less desired. Even if, by some strange chance, the shift in the relative desirability of products were such as to diminish the world demand for all of the current exports of a productively diversified country, and to increase the world demand for all of its imports, it would be open to such a country to expand the output and reduce the import of such goods as it was producing, as well as importing, on the margin of indifference with its exports (and concurrently, perhaps, contract the output but not the export of the goods it had hitherto been exporting) so as to preserve the pre-existing price relationships. And, if this were not feasible in any considerable degree in a given country, other countries, on the margin of indifference in the production of the now relatively less and the now relatively more desired commodities, would shift to the latter and, in so doing, preserve an unimpaired market, in the face of a declining world demand, for the original exports of the given country even while they continued to furnish it with imports of increased world demand on the same terms as before and to the extent of its purchasing power. Whenever, moreover, the shift in world demand is so great as to be incapable of compensation by such shifts in supply, and therefore leads to a change in normal price relationships (dependent upon a shift in the focal national production of one or more commodities), it is not so much through the actual alteration in prices which would then occur as in the consequent expansion of the lists of exports, and contraction of the lists of imports, or both, in countries adversely affected (with the opposite phenomena obtaining in the favored countries), that equilibrium in the international accounts is maintained.[24] This fact makes superfluous, for *normal* values, that discussion of "national elasticities of demand" which occupies so prominent a place with the writers of the neo-classical school. Their notions on elasticity are, in any event, dubious, but comment on the matter will, for the moment, be postponed.

Under conditions of constant cost in the several countries then, the sole influence of demand on (normal) international prices is in the determination of the country that will be the marginal national producer of any given product (and will thus establish its price, against the other commodities it produces, in identity with the cost ratios in that country). This follows from the fact that no change in demand, unless it be so great as to transfer the margin of production from one country to another (and, therefore, change relative marginal costs), will have any effect whatever on the (normal) ratio of exchange.

The Neo-Classicists on Costs

Because (normal) ratios of exchange cannot alter except as a result of a change in normal marginal costs;[25] because they will always shift in precisely proportionate response to such a change; and because demand can vary widely without affecting either normal costs or the normal ratio of exchange; it seems fair to say that costs are the sole determinant of the (normal) ratios of exchange and, certainly, that the character (urgency, elasticity, and the like) of reciprocal national demand schedules for foreign products is either wholly irrelevant or that it is relevant, if at all, only through the mediation of costs. Yet, in defense of the classicists against earlier criticism from me, Profesor Viner alleges that, though the exposition of Mill and his followers was "defective," the defect was not that they exaggerated the importance of reciprocal demand in the determination of the terms of trade which, Viner avers, is logically impossible,

[24] That is to say that not only the volume but the *range*, or variety, of potential exports would expand, and that of potential imports contract, automatically, in all countries adversely affected by an alteration in the ratio of exchange. The converse would, of course, happen in all countries favorably affected. The stronger the movement in the international balance, or net "terms of trade," adverse to any country, the longer becomes its list of potential exports and the shorter its list of potential imports.

[25] That rarity, a limbo ratio, is excluded as not embodying normal values.

but that, whatever they may have known, they did not sufficiently emphasize the influence of cost conditions on reciprocal demand.[26]

What may have, in this matter, been a valid criticism of Mill was, Viner says, much less applicable to Marshall, Edgeworth, and other followers of Mill, who "were aware of the fact that the greater the number of countries and the greater the number of commodities, the greater is the influence of cost conditions on the reciprocal demands and therefore on the terms of trade, and the smaller, therefore, given the cost conditions, the range of possible variation in the terms of trade as the result of given changes in the basic utility conditions."[27] Viner then goes on to say that the first quotation following shows that Marshall appreciated the importance of multiplicity of commodities and of countries in causing the reciprocal demands to be elastic and therefore in restricting the range of variation of the terms of trade, while the second quotation, from Edgeworth, shows that Bastable and Edgeworth both recognize the similar effect of multiplication of countries. The quotation from Marshall is:

"It is practically certain that the demand of each of Ricardo's two countries for the goods in general of the other would have considerable elasticity under modern industrial conditions, even if E and G were single countries whose sole trade was with one another. And if we take E to be a large and rich commercial country, while G stands for all foreign countries, this certainly [sic; a misquotation for 'certainty'] becomes absolute. For E is quite sure to export a great many things which some at least of the other countries could forego without much inconvenience: and which would be promptly refused if offered by her only on terms considerably less favorable to purchasers. And, on the other hand, E is quite sure to have exports which can find increased sales in some countries, at least, if she offers them on more favorable terms to purchasers. Therefore the world's demand for E's goods . . . is sure to rise largely if E offers her goods generally on terms more advantageous to purchasers; and to shrink largely if E endeavors to insist on terms more favorable to herself. And E, on her part, is sure on the one hand to import many things from various parts of the world, which she can easily forego, if the terms on which they are sold are raised against her; and on the other to be capable of turning to fairly good use many things which are offered to her from various parts of the world, if they were offered on terms rather more favorable to her than at present."[28]

The quotation from Edgeworth runs thus: "The theory of comparative costs is not very prominent from the mathematical point of view. . . . That the point of equilibrium [determining the terms of trade] falls between the respective [trade] indifference-curves is the geometrical version of comparative costs. The expression which occurs in some of the best writers, that international value 'depends on' comparative cost, is seen from this point of view to be a very loose expression. (No doubt, as Professor Bastable has pointed out, when there are numerous competing nations, the limits fixed by the principle of comparative cost are much narrowed and accordingly it becomes less incorrect to regard the principle as sufficient to determine international value.)"[29]

It is difficult to see how these quotations warrant Viner's assertion that the neo-classicists he quotes recognized the importance of cost. The word "cost" does not even occur in the quotation from Marshall while, in that from Edgeworth, the role of cost is minimized in only slightly lesser degree. If this is the best that can be found in the leading classical and neo-classical writers in recognition of the importance of costs (and, apart from some lip-service, I think it is), the charge that they neglected, or even spurned, costs in their discussion of international values would seem to be abundantly proved.[30]

Reciprocal Demands and Costs

Viner himself states that cost conditions can operate on the terms of trade only intermediately through their influence on the reciprocal demands and that the terms of trade can be directly influenced by reciprocal demands *and by nothing else*.[31] This seems to me to be casuistical. Reciprocal demand is the same thing as reciprocal supply and it would be just as correct to say that the terms of trade can be directly influenced by reciprocal *supplies, and by nothing*

---

[28] Viner, *op. cit.*, pp. 550-551, quoting from Marshall, *Money Credit and Commerce*, p. 171.

[29] Viner, *op. cit.*, p. 551, quoting from Edgeworth, *Papers*, II, p. 33. The sentence placed in parentheses appears in the original (in Edgeworth) as a footnote.

[30] "Why," says Edgeworth, in a passage approvingly quoted by Viner, "should there be any correspondence between cost and value [in international trade] in the absence of the conditions, proper to domestic trade, on which that equality depends?" (*Studies*, p. 487).

[31] Viner, *Studies, op. cit.*, p. 549.

else. Since reciprocal supplies surely depend on costs, this would bring out the fact that there is no demand for anything without an offer of a *quid pro quo* and that the real question is what determines the *quid* that will be offered *pro quo*.[32] Terms of trade *are* (rather than are determined by) reciprocal demands (reciprocal supplies), and Viner's assertion could be paraphrased in the words "the price of goods can be directly influenced only by what they are offered for and by what is offered for them." This truism is, in fact, about the sum of the classical doctrines on international values. It is as valid, and about as valuable, a statement as the assertion that the temperature of any body can be directly influenced only by the degree of heat it harbors. Because the classical economists were dissatisfied with such superficiality in their theory of *domestic* values they there sought *causas causantes* in costs.[33] A resort to costs is equally necessary to rescue the theory of international values from inanity.

Viner declares me in error because, so he alleges, I fail to see that cost conditions can operate on the terms of trade only intermediately through their influence on reciprocal demands.[34] This is an unwarranted charge. I would no more deny that costs can operate on the terms of trade only through their influence on reciprocal demands (reciprocal supplies) than I would deny that a current of electricity can operate only through a conductor. But I would not on this account say that it is the conductor rather than the electricity that is the cause of the shock. If we were to halt in a search for causes because they can operate only intermediately, through some conductor, the progress of science, which is a search not for proximates but ultimates, would long since have been brought to a close.

Viner's contention arises from the inevitable tendency of adherents of the classical school to think of market rather than of normal values. In *market* values, where costs can be relevant only so far as they affect the psychology of the bargainers, emphasis is properly laid on demand. But for *normal* values, where demand can be relevant only so far as it affects costs, this is a wholly perverse procedure. For *market* values it would be fair to say that reciprocal demand (or rather desire) is the *sole* determinant of exchange ratios (if we may assume that given supplies are in being and are offered against each other without reservation). For *normal* values it is at least

---

[32] A desire not accompanied by an adequate offer is a desire only, not a demand.
[33] These, if we chose, could be called "indirect" influences.
[34] Viner, *Studies*, p. 551.

equally fair to say that *cost* is the sole determinant of exchange ratios. The adjustment of relative supplies, to bring marginal values into line with costs, is indeed the essence of the notion of normal values, and it is, to repeat, with normal values that the classical economists affected to deal. Costs operate on the (normal) terms of trade, intermediately if you will, through their influence on reciprocal demands (supplies). But, on the assumption of constant costs within any national entity (an assumption to which the classical economists generally adhered), reciprocal demands, or changes in them, do not ordinarily affect the normal terms of trade at all, while, on the assumption of variable costs, they can affect the normal terms of trade only through their influence on those costs. The mediacy of demand, if present at all, is distinctly more remote than that of costs as a factor in the determination of normal values. Even, therefore, on his own premises, Viner's disparagement of costs would seem to be wholly unjustified. In these circumstances, and when we are dealing with norms, it would appear that instead of saying, with Viner, that cost conditions can operate on the terms of trade only intermediately through their influence on reciprocal demands it would be more appropriate to turn it the other way round and say that reciprocal demands can operate on the normal terms of trade, if at all, only intermediately through their influence, if any, on costs.[35] It is a change in (marginal) costs which is *always* the condition of an alteration in the (normal) ratio of exchange whereas the many changes in demand which do not alter the one will not alter the other.

Until, at any rate, reciprocal demands and costs come into identity, it is only through its (possible) intermediate influence on costs (variable cost conditions) that demand (reciprocal or otherwise) can ever be said to be even a partial, and remote, determinant of normal international values. Reciprocal demand and costs will come into identity at the moment that (normal) values, based on costs, become established in the market and the relative marginal ophelimities of the various products have, *through changes in relative*

[35] Viner's assertion (*op. cit.*, p. 552n.) that "if . . . cost conditions are left unchanged but . . . utility assumptions altered, the equilibrium terms of trade can be changed, within broad limits, in whatever degree and direction is desired" is flatly untrue if, by unchanged "cost conditions," he means that the cost of the marginal supply remains unaltered during the change in utility assumptions, and, even if he does not mean this, his implication that demand conditions are of *primary* importance is baseless.

supply in response to vicissitudes in demand, been brought into correspondence with relative costs. At this point reciprocal demands, reciprocal supplies, costs, marginal utilities, and values are synonymous
terms, with costs the (not quite immovable) lodestone to which the
(volatile) reciprocal demands, reciprocal supplies, marginal utilities, and values have been attracted. To explain normal values it
would then be necessary to explain *normal* reciprocal demands and
this could not be done without reference to costs at the margin of
indifference between the output of one product and another. Since
the final reference must be to costs it would seem appropriate to
speak of costs as the determining factor.

The fact is that the classical and neo-classical writers on international values did not establish any value *norms* at all. Their failure
to stress, or even recognize, commodities produced in common by
two or more trading countries made impossible a resort to costs as
the determinant of normal values and restricted their use of costs
to the establishment of widely divergent limits within which the
ratio of exchange must lie.[36] Having no focus of (normal) values
in common costs, no margin of indifference in the production of one
commodity or another, and therefore no possibility of adjustment
of supply to changes in relative values within wide limits, the classicists were forced back upon what Mill declared to be an "anterior"
law of values, the law of reciprocal demand. This so-called "anterior"
law is the law that applies to *market* values (supplies being given)
and, particularly, to those commodities such as "old masters" the
supply of which cannot be affected by new production, or its renunciation, no matter what shifts in value might occur. It could never
be a law of *normal* values, which must rest on something much less
volatile than demand, and it was necessarily supplemented by the
law of costs when, as in their theory of domestic values, the classicists
sought to establish such norms. If, as the classicists believed, they
could not appeal to costs in their discussion of international values,
they ought, in logic, to have said that normal values in this field are
non-existent. The classical theory of international values is, in fact,
a theory of market values rather than of norms and, as will presently appear, not a good theory at that.

[36] These limits are set by the different cost ratios between commodities in each
of the trading countries and it might be conceded that this provided a *very* remote
approximation to norms, a normal *zone.*

The "Equation of Reciprocal Demand"

Mill's exposition would have been stronger if he had made the terms of the international exchange of goods dependent not upon any "equation of international demand" but upon the maximization of the volume of transactions. In the simple case he took, with the citizens of England wholly specialized in cloth and those of Germany in linen, there is *at any moment* (that is, at any given status of demand) something that could properly be regarded as an optimum ratio of exchange. At any rate on one side of, rather than at, this optimum the purveyors of linen would be ready to do more business but the purveyors of cloth would not be ready to do as much, whereas, at any rate on the other side, the purveyors of cloth would be ready to do more business while the purveyors of linen would not be ready to do as much. This, therefore, is the rate at which the largest possible number of transactions could be carried out and, with effective competition (even without mobility in the factors of production), it would be realized. This, of course, is plain market value theory in a regime of (limited) competition, and this, in fact, constitutes the valid content of the classical theory of international values. All that the classicists, or neo-classicists, added to this, in their attempt to establish normal values, was to set (remote) limits on the fluctuation in the exchange relationships.[37] If supply be absolutely invariable, or if, at the moment, there is no way of changing it adequately in response to any shift in demand, there is no definable limit on the movement of the relative values of various goods. The *market* values of internationally exchanged commodities may therefore move in any degree, even quite outside the range set by comparative costs, during any period in which supply is in more or less flagging adjustment to an altered demand. Though, in England, 10 units of cloth could be produced as readily as 15 units of linen, and, in Germany as readily as 20, a sharp shift in demand, with the impossibility of *suddenly* shifting the relative supply of the two textiles, even at one of the limiting ratios of exchange, might result in a market ratio, at any moment, of 25, 50, or 100 units of linen, or of 10, 5, or 2, of such units, for 10 of cloth. This, the classicists correctly said, is not true of *normal* values which cannot, at most, go outside the

[37] This much had been attained by the time of Ricardo and, so far as normal international values are concerned, the accomplishment of his successors in the classical school was nil.

range of 15 to 20 linen for 10 cloth since, for reasons made plain in Chapter II of this book, the supply of the relatively appreciating commodity could, at one or the other of these limits, be indefinitely expanded at constant cost in, and at the expense of, the other. But, whatever the variations in the ratio *within* the limits set by divergent relative costs, no producer in either country would find it worth while to transfer any resources to the commodity hitherto exclusively produced in the other since, at any such ratio, there would be no producers on the margin of indifference as between the one product and the other. The fact that variations in the ratio, within the limits, could have no effect whatever on the relative supply of the two commodities means that, *within* (as well as beyond) the limits, there can be no normal values and this, in turn, means that, in the classical analysis, there can be no normal values at all.[38]

The classical and neo-classical writers seem to suppose that some sort of norm will issue out of the necessity for an equation of reciprocal national demands or, at any rate, that this equation is a determinant of international values. Such an equation, though an accompaniment of, is, in fact, wholly irrelevant to, the establishment of normal, or any other, values. One might as well speak of the "equation of reciprocal local demands" as a determining condition of the normal ratio of exchange of domestic commodities produced in separate areas of a national economy. Yet this has rightly never been a feature of the theory of domestic values, market *or* normal.

Assuming that would-be buyers must pay for the goods they wish to purchase, on pain of not getting them, there will always be equilibrium in the national or international accounts no matter what the ratio of exchange of products may be. The empty concept of the equation of international demand as a *causal* factor is nevertheless cherished with astonishing fervor by members of the classical school who regard its discovery, or invention, as a supreme intellectual achievement.[39] Whether as cause or effect the classicists' concept of the equation of international demand was accompanied not only by the fantastic construct of exclusive national blocs of goods exchanged against each other but by highly unrealistic notions of the manner in which presumptively evanescent equilibria in the total values of

[38] This statement might not be *irrefutably* true if Mill had not characterized as abnormal the one case in which he was dealing with a (potentially) normal value.

[39] Edgeworth, for instance, is fulsome in his praise of the chapter in Mill in which the concept is developed as the key to international values.

these exchanged blocs of goods were, after intervals of dislocation, successfully established. The intervals of dislocation were not—could not be—periods of deviation from a normal ratio of exchange based on costs, which, in their minds, did not exist, but rather periods in which the value of the goods exchanged internationally would not equate, or, to put it more familiarly, periods in which there would be an excess in the exports or imports of any given country which could not be cured except by a shift in the "terms of trade." It is clear, however, that in "cash," i.e. bilateral or, in the legal phrase, "executed," transactions (which was the type of transaction assumed in the development of the fundamental classical analysis), disequilibrium between the values of the imports and exports of any country is never possible. Every single transaction involving exports and imports, is, under these conditions, a finished and balanced transaction (with the export and the import each the *quid* for the *quo*) and this must, therefore, be true of their sums. But if, regardless of the terms of exchange, the total of exports and imports *must*, on the assumed conditions, equate, it is ridiculous to assert that the "equation of international demand" is of any relevance in the establishment of those terms. Viner makes a loyal and valiant but, as it seems to me, unsuccessful effort to rescue Mill, and his successors, from the charge of undue reliance on this equation.[40]

Disequilibrium as a Phenomenon of Monetary and Credit Morbidity

Disequilibrium in the international accounts is purely a phenomenon of monetary and credit morbidity. It arises only when the residents of one country have bought abroad, on deferred obligations, more goods than their current and prospective acquisitions of foreign currencies will cover.[41] If the creditors are unable, or reluctant, to foreclose, they may continue to supply the debtors with goods, and acquire additional deferred claims against them, in the hope that the process will, sooner or later, be reversed. The "dis-

[40] *Studies, op. cit.*, pp. 536 *et seq.*

[41] No reference is here intended to international financial transactions volitionally and deliberately entered upon by both parties. Any such lending and borrowing should be included as an element in the international *balance* as a current international liability of the lender and asset of the borrower. A true lack of balance may occur, however, whenever a portion of what were intended to be merely short-term voluntary credits are perforce extended in term.

equilibrium" in the international accounts may, in this way, be indefinitely prolonged and it has, in recent times, often been unconscionably so prolonged through the failure of the debtor country either to reduce, by deflation, the monetary cost of domestic *factors of production* and, therewith, the domestic currency cost of output, or to lower, by exchange devaluation, the purchasing power of its currency over international commodities. The trouble, in either case, is a low internal, relative to the external, value of the currency. The citizens of the debtor country are then impelled to consume all goods to a greater value than they are producing, and this excess consumption expresses itself particularly in imports, or in exportable commodities, both of which are relatively cheap in the debtor country's currency. The consequent large domestic consumption of exportable commodities reduces the potentiality of export and so operates, as an added impulse, to keep the disequilibrium in being. But, provided the foreign creditors refuse, forthrightly, to extend further favors, the international accounts, so far as current transactions are concerned, must come into balance through the sheer inability of the (former) debtor country any longer to acquire imports to a value in excess of its receipts on exports. This is true not only irrespective of the international ratio of exchange ("terms of trade") but also of the character of "reciprocal national demands," their "elasticity" or "inelasticity," the "essential needs" of the importers, or any other of the obfuscating phenomena with which the matter has been, and continues to be, surrounded. If the fact were widely recognized that disequilibria in the international accounts is attributable, in nearly every case, to a discrepancy between the internal and external value of currency units, accompanied by more or less surreptitious extensions of international credit, there never could have been any confusion as to how a disturbed equilibrium was to be restored or any notion that equilibrium in the international accounts is a *conditioning* factor in the establishment of the normal international ratio of exchange. Elimination of the credits will automatically restore equilibrium; there is no reason to suppose that this would affect the normal international ratio of exchange of products; and, whether it does or not, equilibrium will forthwith appear.[42]

[42] A case in point is, again, the German situation after World War I. It was then ardently contended (not alone by Germans) that Germany *could* not balance

The sole cause, in ordinary times, of a persistent adverse disequilibrium in the international accounts of any nation lies not, as classicists and neo-classicists alleged, in an anomalous relationship between the prices of its imports and the prices of its exports but, as just noted, in the discrepancy between the internal and external (i.e. foreign exchange) value of its currency. Whether under gold standard conditions or an inconvertible and independent currency, such a disequilibrium is indubitable evidence that the purchasing power of the money of the debtor country is excessive over international, as compared with purely domestic, commodities. Both import and exportable commodities will always then be bought in such volume within the country as to bring about disequilibrium between the imports and the relatively small volume of exportable commodities left for actual export.[43]

Under international gold standard conditions gold would, in these circumstances, leave the country in adequate amount (provided the banking authorities refrained from intervention). According to the quantity-theory, price-specie-flow, analysis of the classicists, this would *depress* the (gold) prices of "the paying country's goods" (including exports), and *raise* the (gold) prices of "the receiving country's goods" (including the paying country's imports), and would thus increase the volume of the paying country's exports, relative to its imports, to the degree necessary for equilibrium. But if, as we have earlier remarked, "reciprocal national *demands*" were the determinant of "terms of trade," one would expect the demand for, and the prices of, the imports of the country receiving gold (the

its international accounts since any increase in German exports would not only run into an inelastic demand but would require a prior (presumably equal-value) increase in imports of raw materials for fabrication into manufactured exports. The Germans, for some years, financed a sizable part of their imports through sales of eventually quite worthless mark currency to gullible foreign investors, and the consequent excess of German commodity imports was alleged to be proof of its own necessity. But, when the bottom eventually fell out of the market for marks, equilibrium in German commodity exports and imports was immediately, and automatically, established. cf. Frank D. Graham, *Exchange, Prices, and Production in Hyper-Inflation*, Princeton University Press, Princeton, N.J., 1930, *passim*.

[43] Under the Dawes plan for German reparations, disequilibrium was sure to be perpetuated by remission of the German duty of transfer whenever the internal value of the mark fell below its external value. Both the relatively high external value and the relatively low internal value of the mark were then to be maintained by a process which relieved the pressure on the external value and, at the same time, kept the internal value low by preventing any diminution in the supply of mark currency.

paying country's exports) to *rise* as a result of the recipient country's access of "means of payment," while the demand for, and the
prices of, the imports of the country paying gold (the recipient
country's exports) might be expected to *fall* as a result of the paying
country's corresponding deprivation. This would reverse the position taken by *most* of the classicists, and would not square with that
taken by any of them, on the effects of a movement of gold on the
"terms of trade." The same conflict of views arises within the classical camp with respect to the effects of high vs. low national income
and price levels (the two things are, with certain writers, assimilated
to one another) on the national "terms of trade." One group asserts
that this would depress, and the other that it would improve, the
terms on which the high-income-and-price-level-country would carry
on its international trade.

I leave to the defenders of the classicists the solution of these contradictions. The fact is that the demand for internationally traded
goods is *international* (there is a demand for each and all of the goods
in each of the countries) and there is, therefore, no reason to suppose
that a mere shift in the national *distribution* of monetary purchasing power (without any change in world income) would at all affect
the price relationships between internationally exchanged goods or,
at any rate, that it would affect them in any predictable fashion.
National redistribution of gold will have no inherent tendency to
change the gold prices of *international* commodities or the relationships between them. It will, however, ordinarily exert an effect on
the relationships between the prices of internationally traded commodities *as a whole* and those which are exclusively domestic.
Whereas, when a currently debtor country loses gold to its creditors,
there is no tendency toward a change in the prices of either its exports or its imports or, therefore, in the relationships between them,
the prices of its domestically produced and consumed commodities
will, in the absence of intervention, be likely to fall.[44] This will remove

[44] Both exports and imports are subject to a dual set of influences operating in
opposite directions and, therefore, tending to cancel each other in their effect on
market prices. So far as exports go, the money *cost* in the country losing gold may be
lowered, but the monetary *demand*, in the outside world, will be increased. The
monetary *demand* for imports will be lowered in the country losing gold but their
money *costs of production* in the country of origin will tend to rise. Commodities
not entering international trade will be subject to no such dual influence and will
tend to fall, or rise, with an efflux, or influx, of gold. The discrepancy between prices
and costs for the several groups of commodities in the various countries furnishes
the impetus under which the disequilibrium in the international accounts is eliminated.

that relative, and anomalous, deficiency in the purchasing power of the debtor country's currency over purely domestic commodities (and the correlative excess in its purchasing power over international commodities) which had occasioned the disequilibrium in the international accounts. Producers of these purely domestic commodities will, as a result of the fall in their prices, find it advantageous to shift to the output of goods for export or to those competing with imports. The amounts of both exportable and importable goods *consumed* in the hitherto debtor country will be reduced, in the face of unchanged prices for these goods and a reduced supply of money, at the same time that the amount of international goods *produced* in that country (whether export goods or goods competing with imports) will rise. Balance in the international accounts will be restored through the operation of both factors, with the consequent rise in the number and volume of exports and reduction in the number and volume of imports, all at unchanged prices, in the hitherto debtor country.[45] When balance is achieved the (temporary) discrepancy between the prices of goods in the international and the domestic sectors (in relationship to the prevailing cost ratios) will disappear.

The restoration of equilibrium will, of course, be facilitated by converse changes in the countries with "favorable" balances in the international accounts. There is not only no need, but no probability, of changes in price relationships, between *blocs* of internationally traded commodities, as a condition of equilibrium in the international accounts. *A fortiori*, the necessity for equilibrium in the international accounts can never be a *causal* factor in the establishment of those relationships.[46]

When a country is operating on an independent currency and, through induced international credits of some sort or control of imports, keeps the external purchasing power of that currency (its

[45] The decline in imports will be facilitated both by the reduction in money incomes (while import prices remain unchanged) and by the supply of part of the home demand out of the increased domestic production of hitherto heavily imported commodities. The consumption of purely domestic commodities will also, of necessity, fall, since fewer of them will be produced. Domestic consumption of *all* commodities will thus be curtailed but this is precisely what is essential to correct a condition brought about by the attempt of the country to live beyond its means.

[46] The reader should, perhaps, be warned that the discussion, here as elsewhere, assumes free competition. I would not suggest that actual adjustments are anything like as smooth as those here portrayed, or that they would not deviate, in considerable degree and for more or less lengthy periods, from the pattern here presented. But we are talking about equilibria.

exchange value against other monies) so far above the appropriate relationship with its domestic purchasing power as to promote a persistent deficit in the international accounts, the appropriate mechanism of adjustment is obvious and, with superficial differences, follows much the same course as under a gold standard. A permitted fall in the exchange value of the currency, while having no tendency to alter the (normal) prices of international goods (whether exports or imports of the country in question) when these are measured in a stable *numeraire*, will operate to raise their prices in the domestic currency. The domestic currency prices of purely domestic goods will however, in the absence of extraneous forces, remain unaltered, and the *relative* purchasing power of the currency over these goods will thus be enhanced (which is an alternative way of saying that the relative value of these goods is lowered). The same tendency toward a reduction of imports, a reduction in the home purchase and a consequent expansion in the exports of exportable goods, and a shift of production from domestic to exportable lines or to commodities competing with imports, will then appear, and the restoration of equilibrium in the international accounts will thereafter proceed in the manner outlined, for gold-standard conditions, in the preceding pages.[47] *Mutatis mutandis* the argument applies, in reverse, to the

---

[47] Professor F. W. Taussig in his already cited article published in 1917 (*The Quarterly Journal of Economics*, Vol. XXXI, No. 3, pp. 380 *et seq.*) developed fully, with respect to inconvertible paper monies, the doctrine here set forth but was of the opinion that it could not apply to international gold (or any other such asset) standards. His inability to perceive that, in essentials, the doctrine applied as well in the one case as in the other, and his disposition to regard independent (debt) monetary standards as an aberration, were responsible for his (later) puzzlement over certain adjustments of disturbed international trading conditions under gold standards which had in fact been reached without the price movements which seemed to him necessary. His failure to discard the classical theory of shifts in the relationship between national price levels in favor of a theory of shifts in the relationship between, on the one hand, the prices of domestic goods in any country and, on the other, the prices of international goods (including both the given country's exports and imports) left him, indeed, at a loss to explain the phenomena of adjustment of the international accounts not only under gold-standard but also (though in lesser degree) under inconvertible paper monetary conditions.

Taussig even alleged (p. 399) that the course of prices in trading countries one of which is on a gold standard and the other with inconvertible paper money is, in adjustment to a given disturbance in the international accounts, *precisely the opposite* of that to be expected when both countries are on the gold standard. This seems nothing less than paradoxical and partly depends for such approach to validity as it may have on the selection of the money in which the prices are to be measured and the shifting (general) value relationships between the currencies concerned. Taussig also developed the theory that a paper currency country with a temporarily favorable balance in the international accounts would gain, through

countries with "favorable" balances in the international accounts.

Disequilibrium in the international accounts (a lack of equation of the total monetary values of exports and imports of each of the countries concerned) will thus be cured automatically, and without any necessary, or probable, alteration in the price relationships of internationally traded commodities, provided there is a reasonably free international movement of goods, free movement of a common money material (or of the exchange rates between independent currencies) and international creditors do not insist on throwing good money after bad.[48]

So far is the "equation of international demand" from being a factor in establishing the ratio of exchange (terms of trade) that one can say that the equation would appear even if the ratio of exchange could be (and was) established by arbitrary fiat which, among other things, also prohibited international extensions of credit.[49] It is such extensions of credit, and these alone, which, no

what he stated would be the consequent shift in income and price relationships, *more* than he conceived a gold standard country would gain under similar conditions. This, if true, would be a practically conclusive argument for abandoning the gold standard in the circumstances. It is, however, not true, since the price shifts which Taussig, loyally following classical theory, assumes will take place will not, in fact, occur under *either* of the alternative monetary regimes. There is, indeed, no reason to suppose that a favorable balance of payments, with or without a subsequent influx of gold, will have any persistent tendency to improve, for it, the terms on which the country concerned trades with another country or the outside world in general. The notion that a fall in the exchange value of a currency (the effect of an unfavorable balance of payments) will bring to pass a more or less persistent impairment of the terms of trade of the country in which it occurs and, conversely, that a rise will affect the terms favorably is, however, widespread. (cf. John Parke Young, *The International Economy*, Ronald Press, New York, 1942, p. 179.) There is even some tendency to confuse rates of exchange of currencies with the ratio of exchange of goods. Frictions in competition may justify the view that, for a fairly lengthy period, a country's "terms of trade" may be tied up with aberrational movements of exchange rates, but it seems probable that the presence, and importance, of this phenomenon, if it occurs, have been much exaggerated. The idea that a shift of exchange rates will cause a corresponding shift in the ratio of import to export prices in the countries concerned unwarrantably presumes not only that any given country is the sole (or at least the dominant) supplier of its exports, and the sole (or dominant) consumer of its imports, but also that, in the one case, conditions of supply, and, in the other, conditions of demand, determine market prices.

[48] "The sharp line which many writers have drawn between the international gold standard and other monetary systems proves to be without justification. . . . The time-honored theory of foreign exchange under the gold standard has . . . a more appropriate application to a case of legally flexible exchanges where speculators sell foreign balances and repay debts to highly liquid banks, than it has to a case of a legally simon-pure gold standard where the central bank sells gold but allows . . . commercial bank deposits to remain unchanged." (Fritz Machlup, "The Theory of Foreign Exchanges," Part II, *Economica*, Vol. VII, N. S., No. 25, pp. 41-42.)

[49] To make the fiat "stick" it would, of course, be necessary to control, in totali-

matter what the terms of trade might be, could ever prolong disequilibria in the international accounts.

More or less involuntary international extensions of credit tend to occur whenever any country, by hook or crook, succeeds in keeping the exchange value of its currency above the level which its domestic purchasing power warrants. Because they can get foreign currency cheaply the country's citizens will then always tend to buy abroad more than they can pay for and, because foreign currency will not command much of their own, its producers will prefer to sell at home the exportable products which, if sold abroad for foreign currency, might serve as means of payment for the imports. Some of the foreign suppliers of goods to the country in question will then be compelled to accept claims on the currency of the excessively importing country which will be uncashable in their own money.[50] But this, it should be stressed, is the result not of "wrong" terms of trade but of pathological monetary conditions. The latter can be cured through an automatically attained correction of the relationship between the external and internal value of the country's currency which, typically, will leave the country's exports selling at unchanged values in terms of its imports.

The True Mechanism of Adjustment

It is, then, by changes in the volume or variety of the exports relative to the volume or variety of the imports of any country, without changes in the relative unit values of its exports and imports, that a disturbed monetary equilibrium in the international accounts is typically overcome. International prices are not established at the level which, on the basis of a *given* set of exports and imports for countries A, B, C, and so forth, will produce equilibrium in the international accounts of all the trading countries, but rather in a world context of opportunity costs which determine the volume and variety of commodities which, at a given world ratio of exchange of goods, any country will send out in exchange for the volume, variety, and equivalent total value of imports that, in the current context

---

tarian fashion, commodity supply and demand *within* the various countries. But no control of *international trade* would then be required to secure equilibrium in the international accounts.

[50] They may, of course, get simple compatriots, or their government, directly or indirectly, to buy these claims. The suppliers of the goods can then be paid, in their own money, at the expense of the purchasers of claims to the "weak" currency.

of costs and prices, it can acquire more advantageously by international trade than by domestic production.

It is only a shift in *world* demand for the various internationally traded commodities that could have any possible effect on the free-market normal exchange relationships between them (and even this will have no effect unless marginal cost ratios are thereby altered). When countries produce any commodities in common, demand and supply cannot be divided into reciprocally antagonistic national sectors. It could, for instance, readily happen that, of two countries producing practically identical commodities for export, and with practically identical imports, one had, at a given moment, a "favorable" balance of payments and the other an "unfavorable" balance.[51] On more or less representative classical reasoning, equilibrium in the international accounts could be attained, in the one case, only by a shift in the exchange ratio, between the two groups of goods, which would be the precise opposite of the shift that would be required between identically the same groups of goods in the other. The conclusion, on classical reasoning, must be that equilibrium is impossible. The *real* cause for disequilibrium, however, is that, in the one case, the domestic value (purchasing power over purely domestic goods) of the currency is too low, relative to its exchange value against other currencies and internationally traded commodities, and that, in the other case, it is too high.[52] When these anomalies are corrected the international accounts of both countries will come into balance without any necessary, or probable, prior alteration in the ratio of exchange between the group of commodities that they both export against the group that they both import which, if it occurred, could do nothing to cure *both* of the diametrically opposed imbalances in the international accounts of the countries concerned.

It is possible, when the anomalies just mentioned are corrected, that the former of the two countries may find it advantageous not only to alter the ratio of its purchase, and sale, of international to its purchase of domestic commodities already in being, but also to produce more, and import less, of some (marginal) commodity, or

[51] This would be most likely to happen in the case of two small countries with a very limited list of common exports.

[52] The citizens of the one country therefore buy relatively heavily of imports, and of exportable goods, whereas the citizens of the other buy relatively lightly of both these classes of goods. This is a quite adequate explanation of the excess of imports in the one case and of exports in the other.

even to shift from the import of some commodities, hitherto produced in amounts inadequate to cover domestic consumption, to their export, and that the latter of the two countries will move in the opposite direction. All this may occur without any change in the (normal) price relationships between internationally traded commodities which, to repeat, will not alter unless the change in *world* demand for the various commodities is great enough to bring about a change in the national locus of normal margins of production.[53]

"National Demands" and the Alternative

In a world of trading individuals, free (or even *somewhat* inhibited by national policy) to follow their advantage as they see it, there is, to repeat what has been already said but perhaps not often enough, no such thing as *national* demand and, *a fortiori*, no such thing as *reciprocal* national demand for bales of goods "representative" of each of the national trading entities. The phrase could have any meaning only as between nations organized, for international trading purposes at any rate, as single business units. The latter is a type of "trade" with which this book, along with the classical economists, is not concerned.

How difficult it is for a "classicist" to accept what seems to me the axiomatic assertion made in the preceding paragraph is shown by Professor Viner's reaction to it. In an earlier comment on the matter I had said that "it must be obvious that reciprocal demand is for individual commodities and not for any such uniform aggregate of labor and capital as a unit of the consolidated commodities may incorporate, and that to construct demand schedules for representative bales the physical composition of which is inevitably changing as we move along the schedules, with commodities even shifting from one demand schedule to its reciprocal, is not only to build imaginary bricks with imaginary clay but also to commit the worse fault of assuming a homogeneity in the bricks which, though a logical necessity for the construction of the demand schedules in question, is at the same time a logical impossibility."[54] Of this Viner says:

[53] The shifts within either of the countries in question involve a restoration rather than an alteration of these norms. It was a *monetary* maladjustment which originally disturbed the appropriate cost relationships (measured in money) between international goods, taken as a whole, and purely domestic commodities. When the monetary distortion is straightened out everything else comes into order.

[54] "The Theory of International Values," *The Quarterly Journal of Economics*, Vol. XLVI, 1932, p. 583.

"I understand Graham's argument to be that the theory of international values, as presented, say, by Marshall, is completely vitiated by its use of reciprocal-demand and terms-of-trade concepts requiring for their logical validity a non-existent fixity in the physical composition of the exports and imports of each region, *and that the remedy lies in carrying on the analysis in terms of reciprocal demands for and ratios of interchange between individual commodities.*"[55]

After palliating the classicists' sin as venial, in what in my judgment is an unwarranted *tu quoque* argument, Viner goes on to declare that the alternative that I offer, which he alleges is "analysis in terms of pairs of single commodities," is not satisfactory (except on the assumption that the paired goods are the only commodities entering into international trade or can be held to be "representative" of trade as a whole).[56]

Now I had never imagined, and certainly did not mean to imply, that analysis of a complex international trading situation must be made "in terms of pairs of single commodities." On the contrary, I have for long strenuously maintained that complex trade *cannot* be thus handled, and that one of the very strongest reasons for rejection of the classical doctrines is that the classicists themselves made their analysis in such simple terms (two-country, two-commodity trade) and then erroneously projected their results into complex trading situations. I sincerely regret that my exposition proved so inept that so acute a critic as Professor Viner, doing his best to understand me, should impute to me ideas that I was endeavoring to refute. What I have been trying to say is that, so far as relative demand is significant at all (which is not very far), the normal value relationships between two, three, or hundreds of commodities are determined by the relative *world* (not reciprocal national) demand of individuals for each of those commodities; that the composition of, and ratio of exchange between, the current exports and imports of any given country depends partly on the country's own cost ratios between individual commodities and partly on what the country, with such cost ratios, finds it advantageous, at any time, to export and import in interaction with the evolving world price structure; that the phrase "terms of trade" has many possible meanings;[57] that the

[55] *Studies, op. cit.*, p. 553. Italics mine.　　[56] *ibid.*, p. 554.
[57] Viner, himself, gives an excellent account of the several connotations of the term. cf. *Studies*, pp. 319 *et seq.*

"terms of trade" between any one and any other single country are irrelevant to almost any conceivable purpose and are probably not even susceptible to any form of measurement; that, in the absence of data on relative costs, changes in the price relationship between what were, initially, the exports and imports of any given country are, *per se*, of no significance for any of the purposes for which they are ordinarily used even when the initial exports and imports are maintained; that reciprocal national demands (conceding, for the purpose of argument, that such are conceivable in the individualistic trade with which the classicists affected to deal) are not, in their effect on markets, segregatable from one another; and that reciprocal national demands (however they may be conceived) are as much a resultant as a cause of international values and can, therefore, not serve as a determinant of those values.

Reciprocal demand, says Viner, "is not only an aggregative concept, but it designates an economic force which operates as an indivisible entity. 'Each transaction in international trade is an individual transaction,' but the terms on which it is conducted are set for it by the market complex as a whole. The prices of any particular export commodity and any particular import commodity are functionally related to each other, react upon each other, not directly (except to an insignificant degree) but through their membership in the price and utility and cost systems of the trading world, taken as a whole. In the case of foreign trade, changes in the desires for or costs of particular commodities operate to change the ratios of interchange between these commodities and other commodities only indirectly through their influence on money flows and on aggregate demands and supplies of commodities in terms of money. The reciprocal-demand analysis is an attempt, imperfect but superior to available substitutes, to describe the aggregate or average results of such changes in desires or costs when they affect appreciably a wide range of commodities."[58]

In the former half of this statement (the first sentence excepted) I would concur and cannot see why it should be presented as in any way alien to what I have ever said. With the latter half of the statement I find myself in sharp disagreement. Viner's implication that pecuniarily processed trade would result in a very different ratio of exchange from that which would attend the same trade on a barter

[58] Viner, *Studies, op. cit.*, p. 555.

basis (no matter how refined) would be surprising even to the original proponents of the doctrines that Viner elects to defend.

The classicists', and neo-classicists', zealous advocacy of reciprocal demand doctrine is irrevocably tied up with the fallacious explanation of the operation of the monetary mechanism in adjustment of disturbances in international trade. When, however, Viner says that changes in the desires for or costs of particular commodities operate to change the ratios of interchange between these commodities and other commodities *only indirectly through their influence on money flows* and on aggregate demands and supplies of commodities in terms of money, one is impelled to ask whether it is not incredible that changes in the relative desires for, and costs of, individual internationally traded commodities could have no effect on their relative values unless there had been a prior flow of money, from one country to another, affecting aggregate (pecuniary) demands and supplies.

Professor Taussig (to whom Viner dedicates his book) may perhaps again be cited to show the difficulties in which classical theory involves its devotees. Taussig felt that, on classical theory, the restoration of equilibrium in international trade, following such a disturbance as did not involve a prior distortion of the appropriate relationship between the external and internal value of a currency, would take considerable time, and that it would require substantial international movements of gold (or, in the case of free currencies, a substantial shift in exchange rates). But, as already noted, the facts were otherwise as even Taussig himself was impelled to admit.

"One thing stands out. . . . This is the unmistakably close connection between international payments and the movements of commodity imports and exports. And this closeness of connection, striking in the case of Great Britain, is found again and again in other countries also. International payments, tho they involve between the individuals directly concerned nothing more than remittances in terms of money, lead almost at once to transfers of goods. The movement of exports and imports—the substantive course of international trade—responds with surprising promptness to the balance of international payments as a whole. The promptness is surprising because each constituent transaction . . . is purely in terms of money. When individuals in a country like Great Britain make loans to other individuals (or governments) abroad, they undertake to put at the disposal of the borrowers merely so much of purchasing power, so much 'money.' Yet the recorded transactions between countries show surprisingly little transfer of the only 'money' that moves from one to the other—gold. It is the goods that move, and they seem to move at once; almost as if there were an automatic connection between these financial operations and the commodity exports or imports. That the flow of goods should ensue in time, perhaps even at an early date, is of course to be expected; it is a commonplace in the theoretical reasoning that this must be the ultimate outcome. What is puzzling is the rapidity, almost simultaneity, of the commodity movements. The presumable intermediate stage of gold flow and price changes is hard to discern, and certainly is extremely short."[59]

Taussig's bewilderment, here as elsewhere, failed to shake his faith in the classical shibboleths. He goes on to say: "I find it impossible to see how there can be a complete skipping of the intermediate stage [international gold movements]—anything in the nature of an automatic connection. There is, of course, the case . . . where no intermediate stage is to be expected at all; the case, namely, where those who make loans happen to stipulate also that the proceeds shall be used to buy specified goods of their own or of their associates. But in the 'normal' case, which is exemplified in Britain's trade for the period just examined, purchases of goods are not thus tied to the loans; and it would then seem to be only some sort of roundabout process, some disturbance or readjustment of monetary and price conditions, that could lead to the movement of goods. Being roundabout, one would suppose that it would take time. And yet it appears to require practically none.

"It is true that a searching examination of the presumable links of connection . . . might show that the process was not always so rapid as it seems to be on first inspection. The explanation of the speedy adjustment may be found in the sensitiveness of the British monetary system. It must be admitted, however, that a quick and close adjustment appears to exist in other countries whose systems are less sensitive. So far as I have been able to observe, it is found in the trade of Germany and France also during this very period, the decade or two preceding the Great War [World War I]. One might

59 F. W. Taussig, *International Trade*, Macmillan, New York, 1927, pp. 260, 261. Taussig was examining the British "terms of trade" from 1880 to 1914.

be tempted to say that the sensitive industrial organism always and everywhere shrinks from the loss of its lifeblood, the vital circulating medium; that it turns instinctively to some other way of meeting demands on the industrial structure. But this is no more than a metaphor; it may suggest in what direction an answer should be sought, but gives no answer.

"All in all, we have here a field quite insufficiently explored. The plain outstanding fact is that the exports and imports of goods adjust themselves, if not at once, certainly with quickness and ordinarily with ease, to the sum total of a country's transactions with other countries. The balance of payments is satisfied only to a slight extent by any shipment of specie, chiefly thru changes in the commodity sales and purchases."[60]

Whether the field had or had not been *sufficiently* explored it had by no means been wholly neglected. The question of international movements of gold under a simple specie currency (or of movements in the exchange rate between currencies where an inconvertible paper money is involved) is not, of course, the same question as that of movements in the ratio of exchange between commodities, though, if gold *does* move, it was the belief of Taussig, and other representative classicists, that the terms of trade would, as a direct consequence, undergo an alteration. The two questions, while distinct, are, therefore, in the minds of most of the classicists closely associated. Yet, as we have seen, classical writers were by no means unanimous in their conviction that gold would move. On this matter Viner says:

"Wheatley, as much later Bastable and Nicholson, held that the balance of payments would adjust itself immediately, and without need of specie movements, to disturbances of a non-currency nature, through an immediate and presumably exactly equilibrating relative shift in the demand of the two regions for each other's commodities. Granted [however] that a relative shift in demand as between the two countries may, without the aid of relative price changes, restore an equilibrium disturbed, say, by an international tribute, it is an error to suppose that the shift in demand can ordinarily occur, under the assumption . . . of a simple specie currency, without involving a prior or a supporting transfer of specie from the paying to the receiving country. The new equilibrium requires that more purchases measured in money be made per unit of time in the receiving

[60] *op. cit.*, pp. 261, 262.

country and less in the paying country; as has been shown above, it is by its effect on the relative monetary volume of purchases in the two countries that the relative shift in demands exercises its equilibrating influence. Unless as and because one country becomes obligated to make payments to the other velocity falls in the paying country and rises in the receiving country, these necessary relative changes in purchases and in demands will not occur except after and because of a relative change in the amount of specie in the two countries, and such changes in velocity are at least not certain to occur, nor to be in the right directions if they do occur. Acceptance of the doctrine that a relative shift in demand schedules may suffice, without changes in relative prices, to restore equilibrium in a disturbed international balance does not [therefore] involve as a corollary that specie movements are unnecessary for restoration of equilibrium, as Wheatley, Bastable, Nicholson, and others seem to have supposed. The error arises from acceptance of a too simple version of the quantity theory of money, in which price levels and quantities of money must move together and in the same direction regardless of what variations may occur in other terms of the monetary equation. In its most extreme application this erroneous doctrine has led to the conclusion that if unilateral payments should perchance result in a relative shift in price levels in favor of the *paying* country, the movement of specie will be from the receiving to the paying country!"[61]

In spite of Viner's implication at the end of this passage that a movement of specie from the receiving to the paying country is wholly out of the question, and even ridiculous, Mosak has shown that it is a possibility "not only when the terms of trade turn against her [the receiving country], but even when the terms of trade change in her favor."[62] So far as disturbance and restoration of equilibrium are concerned it is the contention of this book that, on a transfer of income from citizens of one country to those of another, the price relationships between goods will alter, temporarily, pursuant to such shifts in the total demand for the several goods as would occur under unchanged prices. Supplies are, for the moment, fixed, and not only the relative volume but also the character of the new

61 *Studies, op. cit.*, pp. 365, 366.
62 Jacob L. Mosak, *General-Equilibrium Theory in International Trade, op. cit.*, p. 91.

demand will lead to different degrees of deviation of price from the norms set by costs. The price movements, quite obviously, will divide without reference to the national origin of buyers, or of the output, of the various goods. They may temporarily disrupt the international accounts (in unpredictable ways) and lead to gold flows, or exchange rate movements, in any direction. The price movements will, in any case, presently be cancelled by shifts in supply. Part of this shift in supply will be accomplished, in any country with a balance of international payments disturbed by the transfer, through a change in the composition of industry as between domestic and international goods (exportables or goods competing with imports). This will be induced by an appropriate alteration, however achieved, in the relative external and internal values of the currency of the country in question. Any price movement necessary to occasion such a shift will be annulled, without further effect, after the shift has taken place. The altered composition of industry will be the primary factor in the restoration of equilibrium in the international accounts. Prices will eventually take the form dictated by opportunity costs and there is little ground for supposing that these will have been at all affected.

While, in varying circumstances, a "disturbance" in international trade might result either in no movement of gold at all or in a (minor) movement in *either* direction (*mutatis mutandis*, for free currencies, in no movement at all in exchange rates, or in a [minor] movement of the value of any given such currency, in terms of others, in *either* direction) it seems to me probable that the transfer of purchasing power from one country to another, to which it has incurred any out-of-the-ordinary obligation such as a loan or tribute, will not be attended either by complete neutrality in its effect on the world demand for various internationally traded goods or by a shift of demand which will favor the output of the paying rather than the receiving country. The recipients of the loan or tribute will probably not immediately spend the full addition to their incomes but will increase their money balances. If this is so, a (small) transfer of gold from the paying to the receiving country will, under gold standard conditions, tend to develop. (In the case of an inconvertible paper currency the parallel phenomenon would be a slight fall in the exchange value of the paying country's monetary unit.) Either phenomenon, unless "compensated" by action of the monetary authorities, will include that (opposite) shift in the relationship between the external and internal values of each of the respective currencies which will achieve whatever alteration in the balance of payments may be necessary to consummate the transfer of the loan or tribute. The shift will, in any event, be temporary, merely as a facilitant of what would otherwise take place more slowly, and, when the objective has been reached, will be cancelled, or even replaced by a (temporary) movement in the other direction. The latter will tend to be the case where the loan or tribute is an isolated transaction whereas a mere cancellation will be appropriate to the situation in which the loan or tribute is repeated year after year. In the case of repetitive loans or tribute the change in the composition of industry, to which the temporary price movement is an incentive, will be maintained even when the price impulse that was a factor in inducing it is no longer operative.

Viner's adherence to the classical view that there will ordinarily be a definitive change in the relationship between the price levels of the exports and imports of the paying and the receiving countries (conceptually applicable in equal degree to all the commodities in either category) seems to me not only to fly in the face of the facts that puzzled Taussig but, for reasons given in the first part of this chapter, to be, in complex trade, a logical impossibility. Since, in a given constellation of constant costs and on the assumption of intranational freedom of competition, there can be no shift in normal price relationships between *any* of the goods in the national output, and since the normal price relationships between international goods can shift only with a transfer of the locus of the margin of indifference in the production of two or more goods from one national entity to another, the occasions will be rare in which any shift in normal international price relationships can, under the posited conditions, occur. Even when we relax the postulate of constant costs, the normal price structure will reflect movements along given cost curves (according to the volume of output of the various goods), and, except as this *volume* is affected (and then only intermediately through costs), the national origin of demand, its character, and the changes in it, will be of no significance in the structure of prices. For such normal prices we must look to the *cost* structure, and changes in relative opportunity costs (if any) will surely not correspond with the price changes that Viner conceives, or, to put it the other way round, the price changes that he conceives will not correspond with the changes in costs.

The change in opposite directions in the two countries, *in the relative output and purchases of domestic and internationally traded commodities* (which might well be a consequence of the alteration in their relative spendable incomes), would perhaps require for its effectuation a temporary change, in opposite directions in the two countries, in the price ratio between domestic and internationally traded goods (the prices of, and price relationships between, internationally traded commodities tending to remain stable while the prices of domestic goods move, in opposite directions, in the two countries). This would be the consequence of a (small) transfer of money from the disbursing to the recipient country on loan or tribute account, following a temporary lack of balance in the international balance of payments and pending the transfer of output from domestic to exportable commodities in the disbursing, and the converse in the recipient, country.[63] When the shift in relative prices had done its work, and the transfer of gold was perhaps reversed, all price relationships both among internationally traded goods and between the exports and domestic production of each country would then come into correspondence with opportunity costs.[64] With constant cost conditions these would have remained unchanged regardless of shifts in relative demand, and, with variable costs, would have altered without reference to the country in which the goods concerned happened to be produced.

It is important to stress that, so long as the countries continue to produce any given commodity in common there can, with a given constellation of constant costs, be no shift in any *normal* price relationships (whether as between internationally traded goods, from one or another source, or as between these goods, as a whole, and domestic goods in either country) without subversion of the postulates that the classicists themselves laid down. The classicists

[63] The transfer need not be nearly as large as Taussig looked for and did not find. The results could in fact be attained, without any transfer at all, by merely varying the ratios of fiduciary to basic currency.

[64] This would be the full equilibrium which Professor Pigou has distinguished from the exchange equilibrium by which it would have been preceded. (cf. A. C. Pigou and Dennis H. Robertson, *Economic Essays and Addresses*, P. S. King & Son, Ltd., Westminster, 1931, p. 45.) Pigou, however, does not put the matter in the way it is here presented but sticks to classical exposition and, in part, to classical conclusions.

here wandered in the wilderness not only because they were obsessed with the fantasy of "reciprocal *national* demands," as opposing sectors of a total demand any part of which in fact traverses both sectors, but because they were prone to forget that, with shifts in income, the citizens of every country consume a varying share of their own exportable commodities as well as of imports and of domestic goods.

The Transfer Problem

The so-called "transfer problem" came into prominence only after World War I. There had, before this, been many cases of sudden shifts in the international obligations of various countries. The corresponding shifts in the balances of payment were effected, with all but imperceptible disturbance, whether the countries involved were on the gold standard or had inconvertible paper currencies.[65] Why then should the belief have arisen that the "transfer problem," particularly with respect to German reparations, would prove difficult to the point of insolubility? The answer to this question lies, I think, in the fact, to which we have called attention, that Keynes, showing, in this respect, no trace of his subsequent iconoclasm, not only took classical and neo-classical international trade doctrines much too seriously in his discussion of the economic consequences of the Peace of Versailles[66] but "sold" to the world his opinion that the payment of the reparations assessed against Germany would be impossible and would hurt the recipients as much as the Germans. Whatever, on political or other non-economic grounds, might be said against reparations, this opinion not only ran counter to experience but, in its latter part, impugns what had hitherto been regarded as economic sense. Yet Keynes' view was held to be substantiated by events inasmuch as the Germans in fact did not, and

[65] The French transfer to Germany of the indemnity payments after the Franco-Prussian War (cf. Jacques Rueff, "Mr. Keynes' Views on the Transfer Problem," *The Economic Journal*, Vol. xxxix, pp. 388-399); the sharp shifts in the international borrowing position of the United States in the post-Civil-War period (cf. Frank D. Graham, "International Trade Under Depreciated Paper: The United States 1862-1879," *The Quarterly Journal of Economics*, Vol. xxxvi, pp. 220-273); the experience of Canada in the early years of the present century (cf. Jacob Viner, *Canada's Balance of International Indebtedness*, Harvard University Press, Cambridge, Mass., 1924); and the case of Argentina (cf. John H. Williams, *Argentine International Trade Under Inconvertible Paper Money, 1880-1900*, Harvard University Press, Cambridge, Mass., 1920); may be cited as typical. The passage on pp. 286-288 shows the surprise of economists at the *ease* of transfer.

[66] *The Economic Consequences of the Peace*, Harcourt, Brace, New York, 1920.

were widely supposed to be unable to, pay any substantial net sums in reparations. The "transfer problem," moreover, appeared to become acute (for other countries rather than Germany) in the decade of the '30's. This had nothing to do with reparations but the complaint of a "shortage of dollars" began then to be chronic.

It is, I think, fair to say that there was no "transfer problem" until it was manufactured and, to show the process of manufacture, it is perhaps best to start with the phenomenon of "dollar shortage." A "shortage of dollars" means that the citizens of many foreign countries are at any time acquiring fewer claims against Americans than are required to cover the claims that Americans are acquiring against them.[67] This means only one thing, viz., that the dollar is then available to them (so far as rationing permits) at less than its value in a free market. Or, to put it more specifically, the exchange value of the dollar against foreign currency is, by one or another means, then being held below what its relative purchasing power (or below what equilibrium in the international accounts) would warrant. We can thus say either that, at the then current national price levels, the dollar is undervalued on the exchanges or that, at the then current exchange rates, the price level in the United States is too low (or, if we choose, that price levels in the countries complaining of "a shortage of dollars" are too high or that the exchange value of their currencies, against dollars, is too high). These all mean an undervaluation of the dollar on the exchanges relative to the requirements of equilibrium or to the respective domestic purchasing powers of the dollar and the other currencies concerned.[68]

People will always bid for the relatively cheap thing and, if that

[67] The discussion is not directed to the (post World War II) conditions prevailing while this is written. These constitute a special case with which I am not here concerned. It is the inter-war period that is in question. I cannot, however, refrain from saying that the "dollar shortage," persisting so long after World War II is not only a consequence of destitution in Europe but also of overvaluation of European, and other, currencies against the dollar. Many countries *not* devastated by the war are also short on dollars and some of them have more or less deliberately, if not voluntarily, maneuvered themselves into this position. This is especially true of Sweden and Canada. cf. Friedrich A. Lutz, *The Marshall Plan and European Economic Policies*, Princeton University, International Finance Section, Essays on International Finance, No. 9, Princeton, N.J., Spring, 1948.

[68] Abstraction is made of conditions of panic attended by flights from other currencies to the dollar. These flights, if unchecked, would lead to a collapse in the exchange market and to an *over*-valuation of the dollar relative to current domestic purchasing powers of the currencies concerned, but, on the other hand, the relatively low actual exchange value of the dollar persistently encourages such flights.

relative cheapness is somehow maintained, the bids will always exceed the offers. In the case in question the holders of the currencies of the countries complaining of a shortage of dollars can get more for their money by buying dollars, and spending these dollars in the United States, than they can get by using their money in any other way. So long as this condition obtains, that is, that dollars are sold at unduly low prices, the shortage will persist. The holders of currencies overvalued in exchange against the dollar will not only buy all the dollars they can get, in order to import from the United States, but they will also buy, much more heavily than usual, the goods that are, at home, cheaper than in the United States, that is to say, the exportable products of their own country. With their imports thus persistently stimulated, and exports retarded, it is small wonder that the shortage of dollars in the countries concerned becomes chronic.

There is a perennial shortage of any valuable thing in the sense that not everyone can get all that he wants of it on terms satisfactory to him. But in a free market there is, on the other hand, *never* a shortage of anything in the sense that the amount offered, at the price obtainable in such a market, falls short of the amount demanded at that price. It is, in fact, the function of (upward) price movements to eliminate any such shortage.[69] The shortage of dollars, in the market sense, is explicable on precisely the same grounds as the shortage of any other economic good the price of which is kept below what a free market would establish.[70] We should never forget that exchange rates are prices.

[69] It may be worth while to call attention to the disappearance of "shortages," practically overnight, when price controls were removed in the United States in 1946. This occurred in face of the fact that there was, in many cases, no increase in supply and no shifting of demand schedules to the left. There will *always* be a "shortage" under controls since the very purpose of the control is to hold down the rise in prices which would otherwise occur. *At the control price,* more of the commodity is *ipso facto* demanded than will be supplied: the free market price is the price that automatically brings the amount demanded and the amount supplied into equilibrium.

[70] The shortage of dollars (in the outside world) is frequently attributed to the restrictive policy of the United States on imports of commodities (cf., e.g., Hal B. Lary et al., *The United States in the World Economy,* U.S. Dept. of Commerce, Bureau of Foreign and Domestic Commerce, United States Government Printing Office, Washington, 1943, p. 22 and *passim*). The protective tariff structure of the United States is deplorable but it is not responsible for this particular evil. A protective tariff, in an otherwise free market, will reduce exports as much as it reduces imports. It has no effect, therefore, on the *balance* of payments, It must, of course, be conceded that it is possible for a country to build up international financial

In the short reign of the inter-War international *gold* standard (1925-1931) the dollar was undervalued on the exchanges. The American price level was low, relative to those of some commercially important foreign countries, at the exchange rates against the dollar that the countries of those currencies had undertaken to uphold. In the absence of a rise in American prices their only chance of currently earning an adequate supply of dollars, while still maintaining the gold standard and reasonable freedom of trade, was to reduce their own price levels, that is, to raise the domestic value of their currencies to correspond with the value in dollars. This they did not do and the shortage of dollars therefore continued until the gold standard broke down. So long, thereafter, as the countries concerned did not try to support the exchange value of their currencies above equilibrium level they did not, of course, run short of dollars. But, as soon as they tried such support, and thereby again overvalued their own currency *vis-à-vis* the dollar (an undervaluation of the dollar), the shortage reappeared. It was then necessary to establish a whole range of controls to keep their citizens from using their money to buy dollars when these dollars were, by the

---

obligations which, without inflation of the monetary unit in which they are denominated, are too great to be carried on a vehicle of restricted trade. The World War II international borrowings of Great Britain are probably in this category. A freely trading world would be of help to the British in the attempt to meet these commitments but it is doubtful whether, without scaling down, they could, even then, be amortized.

The thesis that there is a more or less inevitable *chronic* shortage of dollars in the extra-United States world is explicitly stated by Charles P. Kindleberger in a chapter on "International Monetary Stabilization," *Postwar Economic Problems*, S. E. Harris, editor, McGraw-Hill, 1943, pp. 375-395. Kindleberger says that "the United States can produce a variety of producers' and consumers' goods with a price and quality advantage so great as to be almost absolute" (p. 379). I find it hard to give any significance whatever to this sentence (which, so far as it is intelligible, strikes me as a masterpiece of understatement). It certainly fails of its apparent intention of corroboration of the author's thesis that a chronic "shortage of dollars" is normal "because the world wants American products in order to enjoy a high standard of living" (p. 394). Who is there who does not want American, or any other, products in order to enjoy a high standard of living? If this is what Kindleberger means by a "shortage of dollars" we can be sure that not only foreigners but Americans will be short of dollars (no matter how plentiful, and cheap, they may become) until the end of time.

The one point on which I would agree with Kindleberger is that "a reduction of the American tariff is not . . . an adequate solution for the world shortage of dollars" since it seems to me that the tariff is all but completely irrelevant to the question of *disequilibrium* in the international accounts.

countries' own policy, offered (to preferred purchasers) at unduly cheap rates in the domestic money.[71]

The penchant for controls arose, at least partly, from the conviction, buttressed by fallacious classical theory, that a relaxation of the restrictions would shift the "terms of trade" sharply against the country imposing them. The notion was that a fall in the exchange value of the currency of such a country would result in the sale of its exports at ruinously low prices in terms of its imports. It has even been gravely discussed whether equilibrium in the international accounts of such a country could ever, on a free basis, be attained, since the relative fall in the value of an increased physical volume of "the country's exports," attendant on an inelastic foreign demand for those exports (and an inelastic domestic demand for "the country's imports") might, it was alleged, bring about a situation in which the debit balance of the country on international account would grow, in a vicious spiral, with a decline in the exchange value of its currency and the alleged cheapening of the prices (to foreigners) of its exports.[72]

Disregarding immediate effects (on which something will later be said) all this may be characterized, forthwith, as solemn nonsense. In the first place, no country, as already pointed out, can

71 I would not be held to maintain that exchange control is never desirable or necessary. But the crises for which it could probably be justified were indefinitely prolonged by the very controls used to assuage the crises. So long as the controls were maintained the tension appeared to persist. It is true, however, that, though Americans frequently deplore the shortage of dollars felt by much of the outside world, they do not really want the problem solved. The United States is still so mercantilistic in attitude as strongly to incline toward a "favorable" balance of payments and this, if realized, inevitably involves a shortage of dollars in the outside world. Yet even the Department of State, and the Treasury, which like to think that they are emancipated from mercantilist ideas, are wont to bring to bear such pressure as they can to prevent the currency devaluation abroad (raising of the exchange value of the dollar) which would clear up the dollar "shortage."

The remarkable alleviation of the British adverse balance of payments, after the devaluation of the currency in 1931, is brought out in an article by G. D. A. Mac-Dougall, "Britain's Foreign Trade Problem," *The Economic Journal*, Vol. LVII, pp. 69-113.

72 Professor Gottfried Haberler suggests ("Symposium on the International Monetary Fund . . . ," *The Review of Economic Statistics*, Vol. XXVI, p. 191) that the remedy in this situation would be to raise, rather than lower, the exchange value of the debtor country's currency. If, as is asserted in this book, the difficulty arises solely from the fact that the external value of the debtor country's currency is too high relative to its internal value, it would indeed be remarkable if an *increase* in this disparity would effect a cure. Yet Haberler's suggestion is a perfectly logical inference from classical theories, though, from a lively sense of reality, it has never been tried.

possibly maintain an unfavorable balance of international payments unless, by some means, it can persuade foreigners to offer goods to it *gratis* or on ever more dubious credit. No matter what happens to its exports, its imports will, in the absence of any such favors from abroad, necessarily fall to the amount which can be covered out of the proceeds of its exports, however exiguous these may be. If, on the other hand, it can obtain goods *gratis*, or on ever more dubious credit, there is no real lack of balance in its international accounts, no incontrovertible "shortage" of dollars or any other foreign currency, and no undue pressure on the exchange value of its own.

A balance in the international accounts will, *somehow*, be achieved. The only question is on what terms. It is here that the classical theories have been most misleading. The terms will come into the appropriate relationship with opportunity costs in a world-wide web of competition. The relevant comparison, as already suggested, is not between the price levels of exports and imports (since, under free competition, normal relationships will here tend to remain unchanged, in the absence of changes in cost, regardless of temporary market phenomena or movements in the foreign currency value of the money of the country concerned) but between the price level of domestic and international commodities (a relationship which will be altered by such movements). When the foreign exchange value of the currency of any country is permitted to fall, as a result of a persistent unfavorable balance of payments, the citizens of the country in which this phenomenon occurs will find foreign goods relatively expensive and they will also find it more advantageous to sell exportable goods in foreign rather than in the domestic markets. Their imports will cost them more in their own currency, and so check demand, but they will also get more of that currency for the goods they export. Both factors promote equilibrium in the balance of payments and, irrespective of elasticities of demand, will redress the situation.

The problem of transfer, in *practice*, arises solely from the fact that many countries seek both to have their cake and to eat it. When their earned, and available, real income is, for any reason, reduced, they resort to "controls" in order to keep money incomes unchanged. If, at the same time, they endeavor to maintain a fixed exchange value for their currency against those of other countries not so affected (or affected in the opposite direction), disequilibrium in the international accounts is certain since their citizens will then inevitably seek to purchase both more imports, more domestic commodities, and more of their own exportable goods, than their output will cover. All of these phenomena operate to reduce the ratio of exports to imports. The more or less artificially maintained external value of the currency of such a country (supported, perhaps, by exports of gold, or the use of other capital, or by *ad hoc* borrowing, none of which is accompanied by adequate domestic monetary restriction) will, in having been held above the (falling) internal value, encourage the purchase of *international* goods (both imports and potential exports) which, as a result of the monetary policy, are relatively cheap, will promote the growth of domestic goods industries (at the expense of the output of exportables or of goods competing with imports) where prices, as a result of the same policy, are comparatively high, and will thus *evoke* disequilibrium in the international accounts.[73] When the disequilibrium (which could always be cured by raising the internal, or lowering the external, value of the currency) persists, and recourse is had to measures designed to prevent the citizens from using their money as the monetary policy of the authorities impels (with restraints or prohibitions on imports and discouragement of purchase of exportables), the underlying maladjustments are maintained and even intensified. There is no benefit in all this, quite the contrary, and, among its evils, it has led to the conviction that foreign trade must be managed or it will go awry. The truth is just the opposite. If restraints are put upon the purchase of imports and exportables, citizens will use their thus unspent income to bid up the prices of domestic commodities and so promote their production at the expense of exportables and goods competing with imports. The distortion of output in the country concerned is thus exaggerated and the lack of balance in the international accounts confirmed.

Instead of speaking in terms of discrepancy in the internal and external values of any given currency, disequilibrium could be explained in attempts to keep the money income of the citizens

[73] In these circumstances the political authorities often complain that it is impossible to get an adequate number of workers to enter the export, or potential export, industries. This reluctance on the part of the workers is of course attributable to the fact that, under the existing monetary policies, enterprisers, or potential enterprisers, in those industries cannot offer sufficient inducements to attract workers from the over-developed domestic-commodity industries.

of a country of adverse balance of payments above the appropriate relationship with the money income of countries of favorable balances of payments. (The appropriate relationship is that
which prevails between the respective earned *real* incomes of the
countries concerned on the basis of the current barter ratios of
exchange between goods.) These attempts to hold the money income of any country, relative to others, above the share of world
real income to which the country's productivity, on the basis of
the current barter ratios of international exchange, gives it title,
occur under both the gold standard (with such "controls" as
prevent a downward adjustment in the amount of money, and
money incomes, in countries losing gold) and under inconvertible
currency conditions (with various expedients to maintain, above the
appropriate level, the foreign currency value of their money). When
a country thus holds its relative money income above its relative
earned real income, its citizens are always impelled to spend more
on *all* commodities (exportables, imports, and domestic commodities)
than they can currently afford, though this fact is by no means
obvious to them. It shows up, however, in an inability to pay for the
full demanded volume of imports except through drafts on any such
reserve of international purchasing power as the country may happen to possess.

That disequilibrium in the international accounts under "normal"
conditions is all but universally attributable to currency "management," or mismanagement, in the one or more of the national jurisdictions concerned is recognized by Professor Lionel Robbins in his
Economic Planning and International Order.[74] But Professor Robbins is almost alone among the neo-classicists in intimating that,
but for this, the problem of "transfer" would not occur.[75]

Elasticities of "International Demand"

Elasticities, or inelasticities, of demand have no bearing on the
normal ratios of exchange of international commodities or, in any
event, on the relationship between those ratios of exchange and
evolving (marginal) costs. The *character* of demand schedules is,

---

[74] Macmillan, London, 1937, pp. 270-280.
[75] Since these lines were first written, and while this book was in press, John Jewkes,
Roy Harrod, and Gottfried Haberler have, on various occasions, shown a partial
or complete concurrence with Robbins in this matter.

per se, an irrelevance in equilibrium conditions: in a discussion of norms elasticity has no place.[76] Most of the modern writing on international trade phenomena, however, has dealt with monetary pathology and, in the absence of any real norms in the classical theory of international trade, pathological conditions, once established, are assumed to be more or less self-perpetuating. Because, in the classical theory, there are no standards set by costs, the influence of demand is exalted, and relative demands for the various commodities (gathered into national composites), as well as the *character* of the demand for each of them, become of overweening presumptive importance. The market values at any time current are held to be definitive, in the sense that they are not subject to correction from changes in relative supply. Anything that may happen in the "short-run" is thus inevitably projected into the indefinite future. The "long-run" is regarded as a continuum of a series of discrete market situations each of which is solely determined by the demand situation currently prevailing.[77] On this view of things elasticities of demand take on a significance wholly disproportionate to their real influence, and modern theorizing has become quite unduly concerned with them.

[76] An inelastic demand for any commodity, together with an inelastic supply, has no general tendency to *depress* its market price but merely leads to great price vicissitudes and, therefore, to large deviations of market price, in either direction, from current cost ratios. Any country more or less completely specializing in any such commodity (or narrow group of such commodities) is subject to great ups and downs in prosperity. If this is regarded as, *per se,* an evil, there is a case for diversifying protection as insurance against alternations of prosperity and depression even if, as will presumably be the case, the national income, as an average over the years, is thereby somewhat reduced.

Properly conceived we may speak of elasticity of demand as applicable, at any moment, only to a single good and in terms of the response in the amount of that good demanded with variations in its price, or the response in price with variations in the amount supplied, *when all other circumstances remain unchanged.* Elasticity of demand has no real meaning except with reference to a given demand function. A useful purpose may perhaps be served by the extension of the concept from price to income elasticity in which we seek to discover what will happen to the amounts of a given good demanded, in correlation with fluctuations in general *income,* all else remaining unchanged. But the concept becomes wholly unmanageable when it is stretched to apply to the "reciprocal national demands" of various countries for "each other's goods" in circumstances in which, among numerous other objections, the *relative* incomes of the two countries must be presumed to alter as a result of the price changes in the relationship between the blocs of goods compared. cf. Oskar Morgenstern, "Demand Theory Reconsidered," *The Quarterly Journal of Economics,* Vol. LXII, pp. 165-201.

[77] This, of course, is an example of the confusion of the technical meaning of "long-run" with its "common sense" meaning. For an extended discussion of the matter, see Appendix A.

There is, of course, no doubt that, in a situation where international short-term credits are initially readily available to any given country, the balance of claims and counter-claims between the citizens of that country and the outside world may, for one reason or another, become seriously disrupted, or that growing resistance in the outside world to further extensions of credit would result in so rapid a loss of gold, or fall in the exchange value of the currency of the debtor, as to be gravely disturbing not only to the monetary system of the country in question but to the international price structure and the course and composition of international trade.[78] There can be no compelling objection to a "debrutalization" of adjustment, through offsetting techniques in the monetary system of the country concerned, but if, in this process, the adjustments are indefinitely postponed, a chronic lack of balance in the country's international accounts may develop and, along with a parade of alleged inelasticities of demand, will almost certainly be used in vindication of the "necessity" for an indefinite extension of controls both in space and in time.

The difficulty is likely to arise, and be most acute, in countries specializing in the export of a single commodity, or a narrow group of commodities, of which the world supply is slow to change relative to incomes. If, then, a world-wide depression of incomes occurs, the (world) prices of such commodities will often fall much beyond an average of all commodities (and especially of those imports, of the countries in question, for which supply may respond quickly to demand). The consequent disequilibrium in the international accounts of countries so placed is, however, not primarily attributable to the character of "reciprocal national demands" but to the character of *world* demand and the peculiar composition of production in the various countries. The plain fact is that, with the relative fall in the prices of the exports of any such country, its national income is severely cut. The existing money supply then becomes relatively redundant. Under an "unmanaged" gold standard (with gold used as currency), an efflux of gold would occur and would continue until the fall in gold incomes in the country, and a shift in the relationship between the internal and external value of its gold currency

[78] There might be a strong tendency toward exchange-rate over-compensation of a favorable or unfavorable balance of payments, which, if uninhibited, would set up a functionless, and therefore undesirable, oscillation in the relationship between any country's exports and imports.

(the purchasing power over domestic and international commodities respectively), would, in the manner already outlined, establish equilibrium in the international accounts. If, on the other hand, the country is operating under an independent currency, it has a choice of inducing a sufficient degree of deflation to preserve the exchange value of its money, against the currently "strong" currencies, or of permitting the foreign exchange value of its own currency to decline. Whatever the evils that may issue from any adverse combination of elasticities of demand or supply, however, they cannot be held accountable for a persistent lack of balance in the international accounts. Such an unbalance is always at least *prima facie* evidence of a distorted relationship between the current internal and external value of the currency of the country concerned and the trouble can be cured only by a readjustment in that relationship. This will attain a balance in the international accounts. The country must accept what it can, at most, merely dissemble, viz., a sharp reduction in real income, until it can escape the adverse consequences of a fall in the relative value of its exports through a shift in the composition of output (either within or outside its own borders) toward the commodities of high, and away from those of low, relative value.[79]

The correlative of the situation previously discussed appears in Great Britain, and other countries, when world money income *increases*. The momentary British "terms of trade" (meaning, here, the price ratio between British exports and imports) move adversely to Britain in times of world-wide prosperity—even as they move in Britain's favor in times of world-wide adversity.[80] The world supply of the goods Britain imports is not very readily expansible (largely because it does not shrink much in times of depression) while the world supply of the goods Britain typically exports has, in the pres-

---

[79] Professor F. A. Hayek is right in saying that "it is a delusion to believe that a country can . . . avoid the necessity of adapting itself to changing conditions by . . . changing the external value of its currency." ("A Regulated Gold Standard," *The Economist*, Vol. cxx, No. 4785.) But an appropriate change in that value will nevertheless bring about the required adaptation, which will otherwise require a change in the *internal* value of the currency.

[80] cf. Randall Hinshaw and Lloyd A. Metzler, "World Prosperity and the British Balance of Payments," *The Review of Economic Statistics*, Vol. xxvii, pp. 156-169. "Short-run" alterations in the "terms of trade" are, of course, in process from day to day, with every shift in the market value relationships of internationally traded commodities. Even these, however, are a function of world, not of reciprocal national, demand.

ence of excess capacity, been enlarged with comparative ease. The prices of the former group of products have therefore risen relative to the latter whenever world demand (and supply) has increased, with the converse the case whenever world demand (and supply) has decreased. Whatever the price elasticity or inelasticity of demand for the world's products, in Britain and elsewhere, the British, as others, cannot, in the absence of gifts, acquire more goods than they can pay for, and equilibrium in the international accounts will automatically appear provided the external and internal values of the pound sterling, or other similarly placed currencies, are brought into appropriate relationship. Elasticity, or inelasticity, of demand have in fact no meaning except so far as the would-be demander has adequate purchasing power.

The short-term movements in the "terms of trade" for any country, in ups and downs of world income, will depend upon how nearly the division between its imports and exports corresponds with the division between goods of comparatively stable and those of volatile prices. Countries largely dependent on international trade cannot avoid sharp fluctuations in their international income, from a given physical volume of exports, when this correspondence is close. The exchange ratios between the current exports and imports of such countries may reflect maladjustments which may far transcend the *limits* of the normal ratios of exchange of the goods as determined by conditions of opportunity cost. But the "terms of trade" will not, as Marshall asserts, shift back to less extreme ratios because the demand of any large country for a given *range* of products is "normally" elastic. When the problem is persistent, that is, in a sense, "normal," its solution involves the abandonment of classical theory with its unreal, and indeed impossible, trappings of "ideal" commodities, "representative bales" of exports and imports, and reliance on the (allegedly elastic) character of "reciprocal national demand schedules." The fact is that, with any large, and long-continued shift in the "terms of trade," certain products will eventually be dropped from the export list of some of the countries to which the movement in the terms is unfavorable, and will be replaced in the domestic production of such countries by other commodities, formerly imported, which it will now pay to produce at home (either fully or for a larger proportion of consumption than has hitherto been the case). Certain of the former imports may even enter the export lists of such countries. Either movement would be effective, in considerable degree, in preventing any strong and persistent shift in the ratio of exchange of goods, even if only two countries were involved in international trade. But it is much more fully effective, and in a shorter interval, in the world as it is, where many countries are in commercial contact with one another.

Through the operation of linked competition, any shift in the terms at which one internationally traded product exchanges for another, no change having taken place in relative real costs of production, will, within a not very extended period, tend to be counteracted regardless of the elasticity of the current demand or supply schedules of any given country, or countries, specializing in the commodities in question. To take a specific example, such as wheat, it may well be that Argentina, Canada, and some other exporting countries would suffer a very strong adverse movement in the terms on which wheat would exchange for other commodities (no change, let us assume, having taken place in relative real costs of production) without shifting to other commodities in marked degree and thus without materially reducing the supply of wheat put upon the market. But the United States, and other producers of wheat, have many alternatives to wheat production, and, when wheat offers relatively unfavorable returns, such countries will shift, to some extent, from wheat to other products. The pressure on wheat prices having been thus relieved, and the pressure on prices of other products having been increased, the old exchange relationship will tend to be restored.

It is not even necessary that the country or countries in which the adjustment is made be exporters of the product in question. Certain countries may reduce a domestic production which is already insufficient for home consumption and thus increase the demand for imports of this product. With any movement in the terms at which products exchange against one another any country which is a marginal producer of any part of the supply of the commodities against which the movement in the terms has taken place, whether or not it is an exporter thereof, will transfer resources to such of those commodities favored by the movement in the ratio as had formerly been just extramarginal for it. The production of exports as well as of the internal supply, in all countries, of the commodities disfavored by the alteration in the ratio will consequently decline relatively to the production of exports as well as of the internal supply of the commodities favored by the alteration in the ratio. Since, in the actual world, there is a continuous gradation in the advantage of production in any one country of more, or less, of one product rather than another, even a very slight shift in the terms at which products exchange, relative to their opportunity costs of production in any country, will readily set in motion compensating forces.[81] In other words, relative costs apply here quite as much as to individual commodities in a single (national) market. The problem of elasticities of demand (and supply) is, in fact, precisely the same in international as in intra-national trade, and is purely a *market*, not a *normal*, value phenomenon.

The opportunity-cost explanation of normal values is as valid for domestic as for foreign trade and it makes possible that integration of domestic and international values which the classical economists never achieved. The only difference between domestic and international values, on the assumption of mobility of factors of production in the one case and not in the other, is that the relationship between the prices of the various *factors of production*, and the relationship between the price of any of them and the various commodities, may vary considerably from one country to another but not between places in any one country. The relationship between the prices of commodities will however, in abstraction of costs of transport, be the same between countries as in any one of them, and all will be tied into the opportunity cost structure in each country. There are normal values, solely based on costs, in international as in domestic trade, and an opportunity cost of production theory holds, in both, for all (normal) commodity prices. As a result of their use in the output of internationally exchanged commodities it is not unlikely that even factors of production *of a given grade* will command not very divergent prices (in commodities) in all countries.[82] Whether or not this

---

[81] Lloyd A. Metzler, in a chapter on "The Theory of International Trade," *A Survey of Contemporary Economics* (Howard S. Ellis, ed., Blakiston, Philadelphia, 1948), states that my position in this matter (previously published) seems to him "too optimistic." The validity of the criticism would largely depend on changing political institutions.

[82] This is the contention of Ohlin who thinks in terms of variable costs. It would certainly be the case, in very large degree, on the inception of international transactions and, in a well-reasoned article, Paul A. Samuelson contends that under freedom of trade there would be no tendency for the movement to stop short of the same equalization of the prices of productive factors of a given grade as would occur in the case of commodities. ("International Trade and the Equalisation of Factor Prices," *Economic Journal*, Vol. LVIII, No. 230, pp. 163-184.

is the case it is a fact that we need not have *different* theories for the values of international and domestic commodities but, for domestic values, merely a supplement to the more general theory in a wider extension of competition.

The relative prices of commodities which must be consumed *in situ*, or are otherwise precluded from moving in international trade, may vary in any degree from country to country and will typically be high in one country, as compared with another, whenever the ratio between the efficiency of their production in that country is low relative to efficiency in the production of a commodity exported in common by the two contrasted countries (the relative efficiency of the other country in the same commodities serving as measurer). The chain of causation, expressed in monetary terms, runs as follows: The money value (in any given currency) of any export is determined by competition, on the basis of opportunity costs, in an internationally trading complex, and the money values of the opportunity-cost induced exports of any country, along with efficiency of production, determine the height of money wages that can be paid in the country in question. The same money wages will, under competition, be paid to a given grade of labor whether it is employed in export or in other industries. This will be true regardless of the efficiency of the labor in industries putting out goods incapable of export. If, in the construction of non-exportable houses in two countries producing common exports in an efficiency ratio of 2 : 1 the efficiency of labor in the former country is twice as great as in the latter, then, on the assumption that labor costs are representative of costs in general, the price of a house of given quality will be the same in both countries; if efficiency in construction is more than twice as great in the former as in the latter country the price of a house of given quality will be less, and, if efficiency in construction is less than twice as great, it will be more, in the former than in the latter country. But while such prices may differ widely from country to country they are all linked to the prices of internationally traded commodities.

The points to be stressed are that the international and the domestic value (price) systems are indissolubly associated; that both are based on opportunity costs; that these costs determine what products shall be exported and imported from, and to, any given country; that opportunity costs shift until the *number* of exports, in the evolving volume for each, is sufficient to cover the costs of the so-determined imports on the basis of the current international ratio of exchange (with which both exports and imports interact) ; that, in a given constellation of constant costs and qualitative composition of national outputs, neither the normal price relationships between the exports and imports of any country, nor, except in the process of adjustment, those between international goods and the goods which do not enter international trade, can alter no matter what the changes in demand may be; that, where variable costs are present, the shift in price relationships, attendant upon shifts in the relative demand for various individual commodities, will conform to the evolving marginal cost pattern; and that there is not the slightest reason for supposing that any such changes will run along national lines. Since, in a given constellation of costs, it would not be possible in complex trade for the prices of the exports of any given country to change definitively either in relationship to the prices of imports or of domestic commodities without persistent disruption of both external and internal equilibrium, the classical theory of international values, which posits such changes, cannot be a theory of norms—and even controverts its own postulates.

The whole climate of thinking on international trade has been conditioned by classical concepts and the atmosphere is so murky as to have led to highly distorted conclusions even on short-run policy. The classical concepts are better adapted to "short-run" analysis than to norms, but even short-run analysis is inevitably faulty if it leaves out of account the forces *always* operating to bring market prices into line with current norms. In any aberration of market prices there are two sets of forces, *working in opposite directions,* and the "long-run" forces are the more important. They must be taken into account in assessing the situation now or in the immediate future. The classical theory of international values, therefore, is not only useless as an exegesis of equilibrium conditions but, even as an explanation of market phenomena, is in urgent need of supplement and revision. There can be no useful purpose in developing a theory of market values which leaves out of account persistently operative forces which, in great degree, affect not only the values of today but, still more, those that will appear on the morrow.

APPENDIX A

ON NORMAL VALUES AND OPPORTUNITY COSTS[1]

No one, perhaps, ever doubted that a thing must have utility (in the sense of a potentiality of satisfying some human desire) if it is to have any value. But on Adam Smith and Ricardo the fact that many obviously useful things have little or no value, whereas some of the things that appeared to them to be all but useless have a high value, forced the conclusion that utility was not only an imprecise but even a negligible *determinant* of exchange value. They therefore resorted to cost, as the significant determinant of value, in spite of the fact that analogous objections might seem to apply to cost inasmuch as many things of great cost have no value while many costless things have great value. They were, moreover, not very sure of the nature of cost. Smith was quite hazy in the matter and jumped about—from labor cost, to money outlays in the productive process, to the cost of subsistence, and so forth—in his search for a measure. Ricardo and his followers were more consistent and made a valiant but futile attempt to reduce, or assimilate, all cost to labor or pain.[2] J. E. Cairnes, in the doctrine of non-competing groups, and many other writers in more general criticism, pointed out that labor cost is untenable as a criterion of value, and the next development was the complete abandonment of costs, and a reversion to utility, as the sole explanation.

The new school, led by Jevons, Walras, and the Austrians, removed the previous difficulty in the utility thesis (the difficulty that had proved a stumbling block to Smith and Ricardo) by pointing out that it is the utility of the "final" (or "marginal") small increment of any supply, rather than the utility of the supply as a whole, which is significant in the determination of unit value.[3] In their rejection of cost as a determinant, some of them went on to assert that cost is purely a

---

[1] This appendix is not free of repetition of some points treated, in less detail, earlier in the book. It seemed better, however, to risk the boredom, rather than the incredulity, of the reader.

[2] That values are not necessarily associated with pain is shown not only by the fact that relative values (including normal values) bear no determinate relationship to the pain incurred in the production of the various valued commodities but also by the fact that things might, and in all probability would, be valuable even if the production of all of them were painless. This does not mean that cost (of some sort) is not significant for values but that pain is not very significant in the determination of the relevant cost. Pain is, without doubt, a cost, and even opportunity cost may often be put in terms of pain but pain is far from essential to cost and has no special place in the catalog of costs. Almost as much could be said of labor.

[3] The credit for *origination* of the marginal analysis should rather, perhaps, go to Longfield, von Thünen, or Cournot.

result, and never a cause, of the value of final (consumers') goods, and that the other goods involved in the productive process get their value, derivatively, from these consumers' goods.

But marginal, or any other, utility is dependent on desires, and desires are notoriously fickle. They are subjective and variable, whereas costs can usually, if not always, be expressed in objective terms, rest on more or less unalterable physical facts, and, over short periods at least, are stable. Desires are, indeed, so fickle that it would seem impossible, in the present state of knowledge, to subject them to principle. Marginal utility therefore, if taken as the unique and final explanation of value without any recourse to cost as a determinant of (normal) utility, sweeps away the structure of normal values (the heart, and almost the whole, of classical economics) and would seem to remove, at a stroke, the pretension of economics to be, in any sense, a science.

The marginal utility of a unit of any good rests, however, not only on the current desirability schedule for the good but also, in part or largely, on the supply (and even on the supply of other goods). The amount of a good currently, and even prospectively, supplied is, indeed, a major factor in its marginal utility at any moment. This consideration leads us to ask what determines the amount currently and prospectively supplied. Jevons himself gave the answer to this question when he said:

> Cost of production determines supply.
> Supply determines final degree of utility.
> Final degree of utility determines value.[4]

But, if this is so, we are back to the proposition that the *causa causans* of value is (some sort of) cost of production.[5] This is what the classicists had always contended. The marginal utility doctrine would seem, therefore, to be, at best, an alternative to, rather than a replacement of, the classical theory. This is true, so far as normal values are concerned, and, for such values, the long controversy between the marginal utility and the cost of production schools is nothing but logomachy.[6]

[4] W. Stanley Jevons, *The Theory of Political Economy*, 3rd edn., Macmillan, London, 1888, p. 165. The passage cited first appeared in the second edition, apparently in response to criticisms of Jevons' original neglect, or repudiation, of cost as a factor in value.

[5] This is true, of course, only of normal values. *Market* values bear no determinate relation to current cost of production though they are affected by it. The amount of any good currently demanded at any given price, and the price itself, will always vary, in some degree, as potential purchasers expect, or doubt, an early restoration of the norm. The market price will always stick closer to the norm than would be the case if the *concept* of a normal price were absent.

[6] For a brilliant discussion of the determinants of value cf. Frank H. Knight, "Marginal Utility Economics," *The Ethics of Competition*, Harper, New York, 1935, pp. 148-160.

Marginal utility and cost of production are not however, as Marshall suggested, two blades of a pair of shears about which it would be futile to argue that the one rather than the other did the cutting.[7] Values are not determined impartially and coincidently *both* by marginal utility and by cost of production, even though cost of production usually affects marginal utility and marginal utility sometimes affects cost of production. In the case of variable costs, however, Marshall's contention is not without validity.

Jevons and his confrères are right in their contention that the proximate determinant of all *realized* values is marginal utility and nothing else.[8] In dealing with normal values, however, we are concerned not with proximates but with ultimates, not with current marginal utilities but with the marginal utilities that would exist under conditions of equilibrium. Equilibrium, after any disruption, would be attained through an expansion or contraction of supply to the point where marginal utility moves into correspondence with marginal cost, when no producer, with demand as it is, will have any incentive to change the then attained rate of output. With marginal utility, at equilibrium, identical with the cost of production of a unit of any reproducible good, it is a matter of indifference whether we say that it is marginal utility or cost of production that determines (normal) values at the only point at which normal values can, in fact, emerge. Either, without the other, furnishes a complete explanation.

When we are dealing with *market* values we cannot but speak in terms of marginal utility since, with respect to these values, cost is sometimes of no relevance whatever and is, at others, of no immediate interest. The (original) cost of irreproducible goods, for instance, is without significance for their market value, and the cost of monopolized goods is on no more than bowing terms with the prices at which they sell. The market values of other goods, moreover, are but more or less remotely associated with their cost of reproduction according as contemplation of that cost exerts a weak or powerful influence on bids and offers. When, on the other hand, we are dealing with *normal* values we must resort to costs since we cannot otherwise know what would be the marginal utility of a unit of any commodity under conditions of stable equilibrium in free competition. Since cost schedules are stable (in a given state of the industrial arts), and objectively measurable, and since

[7] Instead of in terms of marginal utility and cost of production Marshall tends to express his views in terms of "Demand" and "Supply." Since the demand for one good implies the supply of another, "Demand" and "Supply," as discrete concepts, cannot appropriately, or even meaningly, be used in general equilibrium analysis.

[8] Refinement of the marginal utility analysis (by Böhm-Bawerk for example) makes the price of any commodity, offered for sale without reservation, a reflection (with an infinitesimal addition) of its marginal utility to the highest excluded bidder.

cost is the lodestone to which marginal utility and market values, despite their inherent flightiness, are constantly attracted, cost is the only possible criterion of normal values.[9]

Marshall asserts that while "marginal costs do not govern price . . . it is only at the margin that the action of those forces which do govern price can be made to stand out in clear light. . . ."[10] I hope I am taking no undue liberty with this when I interpret it to mean that, while marginal costs do not proximately, precisely, or even predominately, govern *market* price (value), they are the exclusive governor of *normal* price (value), and that normal price (value), in turn, loosely governs market price (value) in the sense of establishing a mode around which actual market prices (values) cluster. Marshall further notes that the doctrine of Adam Smith, and other economists, on the normal or "natural" value of a commodity has been much misunderstood[11] and says that normal or "natural" value is the *average* value which economic forces would bring about if the general conditions of life were stationary for a run of time long enough to enable them all to work out their full effect. This seems to me as much of a misconception as any that Marshall could have been castigating. No averaging procedure can be relied upon to give normal values, and normal values might never be exactly reflected in the market no matter how long the "general conditions of life" should remain stationary. Normal or "natural" values are nothing more nor less than cost-of-production values under equilibrium conditions of free competition.[12] To these normal values market values are always in process of unsteady appropinquation since, in spite of the strong underlying tendency toward perhaps occasionally attained identity, market values persistently and wantonly depart from the norm, on either side, in varying degree, for more or less lengthy periods, and regardless of the stability of the "general conditions of life" (i.e. costs of production).[13]

[9] Costs here and, unless otherwise stated, always in this book are not to be construed in terms of money unless the general value of the monetary unit can be taken to be fixed for the period under review.

[10] Alfred Marshall, *Principles of Economics, op. cit.,* p. x.

[11] *idem,* p. 347.

[12] It will later be shown that no other concept of a norm will hold. All other so-called norms are merely more or less stable market values.

[13] The nearest analogy in the physical world to the relationship between normal and market values is probably that between a massive electrically charged lodestone (if it is possible so to charge a lodestone) and small electrically neutral, or oppositely charged, particles. The positively charged lodestone finds its analogue in normal value (charged with costs of production) which persistently draws the neutral, or negatively charged, market values to it. These however, in random fashion, fly off from the lodestone on contact, and sometimes even before they have reached it, only to approach it once more as the steady and powerful attraction of the lodestone overrides, in something like the square of the distal deviation, the relatively weak, and probably diminishing, power of any given repulsive force. The analogy is by no

Normal values are neither averages of market values, nor futurities, but single current phenomena. They are no less likely to be reflected in the present than in any future market. There is *at every moment*, for any reproducible good supplied under freely competitive conditions, both a market price (value) and a normal price (value), and the latter is not an average. On occasion these prices (values) may be identical but they are nevertheless distinct and separable phenomena, with normal prices (values) in no sense an outcome of (prior) market prices (values). The chain of causation, in fact, runs in the contrary direction. Market prices (values) are volatile but they are nevertheless attached, elastically, to normal prices (values). Normal prices (values) are stable, are not in the least affected by market aberrations however great, and are an outcome not of market prices (values) but of costs.

It is true that, under stable cost conditions,[14] average market values of reproducible non-monopolized goods will more or less closely approximate normal (cost of production) values. This follows from the fact that, whether the current deviation is on the upper or the nether side, market values under competition are always being pulled toward the norm set by cost of production. Desire, like the wind, blows where it listeth and market values are steadily subject to the play of this capricious desire. But whatever the direction of desire, and whether it be strong or weak, there is a steady tendency toward compensation of its effect on values through changes in supply. If the supply of any commodity were indefinitely and instantaneously elastic, at constant cost, no change in demand, whatever its magnitude, intensity, or duration, would have any effect whatever on market value. Market value would then remain in identity with the normal value based on cost because the marginal desirability and utility of the commodity would be kept unchanged (identical with the constant cost of production) through *immediate* changes in supply (in correspondence with whatever

---

means exact since the repulsion in the phenomenological world arises from an acquired likeness while there is no tendency for market values to depart from the norm *merely* because they have, for the moment, become identical with it. Market values, moreover, resemble particles which are persistently receiving new *autonomous and extraneous* charges (often before the effects of the old have been nullified) and these may either be akin, or opposed, to that of the lodestone. In contrast, moreover, with their physical counterparts (where the exactly opposite condition prevails) such extraneous forces will bring market values toward the norm whenever the charge is akin to that of the lodestone (the norm) and will repel them whenever it is different. At any given moment the predominant extraneous forces acting on market values may be working either with or against what we may regard as the *intrinsic* force (cost of production) which ties market values, with an elastic cord, to their norms.

14 Stable cost, it will be remembered, is used, in contradistinction to constant cost, to express costs unchanging through time, a concept with which constant cost has nothing to do. It is easy to have stable costs without constant costs or constant costs without stable costs.

caprice demand might show) of sufficient magnitude to bring marginal utility into line with cost. An approximation to this situation can, to some extent, be attained in storable goods through the use of reserve stocks of any commodity. For other goods, however, supply could never be made perfectly and instantaneously elastic in appropriate response to varying demand, and the range and duration of the potential deviation of market from normal values will, in any given case, then be a function of the inelasticity of both the demand and the supply schedules.

It may, however, be the case that supply will be more elastic when market value is below than when it is above normal value (or *vice versa*). If, for instance, the producers of any commodity can turn to some equally attractive alternative pursuit without difficulty, the supply will be readily contracted to meet a shift to the left in the demand schedule. Market price will then never fall far, or for long, below the norm. If, however, the supply of the commodity in question is not so readily capable of expansion as of contraction, a rise in market value, attendant on a shift in the demand schedule to the right, would tend to be of greater extent and duration than any fall that would attend an equivalent shift to the left. For such a commodity the *average* of market values would tend to be persistently higher than the normal value; whereas, on the opposite supposition as to elasticity of supply, it would tend to be persistently lower. Normal values, therefore, cannot be synonymous with the average of market values.

The use of the word "long-run" is equally objectionable as a synonym for normal values if it connotes a value that, in the absence of unchanged general conditions of supply, would *eventually* come to overt expression in the market.[15] Normal values are not "long-run" in the sense that they will or, under given conditions of supply, would, at long last, appear in the market, but only in the sense that the longer the period over which market values are observed the better is the chance that they will coincide at least once with normal values. There is, however, no tendency, under any conceivable cost conditions, for market values to march uninterruptedly toward such coincidence or, having once attained it, to remain unaltered for so long as general conditions of supply do not change. The degree of coincidence of market and normal values depends, as already noted, upon the *facility of adjustment of supply* to ever-changing demand. There is no reason to believe that this will be steadily progressive over any period of actual time since new disturbances are always interrupting, sometimes to fortify but more often to subvert, the processes of adjustment to former dis-

---

[15] There is, however, so far as I know, no reason for distinguishing between "normal," "natural," and "general equilibrium" values, which may be taken to be wholly synonymous terms.

orders. Distortions and adjustments follow one another in endless succession.

Despite what has just been said it is also misleading to say that "short-run forces" are determinative of market values whereas "long-run forces" are determinative of normal values. The latter part of the statement is true, insofar as "long-run forces" are assimilated to equilibrium cost of production, but the former part is false. The forces operating on market values may be either fleeting or persistent.[16] Cost of production for instance, a "long-run force" and the sole factor in the determination of normal values, is also, in the case of non-monopolized reproducible goods, always a *factor* in market values.[17] The essential thing is not the duration of the *forces* affecting market values but the duration of their *effects*, and the fact is that, whatever the duration of any forces currently influencing market values (even though they prove everlasting), the effects attributable to all of them with the exception of cost of production will be mitigated, and, in due course, nullified, by adjustment in supply.[18] Such *forces* may indeed persist long after their effects on price (value) have passed away. Because cost of production not only affects valuations and therefore demand, but, operating through supply, steadily counters and progressively eliminates the effects on market values of all other forces, whether or not they continue in being, cost of production is a significant factor in market values even as it is the dominant, nay exclusive, factor in normal values.[19]

[16] Desire, as a fluctuating entity, is just as *persistent* as the, relatively stable, cost of production.

[17] If the desire for any wasting and reproducible commodity is not strong enough to warrant its production it will disappear from the list of economically significant things. No matter how strong the desire, on the other hand, the market value will, more or less closely, fluctuate around the cost of production, and will be affected, through potential supply, by that cost.

[18] Cost of production is ever and always in antagonism to any forces (except so far as one of them cancels another) which operate to distort market from normal values.

[19] The terms, "long-" and "short-run," as used in the present connection, have, or at least *should* have, no temporal connotation. (They have been said to refer to "clockless" time, whatever that may be.) It would be better to call "long-run" forces "equilibrating," or "normalizing," forces and "short-run" forces "disequilibrating," or "abnormalizing," forces. No matter how quickly equilibrating or normalizing forces may operate they do not, on that account, move out of the "long-run" category and, no matter how permanent a disequilibrating or abnormalizing force may be, it is still to be classed as "short-run." It is futile to cast aspersions on "long-run" analysis by quoting the late Lord Keynes to the effect that in the "long-run" we are all dead. Keynes in this remark was indulging in a *double entendre* for the word "long-run" and, so far as this was not merely "smart," it was either a lapse with respect to the technical meaning of "long-run," for most price concepts at any rate, or was intended to be an objection to all analysis more fundamental than that in which Keynes was, for the moment, interested. "Short-run" phenomena, though not as fundamental,

Normal value is an indispensable concept precisely because it concentrates on the *essential* element in market values and leaves out of account all other factors (whether persistent, recurrent, or innovating) for the reason that, apart from possible induced changes in cost of production (which are taken into consideration under that head), their effects, however great for the moment, are always evanescent.

Marshall has further confused the concept of normal values by saying that: "Four classes stand out. In each, price is governed by the relations between demand and supply. As regards *market* prices, Supply is taken

---

are immensely more complex than "long-run" phenomena and the explanation of a "short-run" situation requires the admission of innumerable forces which, in the "long-run" analysis, can quite properly be left out of account as of ephemeral, and essentially cancellable, effect. Though, at any given moment, the effects of the operation of "long-run" forces may be temporarily distorted, and even, in appearance, overridden, by "short-run" influences, it would be the grossest of errors to assume that they could safely be neglected. "Short-run" analysts, in short, cannot afford to be contemptuous of "long-run" forces, though the converse of this is not necessarily, or even probably, true. We are much more likely to be dead before we get to the bottom of a problem in the "short-" than in the "long-run."

It is the basic, steadily operative, and more or less predictable, character of "long-run" forces which more or less inevitably engages scientific interest and, even though no normal price might ever appear as an actually realized market price in the period to which it applied, or at all, the norm would nevertheless be of more basic significance than any such actually realized price since it would be the focus of the play of all actual prices however wild the movements of the latter might be. If, for any period, we seek a norm as a basis for estimating the tendency of things, we must assume a given set of fundamental conditions and the almost inevitable thing is to take the set already in being or in process. It is obviously futile to take any set that may have prevailed at some past time (which, in spite of the dictum that history repeats itself, we may safely assume will never be duplicated) and no one knows, or can make a reasonable guess about, future conditions, to many of which there is, in even the most unclouded minds, not the slightest clew. Taking then the fundamental conditions at any time in being and in process, (or at least those that we consider relevant, or important, to the purpose in hand) we must, for the purposes of analysis, "freeze" them, that is, we must assume, at least provisionally, that they will remain unchanged during the period for which we are attempting to establish a central tendency, a norm. It would, of course, be possible to assume that they will change in a predictable way—we sometimes proceed in this manner—but, for the most part, to assume that they will not change at all will lead to results as good as, or better than, those which will issue out of an almost certainly erroneous, even if well-informed, guess as to what *may* happen. After an analysis has been made on the basis of given conditions which, for the purpose of the analysis, are frozen, it is possible to suppose, as taking place, any one of an endless variety of changes, or even a (weighted) combination of any number of them. But this tends quickly to degenerate from a quasi-scientific procedure into something not very different from the technique of crystal-gazing.

The fact that anything like scientific method practically requires a "freezing" of the data has led to the repeated complaint that the bulk, if not all, of respectable economic theory is static whereas the facts are kinetic. In the same sense, however, *any* theory is static, inasmuch as understanding requires that we first get at the forces which are currently and persistently operating rather than at those which are not now in being or are random or ephemeral in their effects. We should, for into mean the stock of the commodity in question which is on hand, or at all events 'in sight.' As regards *normal* prices, when the term Normal is taken to relate to *short* periods of a few months or a year, Supply means broadly what can be produced for the price in question with the existing stock of plant, personal and impersonal, in the given time. As regards *normal* prices, when the term Normal is to refer to *long* periods of several years, Supply means what can be produced by plant, which itself can be remuneratively produced and applied within the given time; while lastly, there are very gradual or *Secular* movements of normal price, caused by the gradual growth of knowledge, of population and of capital, and the changing conditions of demand and supply from one generation to another."[20]

Marshall is, of course, entitled to make any classifications he pleases, and to fashion his definitions as he will, but the logic of the foregoing passage leaves much to be desired. In the first three classes or categories the underlying conditions of supply are assumed to remain fixed, while, in the fourth, the assumption is of change, even wholly unpredictable change, in these conditions. The first category deals with a deviation of market prices from what Marshall would have called a current "long-term" norm, the second with a mitigation, and partial restoration, of that norm, and the third with its *complete* restoration. But, in the fourth category, the *norm* is not a current but a future phenomenon and necessarily obscure. If the full classification is to be used in an analysis of current normal values, of deviations therefrom, and of the tendency toward equilibrium, the first three categories are germane but the fourth is not. If the fourth category is brought to bear on any current problem we get an irregularly, and unpredictably, changing norm which envisages an alteration in the general conditions underlying

---

stance, never understand the forces governing the level of the sea if we were to concentrate our attention on the actual waves and troughs of the surface. The waves and troughs have nothing to do with the general level of the sea but the general level is by long odds the predominant determinant of the height at any time of any particle of surface water (measured from the center of the globe). Static theory is always relevant to kinetics and it is in fact impossible to develop any "dynamic" (kinetic) concepts without recourse to the method, and even the results, of statics. So-called theories of dynamics, on the other hand, are, all but inevitably, mere theories of transitions from one to another status of more or less stable equilibrium. They describe the phenomena that occur, off-stage, between the "stills" which, when assembled, give us a cinematic picture. Such theories are practically bound to assume that the progress from one to another status is steady, or oscillatory, or is, somehow or other, governed by known or posited laws. Such an assumption is, in all probability, not fully consonant with fact. Theories of dynamics therefore suffer from those very deficiencies of statics which they affect to relieve and are promulgated to overcome. (cf. F. S. C. Northrop, "The Impossibility of a Theoretical Science of Economic Dynamics," *The Quarterly Journal of Economics*, Vol. LVI, pp. 1-17.)

[20] *Principles, op. cit.*, p. 379.

the former categories and, since it precludes the positing of data (postulates), its application would destroy the usefulness of the former categories for purposes of equilibrium analysis. No one knows or can, with any precision, imagine what new inventions may issue out of the "gradual" growth of knowledge. Presumptive movements in price norms, and therefore in the market, can, in the presence of these unknowable inventions, not be brought within the range of science. The only "secular movements" of normal price that could by any chance be the subject of a scientific scrutiny are those attributable to forces now in being but currently left out of account in reckoning an *ad hoc* norm because their influence will be negligible over any period with which we are, for the moment, concerned. To go beyond these, however, is to move, definitively, from the realm of science into that of clairvoyance. Marshall's classification thoroughly confuses constant, or variable, with stable, or unstable, costs.

In Marshall's first category of prices (*market* prices) the concept of normality is present only as an underlying, and, to Marshall, more or less irrelevant, phenomenon; in the second, he treats of prices which he asserts are normal for periods under which the existing plant remains unchanged; in the third, he deals with prices which he declares to be normal in the sense that they will, or would, be reached, through changes in the number of plants, provided the existing state of the industrial arts remained unaltered. In the fourth category one might have expected that he would have considered only currently infinitesimal, but persistent, influences on the norm (such as those arising from the very gradual exhaustion of the supply of some appropriate resources) that could, for the purposes of the present generation, be ignored but would have to be considered when we were dealing with the problems our children might have to meet. Instead of doing this, however, he leaps altogether out of the realm of scientific precision into that of pure guessing and he never in fact attempted to handle the problems he here presents.[21] One might well sympathize with his reluctance to enter this rather unchartable field but, if he had been more careful in his taxonomy, there would perhaps have been no reason why he should not have gone on (as he always promised to do) to such of those problems of economic kinetics as could be brought within the range of probability.

There are two types of kinetic phenomena and they should be sharply

[21] Marshall may have been seduced by the motto he sets at the beginning of his book, *Natura non facit saltum*, into believing that all evolution is orderly and that a larger knowledge might give us perfect foresight. But while "Nature" may possibly never make a leap, this is far from obvious of men's minds (as Marshall has here well enough demonstrated) and it seems unlikely, therefore, that we shall ever, with any precision, be able to forecast the course of invention.

distinguished. The one type is reflected in deviations about current norms; the other with the establishment of new norms. The one is a more or less integral part of static analysis; the other may or may not transcend it. The first three of Marshall's categories (together with the suggested addition, which is quite different from that posited by Marshall) cover the whole of any one problem of analysis in which the data are either fixed or are changing according to some known rule: the fourth introduces an endless series of new problems in each of which the basic data will be shifted in presently unknowable fashion. For the solution of any problem it is necessary to assume that changes in general conditions are temporarily arrested, or are taking place at a known rate, since it is impossible to carry on analysis without data (*given* conditions) and, when things are changing unpredictably, we have in effect no *data* at all.[22]

It is not very surprising that Marshall devoted his major attention to the third of his categories.[23] The normal values of this category are, in fact, the heart of classical economics. They not only subsume the values of the two preceding categories but they exclude those of the fourth category as not susceptible to scientific treatment.

Market values reflect nothing but relative desires in a situation where the means of their satisfaction are unalterable.[24] The subjective, capricious, and volatile nature of desires precludes any norm for such values. For periods, moreover, in which the supply can be changed only within the limits of existing plant (Marshall's "short-term norm") it is also more than dubious whether we can properly speak of any value norms, especially when the amount demanded, at the long-term normal price, rises above the maximum capacity of existing plants. Suppose, for instance, that the demand schedule for a commodity moves sharply to the right, and stays there, so that, in spite of a (limited) increase in the amount supplied, the price rises above even the enhanced cost of production attendant on an intensive utilization of existing equipment. All that we can say is that the market price would not then be as high as it would have been if there had been no intensive use of equipment. It will, however, be more or less high according as the shift of the demand schedule to the right is great or not so great and, in the absence of additional supply from new productive units, it could stay, indefinitely,

---

[22] For this reason it seems to me, as to Northrop, impossible to have an *analysis* of persistently "dynamic" phenomena.

[23] cf. *Principles, op. cit.*, p. 380, for a statement of Marshall's intentions with respect to the only volume of the projected four which ever appeared under the rubric *Principles of Economics*.

[24] That is to say that supply is taken as, for the moment, fixed. This would be indisputably true only if the available stock were offered, to the last unit, without any reservation as to price.

above the enhanced cost of production (Marshall's "short-term norm").
Market price, moreover, would vary further with any new enlargement
of demand in the presence of a supply fixed at *maximum* output from the
existing equipment. The cost of production of this, or any other, supply
would be no more, or less, relevant than it is to any other market value.
All that a more, or less, intensive use of equipment could do would be
somewhat to modify the deviations of market from normal price; it
could not establish any norm of its own. There is not therefore, as
Marshall professes, any intermediate norm, between market price and
the norm established in his third category, but simply a series of more
or less stable *market* prices under varying conditions. Marshall's second
category of norms falls to the ground both from the fact already cited
and also from the fact that if demand were, or eventually came to fall,
within the range of such amounts as could be satisfied at any price between the true normal cost of production (that of Marshall's third
category) and the (abnormally high) cost of production attendant upon
the most intensive possible utilization of existing equipment, the market
price of the commodity would still move more or less chaotically between
these costs. With demand volatile there would not be the faintest tendency for the price to settle, even temporarily, at a "short-term norm"
equivalent to a fixed intermediate cost of production.[25] The only true
norm in Marshall's four categories, therefore, is the third.

Under constant cost conditions the normal price, at any given time,
is a unique price. If constant cost conditions remain unchanged over
time (that is, if they are stable as well as constant), this norm applies
no matter what the length of the period under review. When supply
can be indefinitely altered, at constant cost, the vagaries of demand
are a matter of indifference to normal price. It is, moreover, only when
the volatile desire factor in value is compensated by shifts in supply,
whether or not at constant cost but, in any case, carried to that point
of equilibrium at which there is no advantage in a further shift, that
any norms can appear or a systematic theory of values can be developed.

It may be worth-while again to point out that goods which are not
produced by man, or cannot be reproduced, have no normal value, and
that the same is at least partly true of monopolized goods. Their value,
in other goods, may move *indefinitely* in one direction or the other, or
may change direction at any time, without any tendency toward sta-

[25] The market price of the commodity, under the conditions cited, would not only
vary, without a norm, in response to the ceaseless play of demand but would also
be affected by changes in supply (on a long-term-cost basis) as the number of producing units was, perhaps erratically, adjusted to such changes in the amounts
demanded as seemed likely to be persistent. The posited situation, in short, is kaleidoscopic, and kaleidoscopes have no norm. The so-called "short-term norm" is, in fact,
a maggot.

bility or to the establishment of any norm. Marginal utility uncompli-
cated, for irreproducible goods at any rate, by questions of cost, is the
sole relevant criterion of value in these cases. The *market* values of reproducible goods produced under competition perhaps now more fully
share the value characteristics of non-producible or monopolized goods
than was formerly the case. Under modern conditions, the suppliers of
any commodity almost always have a negligibly small use for it in
personal consumption, and it is difficult to effect a rapid alteration in
current output. The amount offered, *at any given moment*, is therefore
likely to be little, if at all, affected by any changes in market price that
may occur (though it will not have been unaffected by *past* changes in
market price). That is to say, little or none of an existing, more or less
inflexible, stock will ordinarily be subject to reservation for the personal
consumption of the producers or for the purpose of regulating the
amount offered, not only now but at a later time, according as the price
tends to move away from the norm. In some cases, indeed, this is scarcely
possible.

Suppose, for example, that Friday is fish-day in a community without
refrigeration, and that the populace has a strong prejudice against
eating fish on any other day. Since "fresh" fish cannot in the circumstances well be held over for a full week, the fish dealers will, late on
Friday, be disposed to sell any fish they may have on hand at any price
that they can get, and will, indeed, not hold back any fish even if prices
fall to something not far short of zero. The *current* supply cannot, on
the other hand, be increased no matter how strong the demand, or how
good the price, may be. The result is that the price of fish, on different
Friday evenings, may show great variations, and seem to have no
norm.[26] Most other goods share in lesser degree the market characteristics of fish.

But men will nevertheless not continue to devote their energies to
supplying the markets with fish, or any other commodity, unless they
can, as a norm, get a price which will offer a reward not less than they
could obtain in some alternative, and otherwise not less attractive,
occupation open to them. They will, on the other hand, divert their attention and resources from other occupations to the taking of fish so
long as the normal return in fishing is superior to that which they could
obtain in other not otherwise more attractive pursuits. Fish, therefore,
and all other reproducible un-monopolized goods, have normal values,
each in terms of the others taken as a whole, or in terms of money of
stable general purchasing power.

[26] The aberrations of price are enhanced by the fact that, from week to week, there
is no stable relationship between the number of fish caught and the resources devoted
to the pursuit.

Market values are held more or less closely to these normal values not only in the degree in which supply is storable and stored (and so subject to reservation or release), or is otherwise elastic, but also in the degree of elasticity of demand. In many cases the elasticity of demand will be greatly affected by the prospect of an early increase, or diminution, in the amounts supplied in response to a rise, or fall, in price. For it is all but inconceivable that some potential buyers of a given good will not find it desirable to postpone purchases at a price greatly above that which they have reason to expect will prevail when an enlarged production has been drawn in, or that some individuals, who had no previous intention of buying now, will not be induced to make purchases at prices greatly below that which is in prospect when some of the present suppliers, forced out by bankruptcy, have withdrawn from production of the goods in question. The normal (supply) price is thus of great importance in limiting the range of fluctuations of actual (market) prices. It is nevertheless true to say that, in any explanation of movements in values in free markets, we may safely ignore supply, as substantially fixed for the moment, and concentrate attention solely on changes in schedules of desire among competent buyers.

In dealing with *normal values*, on the other hand, we can ignore *desires*, or *demand*, not indeed because they are fixed, but because, whatever their variations may be, those variations will be persistently counteracted in their effect on price by appropriate shifts in supply. When a change in the amount of any product recurrently demanded at any given price occurs, and supply at a given cost is, within a shorter or longer period, flexible, the amount of the product offered, whatever the retardations that may attend the process, will be steadily adjusted to an altered, or altering, demand situation. Assuming no change in the general conditions of supply, and constant cost over the range of alteration in the amount "required," the price of the product will, after any disturbance arising from a shift of demand, move toward equivalence with cost of production, *no matter what the shift in demand may be,* and the play of prices will meanwhile show only moderate aberrations around the norm established by the prevailing cost conditions.

If, as Adam Smith pointed out, hunters can always secure two deer as readily as one beaver, the "natural," normal, or equilibrium price of deer in beaver will be two deer for one beaver (one beaver for two deer) regardless of any shift in the relative intensity of desire or the relative numbers of these respective creatures that the populace may desire and demand. The *market* price will oscillate around the two to one ratio and, as a result of the induced alteration in relative supplies on any deviation from this ratio, the marginal utility of deer in terms of beaver will persistently be brought into correspondence with the cost ratio.[27] If the market price of a beaver should rise above two deer, no one, on the margin of indifference as to whether he hunts deer or beaver, would bring in any deer at all but would concentrate exclusively on beaver until market price came into line with the norm. If, on the other hand, the market price of a beaver should fall below two deer, hunters on the margin of indifference would, with the same results, reverse the process.

In dealing with normal values as the central tendency of market values it is, therefore, not valid to take, as a *datum*, existing marginal utilities since, as a consequence of changes or prospective changes in supply, these marginal utilities are in constant flux toward equivalence with relative costs of production. In the state of equilibrium coincidence will occur. Marginal utilities, in short, are a *resultant* of supply (which is dependent on cost) and no theory of values that fails to go behind *current* marginal utilities to their basic causes in costs can be anything but superficial.

In dealing with value norms it would be open to us, if we chose, to speak in terms of *normal* marginal utilities. But this would be but another, and more clumsy, name for costs, to which recourse would, in any case, be necessary in the attempt to discover such normal marginal utilities. The almost inevitable tendency, however, of thinking in terms of marginal utilities is to regard them as variable reflections of persistently shifting *desires*, to analyze the nature of specific desires, and to conclude that the volume, urgency, elasticity, or other characteristics, of desire, or demand, schedules will have a pronounced effect on normal even as on market values. It is, indeed, next to impossible for an adherent of the marginal utility school to recognize that neither the volume nor the character of demand has, under conditions of constant cost, any relevance whatever for normal values. Professor Haberler, for instance, in commenting on a former article of mine, says that my conclusion "that the nature of the demand schedules [in international trade under specified conditions] does not affect the [normal] exchange-ratio is about as logical as to deny that demand, in the usual sense, influences price, on the ground that when there are numerous actual and potential sources of supply, every increase in price will call forth a greater supply."[28] This, quite obviously, is intended to be devastating but, pro-

[27] It may be well to repeat that no matter what desires may be, or how they may alter, the marginal utility of a unit of any commodity can be altered *in any degree* through changes in its supply.

[28] Gottfried von Haberler, *The Theory of International Trade*, translated from the German by Alfred Stonier and Frederic Benham, William Hodge & Company, Ltd., London, 1936, p. 150.

vided we remember that we are talking of normal values under constant cost, Haberler's statement is valid (in a sense he clearly did not intend) solely because the logic of *both* asseverations (or, more precisely, of the asseveration and the denial) is impeccable, and not, as he implies, grotesque. To deny that shifts in demand, under constant cost, have any effect on normal price is not, as Haberler apparently thinks, absurd. On the contrary, it is such plain common sense that even Haberler himself (in quoting Adam Smith on the deer and beaver) accepts it, as at least provisionally valid,[29] only a few pages before he here seeks to laugh it to scorn.

Volume of demand will, it is true, affect normal values when costs of production are *not* constant, but only because a shift in the demand schedule will then alter cost relationships. No value relationship would ever be disturbed not only if the potentiality of supply but also the desire for either term in the value relationship, were infinitely and immediately elastic (an elasticity of unity).[30] We can hardly conceive of anything like an infinitely elastic desire (in which unit price would remain unchanged regardless of supply), and were such a desire ever to appear it would be unlikely long to persist. But an infinitely elastic relative supply, in which price tends to remain unchanged regardless of desire, is the normal outcome of constant costs of production.[31] Those costs are best conceived in terms of alternative opportunities, and there is nothing inherently improbable in the notion that the supply of any

[29] *ibid.*, p. 126.

[30] There is much confusion, in the orthodox literature, between desire and demand. Demand implies not only desire but the offer of an acceptable *quid pro quo*. It therefore implies supply. In this sense supply and demand are identical and both are *synonymous* with value (price). We can not talk about either demand or supply, or both, as *determinative* of value (price). But we can so talk about costs, which determine (normal) reciprocal supply or, what is the same thing, (normal) reciprocal demand.

[31] "Given . . . time for readjustment, including changes in form of capital, retraining of labour, and whatever else may be involved, the law of constant cost is not far from the truth. Under such circumstances [the circumstances significant for normal values] *utility determines quantities produced but cannot affect the final equilibrium price.* On the other hand, the factors of production are hardly transferable *instantly* in any degree; for a very short period the condition approximates that of fixed supply. In so far as this is the case, price is determined by the relative utilities of the supplies as they stand, cost exerting no influence at all. For ordinary producers' calculations the role of cost is certainly far the greater, but the actual quoted price at any moment, the price at which consumers buy from dealers, reflects rather the demand conditions, supply being 'given.' The influence of relative utility as compared with that of relative cost depends on the comparative elasticities of the two curves. In the short run, supply is highly inelastic and demand conditions predominate; in the long run, supply generally has practically infinite elasticity and predominates over demand. . . ." (Frank Hyneman Knight, *The Ethics of Competition*, Harper, New York, 1935, p. 155. Italics mine.)

commodity can be increased within very wide limits through the sacrifice of *given* quantities of alternative products, i.e. at constant cost.

The fundamental cost of any good, to him who would acquire it, is the worth of that of which he will be deprived as a condition of getting the good in question. In economics, at least, everything has its opportunity cost, but once one gets beyond the childish stage of expecting gratification of a wish for the moon, there is, in this, no necessary pain. Since one presumably prefers that which he voluntarily chooses to that which he might have had, he can scarcely allege that what he takes had any net cost in pain.

Suppose that we had a world in which everyone took such delight in the work he was doing as to prefer this work, for a substantial portion of his day at any rate, to any alternative that might be open to him even in an environment in which he need take no thought for his subsistence. It is at least conceivable that the commodity price structure, under these conditions, would be precisely what it would be if work were irksome. In an Arcadia, or Utopia, where everyone was in love with his work, production would be carried on without pain, but the total production of goods of all kinds might—in all probability *would*—be far short of that which was necessary to satisfy all the desires of the inhabitants. That is to say, the goods would not be free. Production of goods in general, and the productive efforts of each individual in particular, would be pushed to the point at which the members of the society severally and as a group, no matter how much they liked their work, would at the moment prefer play, leisure, or sleep, to the prospective result of any further workmanlike activity. If cost were measured in terms of presumptively painful labor (as is customary with the classical economists and many of their successors) the goods produced, up to this point, could not be said to have had a cost, and, since none would be produced beyond this point, none of the goods in being could then be alleged to have had any cost associated with them. But, because the output of any good would have involved the loss of the opportunity to produce, or take, some alternative, every good produced would have had a cost in the sense of the sacrifice of that opportunity. This cost tends to be constant.

"The general rule for the long-run under given general conditions . . . is approximately constant cost, the amount of one commodity which must be given up in order to produce an additional unit of another is generally not much affected by the relative amounts produced. . . . Under these conditions it is evident, first, that no matter what consumer's preference [*sic*: consumers' preferences?] may be or what may happen to them, production will bring prices and relative incremental utilities back to about where they were before, if technical conditions of production remain unchanged; and, second, that anything which happens on the production side, changing the relative productivity of resources in two uses (maintaining the law of constancy with varying output, at the new level), will ultimately establish this new relative productivity as the ratio of exchange and as the ratio of equal-utility quantities of the commodities. It is therefore correct to say that . . . cost determines both price and utility."[32]

It is no doubt true that, if an *enormous* shift in production were required, we could not get increasing quantities of any one good at a constant unit cost in terms of a forgone alternative good. But, within the range of practical probabilities, the assumption of constant opportunity cost, as a typical phenomenon, is nevertheless fully warranted.[33]

Since the classical economists thought of cost of production not in terms of opportunity cost but of labor cost, and it was obvious that comparative labor cost could not be used in explanation of *international* values, they felt forced virtually to abandon cost in their international value theory. Adam Smith said nothing on international *values*. Ricardo was content with the assertion that "the same rule which regulates the relative value of commodities in one country [viz., labor cost] does not regulate the relative value of the commodities exchanged between two or more countries"[34] and merely suggests, by implication, that commodities will be exchanged internationally at *some* ratio within the range set by the difference in their relative labor costs of production in each of the countries concerned.[35] Mill, not unnaturally, was dissatisfied with Ricardo's failure to provide any theory of the determination of the precise "terms of trade" (the exchange ratios between internationally traded products). He therefore attempted, and, as we have seen, without success, to furnish such a theory. Mill repeats Ricardo's assertion

---

[32] Frank H. Knight, "Professor Fisher's Interest Theory: A Case In Point," *The Journal of Political Economy*, Vol. xxxix, Number 2, 1931, p. 196. It is assumed that production is carried on in productive units of optimum size.

[33] It should be noted that this has no necessary relevance to the question of cost *in terms of any given factor of production* as output is altered. All types of factors of production may be released in the case of the forgone good and, if the increasingly required good employs these same factors in substantially the same proportions, constant opportunity cost of production is a hardly rebuttable general presumption.

[34] David Ricardo, *The Principles of Political Economy and Taxation*, Everyman's Edition, Dent, London, p. 81.

[35] Relative labor costs are determined by the ratio between two ratios, that is to say, the relationship between the amounts of two commodities which can be produced per unit of labor cost in one country as compared with the corresponding amounts that can be produced, in the same labor time, in another country. The amount of labor involved to get either commodity, or both, may vary in any degree between the two countries without any necessary effect on the significant ratio. Such variations are wholly irrelevant to the question of *commodity* values (values other than that of the labor).

that the law (i.e. rule) of the proportionality of value to (labor) cost of production does not hold good between commodities produced in distant places.[36] "We must accordingly," says Mill, "as we have done before in a similar embarrassment, fall back upon an antecedent law, that of supply and demand,"[37] as the determinant of the relevant value.

But, if the "law of supply and demand" is antecedent to that of cost of production in the explanation of value, and if the law of cost of production gets Mill into embarrassments which at least twice force him back upon a law of more general application, one wonders why he does not always rely on this "anterior," or antecedent, law. The real reason, earlier noted, is that Mill's whole effort to build a systematic body of economic doctrines would then have collapsed.

Though the demand for, the supply, and the value of commodities are varied expressions for the same phenomenon, and though, in any realized exchange in a free market, marginal demand, marginal supply, and price are the same thing, it is common to speak of spontaneous shifts in the relative marginal desirability of goods as changes in demand and of induced shifts as changes in supply. (In the former case desire *schedules* are altered by the change in desires while, in the latter, they may remain unchanged and, to get marginal utility, we merely move along a given schedule.)[38] But, under conditions of constant cost, it makes no difference, to value, whether or not demand schedules are altered since the marginal desirability of a product always tends to revert, through shifts in relative supply, to an unchanging relationship against other products. When, in a word, a change in desire schedules becomes exactly offset by shifts in the relative quantities of the several goods brought to market, marginal demand, marginal supply, and price relationships settle at their identical norm and it is only the comparative total quantities of the various goods consumed (demanded) and produced (supplied) which are affected. It is simply not true that, when the desirability of one good rises relatively to another (so that, at any ratio of exchange, more of the first good will be "demanded," relative to the second, than had hitherto been the case), the (normal) price of the first good must rise in terms of the second. A rise in the *total*

---

[36] John Stuart Mill, *Principles, op. cit.*, Vol. II, p. 126. It is clear that much more labor went into the production of imports into England from low wage countries than into the English exports, of equal value, for which they were exchanged.

[37] *ibid.*

[38] We cannot properly speak of a change in demand except in the schedule sense, but this is not true of supply. Demand can be adjusted to varying supply, *at a given price*, only through a shift, left or right, to a *different* demand schedule. But supply can be adjusted to varying demand, *at a given price*, through movements along a given (under constant cost, horizontal) supply schedule. This is why costs are determinative of, and demand irrelevant to, normal values.

demand for one good relative to another does not necessarily imply a rise in the relative *marginal* demand (or price). Value, therefore, can never be *explained* in terms of supply and demand. For an *immediate* explanation we are forced to marginal desirability (utility).[39] But, for an *ultimate* explanation, we must go to cost. Where supply cannot be changed, and cost is therefore irrelevant, the immediate (marginal utility) explanation is also ultimate but, where supply can be changed, we have not got to the heart of values until we have followed the movement of supply, and the thereby induced changes in marginal utility, until no one has any interest in a further shift of output. This will be the case when marginal utilities have been brought into conformity with fixed, or determinate, costs.

Only so far as we thus rest our explanation on costs is it possible to imagine anything in the nature of a stable equilibrium and normal values. In his attempt to develop a systematic exposition of value Mill, therefore, could not but resort to cost. He did so with regard to values in general. In reluctantly (and erroneously) abandoning cost-of-production analysis as inapplicable to the determination of *international* values he might have been expected to recognize that he must cease to pursue systematic precision and must join Smith and Ricardo·in leaving the matter of international values indeterminate. This his ambition would not permit since it would have precluded his saying anything about those norms of value (the central tendency of market values) which he was eager to establish and which, in the effort to make a science of economics, he felt he must seek in the international as in the domestic field. When he lost hold of cost of production, and reverted to "supply and demand," he was, nevertheless, inevitably back in the swamp from which, in domestic values, he had sought to escape on the (labor) cost-of-production causeway.

In his vain endeavor to find a new bridge Mill developed the concept of the "equation of international demand." His rather elaborate exposition of this doctrine boils down to nothing more than a statement of the obvious fact that things are equal in (market) value to the things for which they are exchanged. This will, of course, be true regardless of the terms (or the variations in them) on which the exchange takes place, but Mill apparently convinced himself that, somehow or other, the equation (which is an obvious result) was causal in the determination of the terms. He was however, in his first essay at the problem, not very successful in convincing some of his contemporaries and he sought to meet their criticisms (which he had come to accept

---

[39] The marginal concept was not developed until after Mill's day and he (loosely) uses "demand and supply" in its place. The concept of marginal desirability must, here at any rate, be taken to involve a contrast between alternatively available goods.

as, at least partially, valid) in a second essay.[40] This second attempt is, on the whole, a good deal less satisfactory than the first.[41]

In the transition to an exposition in terms of "supply and demand," rather than cost, Mill carried his shift in terminology somewhat farther than the shift of base would seem to require. He replaces the phrase "supply and demand" with "reciprocal demand." In a barter transaction (and international trade theory has almost always, and, as we have seen, for excellent reasons, been set forth in barter ratio, rather than in monetary, terms) there is, of course, no conceivable difference between supply and demand. Each of any two bartered commodities may be thought of as having been either supply, or demand, or both. In other words, supply is demand and demand is supply. There can, therefore, be no *objection*, in the development of the theory of international values, to the replacement of the phrase "supply and demand" with the words "reciprocal demand." But it would seem to have been equally logical to employ the phrase "reciprocal supply" which is, at any given moment, the same thing as "reciprocal demand" but is, in the ordinary reader's mind, much more readily applicable to the concept of norms and, therefore, much more in consonance with Mill's thought on value in general. Why then did Mill employ the words "reciprocal demand" rather than "reciprocal supply"?

There can be little doubt that, in the choice of the form "reciprocal demand," Mill was, in his own mind, assimilating the conditions of international trade to those of the market for "old masters" where the supply of the designated goods is absolutely fixed, and values therefore, without a norm, shift with every alteration in the quite unanchored vagaries of desire.[42] This was an error so fundamental as to have perverted the whole of Mill's reasoning on international values. His reasoning, nevertheless, was adopted by all the neo-classicists and is still almost universally accepted by students of the theory of international trade.[43]

[40] In the revision of his *Principles* Mill conceded that "there is still . . . a portion of indeterminateness in the rate at which the international values would adjust themselves." (Vol. II, p. 155.) Jevons spoke of it as the failure of the equations of exchange.

[41] "The attempt made by Mill to amend his theory . . . is, as even he seems to admit, a failure. . . . Professor Edgeworth's authority may be quoted in support of this criticism." (Bastable, *Theory, op. cit.*, p. 29n.)

[42] The statement holds, of course, only within the range of exchange ratios, for internationally traded goods, set by comparative cost ratios in the trading countries. But since Mill thought that exchange ratios, except in barely conceivable cases, would lie somewhere within this range the limitation is all but completely irrelevant.

[43] Alfred Marshall notes (*Money Credit and Commerce*, Macmillan, London, 1923, p. 161) that "some writers have . . . laid so much stress on the word 'demand' . . . as to imply that the problem of international trade is one of demand rather than supply; and this is a reason for emphasizing the interdependence of supply and demand." The concluding words of this quotation fail, in my judgment, to do justice

The supply of most articles in international trade is in no wise subject to the conditions which determine the supply of "old masters" and is, in fact, subject to conditions similar to, though not identical with, those which apply to most of the articles exclusively produced and consumed in the several domestic markets. The sole reason for a theory of international values distinct from that of domestic values is the real or alleged immobility of labor and capital across national boundaries. This immobility is an obstacle to free competition but it is far from eliminating supply (cost of production) as the fundamental factor in the determination of the normal values of international as of domestic goods.

By a strange irony the classical theory of international values, which was much more defective than the classical theory of domestic values, has been widely accepted by modern writers on economics who have been very caustic about classical theory in the domestic field. The dubious, or completely erroneous, labor theory of value (and of cost of production in terms of labor) completely vitiates, for them, the classical theory of domestic values but, since the classicists had abandoned cost of production in their treatment of international values, the classical theories in the latter field have escaped the criticism they so richly deserved. It is true that the classical writers *began* their analysis of

---

to the importance of cost of production in the fixing of marginal utilities, and Marshall, in spite of the note of warning, all but completely neglected the factor of supply in his subsequent treatment of the topic. Supply and demand, moreover, are not so much interdependent as identical. When writers stress demand, and its variations, as a determinant of value they are prone to take into account only a discrete series of momentary situations. Whether they know it or not they are then forced into a discussion of a congeries of market values as if each of them had no history, or prospect, was independent of the past and unassociated with the future. Stocks of goods can then, without much violence to fact, be taken as a *datum*. But if stocks of goods *and their variations* be taken into account, as is necessary if we are to deal with normal values, we are compelled to look to costs. Desires, and their vicissitudes, are then irrelevant since, with adjustable supplies, variations in desires have either no effect on (normal) values or, at most, can affect them only so far as the amount of a good demanded exerts an influence on unit costs. In that case we can still look to costs as our criterion, and, in all cases where reproducible goods are concerned, costs are a factor, even in market values, to the degree of their effect on valuations.

The distinction between supply and demand (a fundamentally invalid distinction for anything but partial equilibrium analysis) arises from the tendency to think one-sidedly, in monetary terms, of but one of the articles in a (trading) transaction (which is, by definition, bilateral). Even the monetary demand for a commodity is a *supply* (of money) and the supply of the commodity is a demand for money. Since, in international transactions, the money of one jurisdiction must necessarily be treated as a pure commodity by the citizens of another (where it is not money) the distinction between supply and demand completely loses any usefulness it might otherwise have. (This is an additional reason for developing the basic theory of international values without reference to money.)

international values with a comparison of the ratios of the labor cost of production of commodities in different countries. But this, which merely set limits on the range of international values, did nothing to establish actual values within those limits, and was, in fact, not necessary to their case. As the *determinant* of those values they relied on what was essentially an unrefined marginal utility analysis (without reference to labor or any other cost of production). Marginal utility concepts had not then been expressly developed but, since they were implicit in the classical doctrines on international values, the marginal utility school was not disposed to be censorious of that part of the classical structure. Marginal utility analysis, however, if it is to proceed from market to normal values, or even to probe at all deeply into market phenomena, must resort, impliedly at least, to some sort of cost.[44] Though this fact was slighted, or expressly denied, by many marginal theorists it does not, for that reason, cease to be a fact. The classical theory of international values was, therefore, not better, but worse, than the classical theory of domestic values and there is no valid ground for its complacent acceptance by the marginal utility school. The classical theory of domestic values can be validated by correcting an erroneous notion of costs but the classical theory of international values cannot thus be restored. The theory must be developed along entirely new lines since it is impossible to correct what is not there in the first place.

Normal values are dependent upon the principle of substitution and this is closely associated with opportunity costs. There can be no normal value relationships except there be a group of producers who, at a given ratio of exchange between two potential products, are indifferent as to whether they go in for the one or the other. As soon as the ratio of exchange between the products shows any *tendency* to deviate from the given position this group of producers will move into the production of the commodity which the deviation favors, and out of that against which it discriminates, and thus will maintain, or restore, the given (normal) ratio.[45]

This assumption of indifference, for producers on the margin, is a

[44] There is little, anywhere in economic theory, on the nature, or determinants, of desires, which are taken as postulates into which it is not the problem of the discipline to probe. This is unreservedly true of a theory of exchange. Attention is there centered only on the means of satisfying desires, whatever they may be, and of bringing them into equilibrium.

[45] Some actual deviation might be necessary to remove an inertia like that of the "old sailor my grandfather knew, who had so many things . . . he wanted to do, that, whenever he thought it was time to begin, he couldn't because of the state he was in," that is to say, the state of indecision which might attend a situation of *perfect* equilibrium. (The jingle is from A. A. Milne, *Now We Are Six*, Dutton, New York, 1927, p. 36, slightly adapted.)

commonplace of the general theory of normal values and it is as valid in international trade as anywhere else. But, in the classical and neo-classical theory of international trade, it finds no place. At the ratio of exchange between internationally traded products which the classical writers typically *assume* (a ratio somewhere *within* the limits set by comparative costs in the respective countries), no producer, *anywhere*, is on the margin of indifference as between the output of one product and another but all would have a comparative advantage in one or the other of them. No *normal* values could then appear. The fact is, as brought out in this book, that the focal points for international values typically lie at the cost ratios, between any two products, currently prevailing in some one of the trading countries (and not *between* those in the several national entities), so that there are always producers who are indifferent as to whether they produce one commodity or another. One of the attributes of this condition is that it is normal for a country to be importing (as well as producing) at least one commodity in the production of which, at the existing ratio of exchange of products, it is at no comparative disadvantage. This situation is at once the condition of the establishment, and the mechanism for the maintenance, of normal values in international trade. The situation, however, is wholly unknown to the classical analysis.

It is through commodities produced in common in different countries that national cost structures are integrated into an international scheme of normal values in which the various national opportunity cost structures are married, and it is impossible, not only in the theory of international values as such but for the integration of the theories of domestic and international values into a *general* theory, to exaggerate the importance of internationally shared production of link commodities. The cost structures in the several national entities are, through such commodities, indissolubly united, and all are brought into conformity with the ratio of exchange of internationally traded commodities which, in a process of interdependence, they help to establish. Cost structures in any country are dependent not on the relative (or, *a fortiori*, on the absolute) labor involved in the production of the various goods but on what it costs to produce any given commodity, in the various countries, in terms of other commodities that might be produced as alternatives. Since a commodity produced in any two (or more) countries is one of the alternatives, for either of them, to commodities they do not *share* in producing, adjustments to disturbances in international trade are regularly achieved not through a shift in national price-level relationships (or, indeed in *any* price relationships, though this, of course, is not precluded) but rather through shifts in output in response to shifting world demand. Only when the dividing line between the exports and imports of any country is raised or lowered (a shift in the national locus of the marginal output of some commodity) will the ratio of exchange of internationally traded commodities be affected (in more or less unpredictable ways).

When we think in terms of opportunity cost it can be conclusively demonstrated that Ricardo, Mill, and the neo-classicists, were wholly wrong in supposing that the same rule which regulates the relative value of commodities in one country does not regulate the relative value of the commodities exchanged between two or more countries. In the absence of such a rule international values would, in fact, be so mercurial as not only to mock any attempt at analysis but also to make impossible any equilibrium, within any country, in the production for domestic and international markets.

It may be well to note again that opportunity cost, *measured in commodities*, is not concerned with absolute efficiencies. It could be possible, in either of two countries of very different productive capacity per worker, to secure two bushels of maize by forgoing the production of one of wheat (or vice versa). The opportunity cost of wheat in terms of maize, or of maize in terms of wheat, would then be the same in both countries regardless of differences in general productive efficiency. It is irrelevant to commodity cost *relationships*, commodity values, and prices, whether it takes the same, twice, or ten times as much labor to produce either of the grains in one country as it does in the other. Opportunity cost, applied to commodities only, has no link with labor cost and is, therefore, not subject to the objection which, as a result of the assumed international immobility of labor, made it impossible to apply the classical (labor) cost theory of domestic values in the international field. Opportunity cost, measured only in commodities, is applicable equally to domestic or to international values since for these costs it is irrelevant whether *labor* is or is not spatially mobile. All that is necessary for a theory of normal commodity values is a knowledge of the terms on which the output of one commodity can be substituted for that of another. The amount of *labor* involved in producing commodities in general, in one environment or another, is of no significance whatever in the matter.

General differences in the labor-time cost of commodities in one environment or another, however, will of course affect relative incomes, prosperity, and the commodity value of labor-time (real wage-rates) in the two environments. The concept of opportunity cost can readily be extended to cover this case inasmuch as the opportunity cost, in sacrificed leisure, will be low for most, or all, commodities in an environment of general productive efficiency, and will be high where the opposite

conditions prevail.[46] But inasmuch as the theory of international trade
and values posits at least an inhibited international movement of labor
(and other factors of production) there is, in that theory, no use for
the extension of the concept of opportunity cost from commodities to
leisure. Labor (and other factors of production) are not brought into
direct competition internationally. Except when specifically noted, the
concept of opportunity cost has, therefore, been used in this book in
the (limited) sense in which it is peculiarly appropriate to the discussion of international values.

The mode of *distribution* of incomes (*relative* returns to the owners
of the various factors of production) in the several countries may,
however, affect their comparative advantages in the production of
internationally mobile commodities from the fact that it may influence
opportunity cost (measured in commodities) within each of the national
units. The pattern of distribution will depend on differing institutions,
particularly with respect to private property and its rights, in one
country and another. But these institutions must, for present purposes,
be taken as given, on the assumption that every country has the institutions appropriate to the disposition of its inhabitants and that there
is no reason to suppose that any other feasible set of institutions would
suit them better. Opportunity costs will then reflect "real" cost relationships no matter how that "real" cost may be construed or measured.

[46] Conversely, the opportunity cost of leisure, in terms of sacrificed commodities,
will be high in the efficient country and low in the other.

APPENDIX B

ON BARTER AND BARTER-RATIOS

IN AN appendix to his *Principles of Economics* (Appendix F) Marshall attempts to show that, where the process of exchange is by barter rather than with the use of money, any equilibrium ultimately attained, as well as the terms on which the transactions, as a whole, will be effected, will probably be very different from those which would obtain in a money economy. Inasmuch as, after each of a series of segregated trading transactions between two individuals (each of whom is presumed to have started with a definite stock of one of the alternative objects of exchange), the marginal utility of the good that either had just given up would, to him, rise, and the marginal utility of the good that either had just received, would, to him, fall, there is clearly some validity in Marshall's contention that the situation will depart from that which would develop in a series of transactions substantially similar except that money (with a presumedly stable marginal utility per unit) is employed. Marshall, however, himself points out that, under different barter circumstances (viz. a great number of traders each in original possession of a stock of one of the commodities), the distinction he makes would not hold in anything like full measure. Any such widely-held stock of a given highly barterable commodity would be analogous to a stock of money and Marshall's concession does not, therefore, much weaken his contention that "the real distinction . . . between the theory of buying and selling [with, and for, money] and that of barter is that in the former it generally is, and in the latter . . . is not, right to assume that the stock of one of the things [money] . . . in the market . . . is very large and in many hands; and that therefore its marginal utility is practically constant."[1]

The distinction is, nevertheless, of minor, or no, significance. In contrasting barter with a trade employing money Marshall makes an irrelevant comparison in assuming, for barter, a series of chronologically juxtaposed transactions between two individuals each of whom starts with a monopoly of supply of one of the commodities, whereas, for money, he assumes a practically perfect, competitive, market. In the latter type of trade none of the (numerous) traders undergoes a series of staccato transformations of his utility schedules, but each buyer, at a stroke, takes that supply of the offered commodity which is sufficient to bring its momentary marginal utility, to him, to an equality with the marginal utility, to him, of the money that he gives in

---

[1] *Principles, op. cit.,* p. 793.

exchange. He then retires from the market until, at some later date, his wants recur. The market is, at any moment, made up of numerous potential buyers, all of whose demand schedules may, for the purpose in hand, be regarded as fixed, and of numerous potential sellers ready to offer their supplies, "at market," i.e. without any reservation as to price. The situation, through time, is that the original buyers are first replaced by a different group, and, as the latter drop out, by others, until, in the course of time, the individuals of the first group straggle back with reconstituted demand schedules. The sellers, on the other hand, have meanwhile replenished their stocks. The market is thus in persistent process of reconstitution, on both the buying and the selling side, and may well, at any given moment, be much the same as it was at an earlier, and will be at a later, date.

This is a very different type of exchange from that which Marshall poses as *representative* of barter since, instead of bargaining, at any moment, about the price at which a single transfer might be consummated (involving the full amount of the two commodities that could, in the circumstances, be exchanged by the trading pair), he supposes the (two) bartering traders to higgle first over the terms of exchange of one small lot of each of the commodities and then, when an agreement has been reached on this, over the terms of a second similar transaction, and so on, until the traders can no longer find any terms on which they can continue to exchange the commodities. The barter ratio of the last consummated transaction will establish *an* (accidental) equilibrium, but not, as Marshall notes, *the* equilibrium. Results very similar (if not identical) to this would, however, have been reached if Marshall had assumed a pecuniarily processed trade of the same character. The fact is that this trade between two (if, after the first transaction, not quite absolute) monopolists, is negotiated on terms which, whether under barter or with the use of money, will solely depend upon the power (of whatever sort) that either of the traders can exert relative to the other. Marshall himself suggests that skill in bargaining (a form of power) will be the decisive factor.

If, even in this very simple "market," the use of money would not make as great a difference as Marshall implies, any difference that there may be is greatly narrowed in more complex trade. If Marshall had brought into his barter picture not only a large number of competing traders, each possessed of a supply of one of the two commodities concerned, but had, in addition, introduced a comprehensive congeries of commodities each of which was "competing" for the potential consumer's nuts, apples, arrows, fish, eggs, hoes, or any other good which he might offer in payment, the distinction between the barter, with persistently reconstituted demand and supply, and a pecuniarily processed equilibrium ratio of exchange would have been reduced practically to the vanishing point. There is, in fact, no reason for supposing that the ratio of interchange of products, or the conditions of attainment of equilibrium, would be any different in a general barter market than they would be in a pecuniarily organized market under similar conditions.

The *awkwardness* of barter, on a small scale, is obvious, but, if barter transactions were carried on in an immense "fair," many of the difficulties would disappear and those that remained would merely inhibit certain transactions rather than establish aberrations of the ratio of exchange, of such commodities as were in fact traded, from that which would prevail in the presence of money.

International trade between countries of independent monetary systems is inevitably a highly developed form of barter since the "money" of one political jurisdiction, which passes to the citizen of another in exchange for delivered goods, is not money to him and must be bartered against his own currency, or used directly for the purchase of goods of the country of issue, if the recipient is to realize anything on its acquisition. The true reason, in addition to this, for expressing the theory of international values in barter ratios of exchange rather than in pecuniary terms is not that the ratios are different in the one case and in the other (that there would be *no* difference was asserted by the earlier classicists themselves), nor even, perhaps, that the use of money *necessarily* vitiates the exposition, but because no actual money has ever been a good *numeraire* and because the international transfer of any money material, common to the currencies of two or more countries, introduces into the accounts an ephemeral balancing item which facilitates the attainment of a more or less spurious, because unstable, equilibrium which should not, but is likely to, be confused with the genuine article. Analysis in terms of money precludes precise assessment of the real gains from international trade. The conditions of equilibrium become quite inscrutable, in monetary terms, when deferred payments are involved,[2] or whenever long-term international loans are offset, in

---

[2] With deferred payments in the picture a formal balancing of the international accounts, in monetary terms, may well fail of realization even when an actual balance has, in fact, been achieved. With fluctuating exchange rates between currencies, an international debt of a given amount in the creditor's currency may be paid off with the use of more or less of the debtor's currency than will have been the equivalent of the debt at the time it was contracted. Since executory international contracts are made by the citizens of any country both in their own and in foreign currencies, and for indefinitely variable periods, it is quite possible, indeed all but inevitable, that, over any given period, the accounts may in fact be balanced though the actual receipts and payments, measured as they must be in any one currency, could not be made to equilibrate at any exchange rate, between the currencies involved, that had prevailed at any time during the period for which the balance is

some unascertainable degree, by an induced (though perhaps involuntary and unconscious) movement of short-term monetary loans in the
opposite direction.

Accurately to assess, in monetary terms, the international ratio of
exchange of goods, and balances of payments, would, nevertheless, be
somewhat less difficult than the classicists supposed if, as was at one
time the case, the currency of any given jurisdiction passed freely in
others. Gold sovereigns, louis d'or, Spanish doubloons and other gold
coins once circulated, side by side, in many jurisdictions other than
those of issue (and certain silver coins, such as the Maria Theresa thaler
and the Mexican dollar, are still used in some foreign jurisdictions).
The problem of translation of one currency into another, which is
often said to constitute an important difference between international
and domestic trade, was then not present. The situation, moreover, was
not greatly altered after nations had begun to show jealousy of foreign
coins (and it became necessary to melt, and re-coin, in order to shift
money from a "native" to a "foreign" jurisdiction) until monetary
"management" was introduced and the internationally equilibrating
effects of an influx of gold were inhibited. But gold is itself a commodity,
and its changing ratio of exchange, against all the rest, affects opportunity costs in countries which are actual or potential producers of
the metal. The value of gold is, in fact, so intertwined with that of
other commodities, and is yet determined on such a unique basis, as to
preclude its use as a neutral measurer of all the magnitudes with which
we are concerned in the theory of international values. If it be felt
that the theory of international values *must* be expressed in monetary
terms it might, therefore, on the whole, be better to use some non-commodity money as a measuring stick.

There seems, however, to be no real case for expression of the *basic*
theory in monetary terms. The world has not yet seen a neutral money
and it is only with respect to the *deviations* from norms, frequently
caused by a morbid money, that an analysis in terms of money is likely
to be useful. So far as money goes we must frequently deal with values
fixed in money,[3] as well as with fluctuating value relationships, but
this calls for an analysis supplementary to that attempted in this

---

struck. Nor would an average of exchange rates be of any help. cf. G. W. McKinley,
"The Residual Item in the International Balance of Payments," *The American
Economic Review*, Vol. xxxi, pp. 308-316.

[3] Long-term international pecuniary contracts usually call for the payment of
fixed amounts of some given money, regardless of fluctuations in its commodity
value, and the obligations under such contracts may have a considerable, and changing, effect on the line dividing exports from imports in any country, with a lesser,
but possibly sensible, effect on the ratio of exchange of international commodities.
This, however, is in the field of pathology rather than norms.

book. For the problems with which the classical economists affected to deal (the problems here attacked), a statement in monetary terms is not only unnecessary but, as the classicists alleged, obstructive. It would have been well if they had paid heed to their own warnings about the money-trap since, in resorting to its use as an essential part of their theory of adjustment to disturbances of equilibrium, they became entangled in meshes about which they had had justifiable forebodings.

When "management" of gold currencies became prevalent, that is to say, when the banking authorities in countries with a convertible paper supplementary currency sought to offset the effects on domestic money incomes of an international transfer of gold, the result was a postponement of called-for adjustments in the volume-ratio (though not necessarily, or probably, in the price-ratio) of exports to imports. The postponement could have been salutary as a smoothing process but it was all too frequently used as a more or less lengthy preventive, with eventual downfall of the monetary standard. Similar attempts to avoid internal adjustments under inconvertible paper monetary conditions, temporarily held in stable exchange relationships against gold or other currencies, had similar results. The upshot, over time, was a series of disequilibrium situations, punctuated by collapses, in which equilibrium was momentarily attained through partial or complete international bankruptcy only to be again lost in a repetition of earlier procedures. With pecuniary systems so handled the attempt to deal with the phenomena of equilibrium, in terms of any actually existing money, would assuredly be vain, and a true equilibrium was, in fact, precluded by such practices. It was then that doctrines on the difficulty, and even impossibility, of attainment of equilibrium began to appear.

In spite of the earlier classicists' belief not only that exchange relationships in international trade might better be expressed directly than through the medium of money, but also, that, if the matter *could* be appropriately expressed in monetary terms, the results would not differ from those of the direct method, the notions crop up, even in highly reputable expositions, first, that the "terms of trade" will affect national price *levels* and second, that national price levels will affect the "terms of trade."

Mill, for instance, asserted that "the countries whose exportable productions are most in demand abroad, . . . and which have least demand for foreign productions, are those in which money will be of lowest value, or in other words, in which prices will habitually range the highest."[4] On the basis of Mill's reciprocal-national-demand analysis of the "terms of trade" this is tantamount to saying that favorable

[4] *Principles, op. cit.*, Book III, Ch. XIX, §2.

"terms of trade" for any country will lead to a high money price level in that country. The only argument that Mill advances in support of this view is that, if (gold) money is imported as merchandise, "it will, like other imported commodities, be of lowest value in the countries for whose exports there is the greatest foreign demand, and which have themselves the least demand for foreign commodities."[5] But suppose, as comparative advantage would determine, that gold is *ex*ported (as merchandise) by a country otherwise in the position that Mill posits. Then, *on Mill's reasoning*, (gold) money, like the other exports, would have a *high* value in the country in question or, in other words, the gold price of commodities would habitually there be low. This would seem to be inconsistent with the possibility of export of the gold. Mill, indeed, confuses *relative* costs with *absolute* prices, and general prices in gold will, in fact, not usually be low in countries which are exporters of the metal.

A money material will always move from the places where its (commodity) value is relatively low to those where it is relatively high, but there is not the slightest reason to suppose that the places where its value is persistently low (which will be where the *comparative cost of its production* is sub-marginal), will have generally favorable, rather than unfavorable, terms of trade. Gold, indeed, may at any time steadily move as an export from some countries where favorable "terms of trade" prevail and, at the same·time, from others where the opposite is the case. It may also be noted that favorable "terms of trade" involve low prices for imports as well as high prices for exports (measured, in each case, according to a domestic cost of production criterion) and, unless the *variety* of imports is greater than that of exports, there is no presumption that prices will, in general, be high in the countries with favorable "terms of trade."

Taussig more or less unquestioningly accepts Mill's view and says (without references) that "it is usually set forth that the country where prices are highest gains most from international trade, and the country where prices are lowest gains least."[6] This, however, suggests the reverse chain of causation to that avouched by Mill. That this is no accident of expression is shown by the fact that Taussig goes on to say that "in buying imported commodities those whose domestic transactions are carried on with many counters [units of money] have an advantage. Foreign goods are not so high in price, and are procured more easily. Conversely, countries with low prices are ill off as regards imported goods, which are bought on hard terms by people whose scale

---

[5] *loc. cit.*

[6] F. W. Taussig, "Wages and Prices in Relation to International Trade," *The Quarterly Journal of Economics*, Vol. xx, p. 497.

of money prices is low."[7] Taussig later goes on to qualify this statement (which, when made, was apparently made unqualifiedly) by saying that it is high money *incomes*, rather than high prices, which will lead to favorable "terms of trade."[8] The qualification is, in any case, a matter of comparative indifference, since, in Taussig's view, the two phenomena were, to some degree, associated, and it can be asserted with confidence that neither the height of money prices (the national price level), nor of national per capita money incomes, has any connection as cause, and that only the latter, in some slight degree, is associated as effect, with the equilibrium ratio of exchange of commodities ("terms of trade"). One ought not to be required to argue this point against a group (the classicists) who generally maintained that the introduction of money made no essential difference to the underlying phenomena. One may point out, however, that, under an international gold standard and free trade, it would be *impossible* for national price levels to show any great dispersion so far as internationally traded commodities are concerned, though national per capita money incomes might, of course, vary in any degree.[9] Every country has some goods that are relatively low in price (exports) and some that are relatively high (imports). So far as the relative height of national price *levels* in the international goods sector is concerned, the matter turns on relative transport costs of imports and exports, and on the *number* of goods exported, in any country, compared with the number of goods imported. A country with a narrow list of exports, as against many imports, would tend to have a relatively high price level in the international goods sector. This happens to be the situation which is in probable consonance with the presumption of favorable terms of trade, but it does not square with the notion that the country's exports are "most in demand abroad" or that its demand for "foreign" products is a minimum. It assumes the dominance of import prices in the general structure and these are, of course, high relative to the prices of the same goods in the countries of origin. But the "terms of trade" are not calculated in this way, and

[7] *loc. cit.* In this quotation Taussig seems to suppose that the ratio of exchange of internationally traded commodities is an outcome of *independently determined* money costs of production.

[8] This, as earlier noted, is in flat contradiction of the usual classical doctrine that economically large (i.e., *ceteris paribus*, rich) countries tend to have *un*favorable "terms of trade," and high incomes would surely lead to a large demand for "foreign" commodities relative to the demand of low-income countries for the exports of the high-income country.

[9] This is also true of inconvertible paper monies when we give any intelligible meaning to the words "high price level" in an international context, for the words must then mean a price level "high" relative to other national price levels when all are measured in the *same* currency (which involves conversion of price levels at current exchange rates between the relevant currencies).

favorable terms merely mean that import prices will be very low *relatively to what the prices of similar goods would be if the equivalent of the imported goods were produced at home.* One may never, therefore, generalize about the connection between favorable terms of trade and a high (domestic) price level for internationally traded goods.

As for goods *not* traded internationally there is no presumption whatever that, whether as cause or effect, they will be relatively high in price in countries enjoying favorable "terms of trade," or large money (or real) incomes. The prices of such goods are purely a function of productivity in these lines relative to productivity in exports (the relative performance of other countries in the same or similar commodities being used as a measurer), and the degree of productivity in commodities that do not enter international trade can scarcely affect, or be affected by, the terms on which those that do are traded. The higher the relative productivity in domestic goods, moreover, the higher will per capita money (and real) incomes be but the lower will be the prices of such goods.

Taussig never seems to be sure whether he thinks that price, or money income, levels are, as he sometimes alleges, really a cause or (the traditional view) a result of the "terms of trade." He says, for example, on the resultant side, that "the general range of [national per capita] money incomes depends fundamentally on the conditions of international trade, *and on those conditions only.*"[10] Are we to conclude from this that per capita productivity is of no influence whatever? Sufficient examples of Taussig's views on the causal side of the matter have already been given. The facts are not only that neither national price levels nor per capita money incomes (except so far as the latter are a phase of total national output) have any causal significance on the (normal) ratio of international exchange ("terms of trade"), but also (except so far as the *number of exports* relative to the *number of imports* is involved) that price levels are never a resultant of the "terms of trade" (which have to do with price, and opportunity cost, *relationships* between commodities rather than with the general level of prices), and that money incomes, though a partial resultant of the "terms of trade," are usually immensely more dependent on physical productivity in both internationally traded and domestic commodities.

[10] *loc. cit.,* p. 510. Taussig had persuaded himself that the United States traded with the rest of the world on terms very favorable to his native land and he thought that this was of great, if not supreme, importance as a factor in American prosperity. (cf. *loc. cit.,* pp. 515-518.) His conviction is almost certainly wrong as is shown by the fact that the United States has a great variety of exports whereas far the larger part of its imports, by value, is made up of comparatively few items. The gains on these may, of course, be large, but the general situation is that which is exemplary of minor gains.

There is, of course, no connection between the relationship of price levels to money-income levels in the various countries of the world. Price levels tend toward equality everywhere, but money incomes vary indefinitely with productivity (of which the "terms of trade" are usually a minor part).

In no case can it be shown that money, *qua* money, will alter any of the (normal) barter ratios, or any of the equilibrium results in amount or distribution of real income, derivable from an analysis from which money has been abstracted. An international money will be so distributed, and the exchange relationships between independent currencies will, under free conditions, so move, as to bring about normal money-price relationships. The normal money-price structure will reflect normal barter-ratios, and these will be solely determined by opportunity costs. All else is an irrelevance and, in any given constellation of costs, the norms will remain fixed except so far as they shift, in correspondence with marginal variable costs, as the output of the various goods is altered, or when, under constant opportunity costs in the various countries, there is a transfer of the national locus of marginal production.

This is not to deny that monetary aberrations, and the lack of a free market in money, may keep money-price relationships from approaching their norms and, more or less indefinitely, disrupt equilibrium in manifold ways. There has, in recent years, been a plethora of writing (mostly in connection with the *soi-disant* "dollar shortage" following World War II) to the effect that free markets, and a free-market fall in the foreign exchange value of a currently debtor country's monetary unit, might not only do nothing to improve its balance of payments but would be likely to make it worse.[11] In any event, so it is asserted, there would be an adverse movement in the country's "terms of trade." The argument makes the most of alleged reciprocal inelasticities of "international demand," and of presumptive fixed composites of national output of mutually exclusive ingredients, and it usually assumes, implicitly, that the only demand for any country's exportables, or imports, comes respectively from the foreign, and the native, populations. What is called demand, moreover, is persistently confused with desire, and involves no recognition of the fact that no real demand can exist without the offer of some *quid pro quo*. (Desire *looks* like demand when commodities are rationed, at low prices, but much of this apparent "demand" would disappear under free market conditions). Though it is alleged that general demand, everywhere, is at the moment strong, the conclusion is almost invariably drawn that, on a fall in the exchange

11 A first-rate study of *inter*-war phenomena in exchange rates is available in Ragnar Nurkse's *International Currency Experiences: Lessons of the Inter-war Period*, League of Nations, Geneva, 1944.

value of a currently debtor country's monetary unit, the *domestic* currency price of its exportables, and the *foreign* currency price of its imports, would remain unchanged. If this conclusion were warranted, the prices of the country's exports would then show a fall in terms of the prices of its imports (both being measured in the currency of any one country), i.e. the "terms of trade," in the accepted connotation of the phrase, would have moved against it. But where, as now, there are *many* countries for which exchange devaluation is in question, and the exports of some are the imports of others (the trade between them covering all internationally mobile goods), any attempt to make a general rule of the contention that the "terms of trade" will so move runs into the impediment of logical absurdity.

"Inelasticities of international demand" doubtless cause short-run difficulties arising from the viscosity of movement of factors of production from domestic goods to internationally traded goods, or *vice versa*, in the currently debtor, and creditor, countries. But most of the data paraded to show these difficulties have nothing to do with price elasticity, but are phenomena associated with a general decline in the monetary demand for commodities (a crisis of liquidity). With a properly functioning money, reciprocal inelasticities of demand for sectors of output collectively covering the whole range of commodities would be impossible, but it is from such alleged inelasticities that most of the trouble is said to issue. The proper approach to the matter is through the improvement of monetary systems. Even with a poorly functioning money, however, inelasticities of demand under free conditions are always in process of neutralization, as a factor prolonging disequilibria in the international accounts, through shifts, in opposite directions, in the output ratio of domestic to internationally traded goods in debtor and in creditor countries respectively.

The case for discriminatory commercial policies, as necessary or desirable for balancing the international accounts, has most recently been emphasized by Thomas Balogh,[12] Paul A. Samuelson[12] and Ragnar Frisch.[13] Their arguments seem to me to be either erudite trumpery or else a proposal to tie two drunks together on the ground that they will thus stagger less than would either alone.

A persistent adverse balance of payments for any country is, in itself, all but irrefutable evidence of discrimination in favor of the home *purchase* of internationally traded as against domestic com-

[12] cf. *Foreign Economic Policy for the United States* (Seymour E. Harris, ed.), Harvard University Press, Cambridge, Mass., 1948, Chs. 25 and 22. See also Ch. 24, by Gottfried Haberler, an excellent chapter skeptically treating the whole concept of "dollar shortage."

[13] cf. "On the Need for Forecasting a Multilateral Balance of Payments," *The American Economic Review*, Vol. xxxvii, No. 4, pp. 535-551.

modities, and in favor of the home *production* of domestic as against internationally traded commodities, total sales in the home market being in excess of produced income. A distorted relationship between the internal and foreign exchange values of the country's currency, along with exchange controls, tends to stimulate purchases from, and retards sales to, those countries toward which the exchange over-valuation of the currency is greatest. Frisch demonstrates that by further discrimination it may, in certain cases, be possible to secure a balance in the international accounts of the country concerned without so great a diminution in the volume of international trade as would occur if all discriminations were removed. But an enlarged volume of *international* trade is not, *per se*, necessarily desirable, and an increase in volume could readily be achieved, through appropriate discriminations, along with substantial net all round loss in real income. Discrimination against such countries as keep their money real if not ideal, in favor of those with a currency that has lost the essential characteristic of real money, its universal "spendability," may possibly achieve a balance more readily, but not more certainly, than would a removal of all restrictions, but it is very unlikely to promote maximum satisfactions. Any form of discrimination may, of course, diminish the net adverse effects of another discrimination which it, in some measure, counteracts, but this is scarcely an argument for discrimination as such. At best, Frisch's "trade matrix" models are a rather noxious intellectual toy.

It should finally be noted that *balance* has nothing to do with efficiency or poverty. Poor men, and nations, may live within their means even as the rich may not. That a country with an "unfavorable" balance of payments will suffer a decline in its standard of living if it proceeds, or is forced, to square its accounts with foreign nations is as obvious as that the standard of living of an individual who decides, or is forced, to live within a given income will decline as compared with a former situation in which he was living beyond his means. But, if this is to be taken as a conclusive argument against balancing accounts, they will, of course, never be balanced until, perchance, the creditors abruptly refuse to lend another penny.

INDEX

347

71, 95, 98, 114, 135, 171, 174, 177, 181; limbo, 35, 45, 54, 68, 72, 75, 151; limiting, 34, 42, 266; normal, 33, 57, 108, 253; stable, 56, 74, 83, 86, 101, 138, 265
Reconstitution of demand schedules, 336
Repetitive loans, 291
Rhineland, 59
Ricardo, D., v, 3, 12, 186, 272n., 309, 326, 328
Robbins, L., 168n., 300
Robertson, D. H., 292n.
Rolph, E. R., 168n.
Rosen, G., 246n.
Rueff, J., 293n.
Russia, 211

Samuelson, P. A., 306n., 344
Schwartz, G. L., 168n.
Sectors of trade, 243
Secular changes, 317
Self-sufficiency, national, 46, 205
Senior, N. W., 260ff.
Services, income from, 156
Shears, analogy of, 311
"Shortage" of dollars, 294ff.
Sidgwick, H., 69n., 144, 145, 254
Silver, 255ff.
Silverman, A. G., 252n.
Simons, H. C., 26
Size, effects of, 58
Small countries, 58, 174, 235ff.
Smith, A., 7, 8, 18, 309, 312, 322, 326, 328
Specialties, exotic, 136n.
Stirling, P. J., 69n., 254ff.
Strategy, possibilities of, 12, 38, 60
Substitution, law of, 27n., 331
Supply, 3, 4, 9, 113, 138, 149, 290; bottlenecks in, 104; elasticity of, 138, 314; fixed, 33, 36; reciprocal, 9
Sweden, 294n.

Tariff Commission (U.S.) Report, 246n.
Taussig, F. W., vii, 4, 8n., 33n., 48n., 50, 187, 189, 242n., 251, 252, 279n., 286, 291, 292n., 340ff.
Taxes, effects of, 163ff.
"Terms of trade," 16, 17, 34, 38, 56, 122, 123, 156, 175, 182, 183, 185, 187, 198, 200, 205, 208ff., 214ff., 220, 230, 269, 274, 280,

297, 303, 326, 343; manipulation of, 38, 41, 134
Textiles, 253
Thornton, H., 154
Thünen, J. H. von, 309
Tin, 255ff.
Tinbergen, J., 149n.
Trade, complex, 10, 90ff., 112, 138, 284; true, 21
Transfer problem, 6, 289, 293ff., 298
Tribute, 183ff., 198, 200, 290

Undervaluation of dollars, 294ff.
Unilateral transfers, 190, 289
United States, 108n., 228, 229, 234, 244, 252n., 254, 294, 297, 305
Utility, and value, 309
Utopia, production in, 325

Values, equilibrium, 7; market, 3, 9, 30, 157, 311; long-run, 7; normal, 3, 7, 8, 16, 36, 268ff., 309ff.
Variety of exports, 209, 236, 265
Veblen, T., 24n.
Venezuela, 228, 229, 246
Viner, J., vi, 4, 5n., 15n., 69n., 139n., 144, 145, 149n., 185n., 186, 189n., 191n., 214, 219n., 230, 252n., 254n., 257n., 258, 260, 261, 263, 266, 267, 269ff., 274, 283, 284, 285, 288, 289, 291, 293n.

Wages, money, 262, 307
Walras, L., 309
Weak-points in ratios, 104
Wheat, 255ff., 305
Wheatley, J., 186, 288, 289
Whisky, 38ff., 253
White, H. D., 252n.
Whittlesey, C. R., 202
Wicksell, K., 187, 188n.
"Wild" commodities, 101, 174
Williams, J. H., 293n.
Wilson, R., 189, 190, 191n., 195
Wu, C., 254n.

Xenophobia, 231

Yntema, T. O., 4n.
Young, J. P., 280n.

Zones of indeterminateness, 8n., 11